Shojo Beat

Skip·Beat!

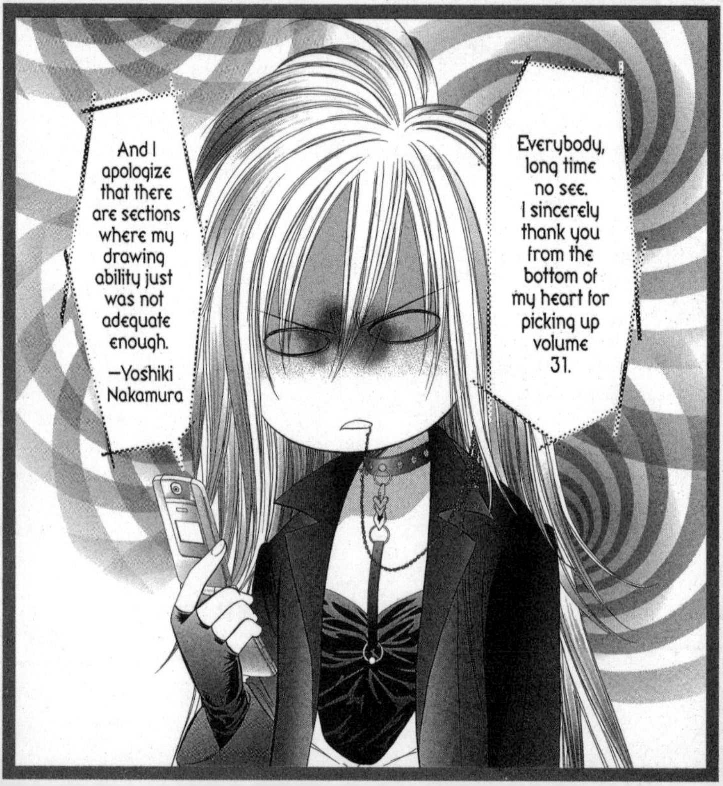

Everybody, long time no see. I sincerely thank you from the bottom of my heart for picking up volume 31.
And I apologize that there are sections where my drawing ability just was not adequate enough. —Yoshiki Nakamura

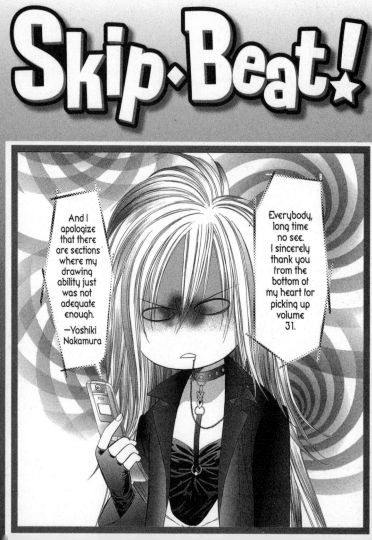

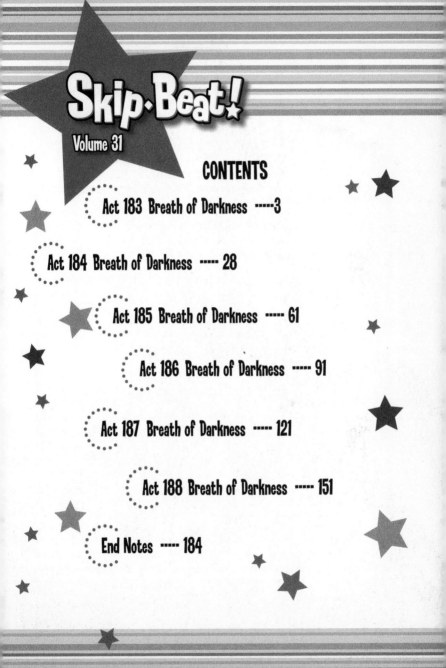

Skip·Beat!
Volume 31

CONTENTS

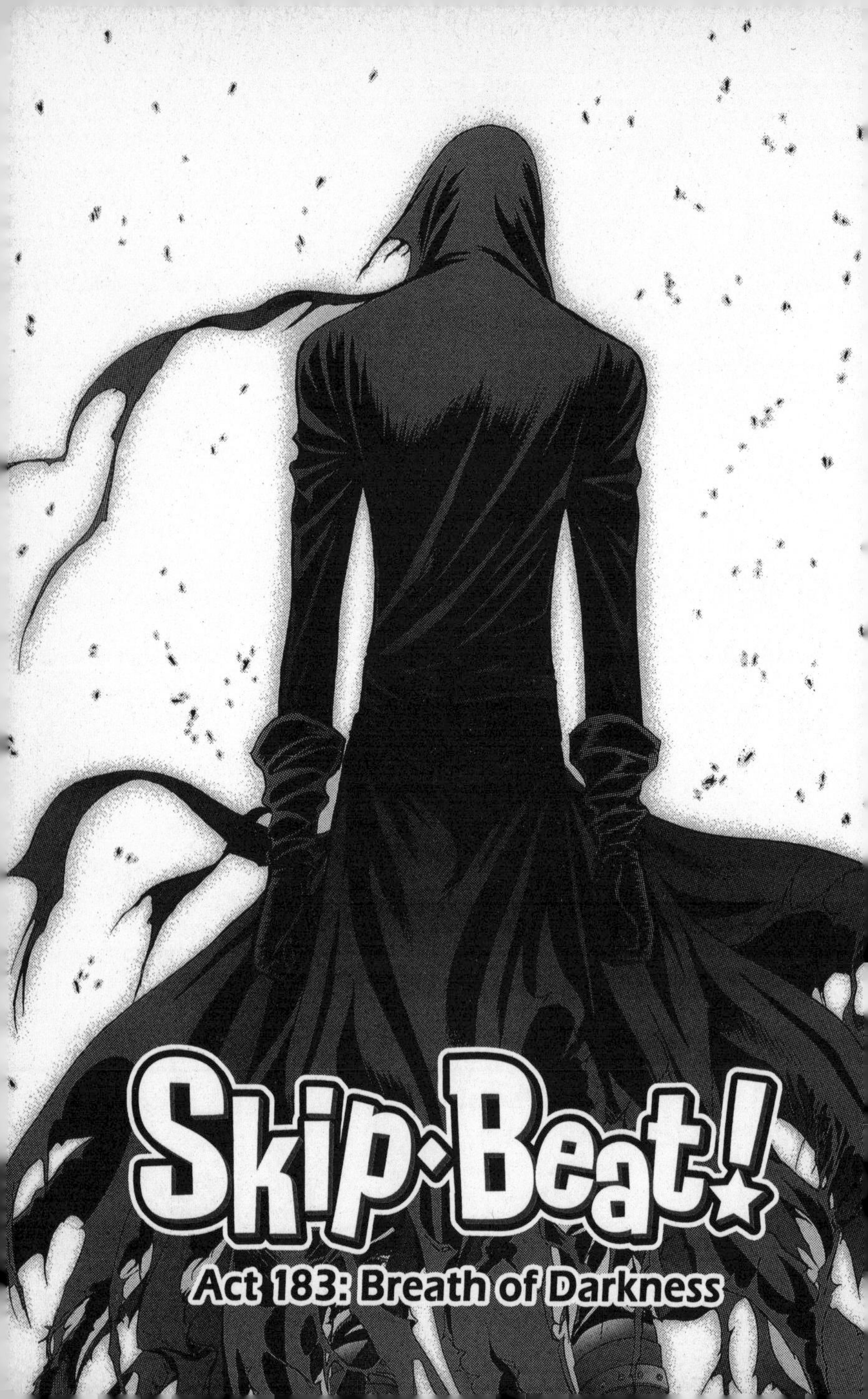
Skip·Beat!
Act 183: Breath of Darkness

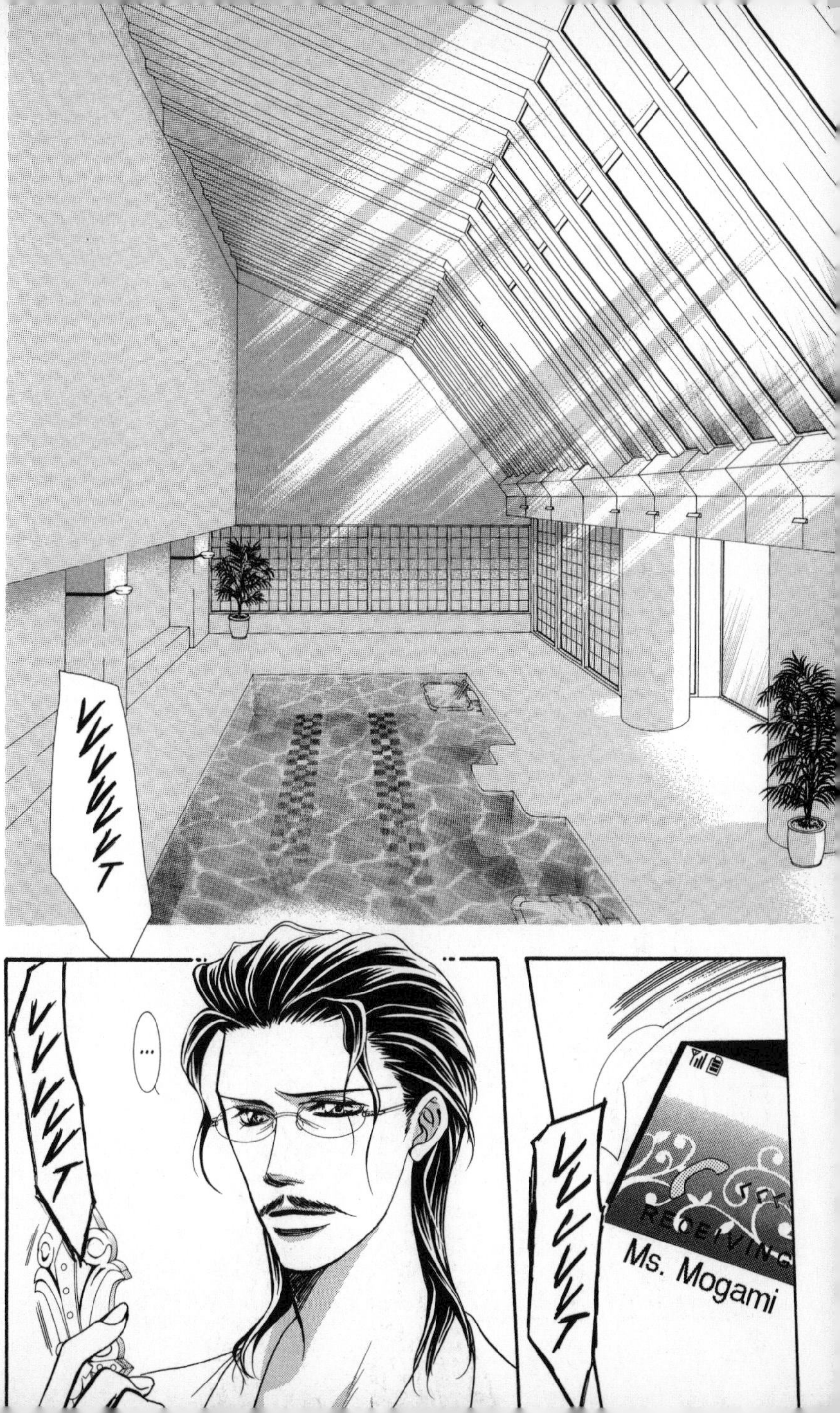
VVVVVVVT
VVVVVVVT
RECEIVING
Ms. Mogami
VVVVVVVT
...

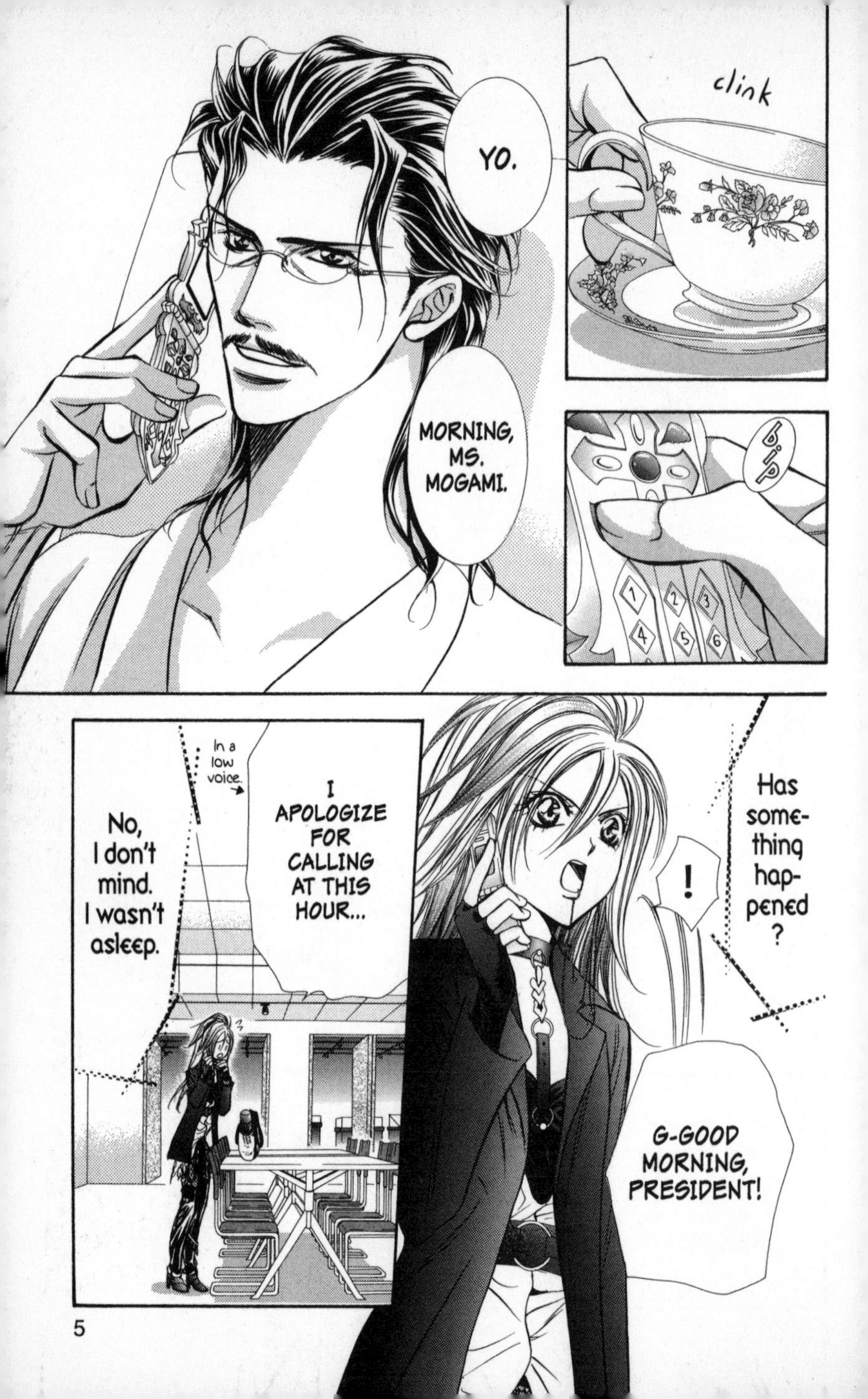
clink
bip
YO.
MORNING, MS. MOGAMI.
Has something happened?
!
G-GOOD MORNING, PRESIDENT!
In a low voice.
I APOLOGIZE FOR CALLING AT THIS HOUR...
No, I don't mind. I wasn't asleep.

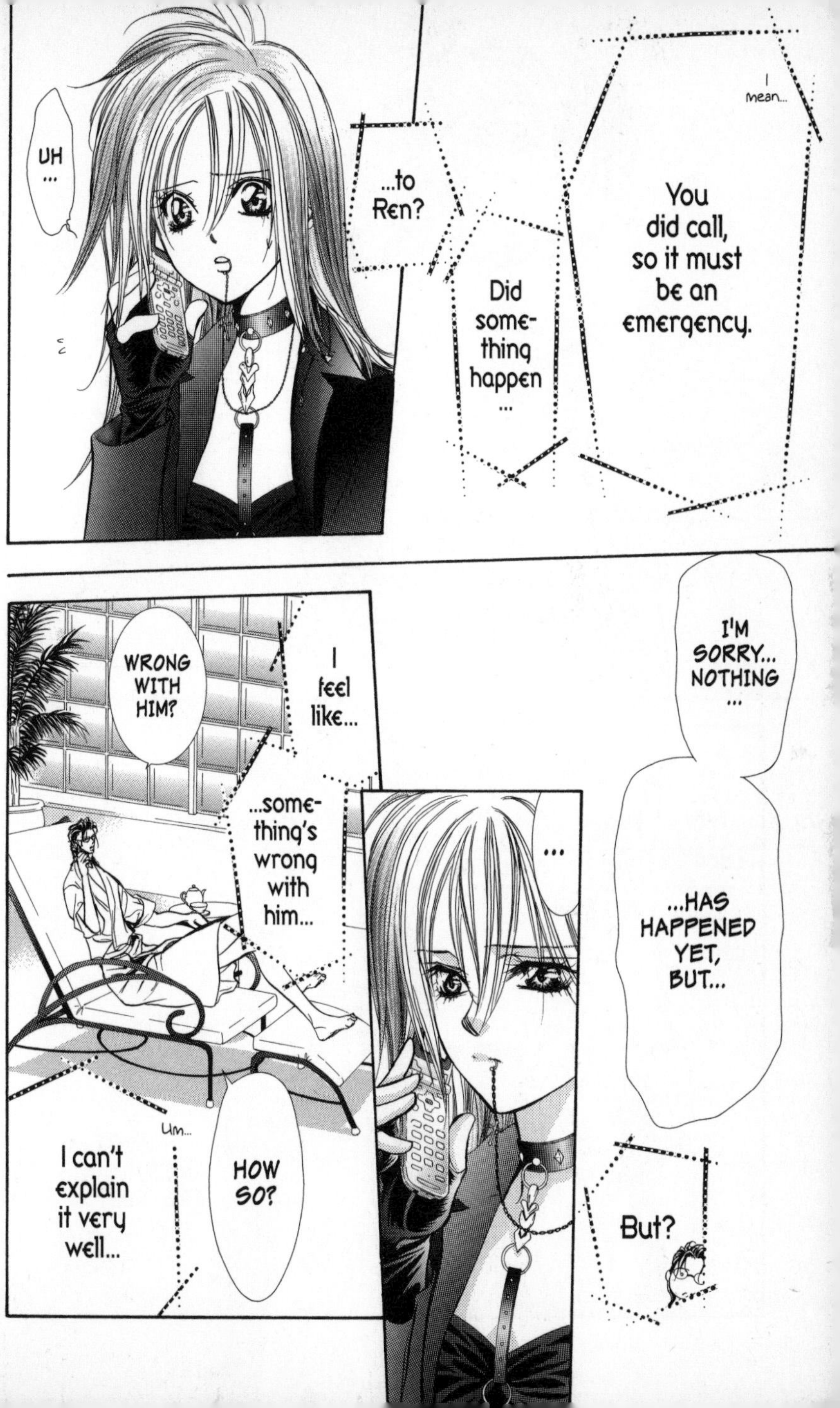
I mean...
You did call, so it must be an emergency.
Did something happen...
...to Ren?
UH ...
...
I'M SORRY... NOTHING ...
...HAS HAPPENED YET, BUT...
But?
I feel like...
...something's wrong with him...
WRONG WITH HIM?
HOW SO?
Um...
I can't explain it very well...

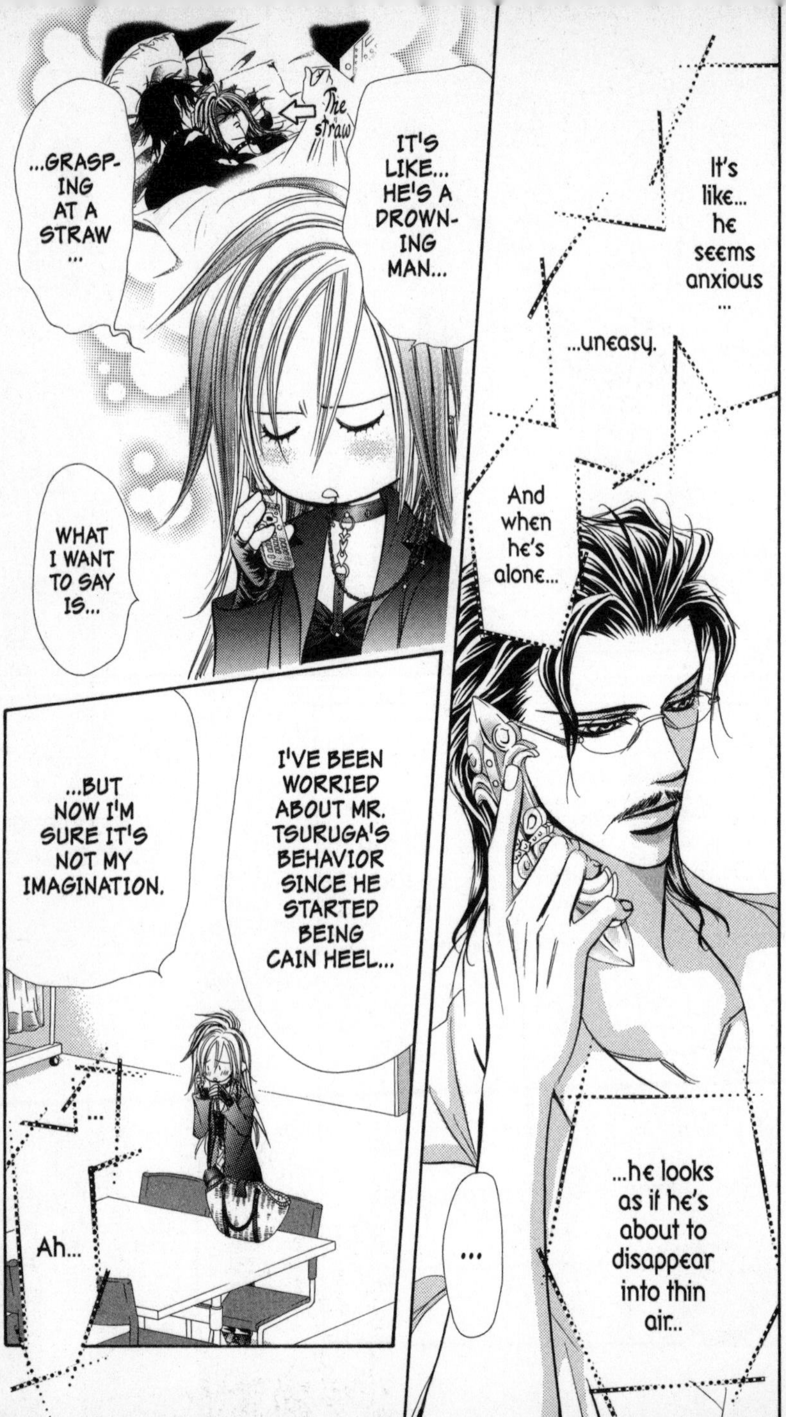
It's like... he seems anxious...
...uneasy.
And when he's alone...
...he looks as if he's about to disappear into thin air...
...
The straw
IT'S LIKE... HE'S A DROWNING MAN...
...GRASPING AT A STRAW...
WHAT I WANT TO SAY IS...
I'VE BEEN WORRIED ABOUT MR. TSURUGA'S BEHAVIOR SINCE HE STARTED BEING CAIN HEEL...
...BUT NOW I'M SURE IT'S NOT MY IMAGINATION.
...
Ah...

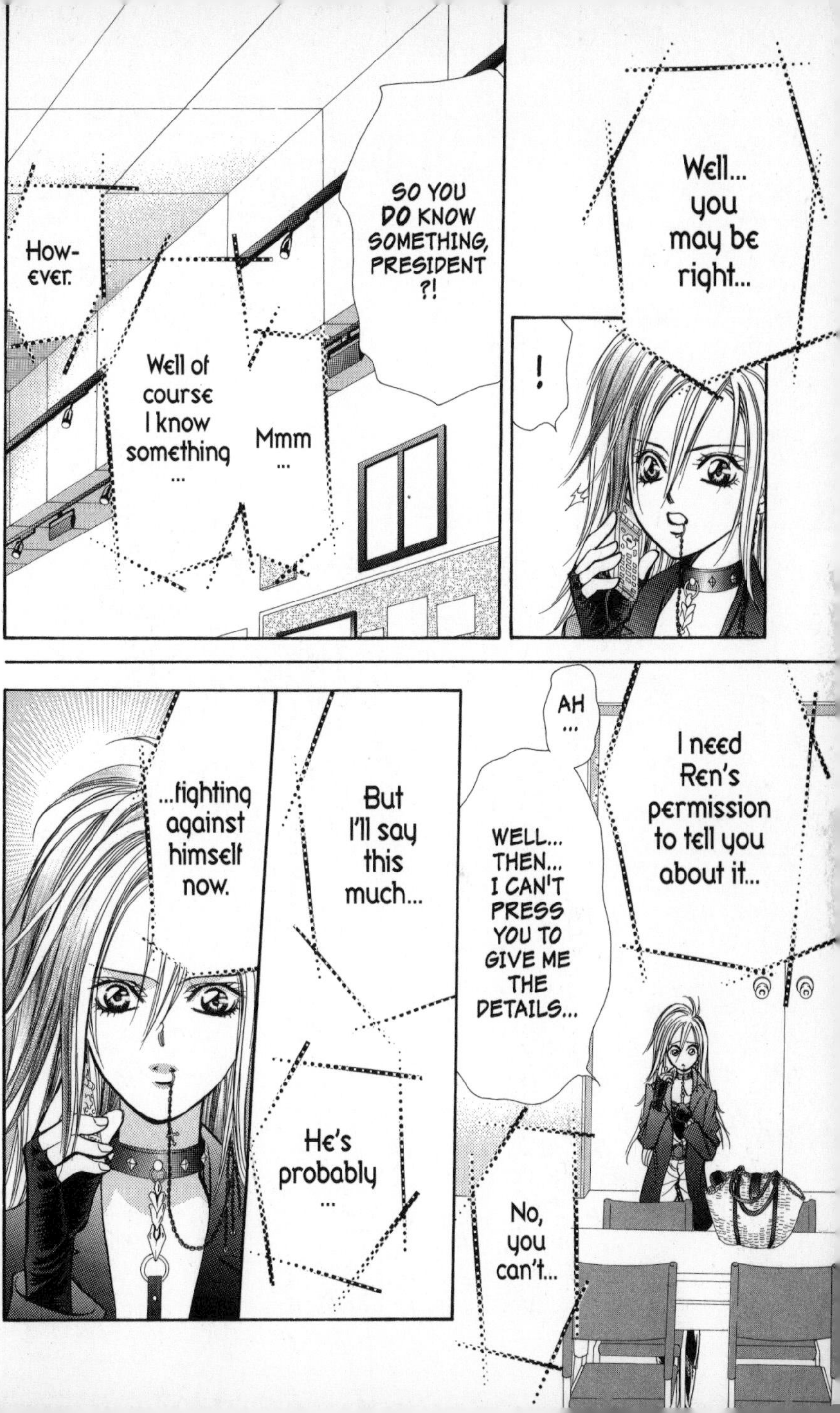
Well... you may be right...
!
SO YOU DO KNOW SOMETHING, PRESIDENT?!
Mmm...
Well of course I know something...
How-ever.
AH...
I need Ren's permission to tell you about it...
WELL... THEN... I CAN'T PRESS YOU TO GIVE ME THE DETAILS...
No, you can't...
But I'll say this much...
He's probably...
...fighting against himself now.

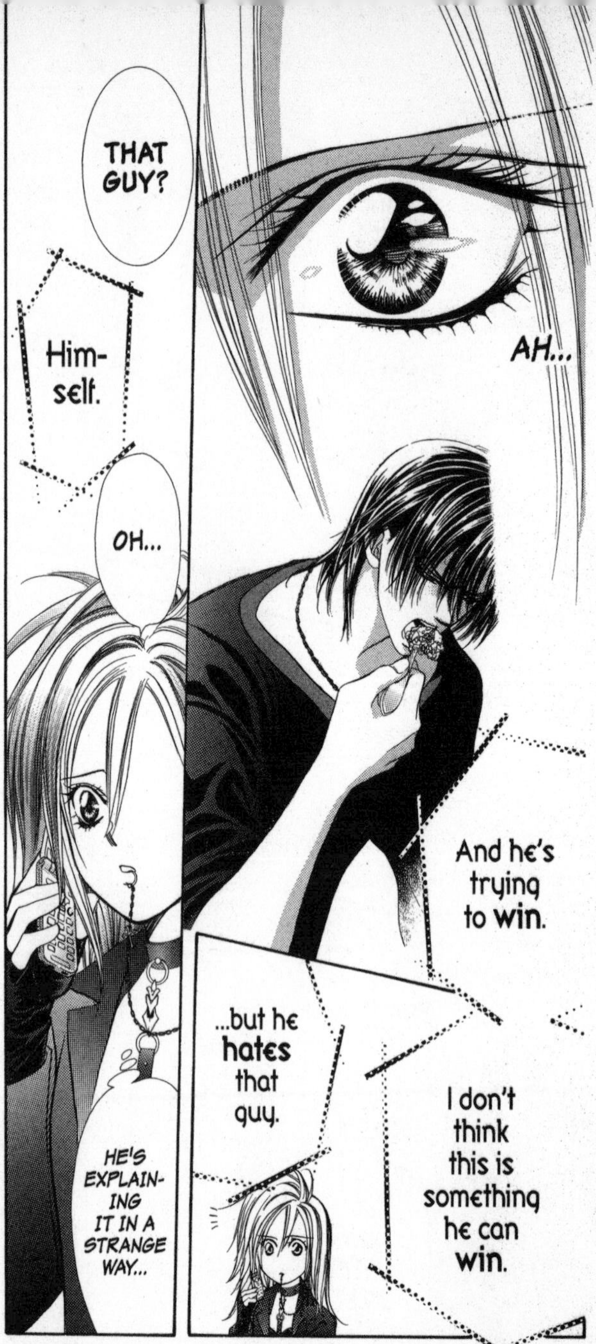
AH...
And he's trying to win.
I don't think this is something he can win.
...but he hates that guy.
THAT GUY?
Him-self.
OH...
HE'S EXPLAIN-ING IT IN A STRANGE WAY...

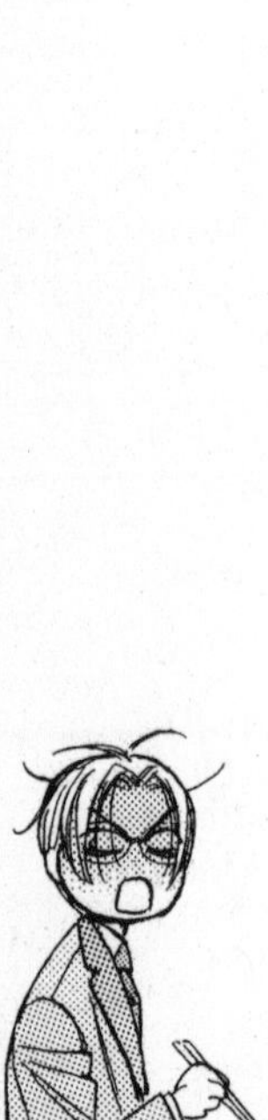

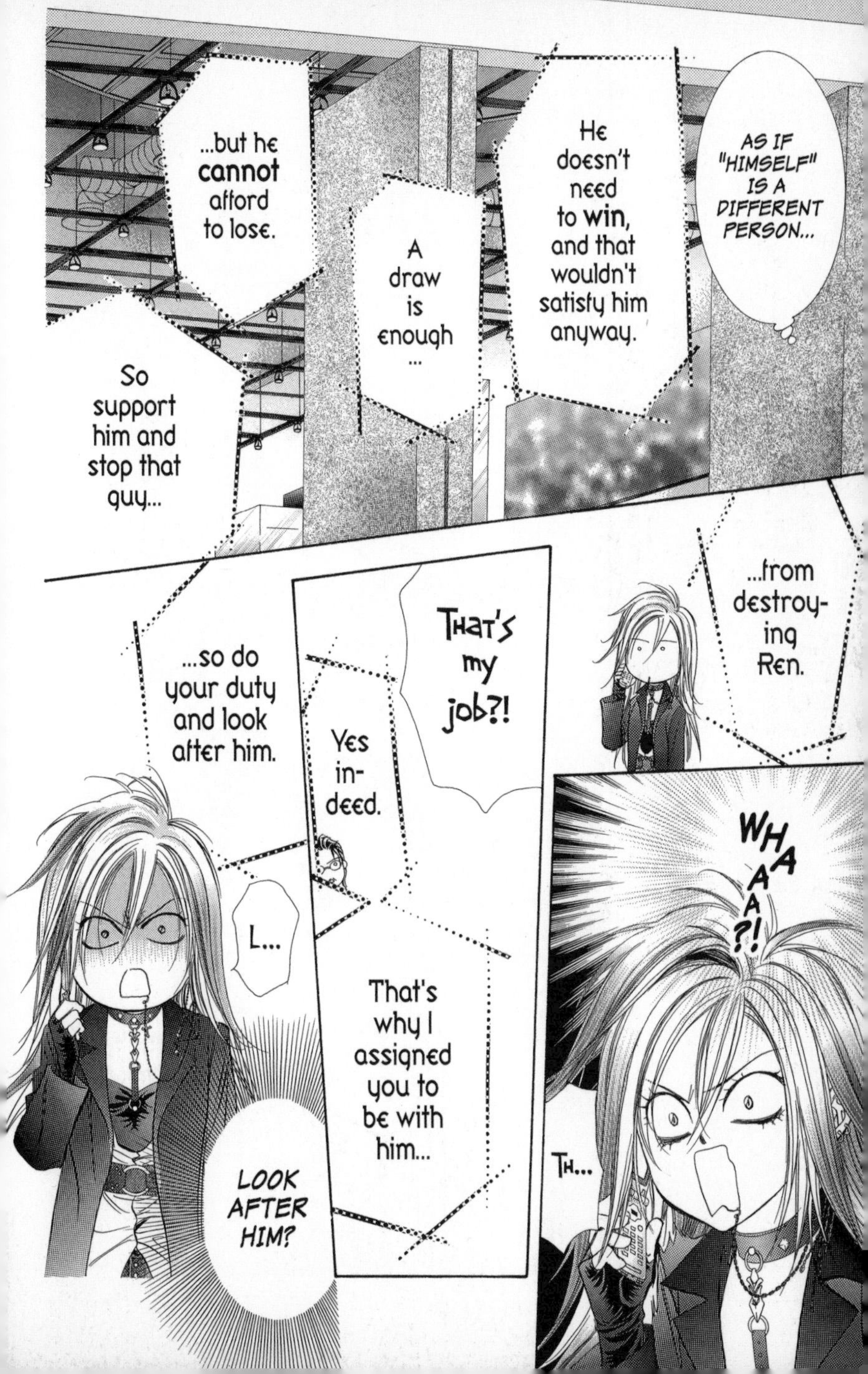

AS IF "HIMSELF" IS A DIFFERENT PERSON...
He doesn't need to win, and that wouldn't satisfy him anyway.
A draw is enough...
...but he cannot afford to lose.
So support him and stop that guy...
...from destroying Ren.
...so do your duty and look after him.
L...
LOOK AFTER HIM?
That's my job?!
Yes in-deed.
That's why I assigned you to be with him...
TH...
WHAAA?!

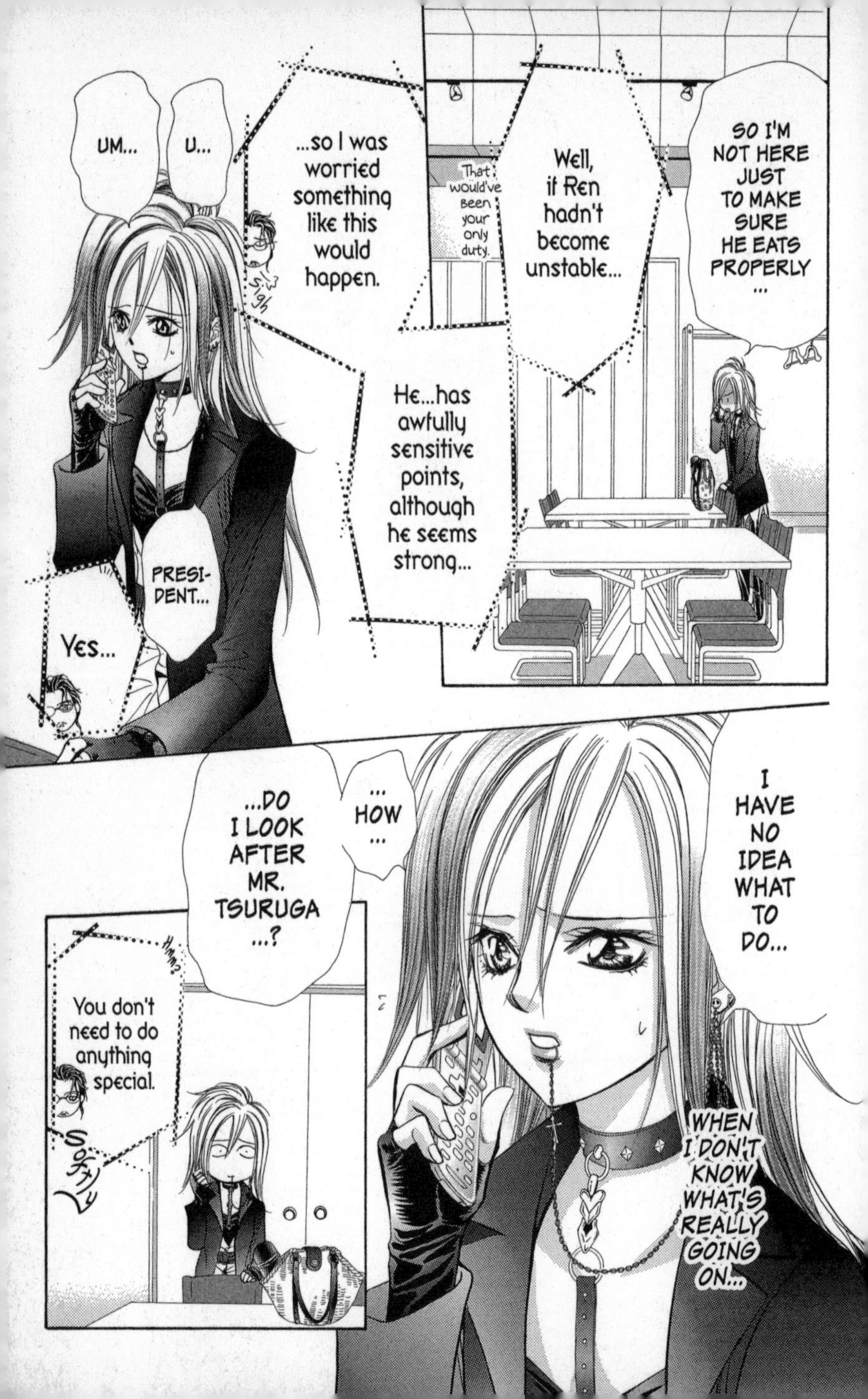
SO I'M NOT HERE JUST TO MAKE SURE HE EATS PROPERLY ...
Well, if Ren hadn't become unstable...
That would've been your only duty.
He...has awfully sensitive points, although he seems strong...
...so I was worried something like this would happen.
Sigh
U...
UM...
PRESIDENT...
Yes...
I HAVE NO IDEA WHAT TO DO...
WHEN I DON'T KNOW WHAT'S REALLY GOING ON...
...HOW...
...DO I LOOK AFTER MR. TSURUGA...?
Hmm?
You don't need to do anything special.
Softly

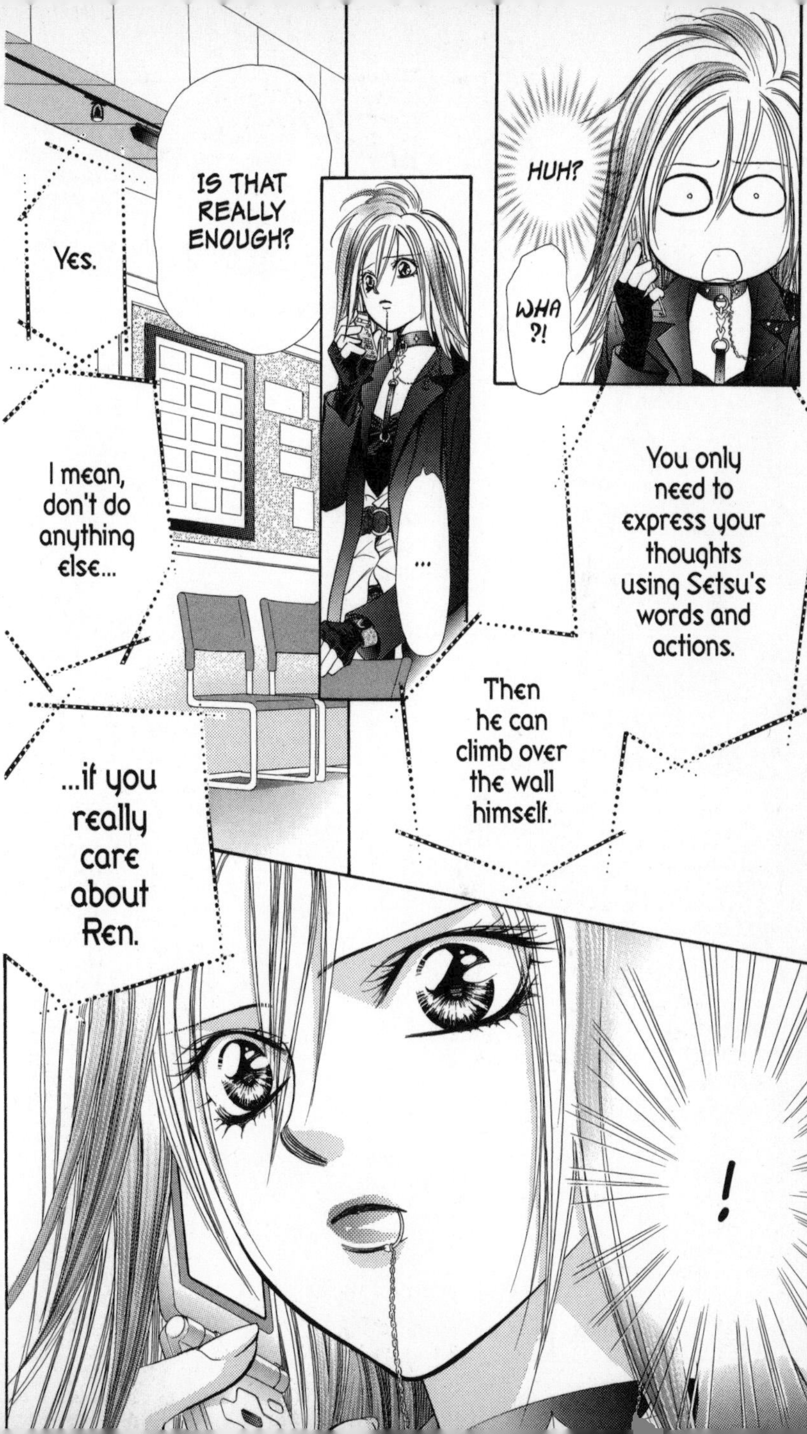
HUH?
WHA ?!
...
IS THAT REALLY ENOUGH?
Yes.
You only need to express your thoughts using Setsu's words and actions.
Then he can climb over the wall himself.
I mean, don't do anything else...
...if you really care about Ren.
!

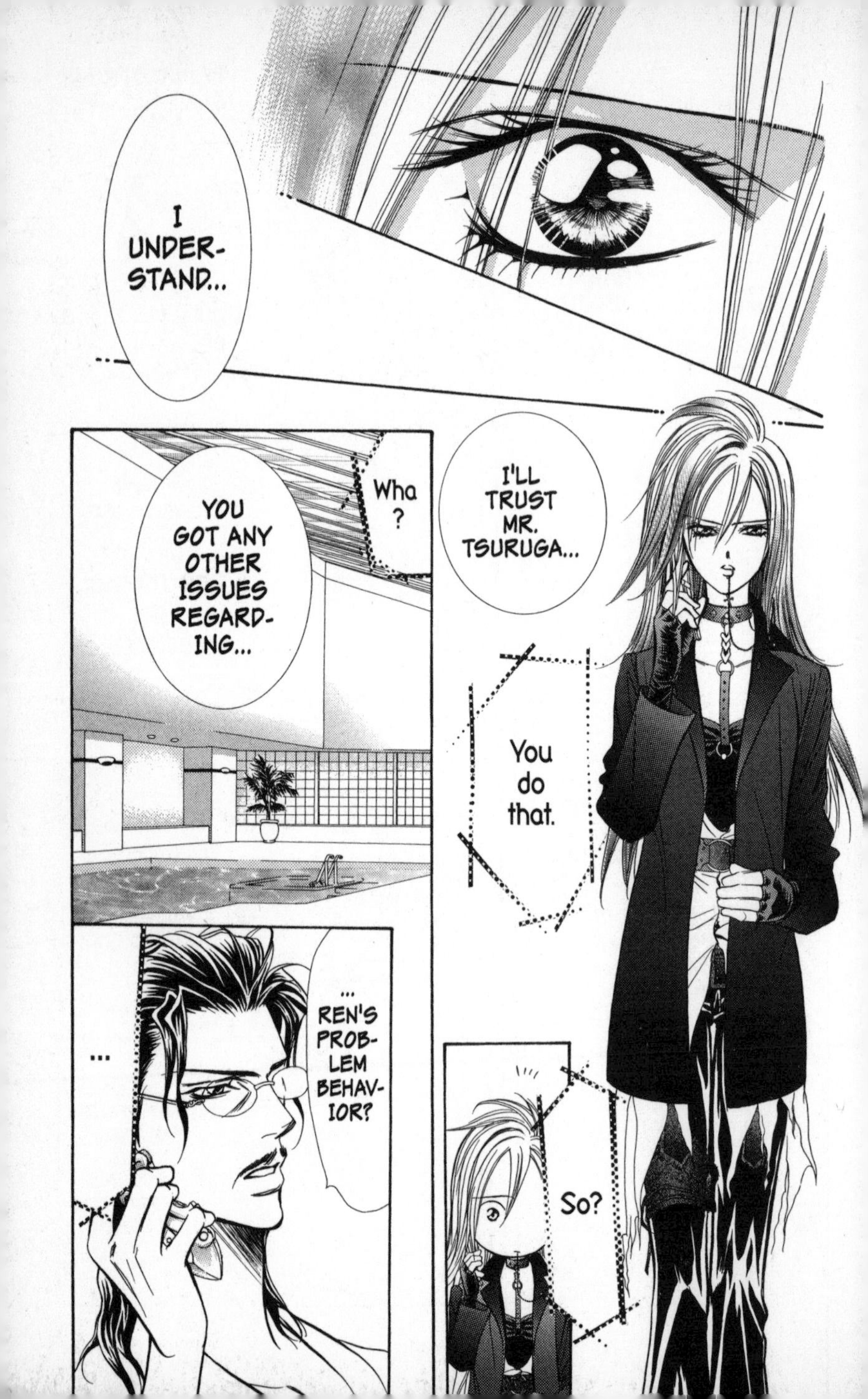
I UNDER-STAND...
I'LL TRUST MR. TSURUGA...
You do that.
So?
Wha?
YOU GOT ANY OTHER ISSUES REGARD-ING...
... REN'S PROB-LEM BEHAV-IOR?
...

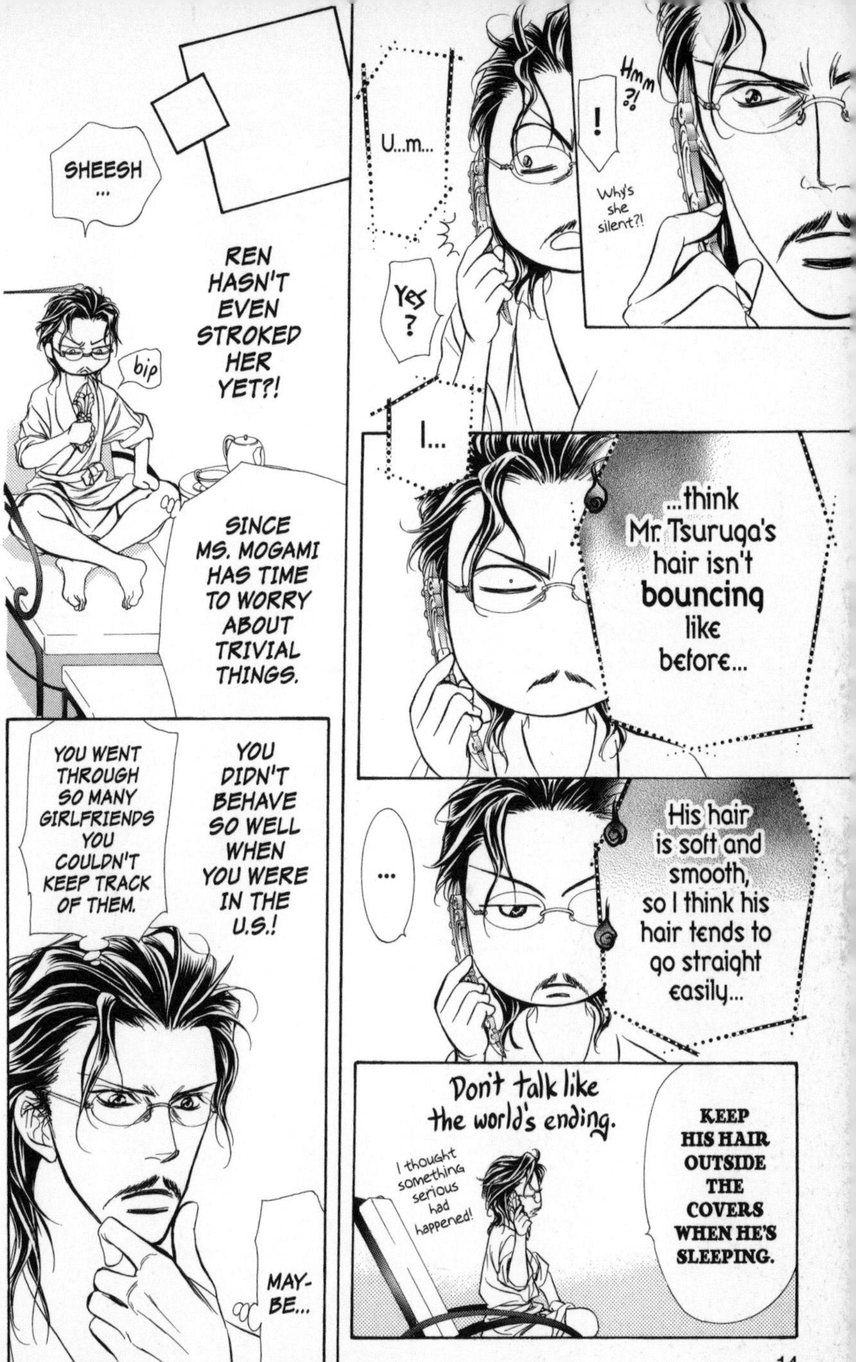
Hmm ?!
!
Why's she silent?!
U...m...
Yes?
I...
...think Mr. Tsuruga's hair isn't bouncing like before...
...
His hair is soft and smooth, so I think his hair tends to go straight easily...
KEEP HIS HAIR OUTSIDE THE COVERS WHEN HE'S SLEEPING.
Don't talk like the world's ending.
I thought something serious had happened!
SHEESH ...
REN HASN'T EVEN STROKED HER YET?!
bip
SINCE MS. MOGAMI HAS TIME TO WORRY ABOUT TRIVIAL THINGS.
YOU DIDN'T BEHAVE SO WELL WHEN YOU WERE IN THE U.S.!
YOU WENT THROUGH SO MANY GIRLFRIENDS YOU COULDN'T KEEP TRACK OF THEM.
MAY-BE...

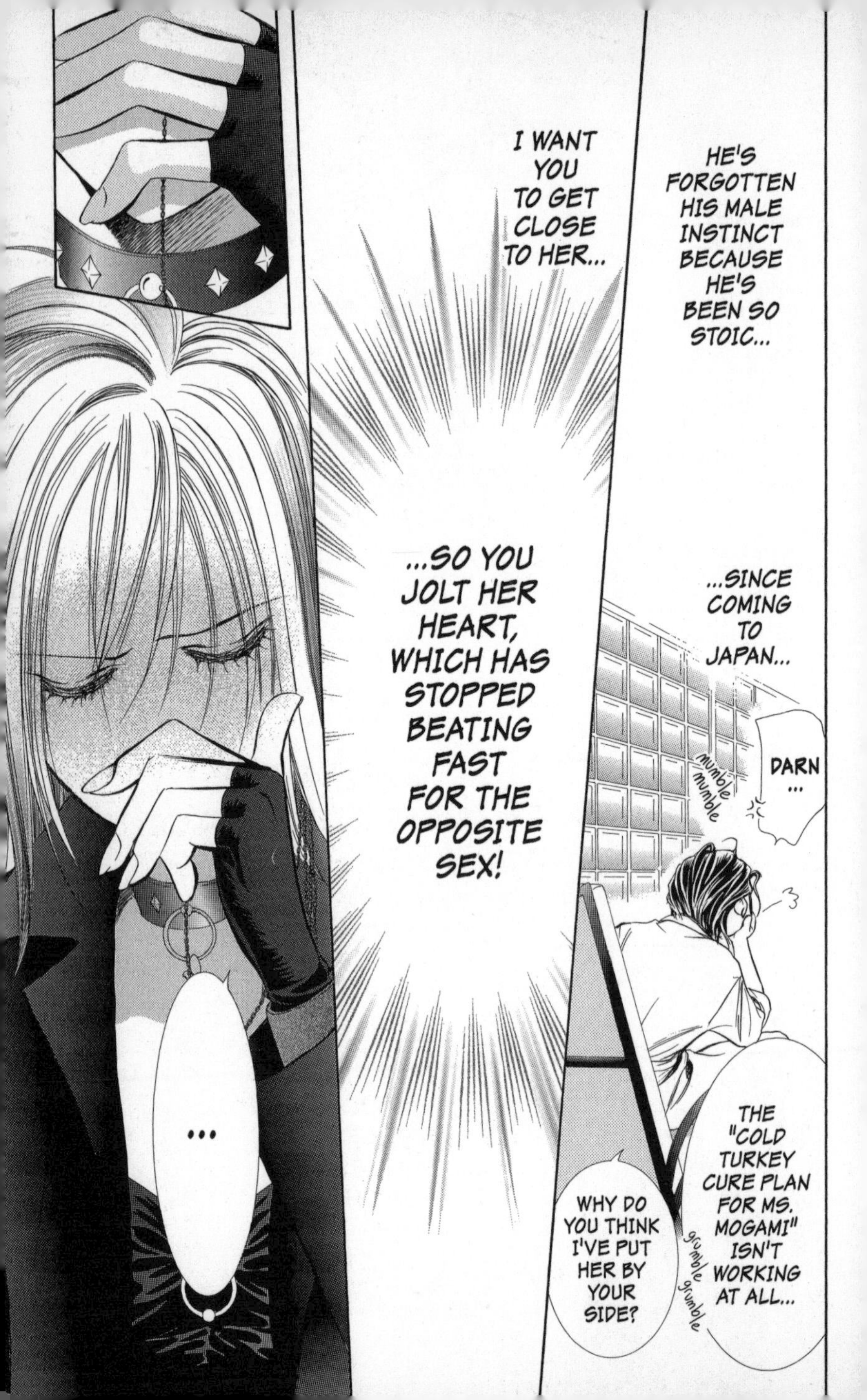
HE'S FORGOTTEN HIS MALE INSTINCT BECAUSE HE'S BEEN SO STOIC...
...SINCE COMING TO JAPAN...
DARN...
mumble mumble
THE "COLD TURKEY CURE PLAN FOR MS. MOGAMI" ISN'T WORKING AT ALL...
grumble grumble
WHY DO YOU THINK I'VE PUT HER BY YOUR SIDE?
I WANT YOU TO GET CLOSE TO HER...
...SO YOU JOLT HER HEART, WHICH HAS STOPPED BEATING FAST FOR THE OPPOSITE SEX!
...

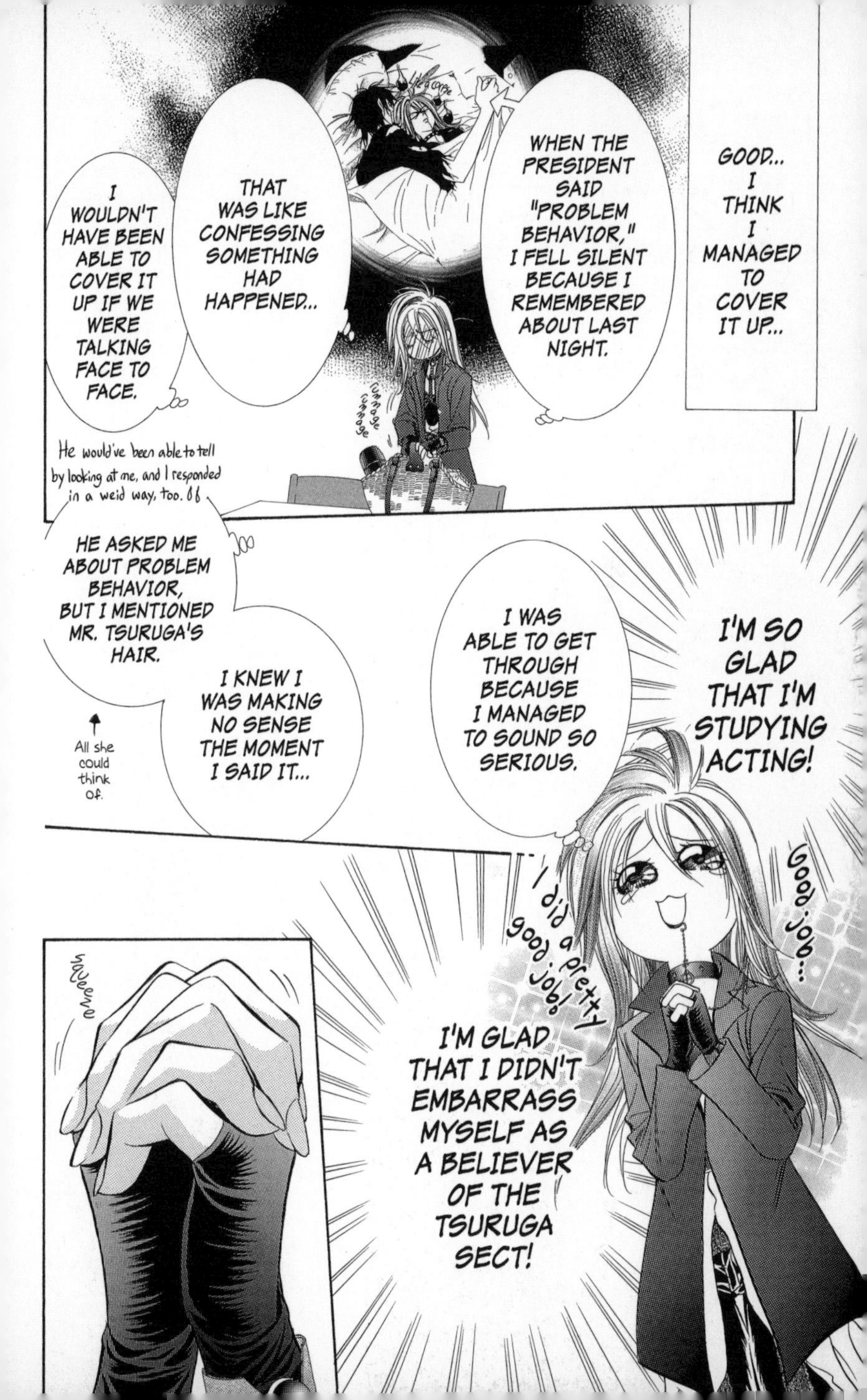
GOOD... I THINK I MANAGED TO COVER IT UP...
WHEN THE PRESIDENT SAID "PROBLEM BEHAVIOR," I FELL SILENT BECAUSE I REMEMBERED ABOUT LAST NIGHT.
THAT WAS LIKE CONFESSING SOMETHING HAD HAPPENED...
I WOULDN'T HAVE BEEN ABLE TO COVER IT UP IF WE WERE TALKING FACE TO FACE.
rummage rummage
He would've been able to tell by looking at me, and I responded in a weid way, too.
I'M SO GLAD THAT I'M STUDYING ACTING!
I WAS ABLE TO GET THROUGH BECAUSE I MANAGED TO SOUND SO SERIOUS.
I KNEW I WAS MAKING NO SENSE THE MOMENT I SAID IT...
HE ASKED ME ABOUT PROBLEM BEHAVIOR, BUT I MENTIONED MR. TSURUGA'S HAIR.
All she could think of.
Good job...
I did a pretty good job!
I'M GLAD THAT I DIDN'T EMBARRASS MYSELF AS A BELIEVER OF THE TSURUGA SECT!
squeeze

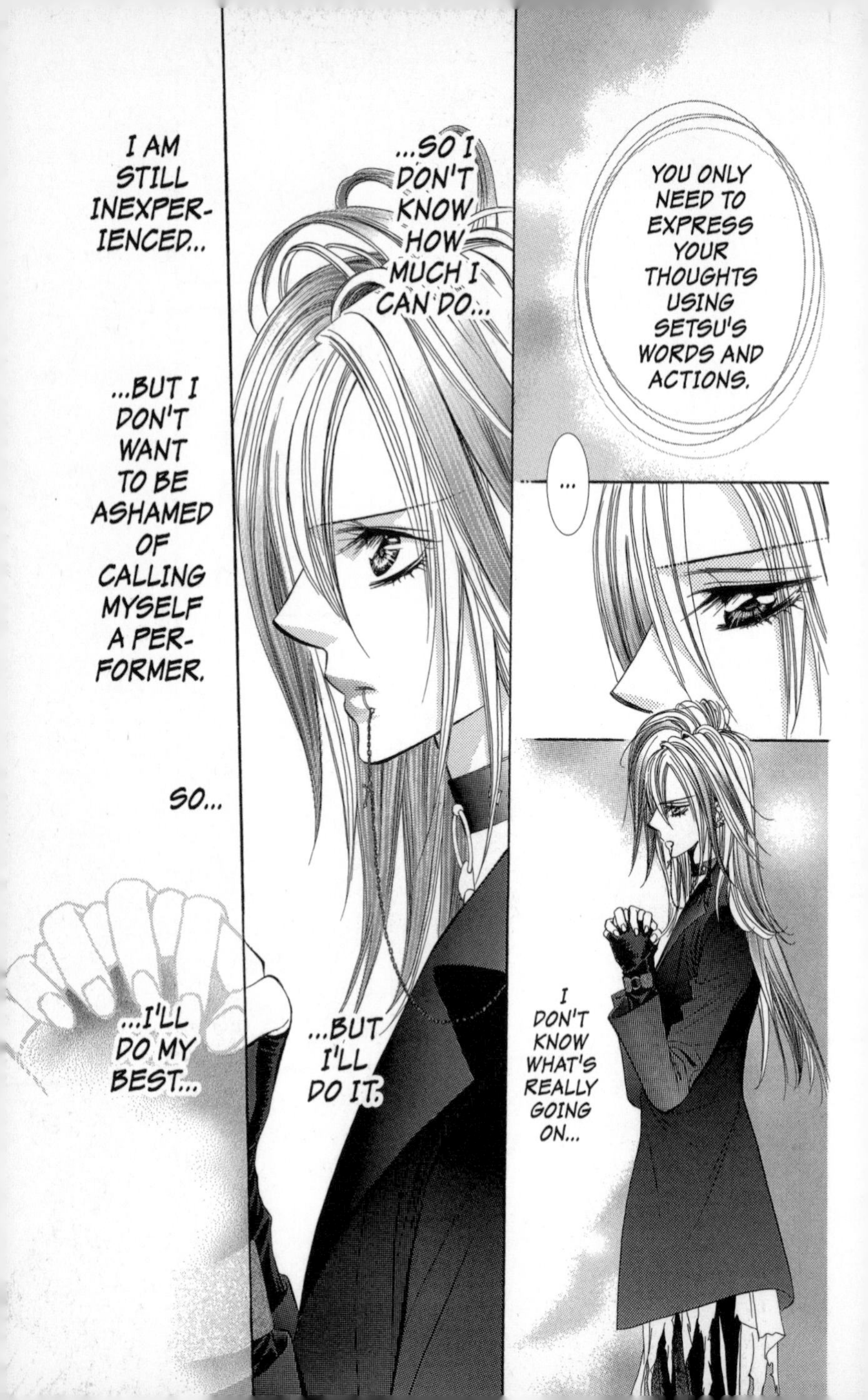
YOU ONLY NEED TO EXPRESS YOUR THOUGHTS USING SETSU'S WORDS AND ACTIONS.
...
I DON'T KNOW WHAT'S REALLY GOING ON...
...SO I DON'T KNOW HOW MUCH I CAN DO...
...BUT I'LL DO IT.
I AM STILL INEXPER-IENCED...
...BUT I DON'T WANT TO BE ASHAMED OF CALLING MYSELF A PER-FORMER.
SO...
...I'LL DO MY BEST...

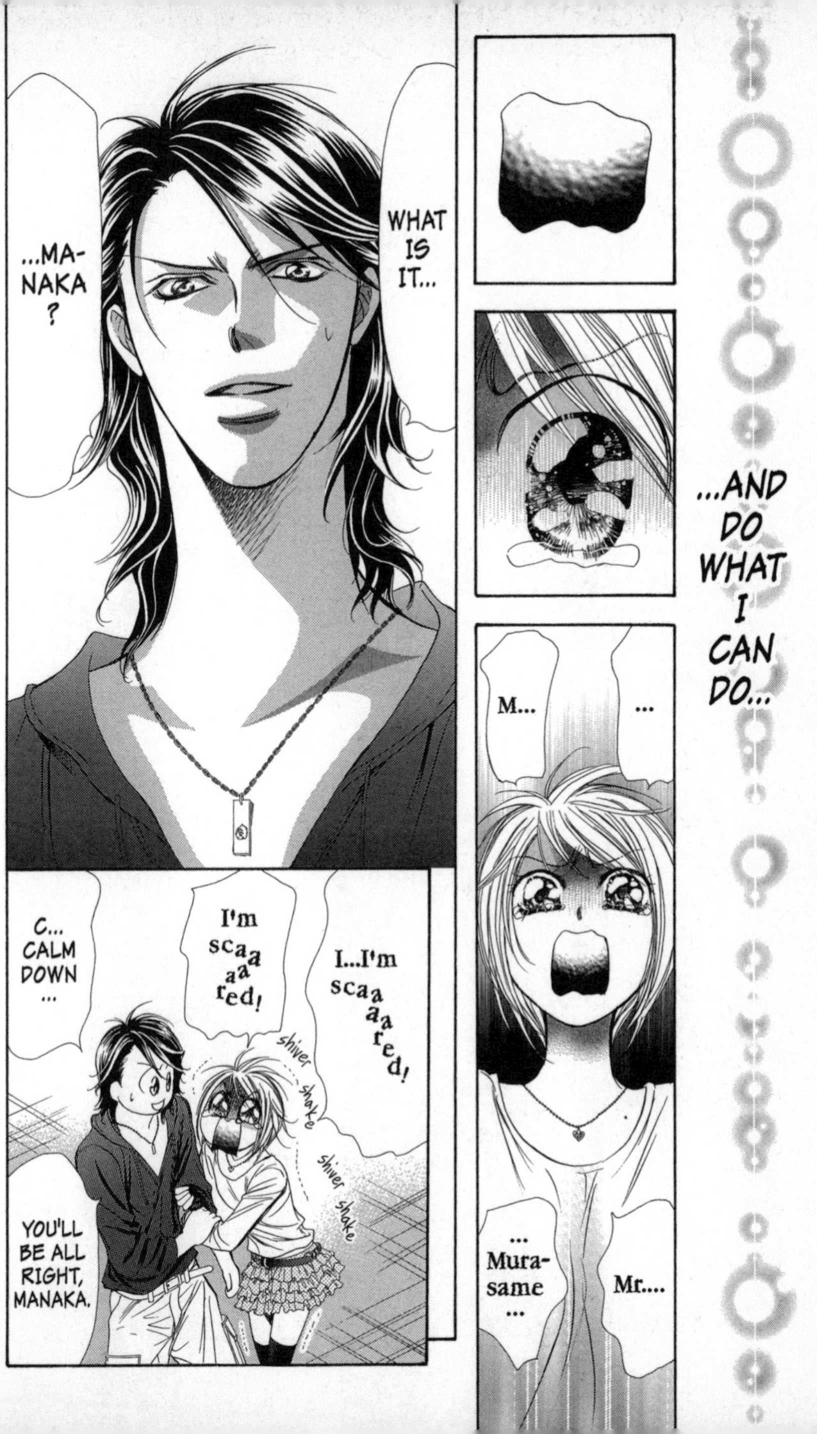

...AND DO WHAT I CAN DO...
...
M...
Mr....
...Mura-same...
WHAT IS IT...
...MA-NAKA?
I...I'm scaaaared!
I'm scaaaared!
C... CALM DOWN...
shiver shake
shiver shake
YOU'LL BE ALL RIGHT, MANAKA.

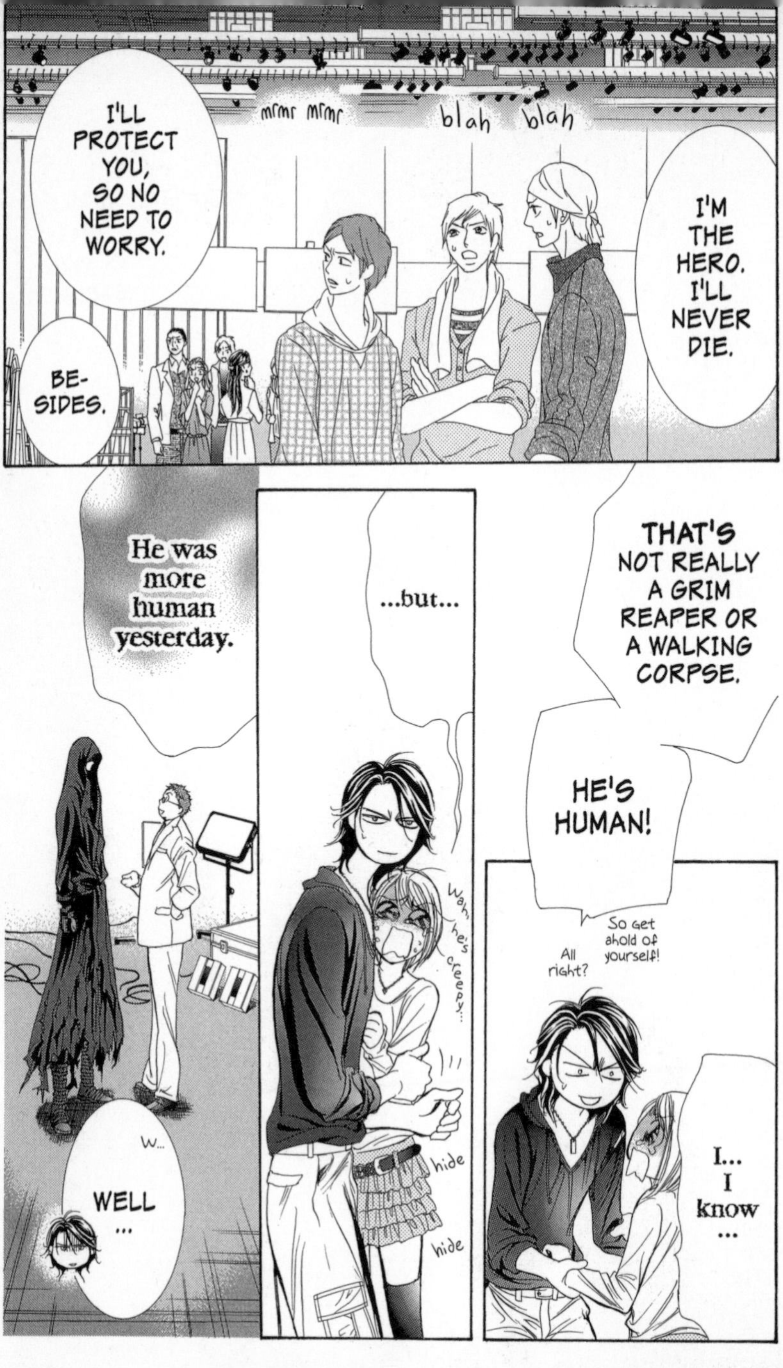
I'M THE HERO. I'LL NEVER DIE.
blah blah
mrmr mrmr
I'LL PROTECT YOU, SO NO NEED TO WORRY.
BE-SIDES.
THAT'S NOT REALLY A GRIM REAPER OR A WALKING CORPSE.
HE'S HUMAN!
So get ahold of yourself!
All right?
I... I know...
...but...
Waah he's creepy...
hide
hide
He was more human yesterday.
W...
WELL...

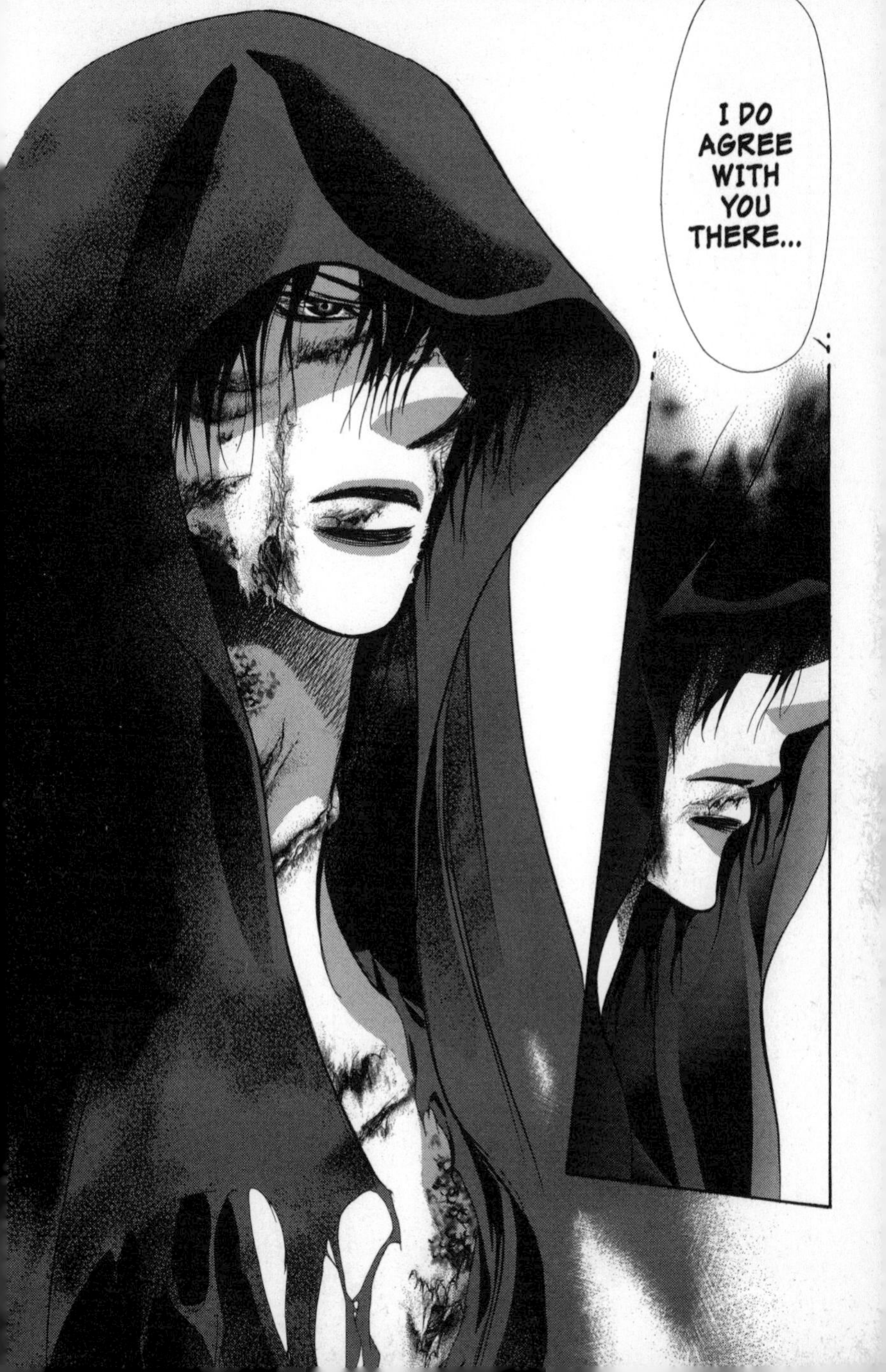
I DO AGREE WITH YOU THERE...

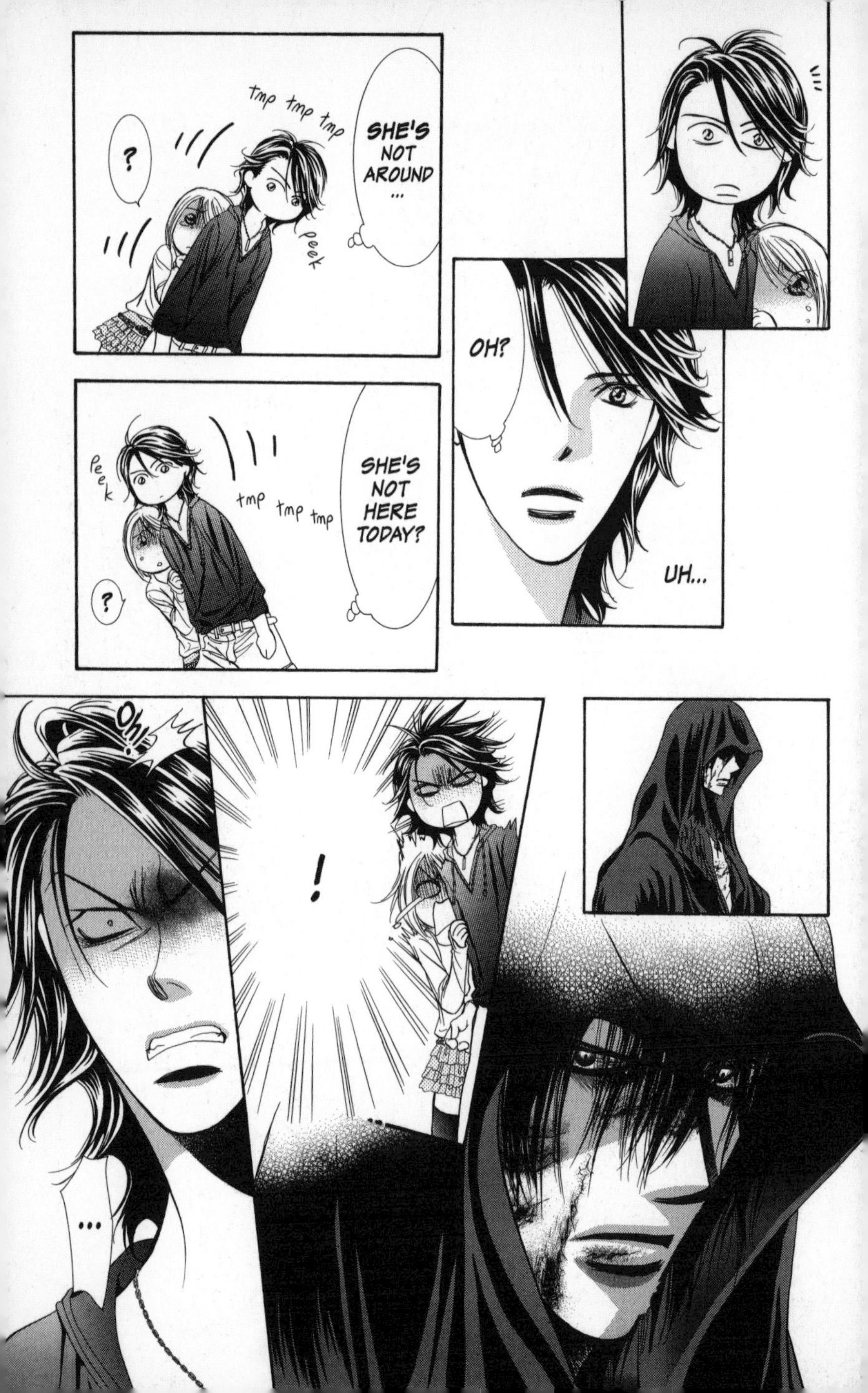
OH?
UH...
SHE'S NOT AROUND...
tmp tmp tmp
peek
?
SHE'S NOT HERE TODAY?
tmp tmp tmp
peek
?
!
...
Oh!
...

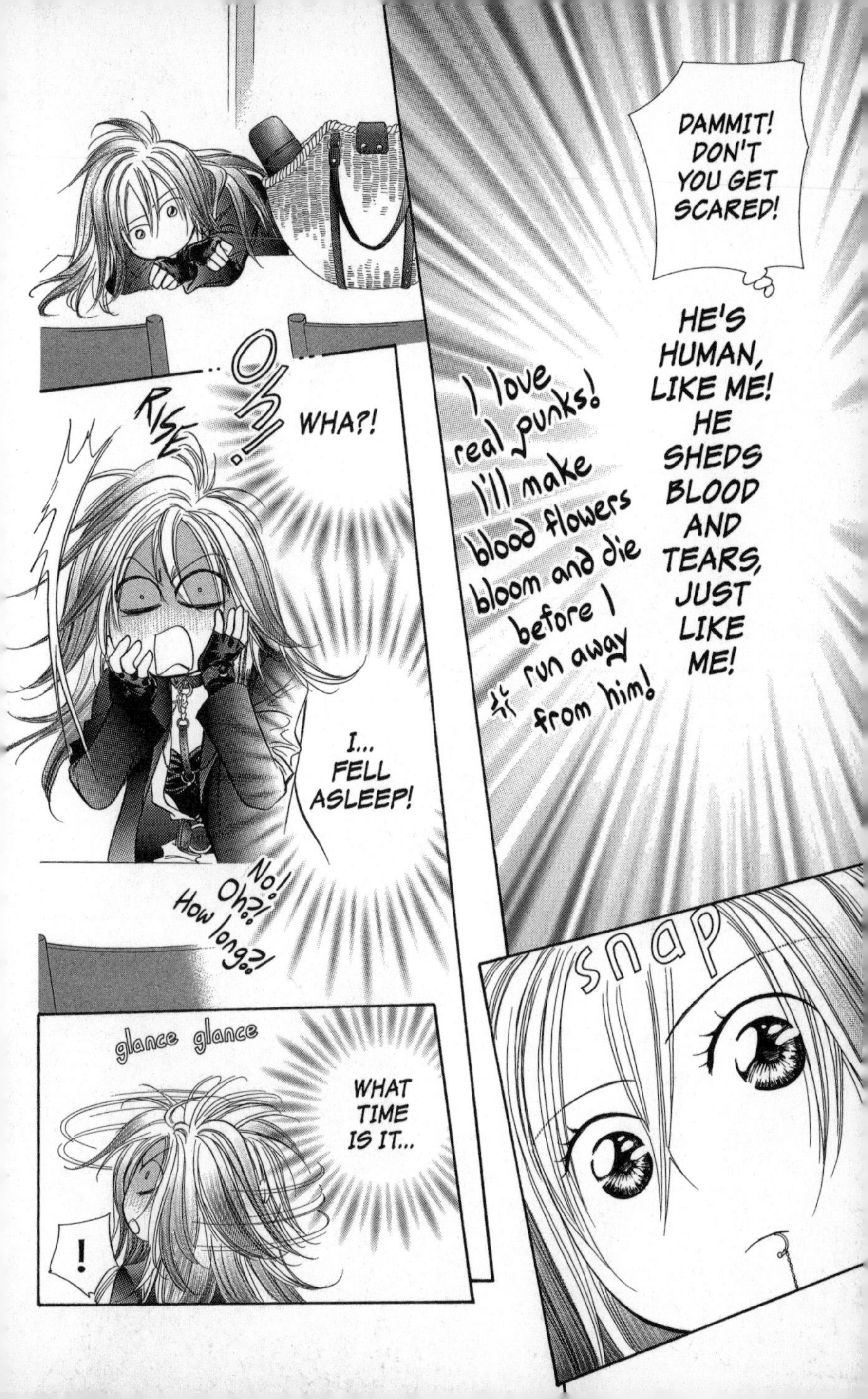
DAMMIT! DON'T YOU GET SCARED!
HE'S HUMAN, LIKE ME! HE SHEDS BLOOD AND TEARS, JUST LIKE ME!
I love real punks! I'll make blood flowers bloom and die before I run away from him!
snap
...Oh!...
RISE
WHA?!
I... FELL ASLEEP!
No! Oh?! How long?!
glance glance
WHAT TIME IS IT...
!

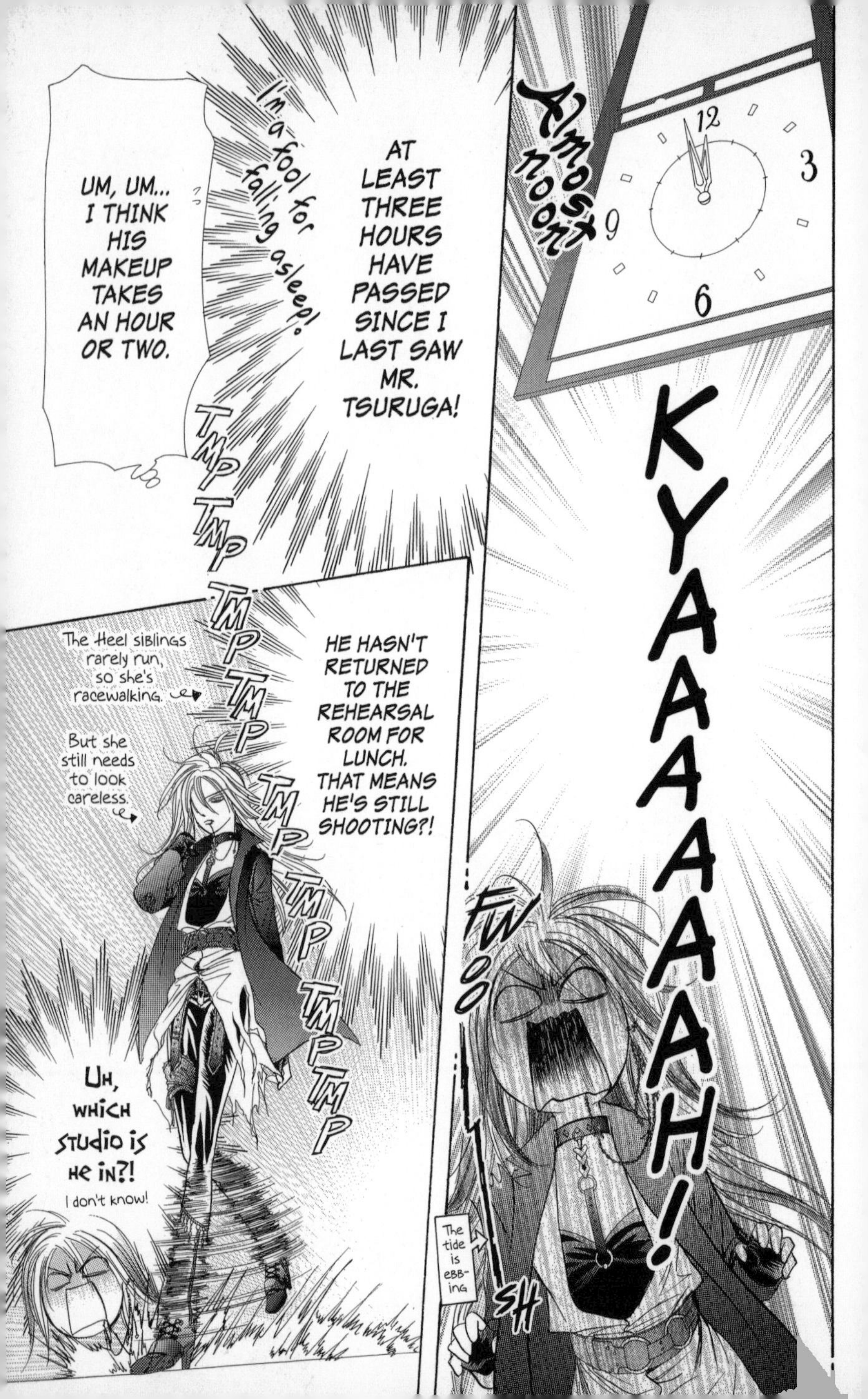
Almost noon!
KYAAAAAH!
FWOOSH
The tide is ebbing
AT LEAST THREE HOURS HAVE PASSED SINCE I LAST SAW MR. TSURUGA!
I'm a fool for falling asleep!
UM, UM... I THINK HIS MAKEUP TAKES AN HOUR OR TWO.
TMP TMP TMP TMP TMP TMP TMP TMP
HE HASN'T RETURNED TO THE REHEARSAL ROOM FOR LUNCH. THAT MEANS HE'S STILL SHOOTING?!
The Heel siblings rarely run, so she's racewalking.
But she still needs to look careless.
Uh, which studio is he in?!
I don't know!

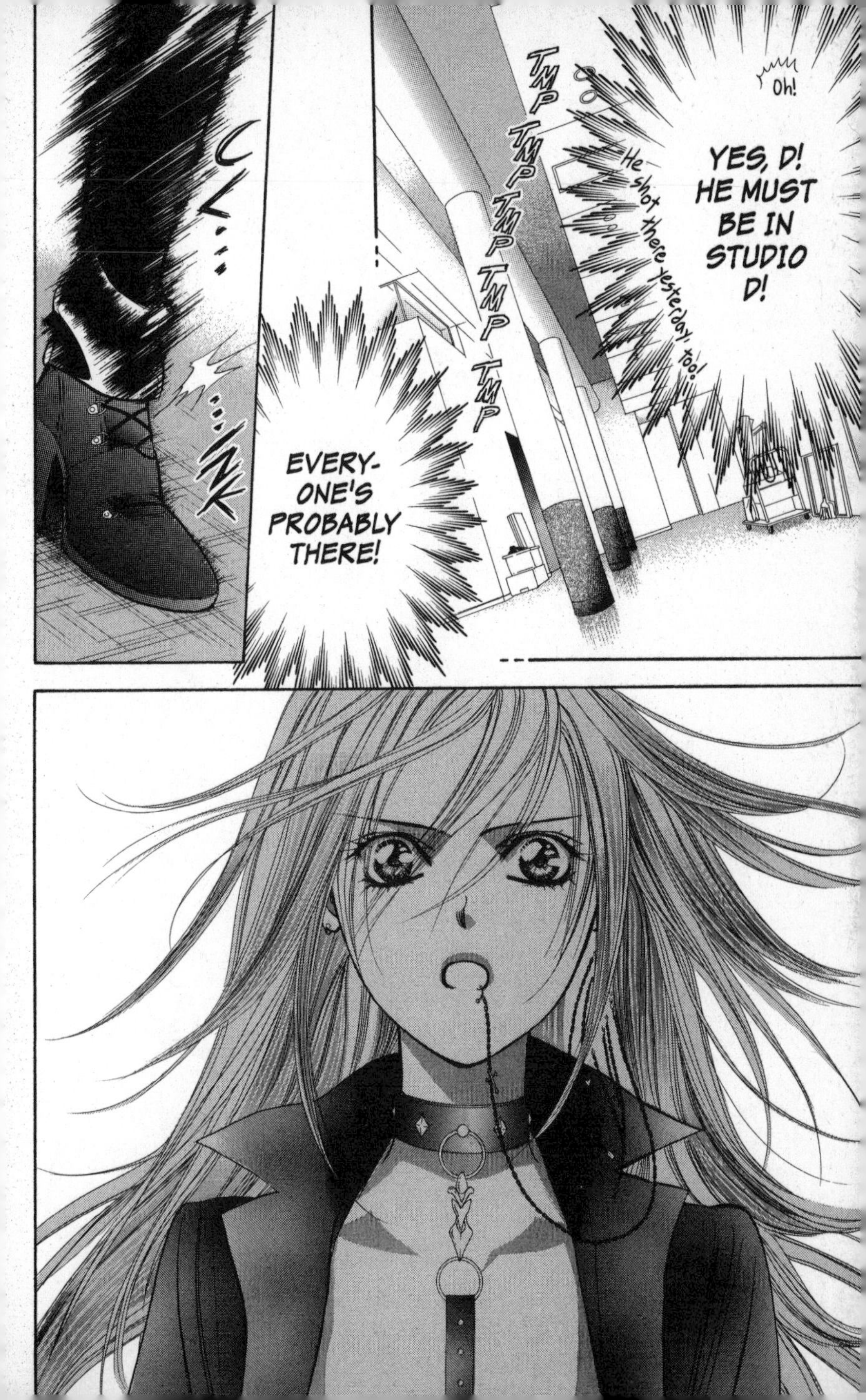
Oh!
YES, D! HE MUST BE IN STUDIO D!
He shot there yesterday, too!
TMP TMP TMP TMP TMP TMP
EVERY-ONE'S PROBABLY THERE!
CL...
...INK

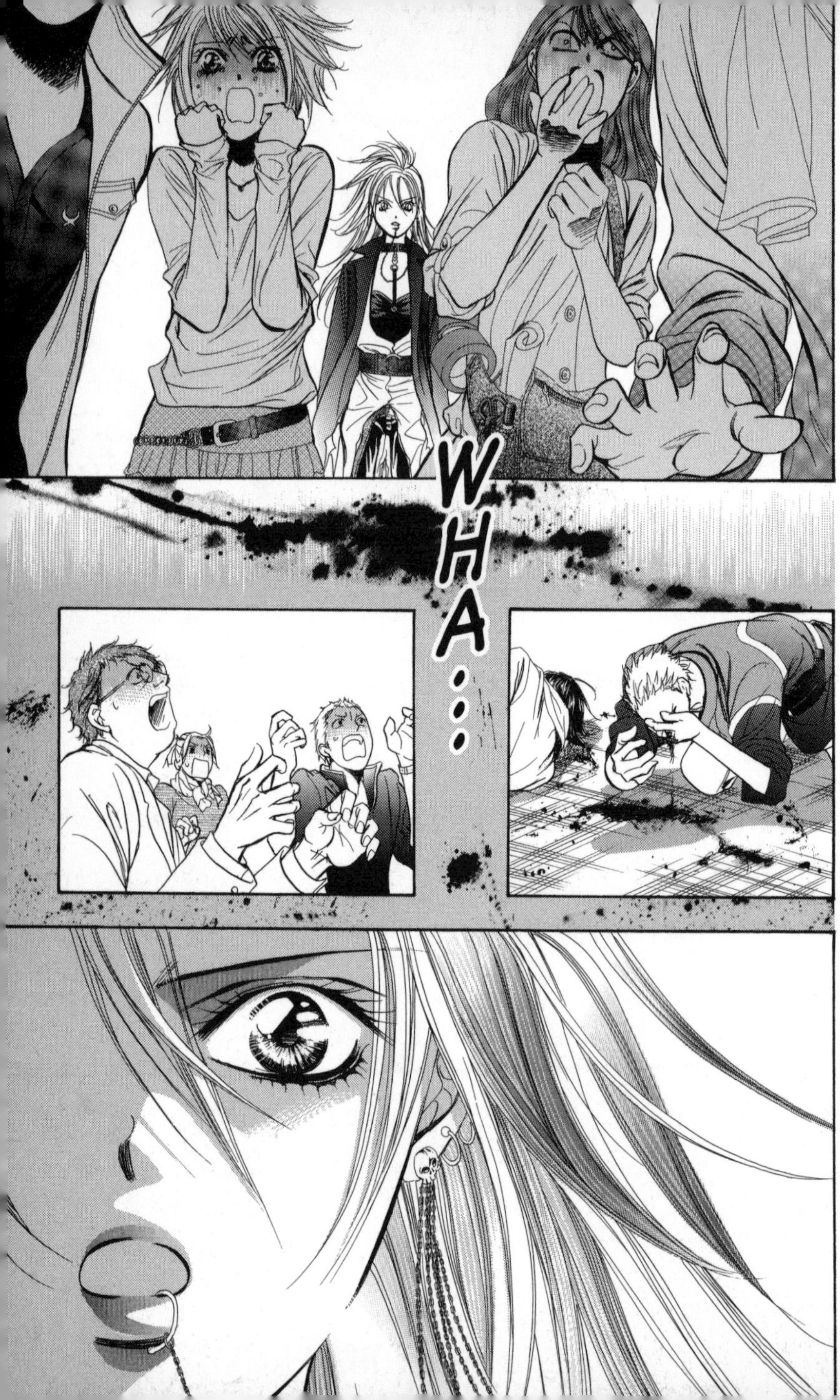
WHA...

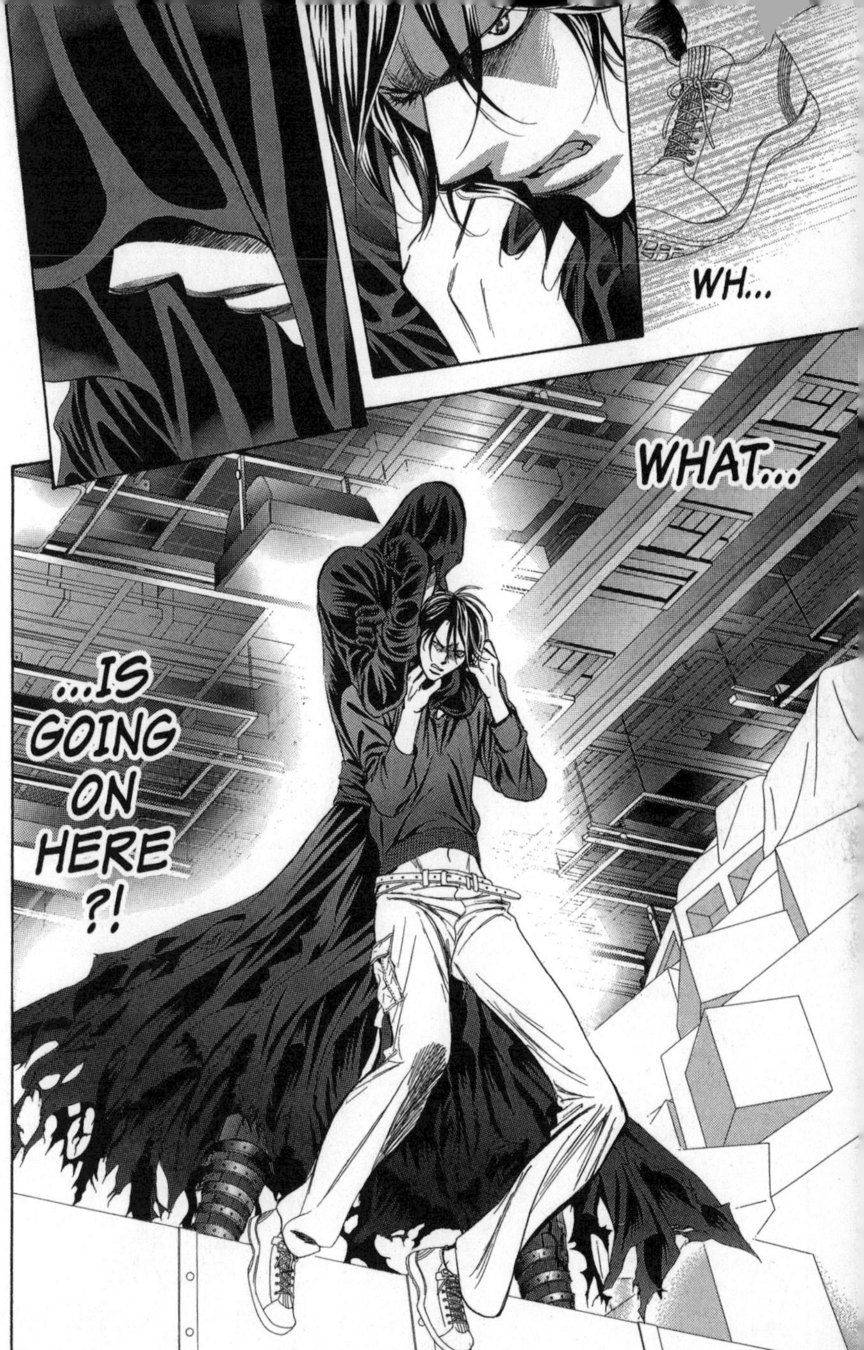
WH...
WHAT...
...IS GOING ON HERE ?!
End of Act 183

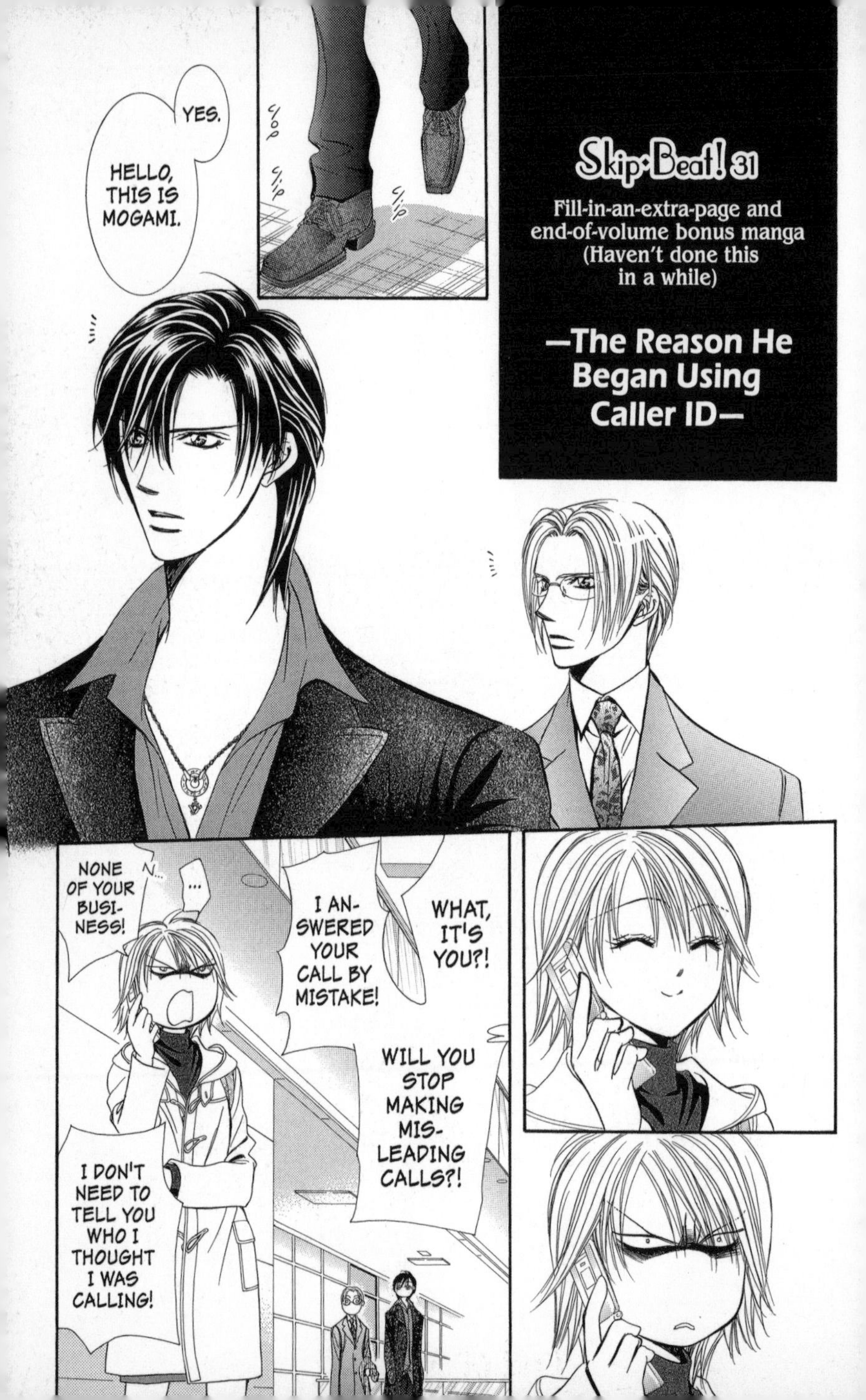
Skip·Beat! 31
Fill-in-an-extra-page and end-of-volume bonus manga (Haven't done this in a while)
—The Reason He Began Using Caller ID—
slip
slip
slip
YES.
HELLO, THIS IS MOGAMI.
WHAT, IT'S YOU?!
I ANSWERED YOUR CALL BY MISTAKE!
N...
...
NONE OF YOUR BUSINESS!
WILL YOU STOP MAKING MISLEADING CALLS?!
I DON'T NEED TO TELL YOU WHO I THOUGHT I WAS CALLING!

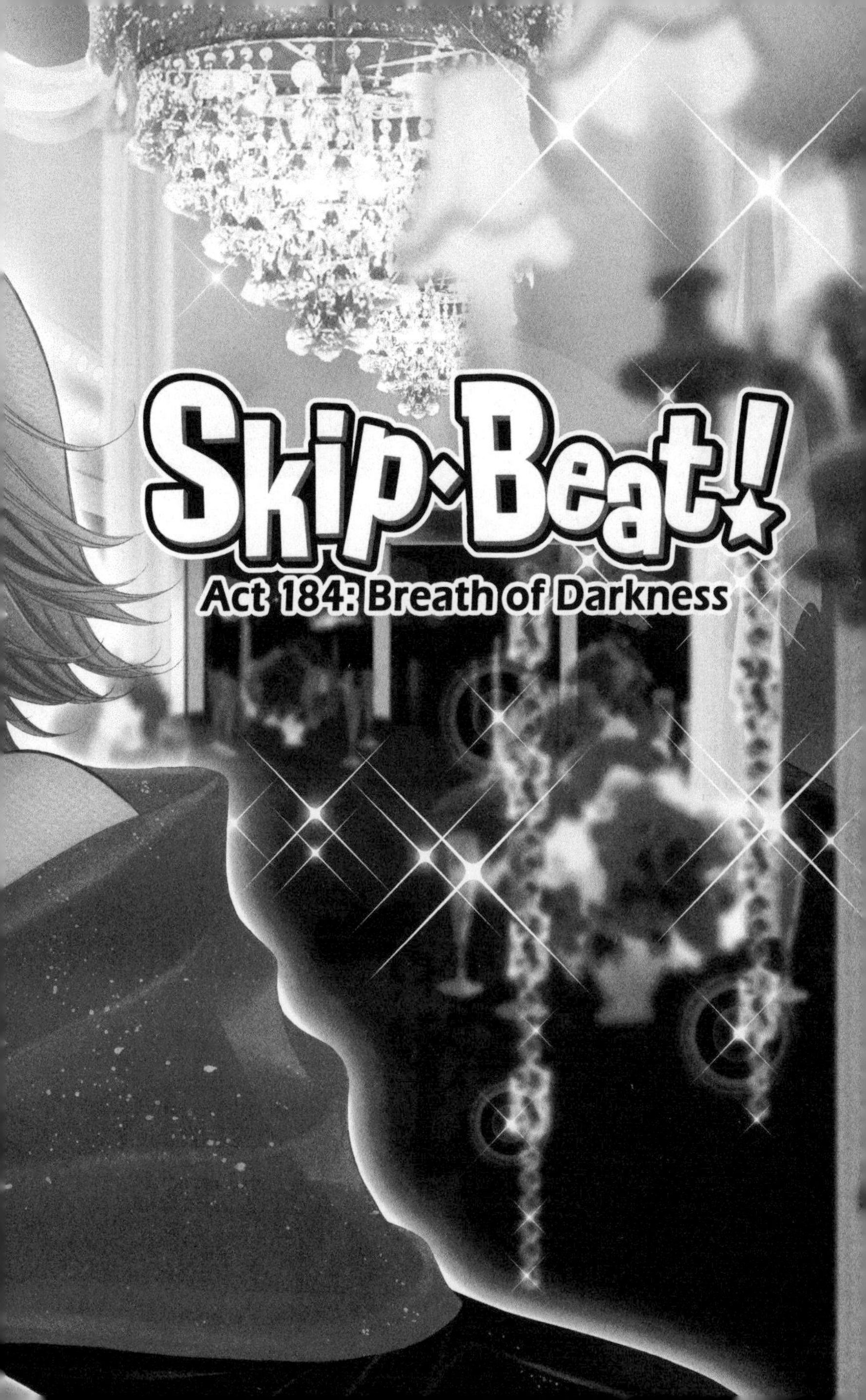
Skip·Beat!
Act 184: Breath of Darkness

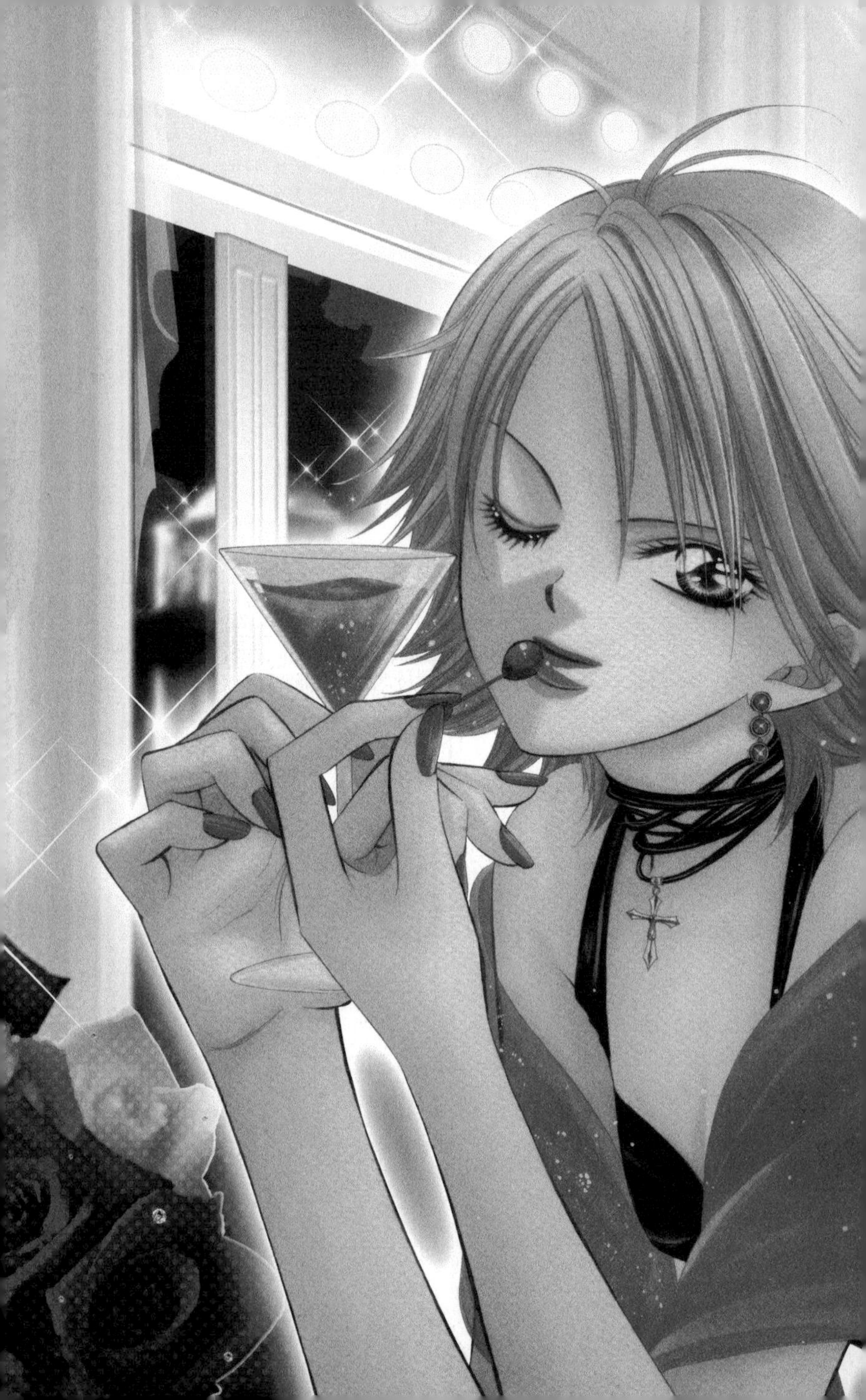

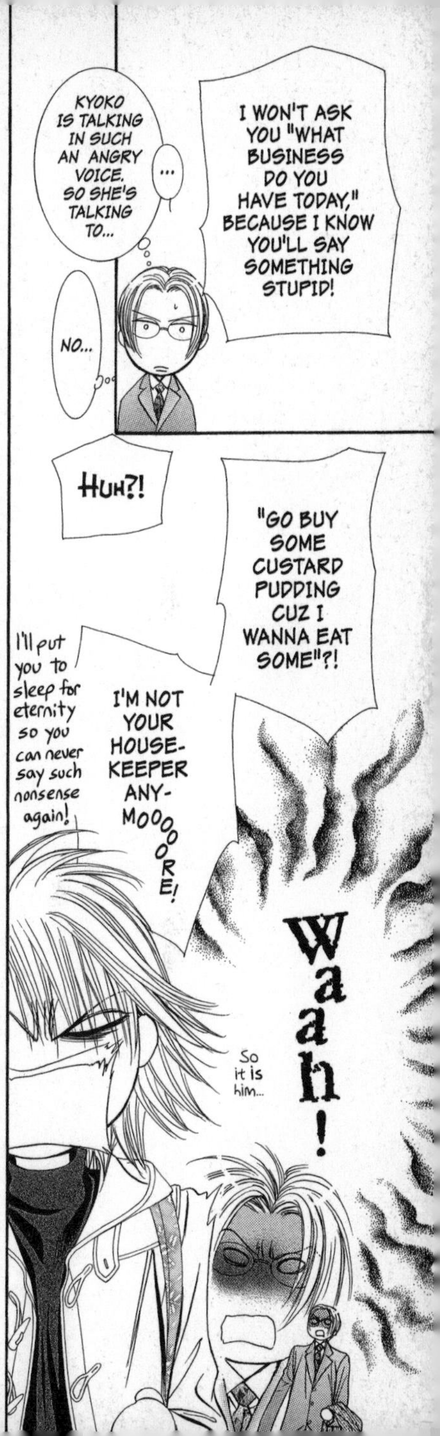
I WON'T ASK YOU "WHAT BUSINESS DO YOU HAVE TODAY," BECAUSE I KNOW YOU'LL SAY SOMETHING STUPID!
KYOKO IS TALKING IN SUCH AN ANGRY VOICE. SO SHE'S TALKING TO...
...
NO...
HUH?!
"GO BUY SOME CUSTARD PUDDING CUZ I WANNA EAT SOME"?!
I'M NOT YOUR HOUSE-KEEPER ANY-MOOOOORE!
I'll put you to sleep for eternity so you can never say such nonsense again!
Waah!
So it is him...

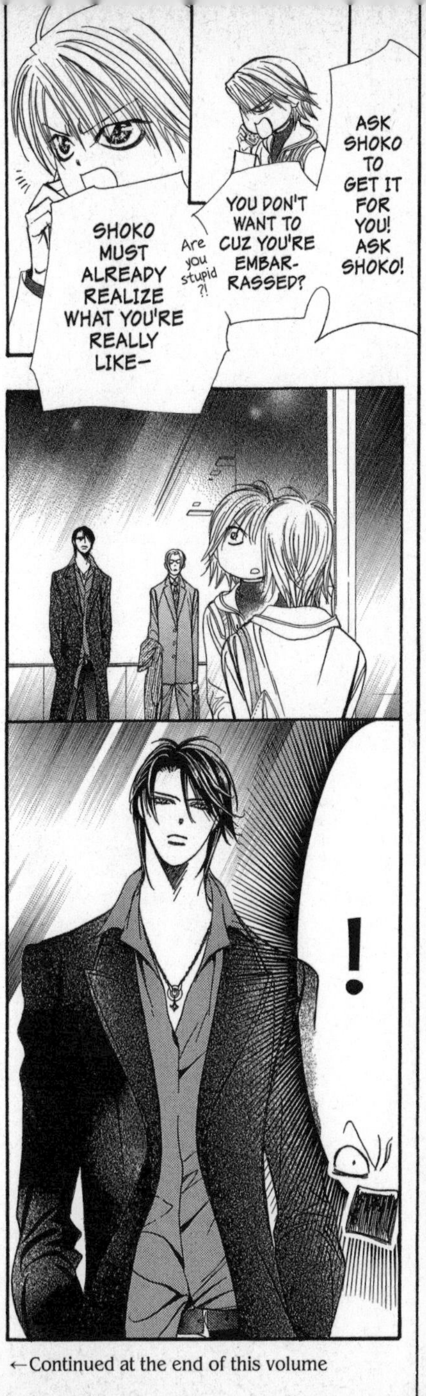
ASK SHOKO TO GET IT FOR YOU! ASK SHOKO!
YOU DON'T WANT TO CUZ YOU'RE EMBAR-RASSED?
Are you stupid?!
SHOKO MUST ALREADY REALIZE WHAT YOU'RE REALLY LIKE-
!

←Continued at the end of this volume

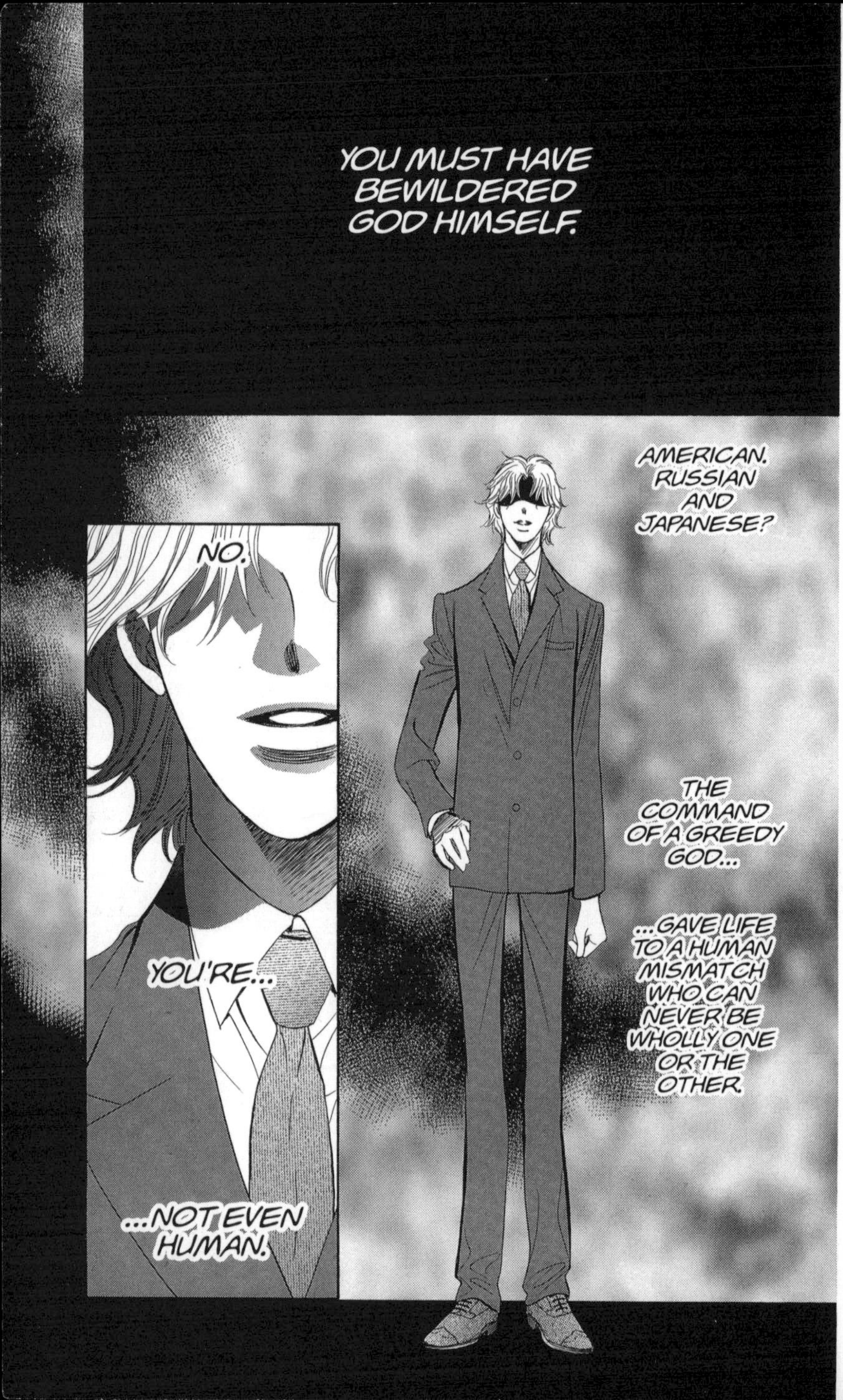
YOU MUST HAVE BEWILDERED GOD HIMSELF.
AMERICAN. RUSSIAN AND JAPANESE?
THE COMMAND OF A GREEDY GOD...
...GAVE LIFE TO A HUMAN MISMATCH WHO CAN NEVER BE WHOLLY ONE OR THE OTHER.
NO.
YOU'RE...
...NOT EVEN HUMAN.

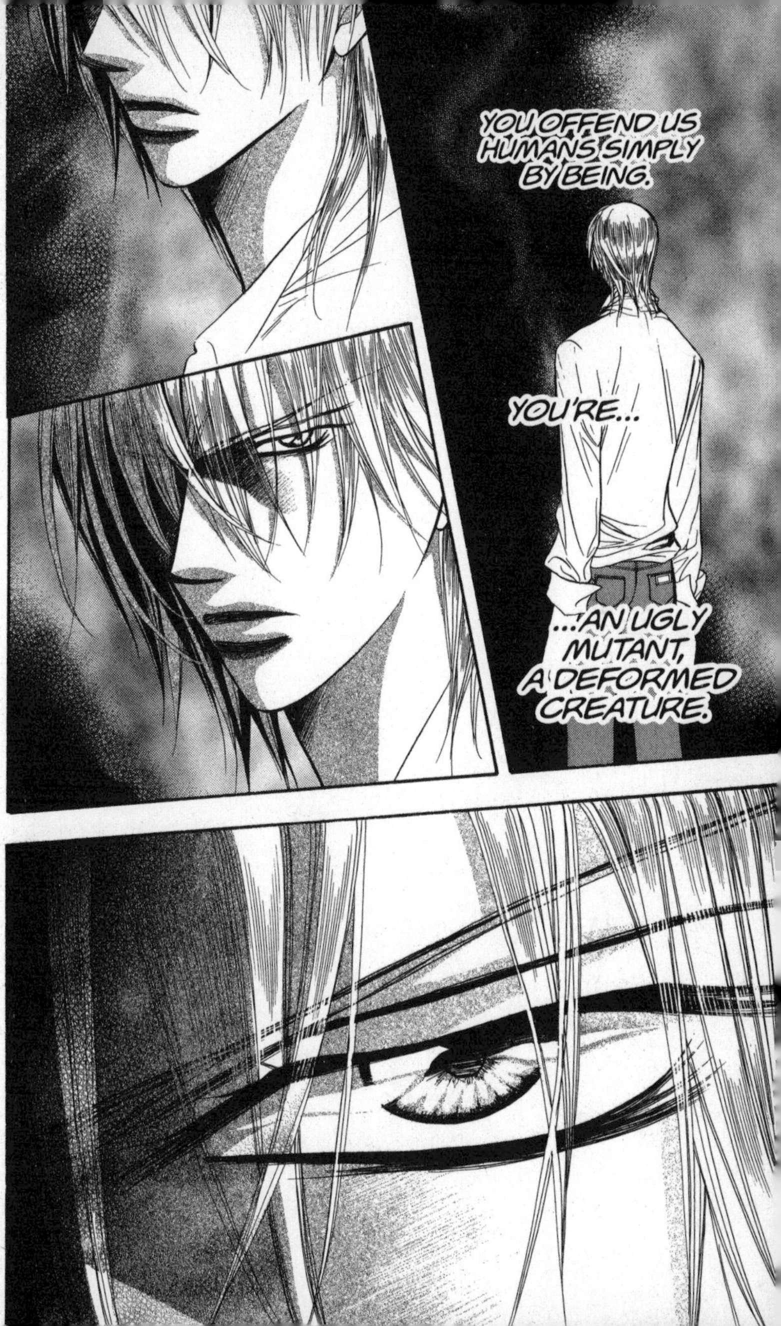
YOU OFFEND US HUMANS SIMPLY BY BEING.
YOU'RE...
...AN UGLY MUTANT, A DEFORMED CREATURE.

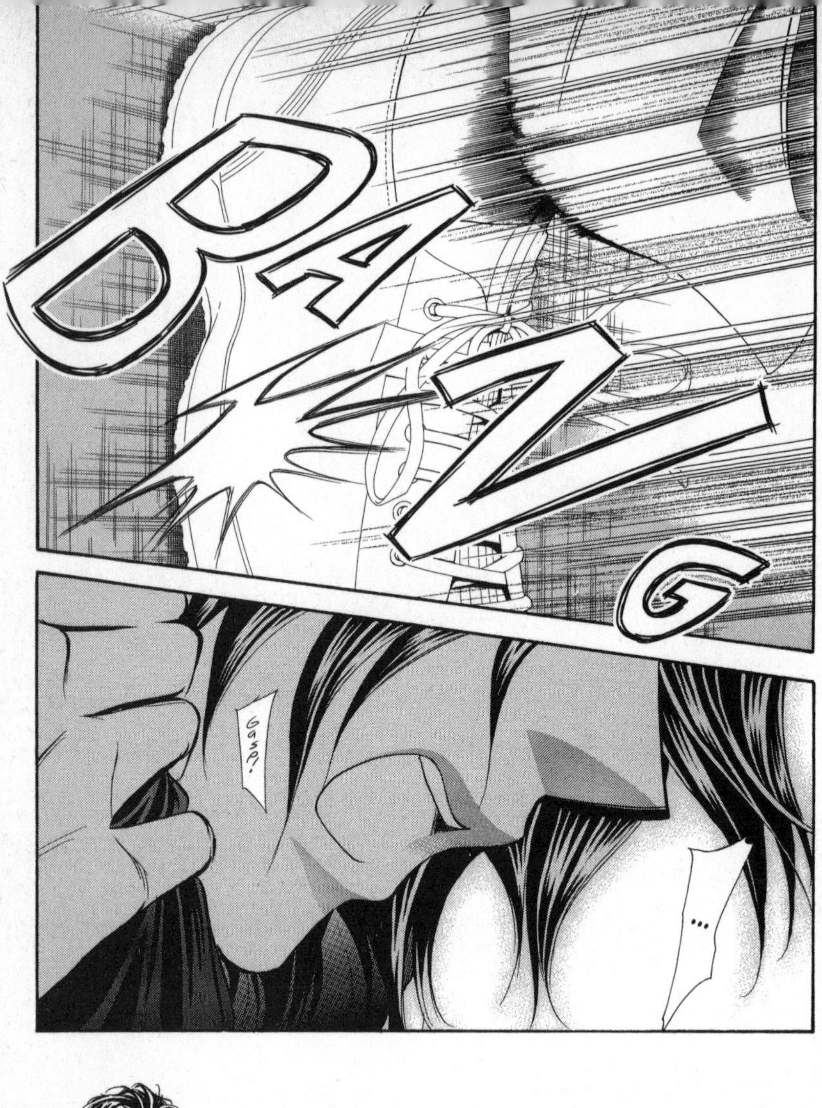
DAZNG
Gasp!
...

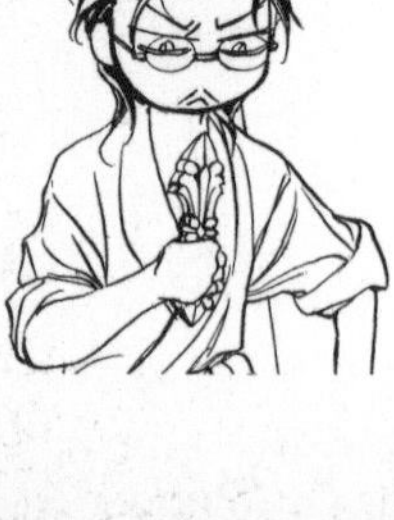

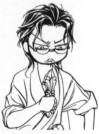

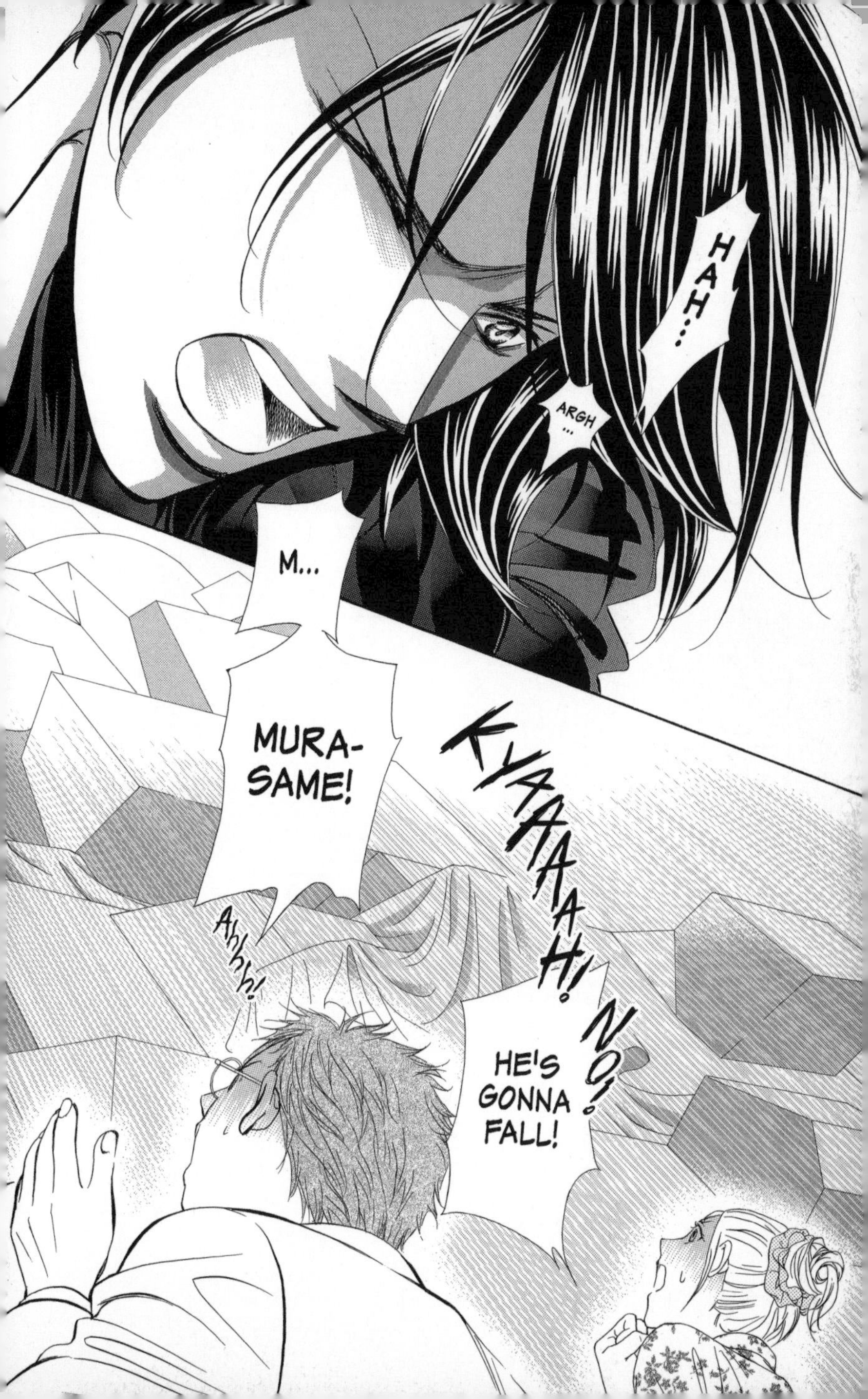
HAH...
ARGH...
M...
MURA-SAME!
KYAAAAAH!
NO!
HE'S GONNA FALL!
Ahhh!

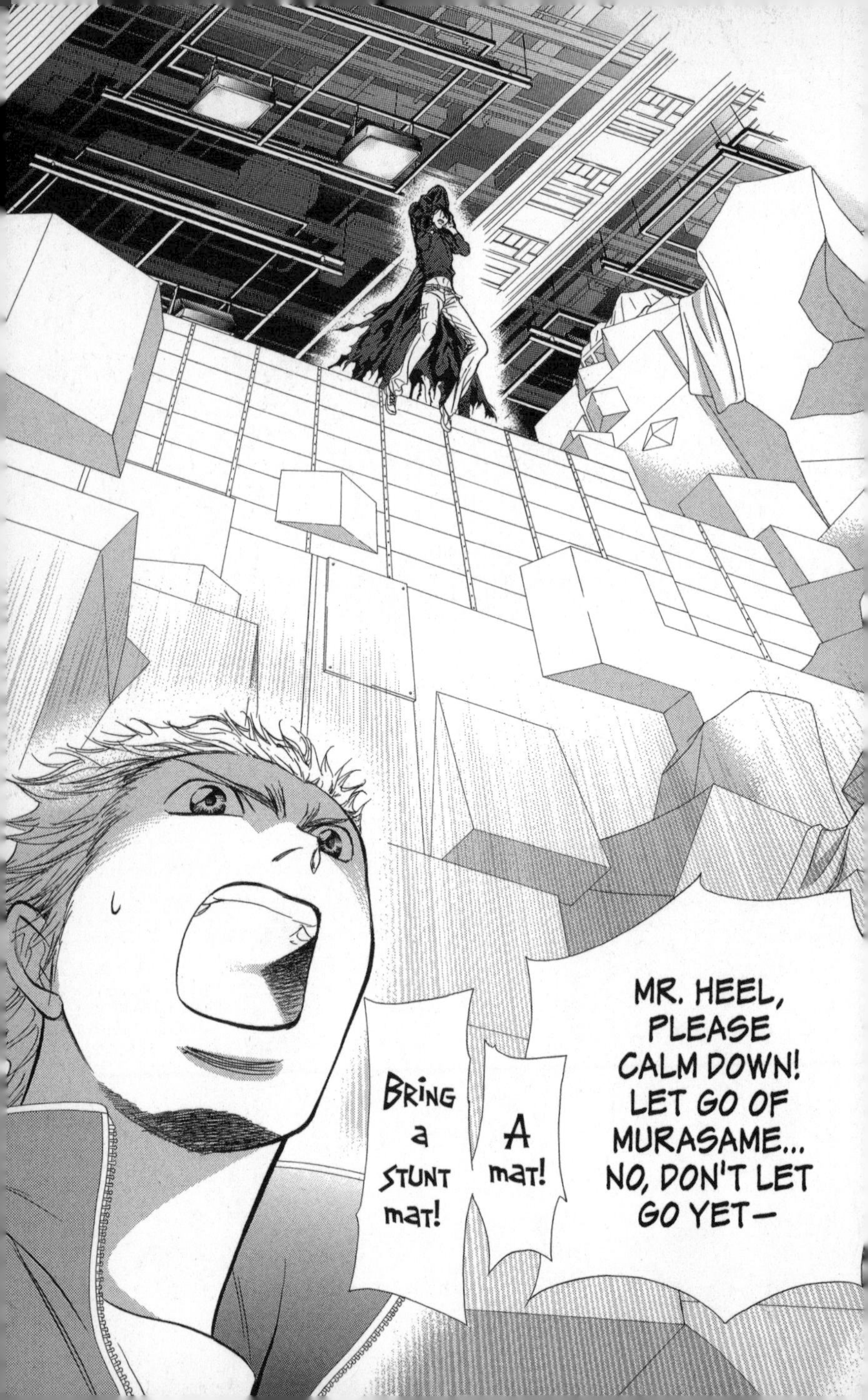
MR. HEEL, PLEASE CALM DOWN! LET GO OF MURASAME... NO, DON'T LET GO YET—
A mat!
Bring a stunt mat!

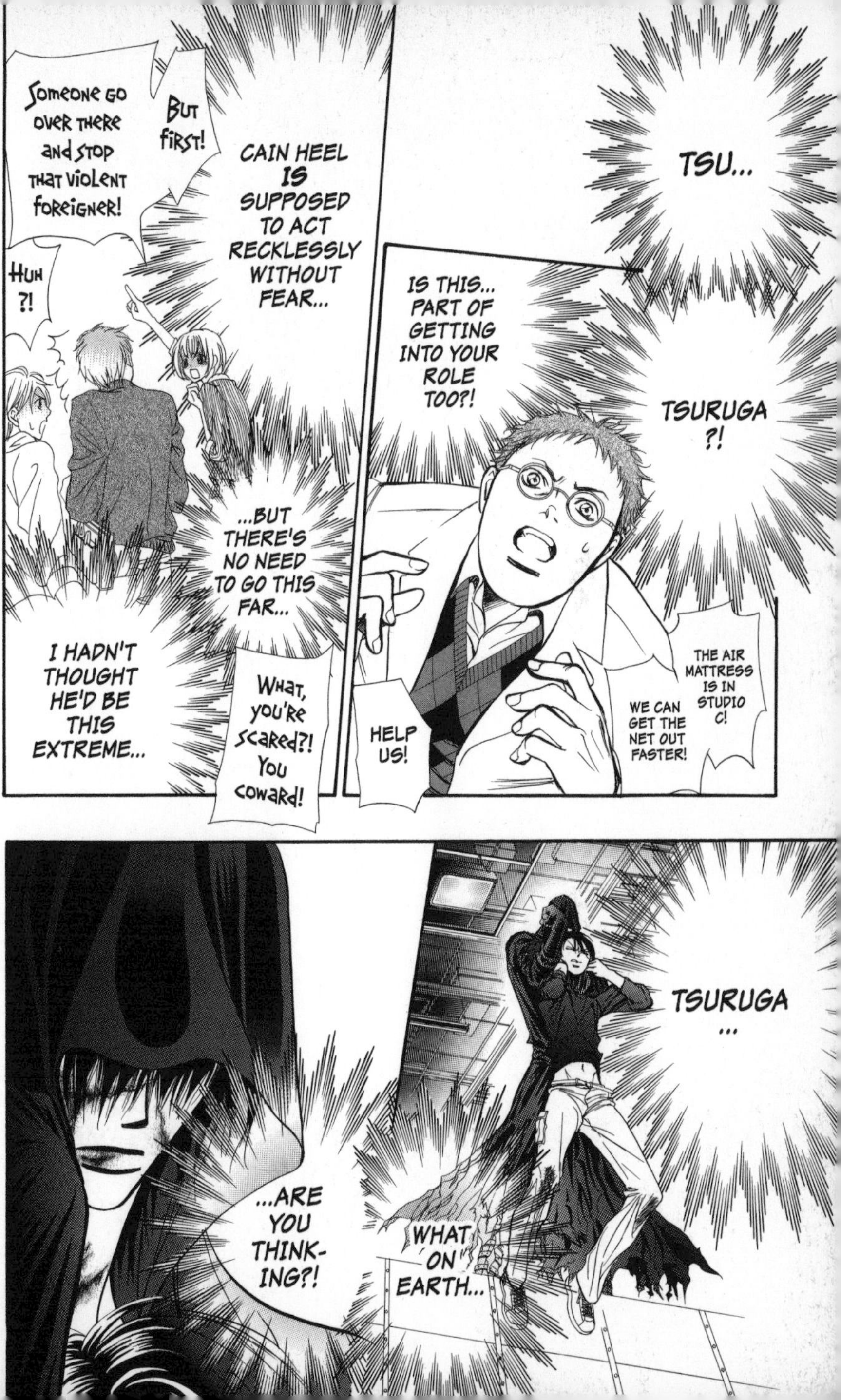
TSU...
IS THIS... PART OF GETTING INTO YOUR ROLE TOO?!
TSURUGA ?!
THE AIR MATTRESS IS IN STUDIO C!
WE CAN GET THE NET OUT FASTER!
HELP US!
But first!
Someone go over there and stop that violent foreigner!
CAIN HEEL **IS** SUPPOSED TO ACT RECKLESSLY WITHOUT FEAR...
Huh ?!
...BUT THERE'S NO NEED TO GO THIS FAR...
What, you're scared?! You coward!
I HADN'T THOUGHT HE'D BE THIS EXTREME...
TSURUGA ...
WHAT ON EARTH...
...ARE YOU THINKING?!

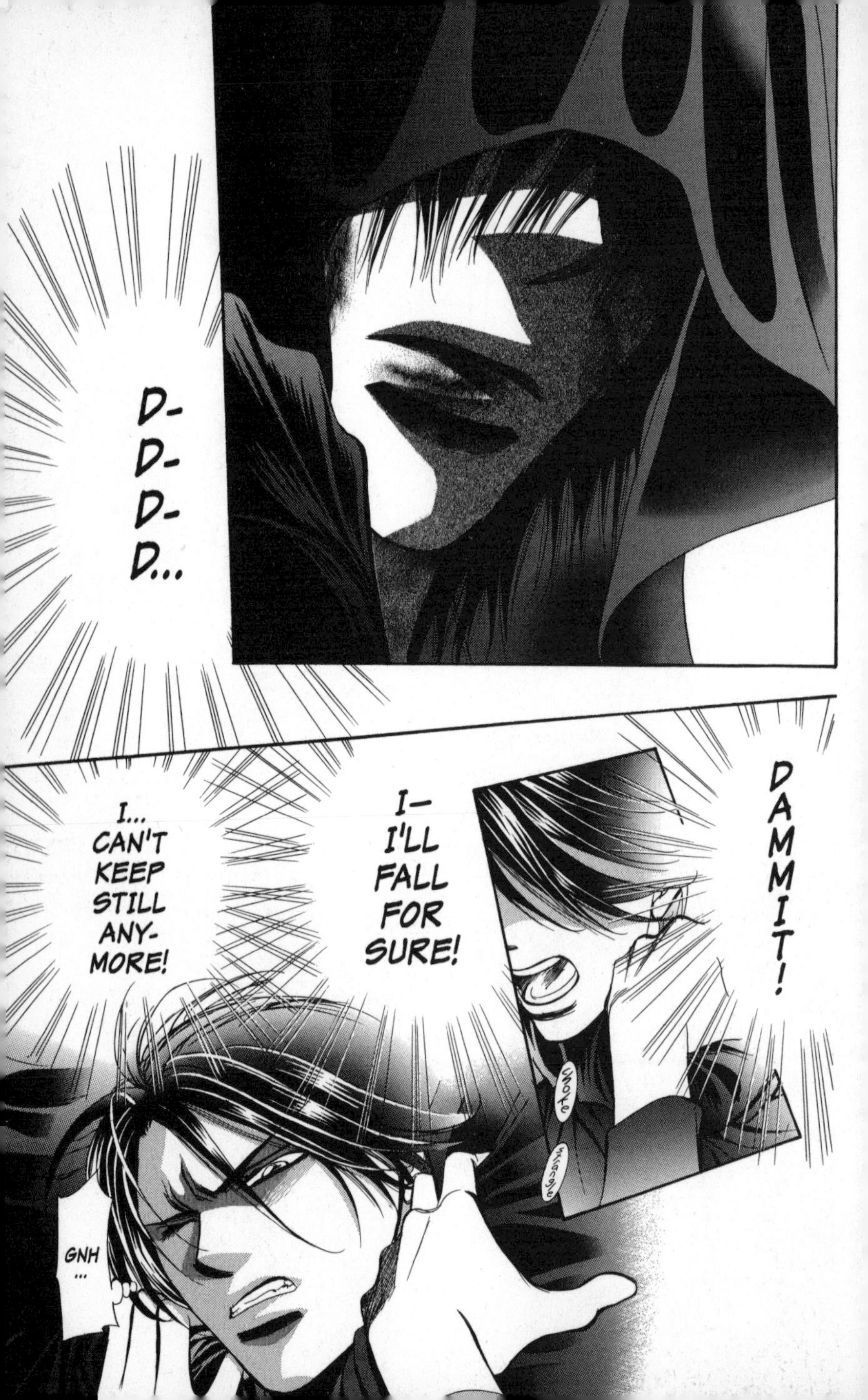
D-
D-
D-
D...
DAMMIT!
I— I'LL FALL FOR SURE!
I... CAN'T KEEP STILL ANY-MORE!
choke
strangle
GNH...

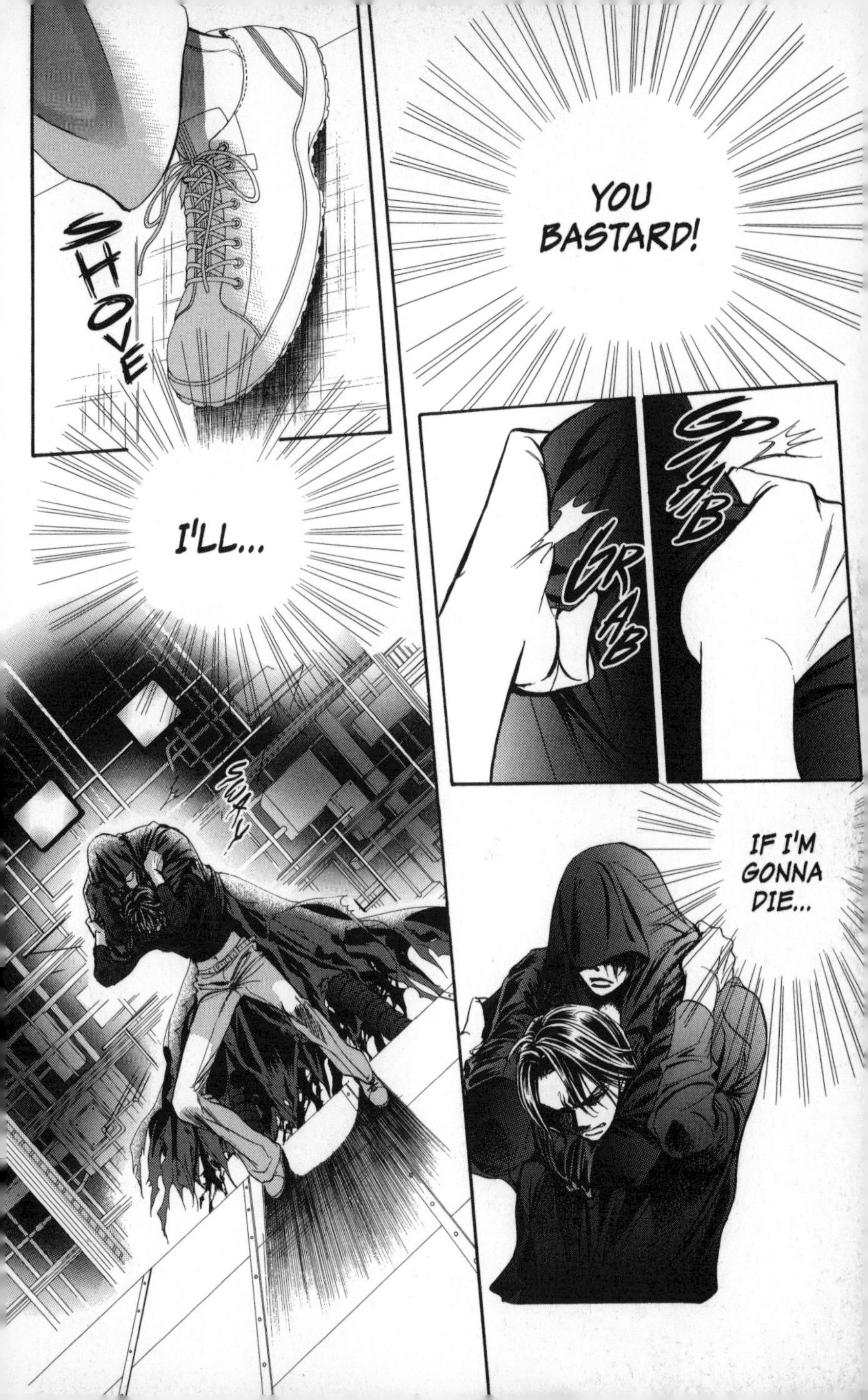
YOU BASTARD!
SHOVE
GRAB
GRAB
I'LL...
IF I'M GONNA DIE...
SWAY

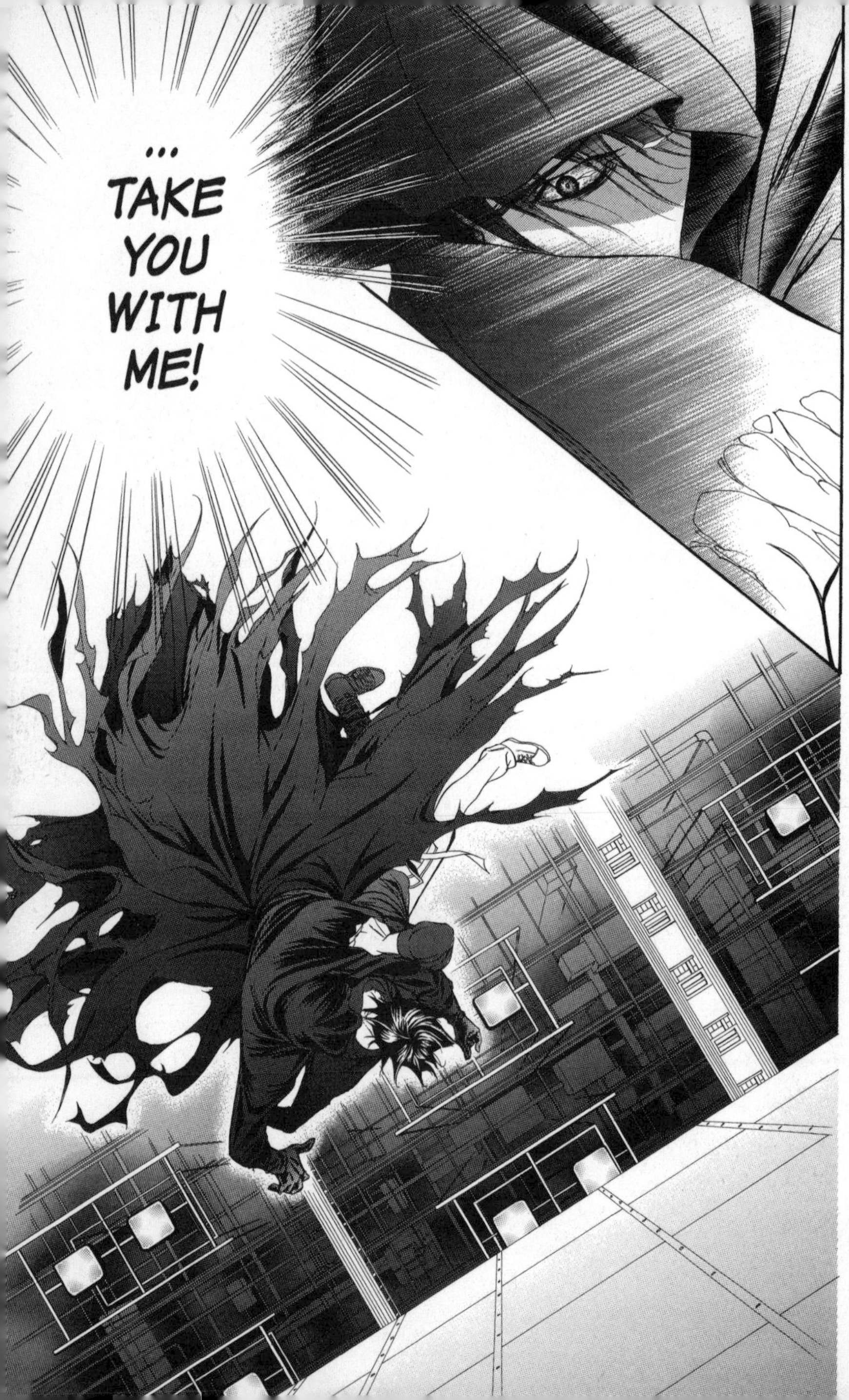
... TAKE YOU WITH ME!

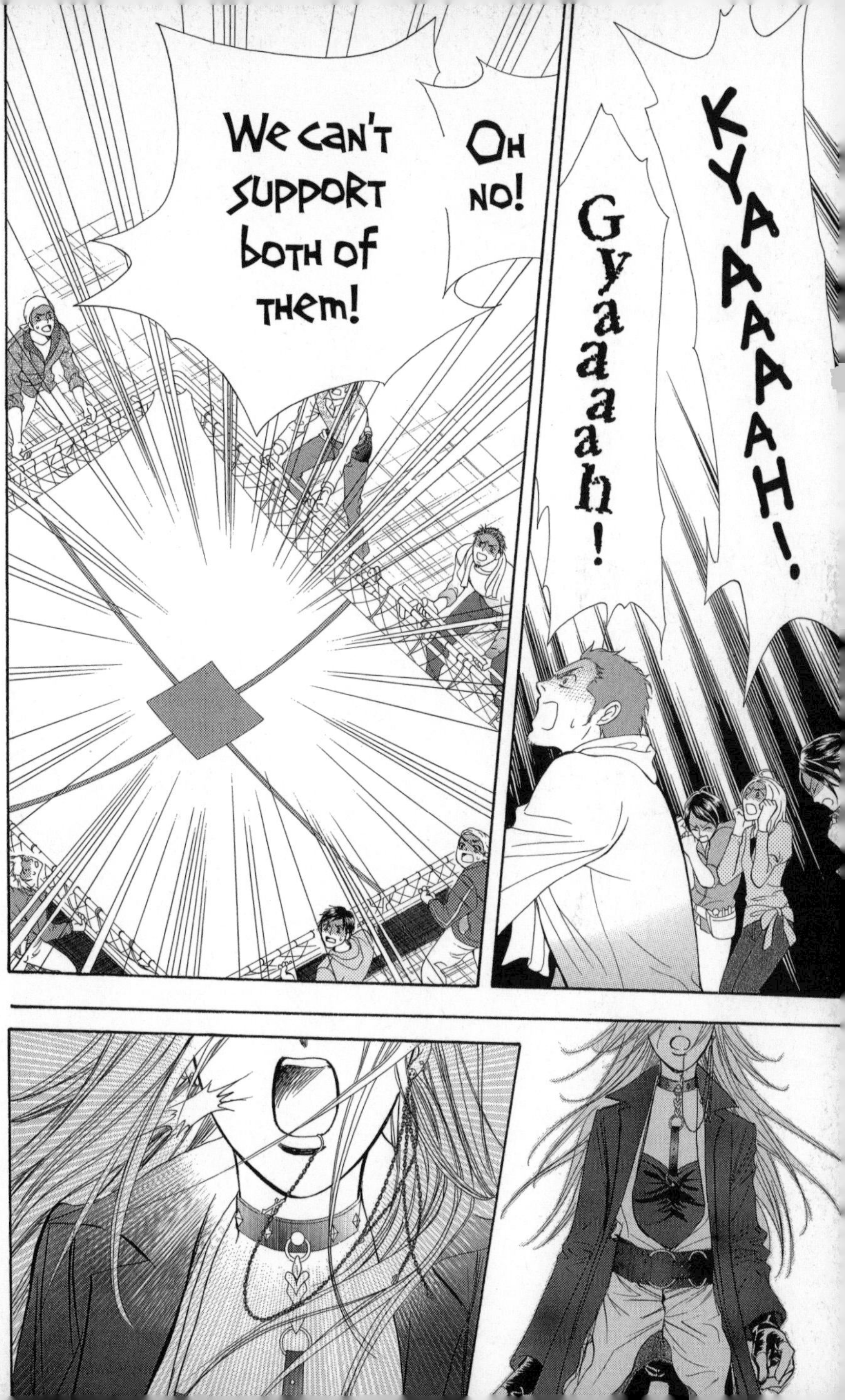
KYAAAAAH!
Gyaaaah!
OH NO!
We can't support both of them!

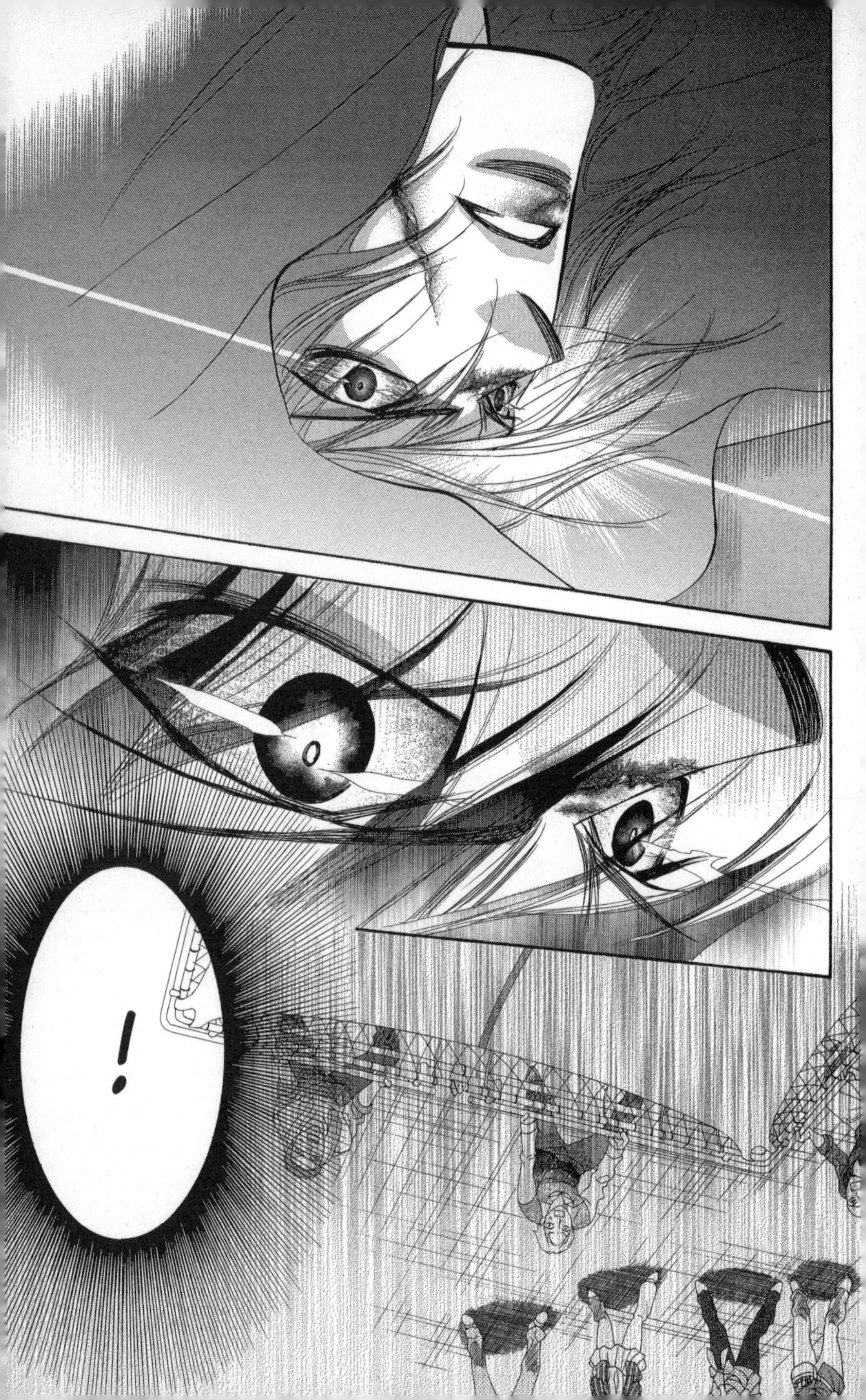
!

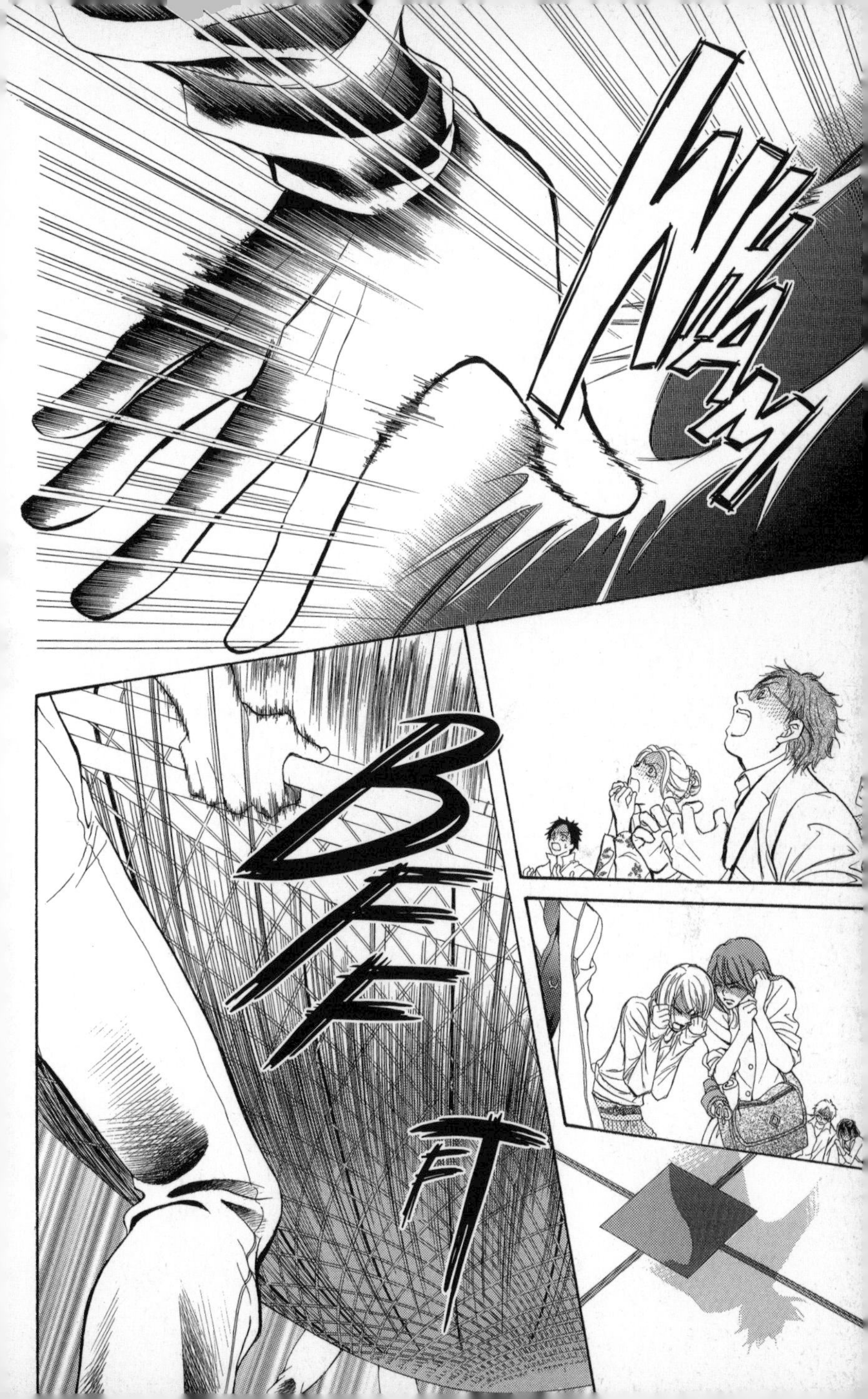
WHAM
BFFFT

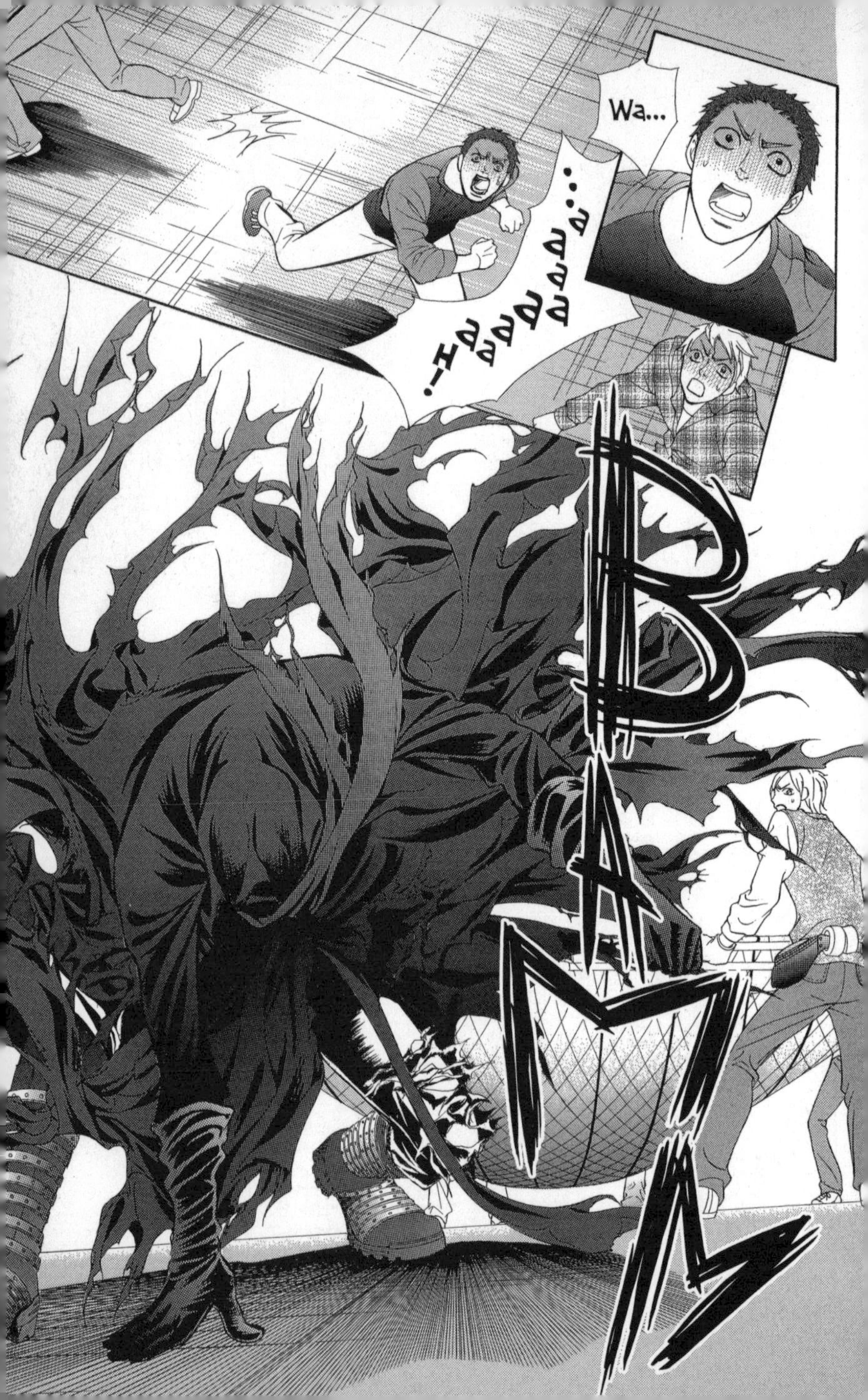
Wa...
...aaaaaaaaah!
BAM

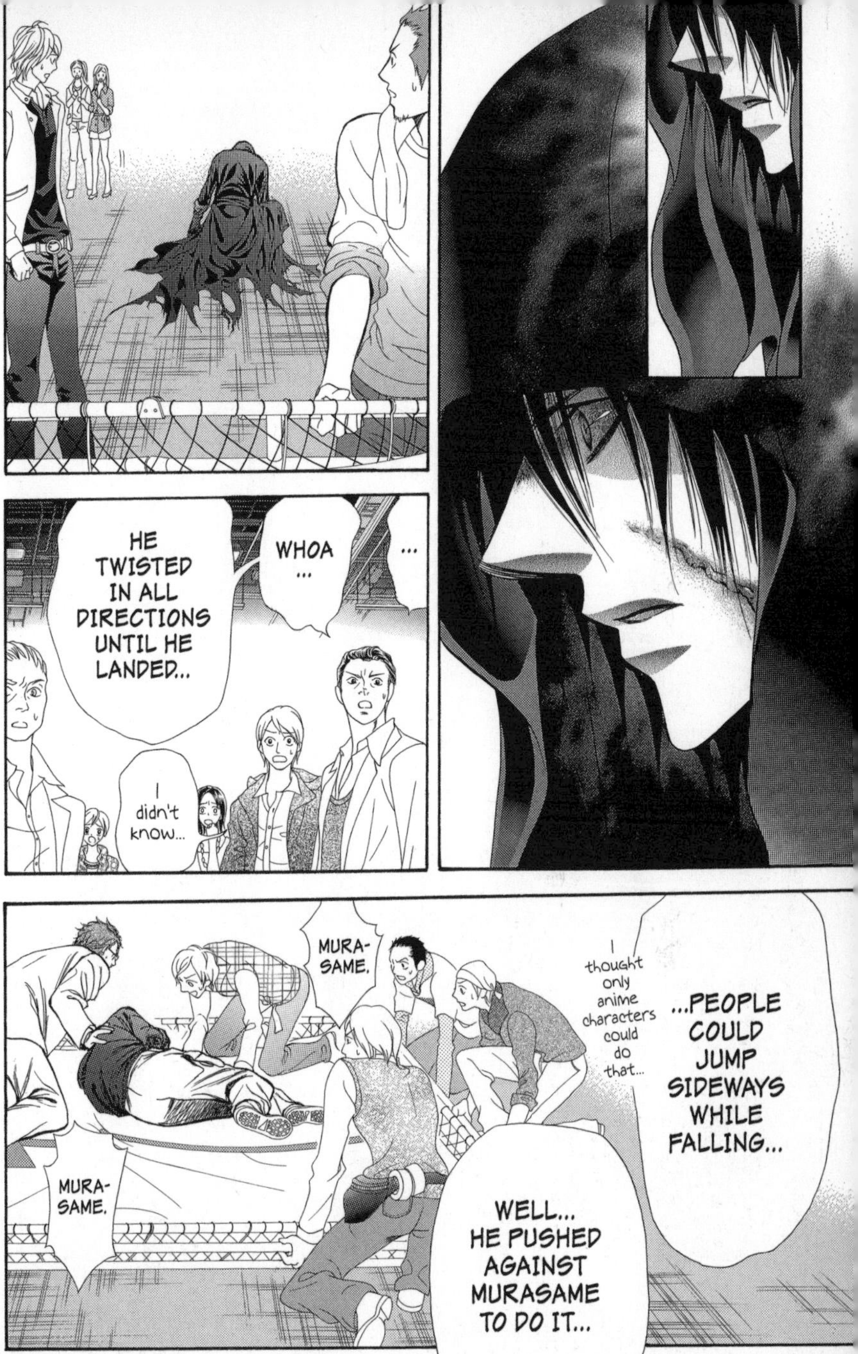
...
WHOA ...
HE TWISTED IN ALL DIRECTIONS UNTIL HE LANDED...
I didn't know...
...PEOPLE COULD JUMP SIDEWAYS WHILE FALLING...
I thought only anime characters could do that...
MURA-SAME.
WELL... HE PUSHED AGAINST MURASAME TO DO IT...
MURA-SAME.

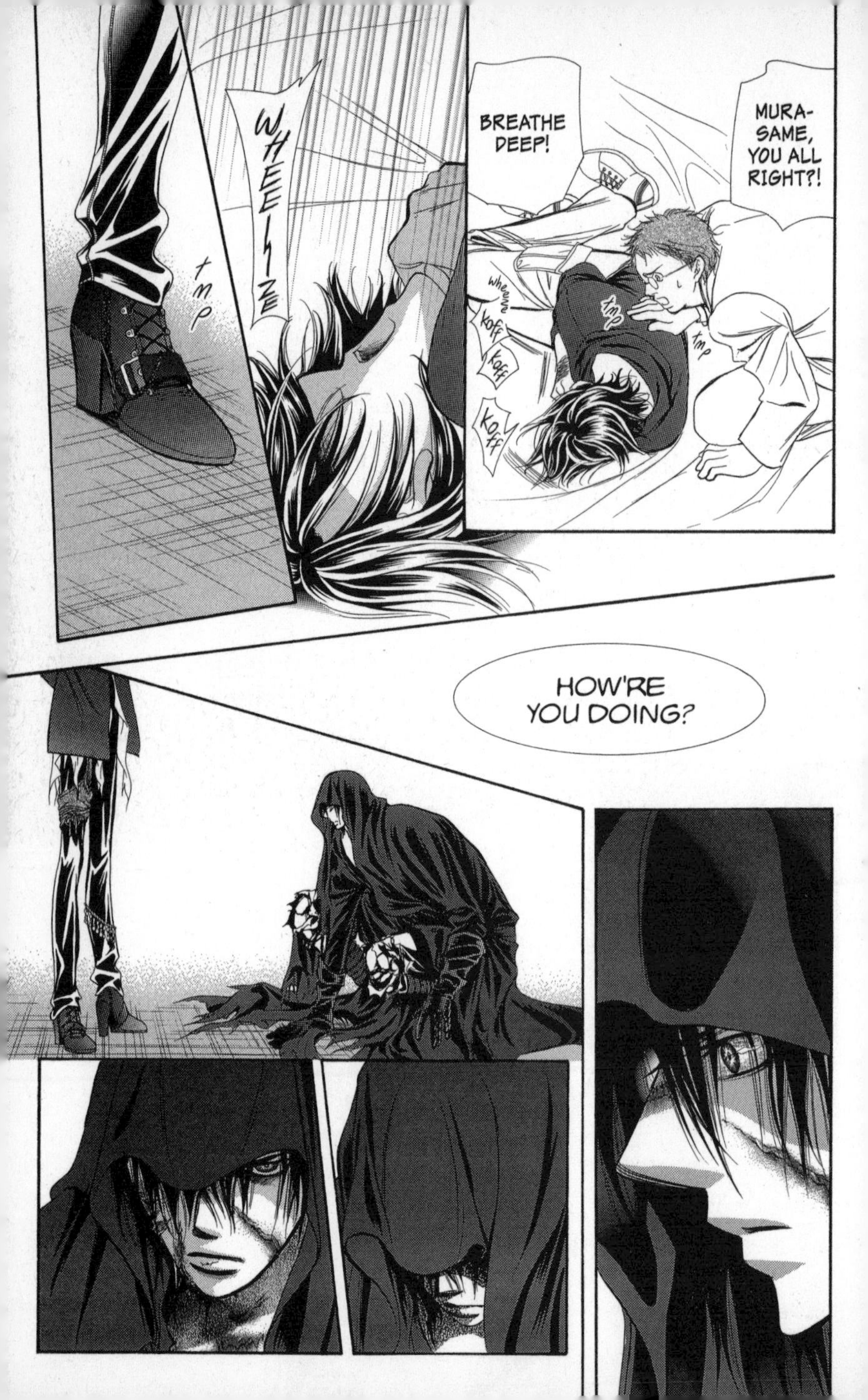
MURA-SAME, YOU ALL RIGHT?!
BREATHE DEEP!
tmp
wheeze
koff
koff
koff
tmp
WHEEEZE
tmp
HOW'RE YOU DOING?

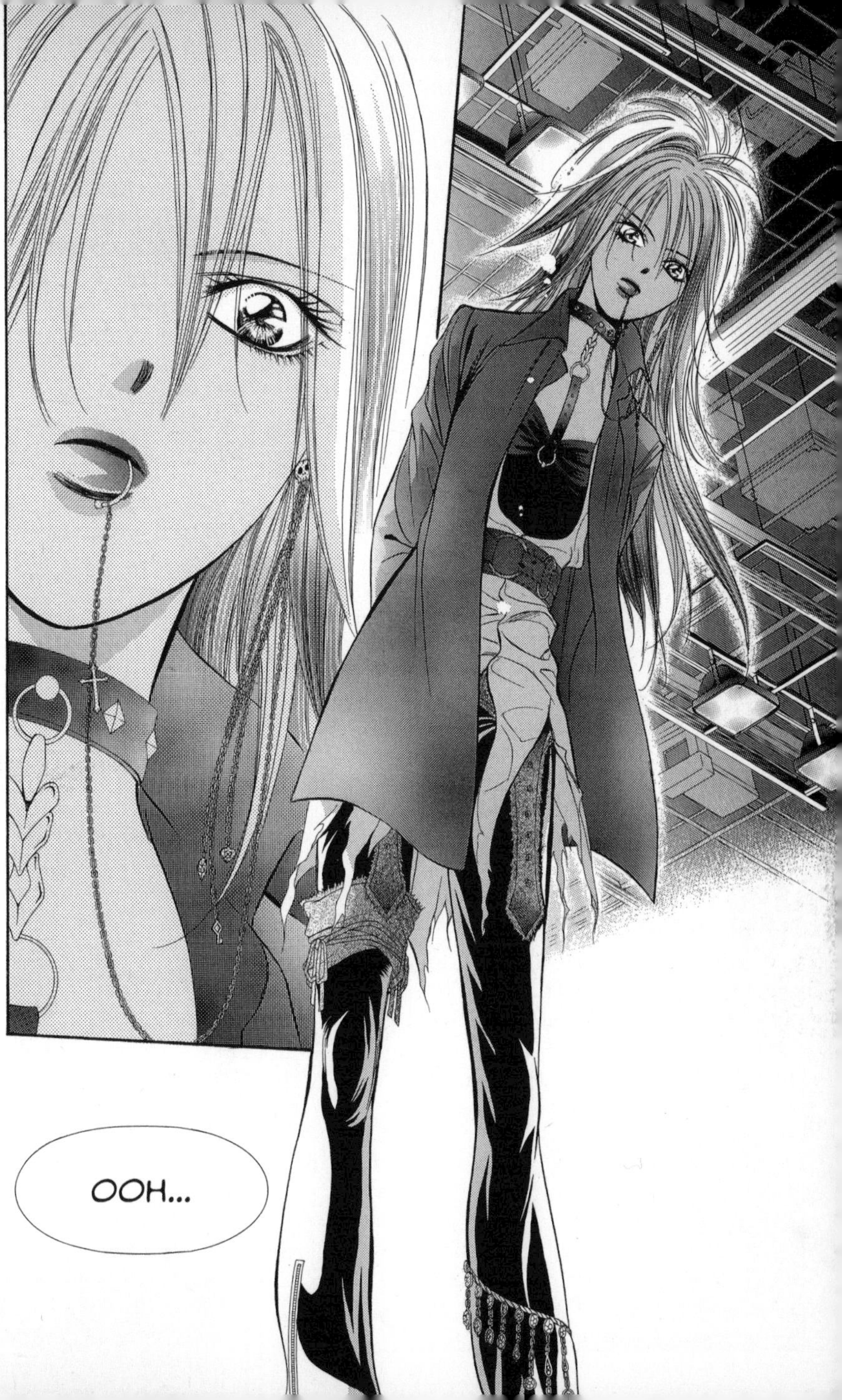
OOH...

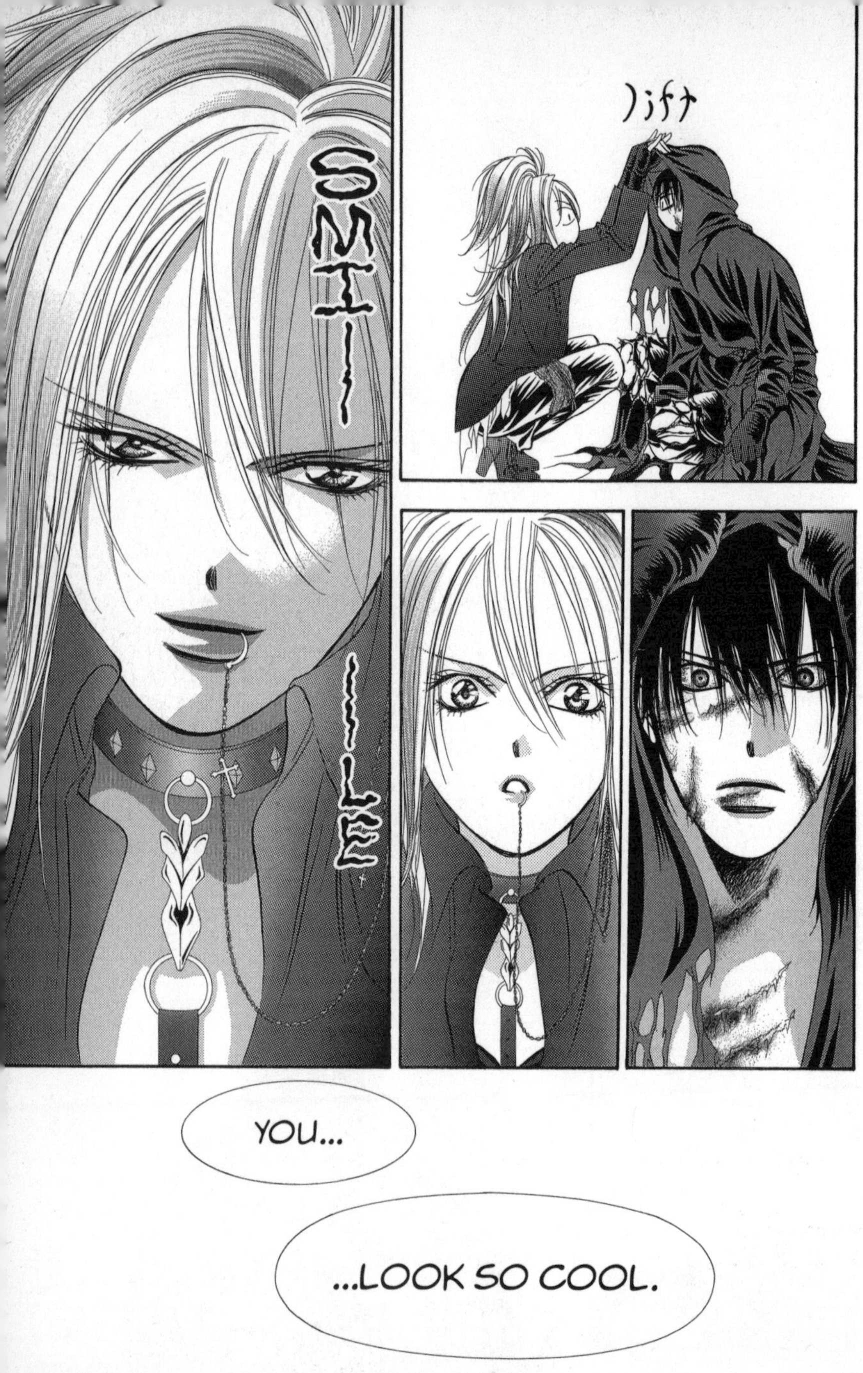
lift
SMI---LE
YOU...
...LOOK SO COOL.

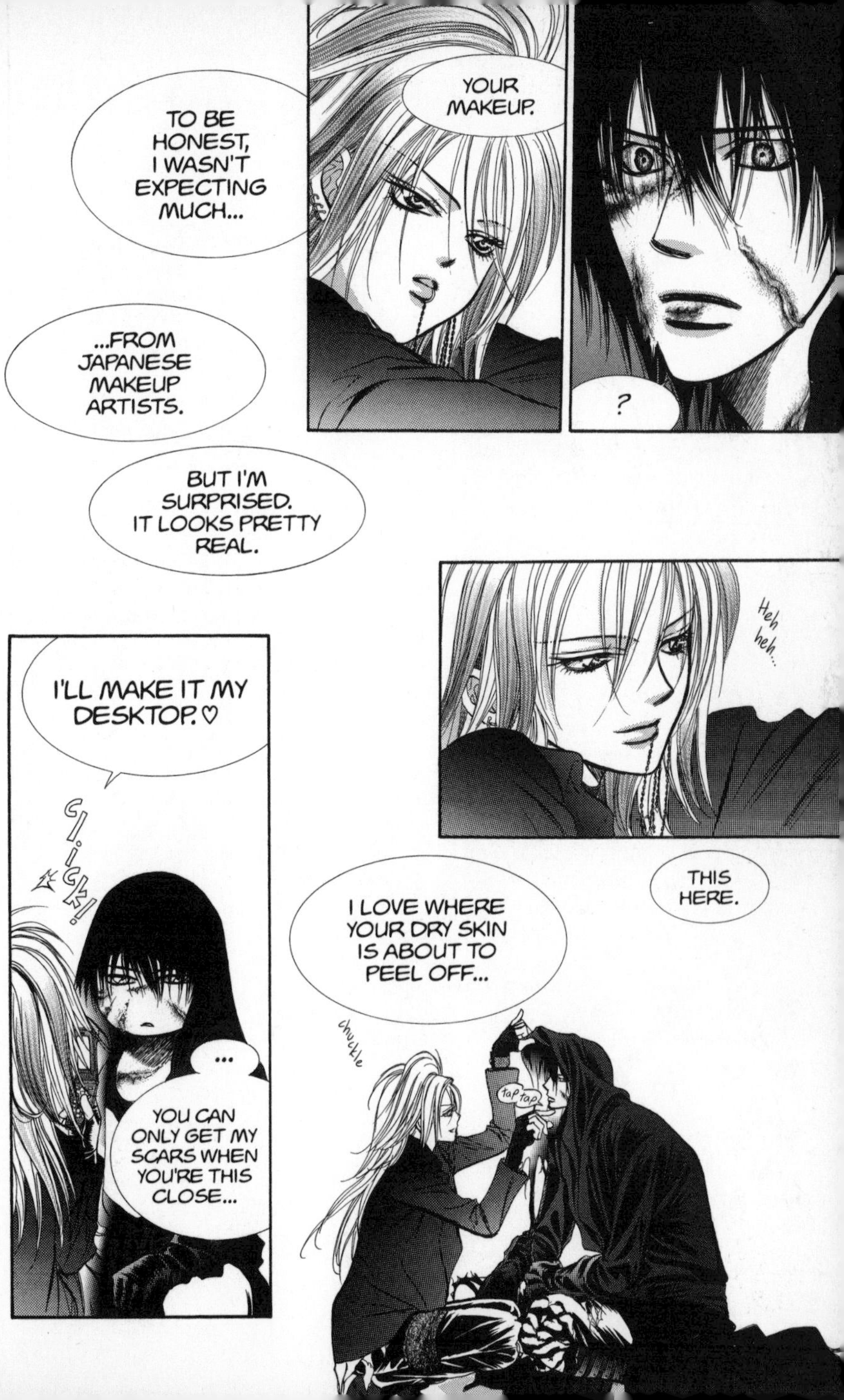
?
YOUR MAKEUP.
TO BE HONEST, I WASN'T EXPECTING MUCH...
...FROM JAPANESE MAKEUP ARTISTS.
BUT I'M SURPRISED. IT LOOKS PRETTY REAL.
Heh heh...
THIS HERE.
I LOVE WHERE YOUR DRY SKIN IS ABOUT TO PEEL OFF...
chuckle
tap tap
I'LL MAKE IT MY DESKTOP.♡
CLICK!
...
YOU CAN ONLY GET MY SCARS WHEN YOU'RE THIS CLOSE...

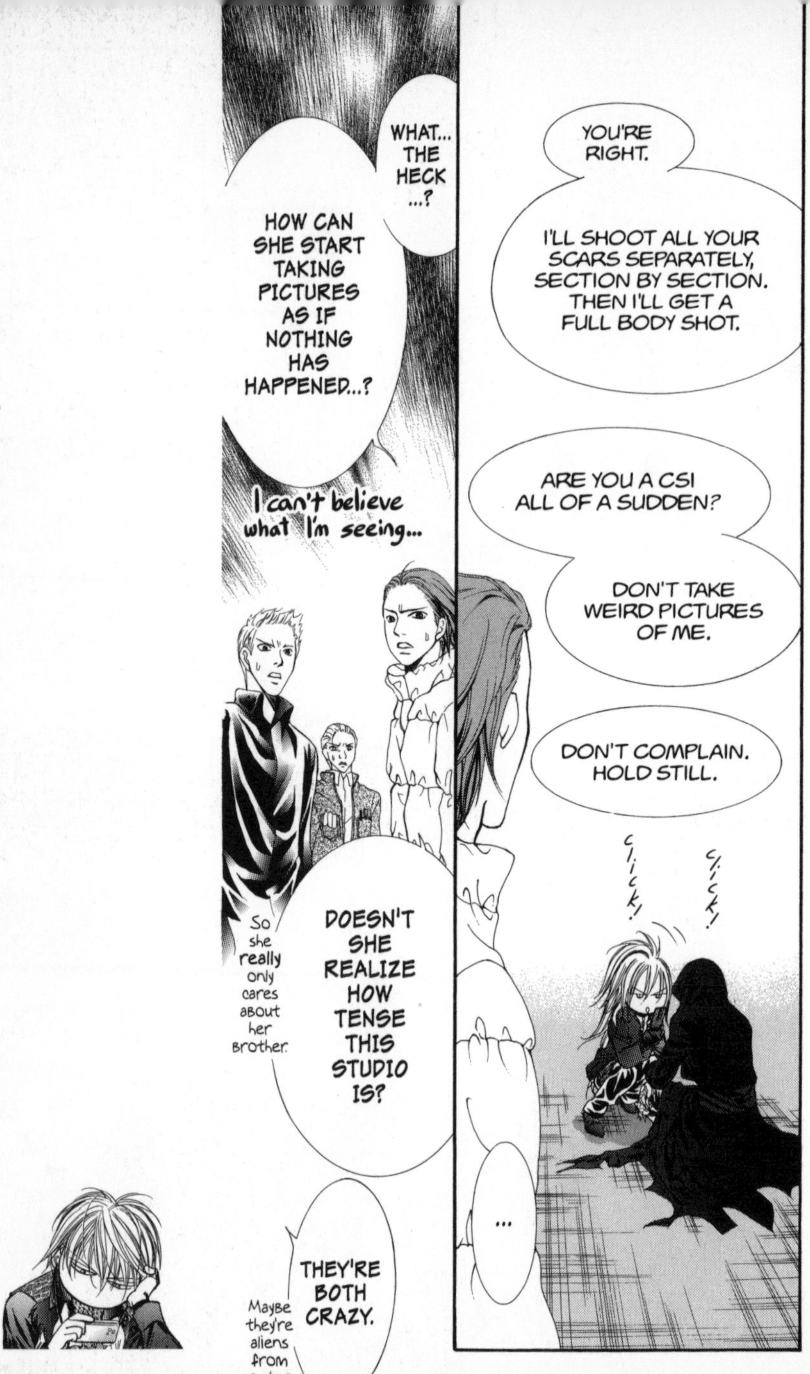
YOU'RE RIGHT.
I'LL SHOOT ALL YOUR SCARS SEPARATELY, SECTION BY SECTION. THEN I'LL GET A FULL BODY SHOT.
ARE YOU A CSI ALL OF A SUDDEN?
DON'T TAKE WEIRD PICTURES OF ME.
DON'T COMPLAIN. HOLD STILL.
CLICK!
CLICK!
...
WHAT... THE HECK ...?
HOW CAN SHE START TAKING PICTURES AS IF NOTHING HAS HAPPENED...?
I can't believe what I'm seeing...
DOESN'T SHE REALIZE HOW TENSE THIS STUDIO IS?
So she really only cares about her brother.
THEY'RE BOTH CRAZY.
Maybe they're aliens from outer space...

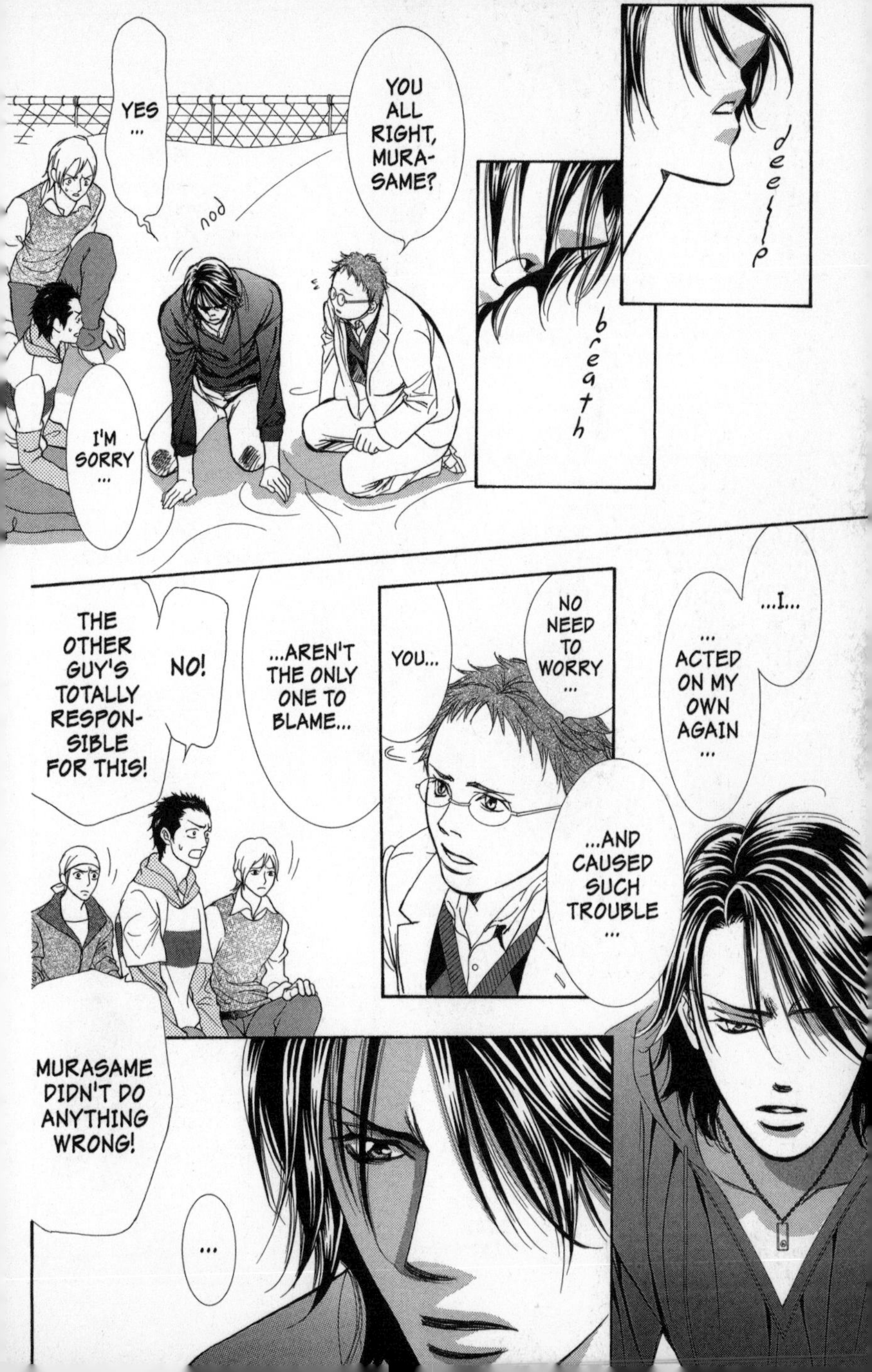
deep
breath
YOU ALL RIGHT, MURASAME?
YES...
nod
I'M SORRY...
...I...
...ACTED ON MY OWN AGAIN...
...AND CAUSED SUCH TROUBLE...
NO NEED TO WORRY...
YOU...
...AREN'T THE ONLY ONE TO BLAME...
NO!
THE OTHER GUY'S TOTALLY RESPONSIBLE FOR THIS!
MURASAME DIDN'T DO ANYTHING WRONG!
...

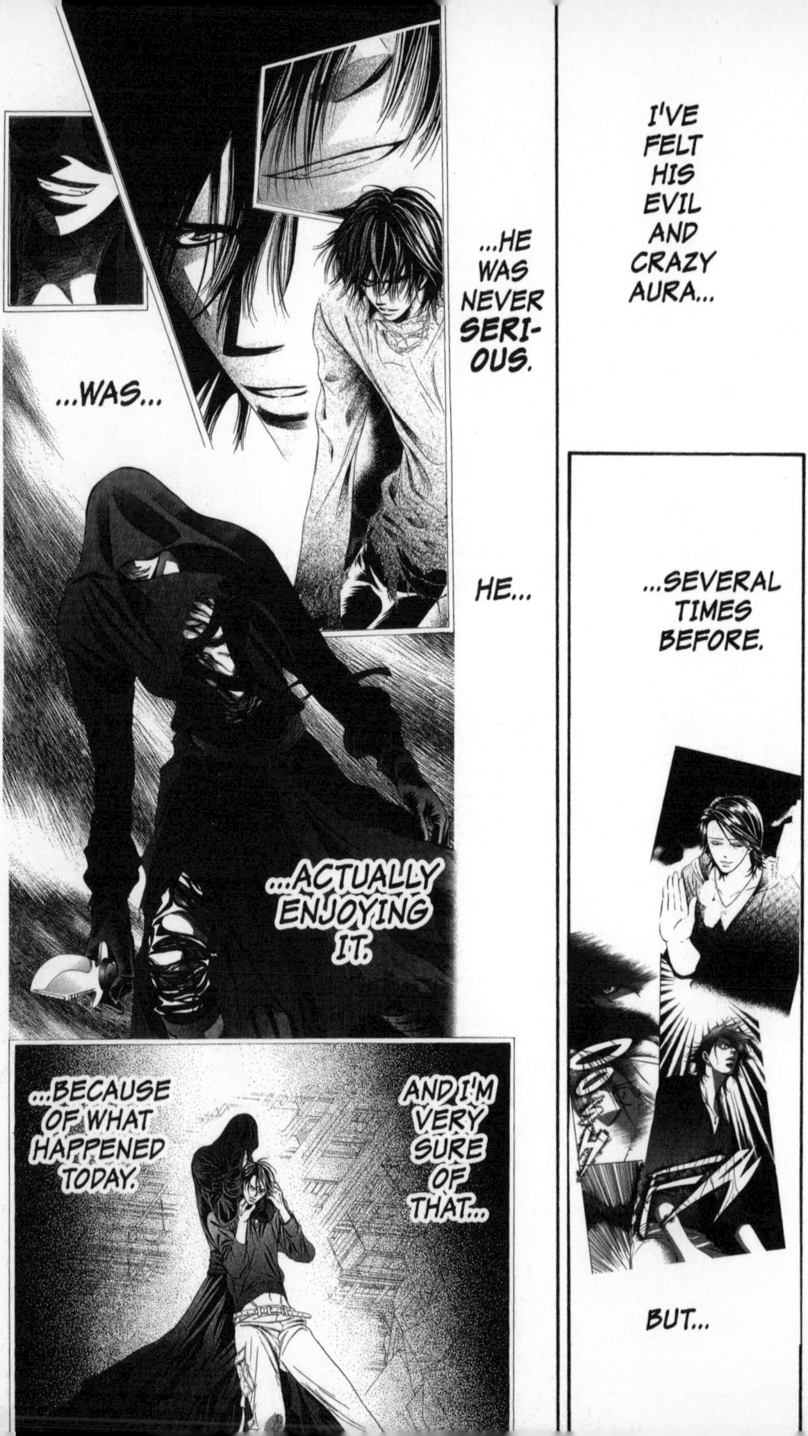
I'VE FELT HIS EVIL AND CRAZY AURA...
...SEVERAL TIMES BEFORE.
BUT...
...HE WAS NEVER SERIOUS.
HE...
...WAS...
...ACTUALLY ENJOYING IT.
AND I'M VERY SURE OF THAT...
...BECAUSE OF WHAT HAPPENED TODAY.

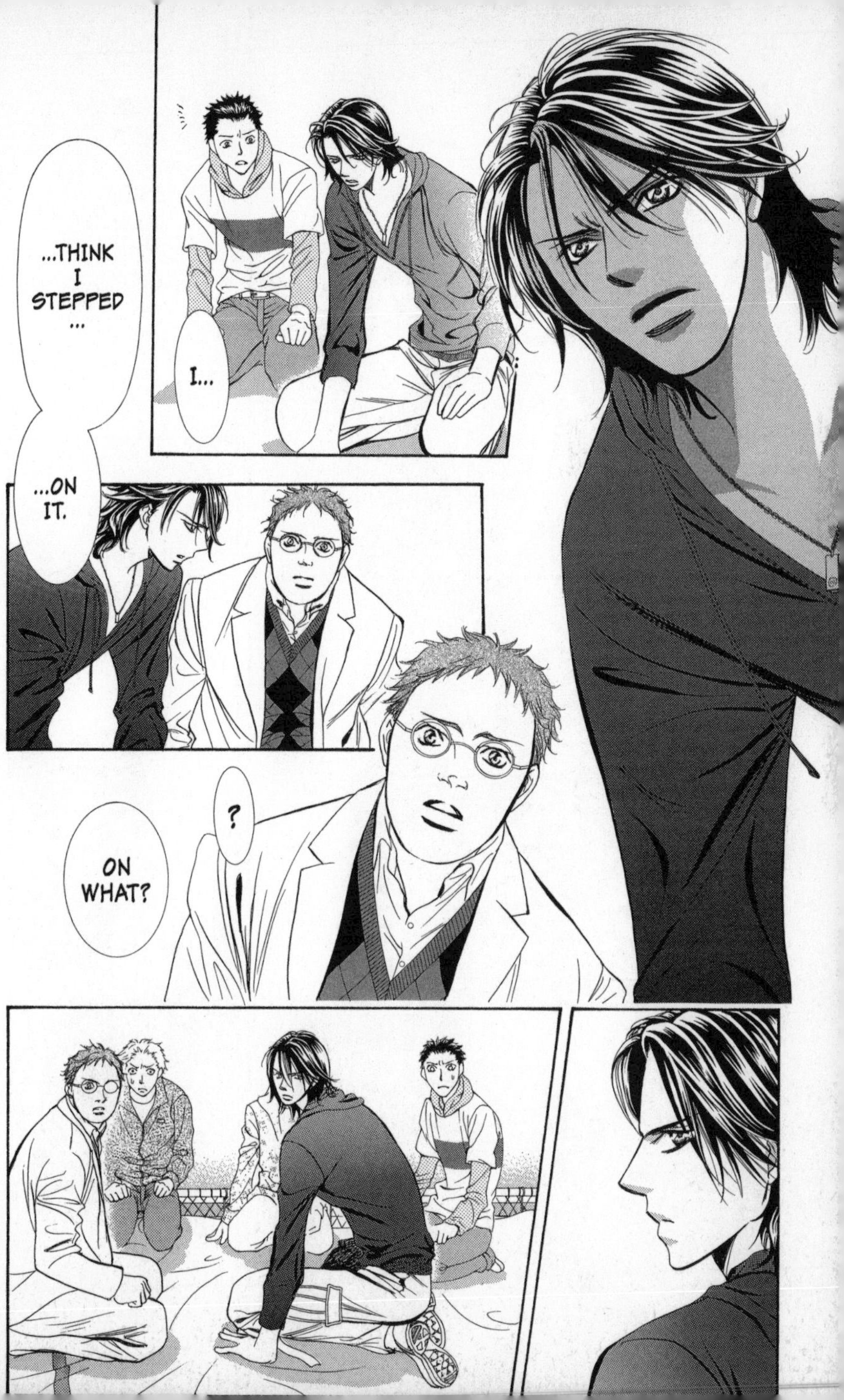
I...
...THINK I STEPPED ...
...ON IT.
?
ON WHAT?

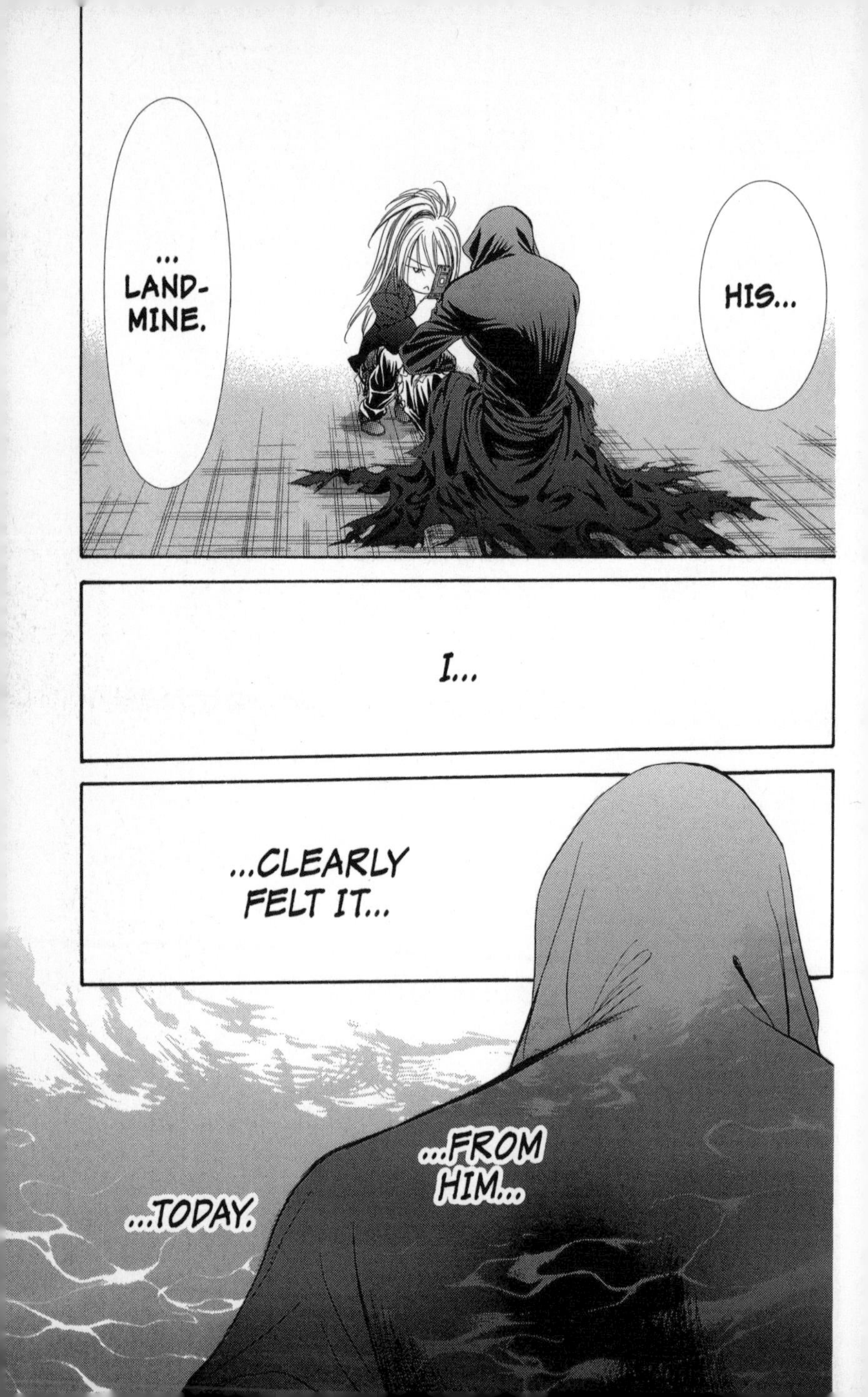
HIS...
... LAND-MINE.
I...
...CLEARLY FELT IT...
...FROM HIM...
...TODAY.

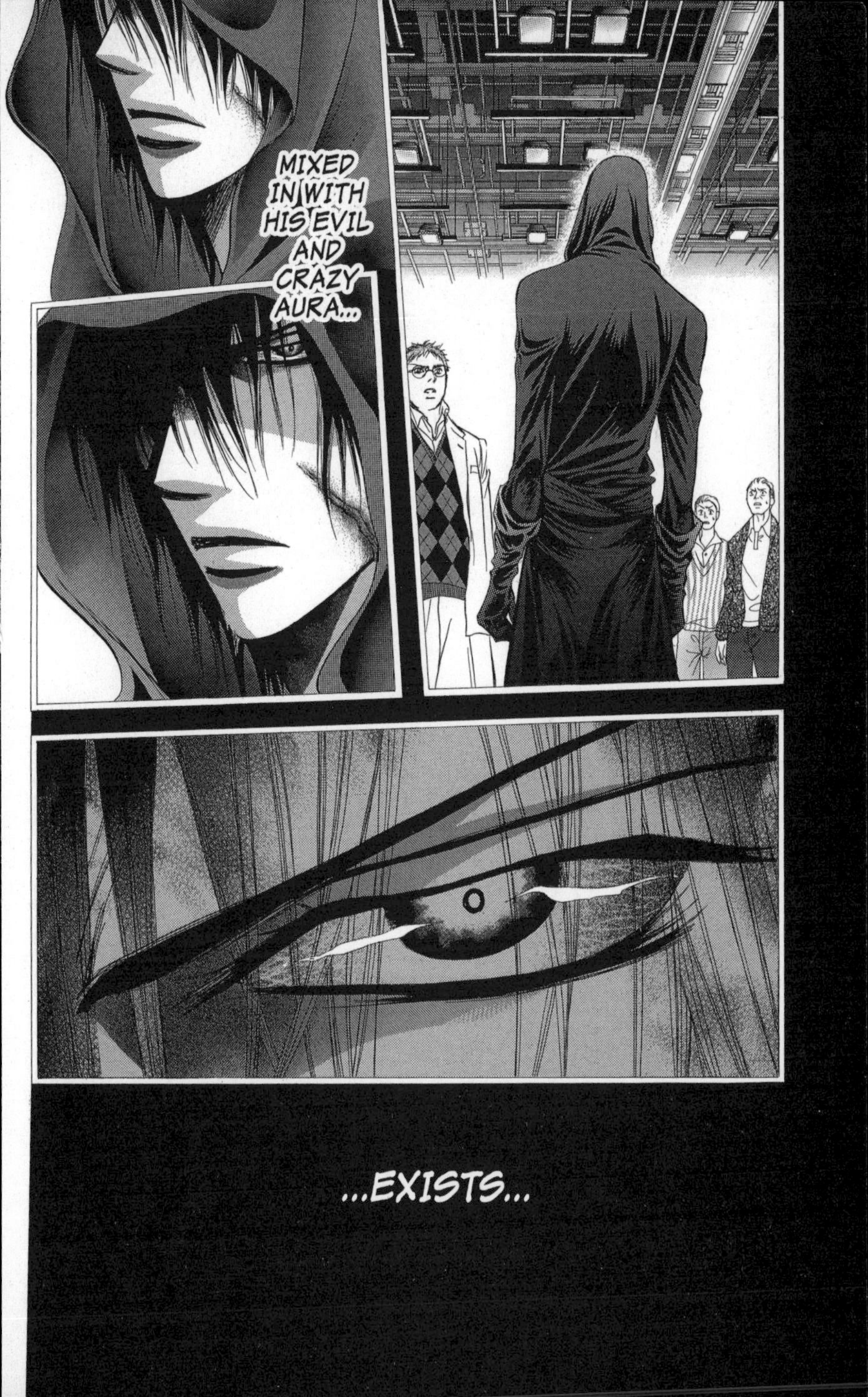
MIXED IN WITH HIS EVIL AND CRAZY AURA...
...EXISTS...

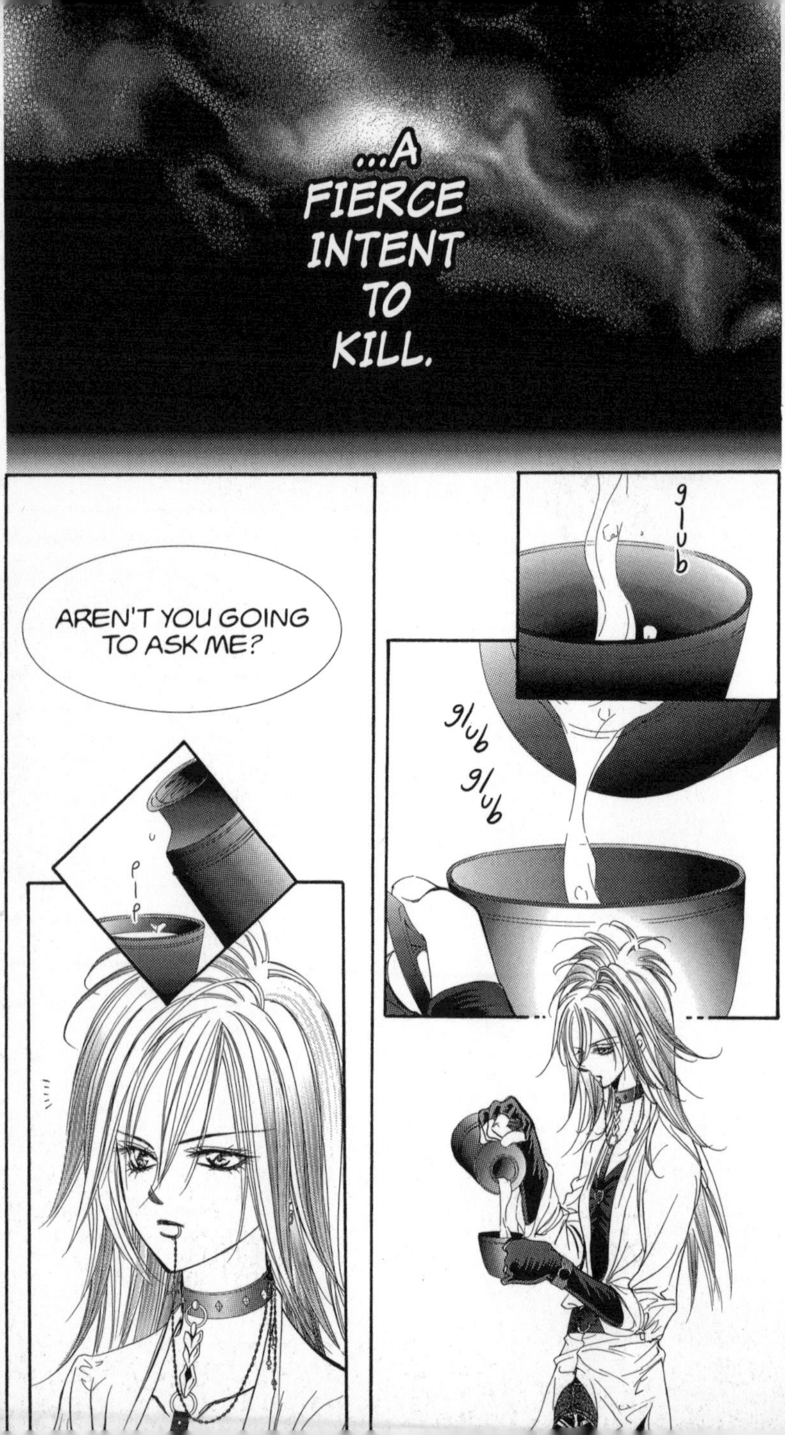
...A FIERCE INTENT TO KILL.
glub
glub glub
AREN'T YOU GOING TO ASK ME?
plip

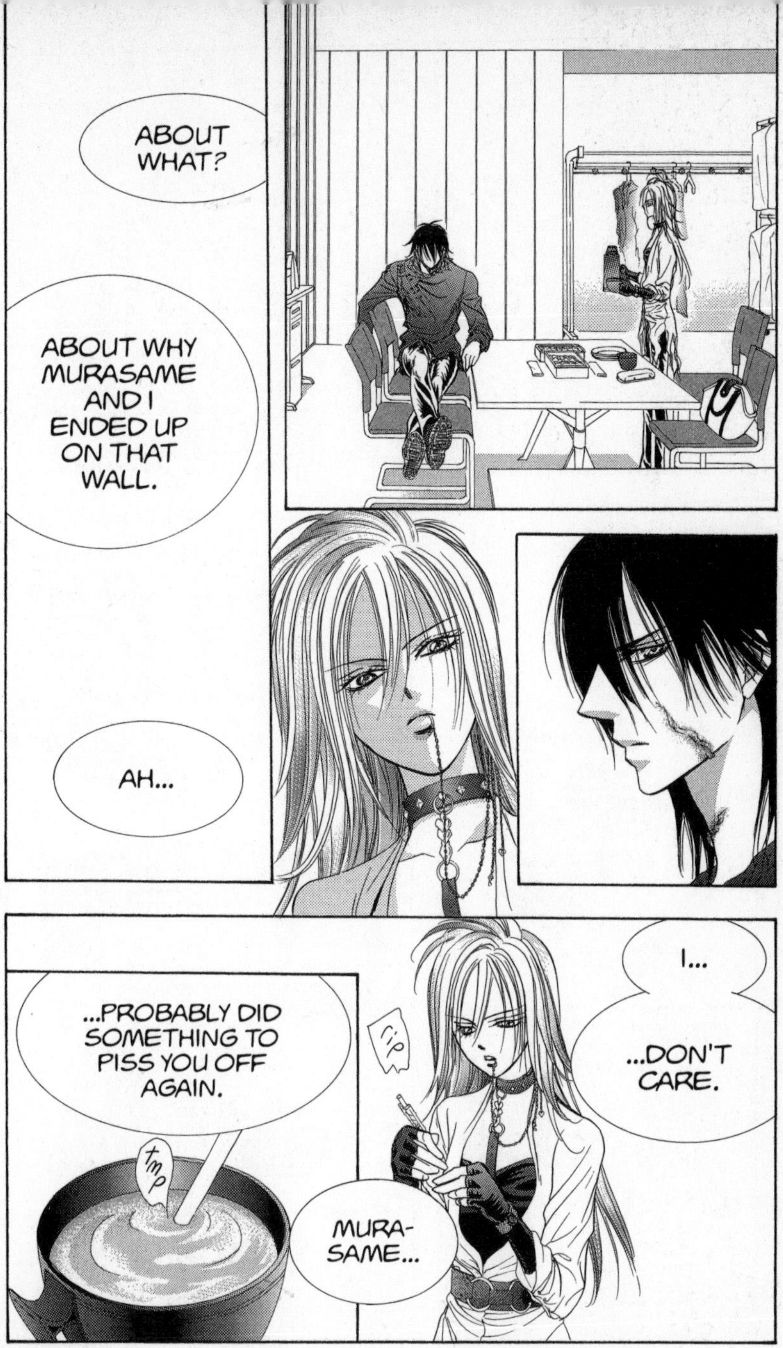
ABOUT WHAT?
ABOUT WHY MURASAME AND I ENDED UP ON THAT WALL.
AH...
I...
...DON'T CARE.
clip
MURA-SAME...
...PROBABLY DID SOMETHING TO PISS YOU OFF AGAIN.
tmp

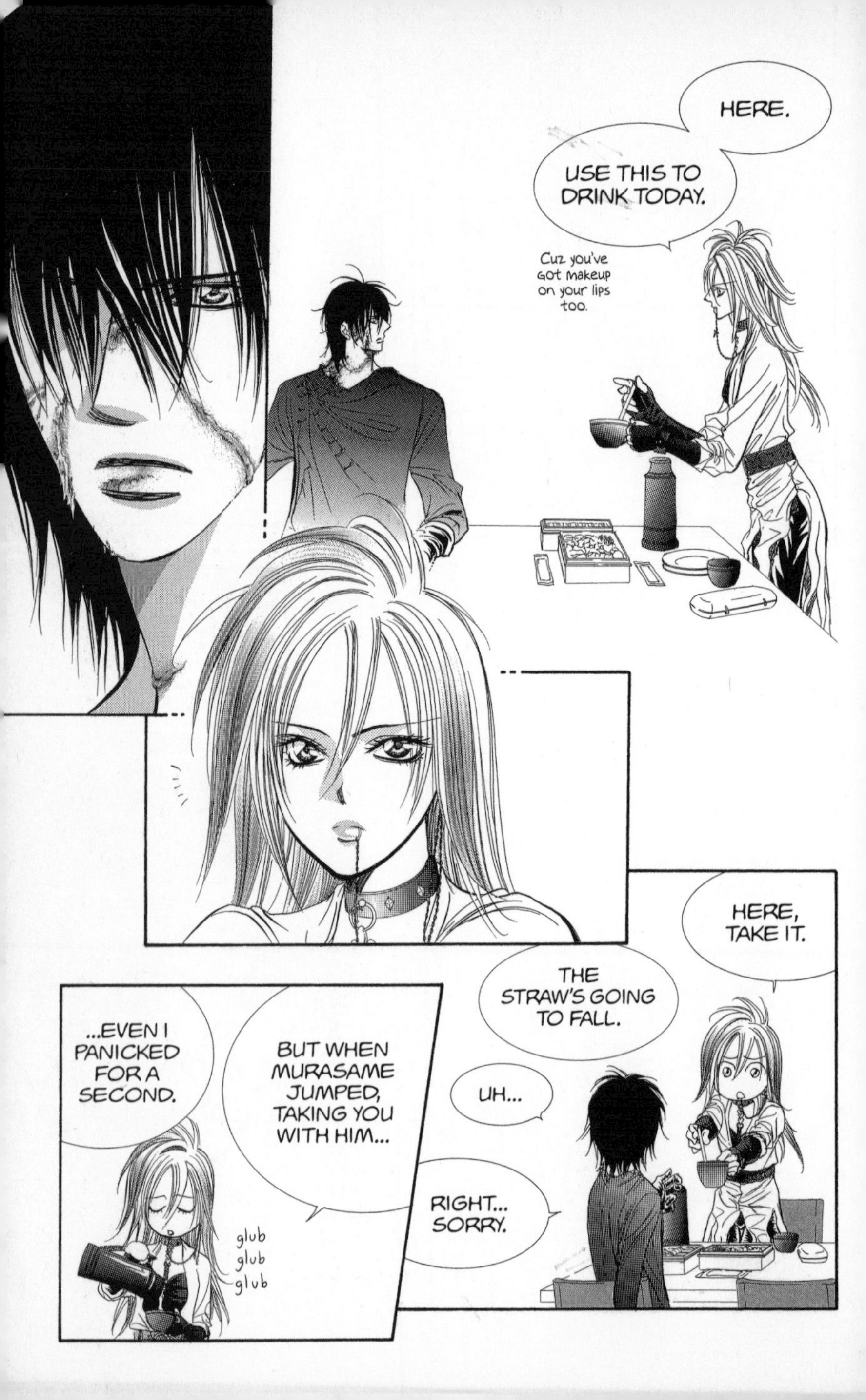
HERE.
USE THIS TO DRINK TODAY.
Cuz you've Got makeup on your lips too.
HERE, TAKE IT.
THE STRAW'S GOING TO FALL.
UH...
RIGHT... SORRY.
BUT WHEN MURASAME JUMPED, TAKING YOU WITH HIM...
...EVEN I PANICKED FOR A SECOND.
glub glub glub

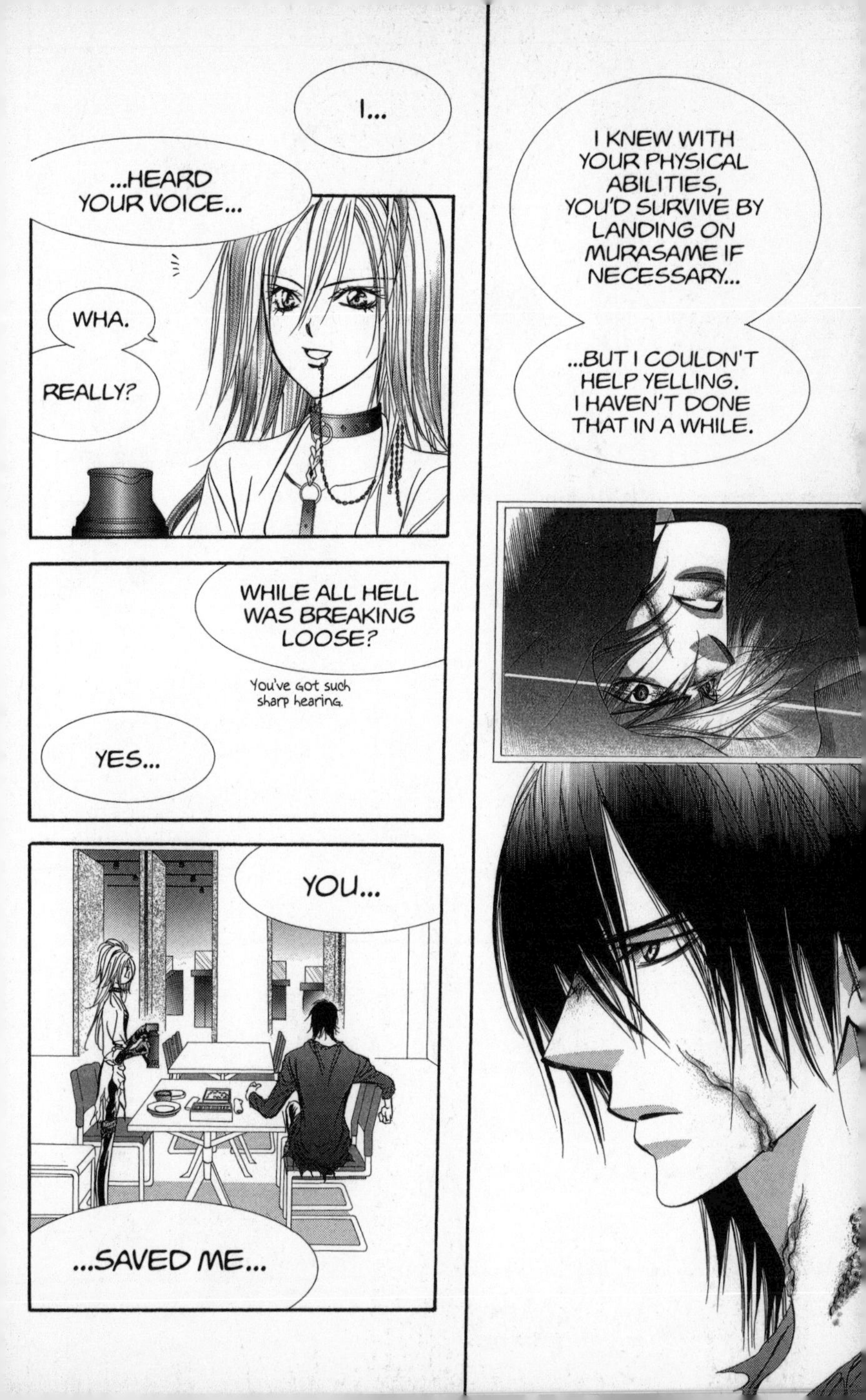
I KNEW WITH YOUR PHYSICAL ABILITIES, YOU'D SURVIVE BY LANDING ON MURASAME IF NECESSARY...
...BUT I COULDN'T HELP YELLING. I HAVEN'T DONE THAT IN A WHILE.
I...
...HEARD YOUR VOICE...
WHA.
REALLY?
WHILE ALL HELL WAS BREAKING LOOSE?
You've got such sharp hearing.
YES...
YOU...
...SAVED ME...

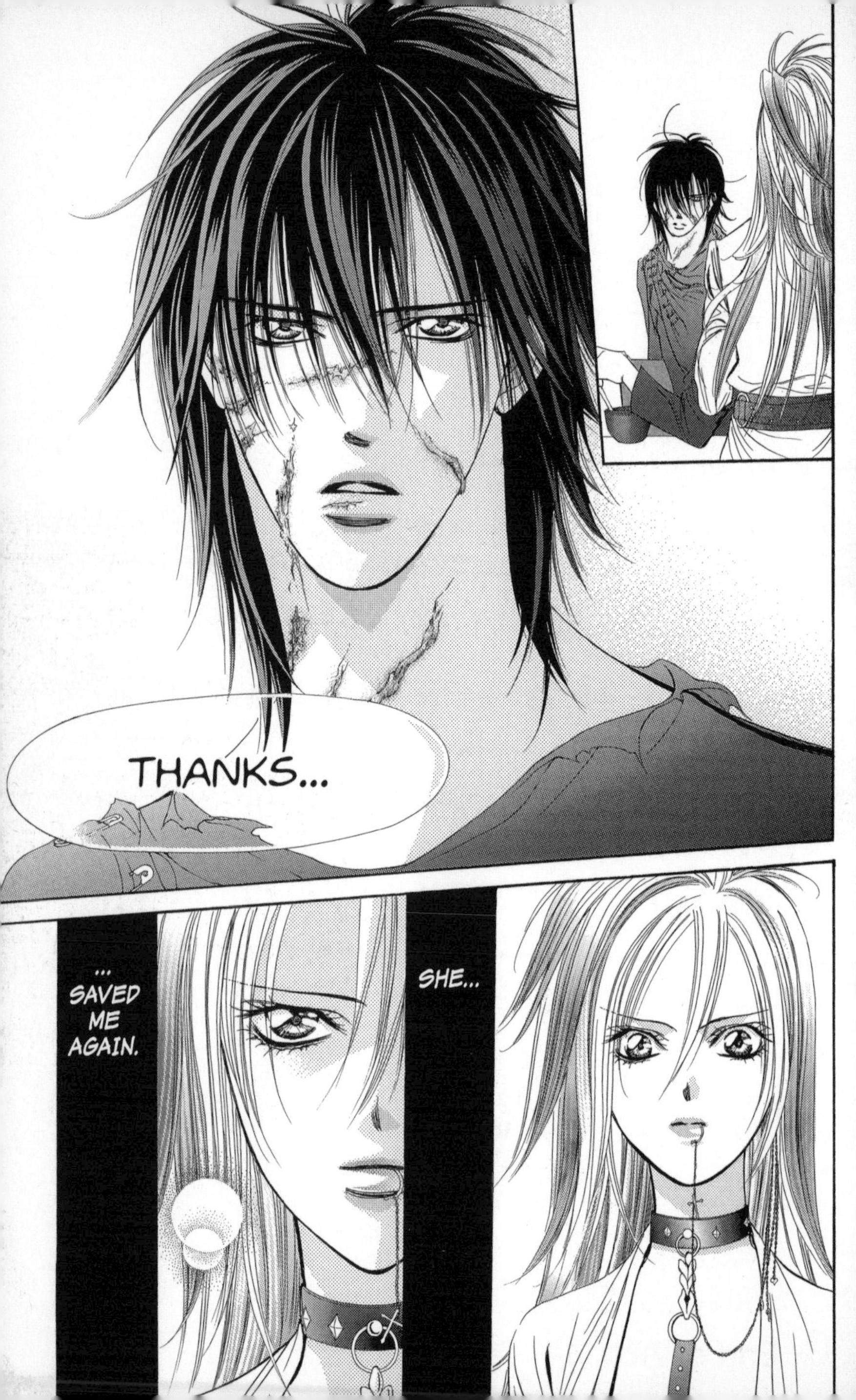
THANKS...
SHE...
... SAVED ME AGAIN.

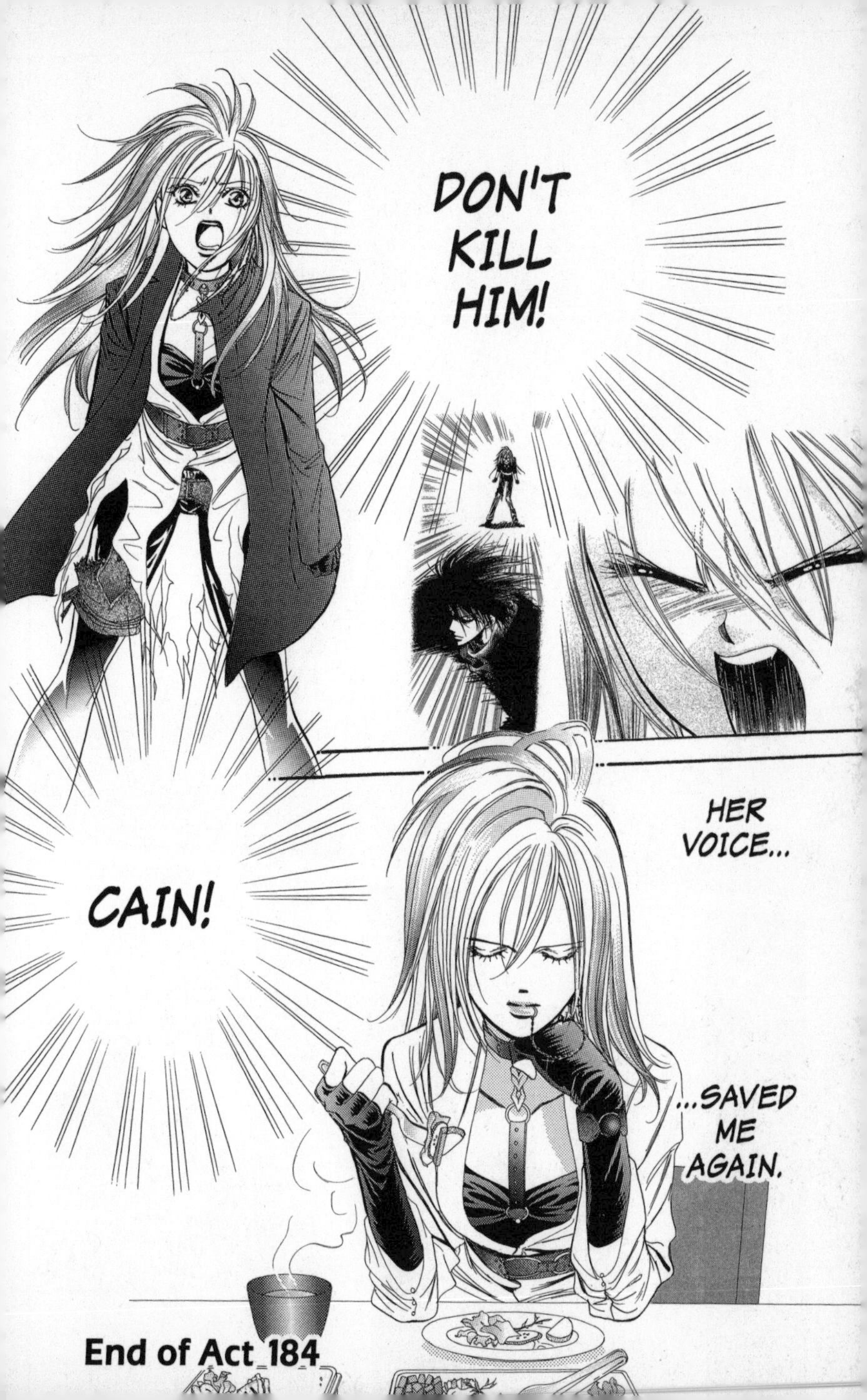
DON'T KILL HIM!
CAIN!
HER VOICE...
...SAVED ME AGAIN.
End of Act_184

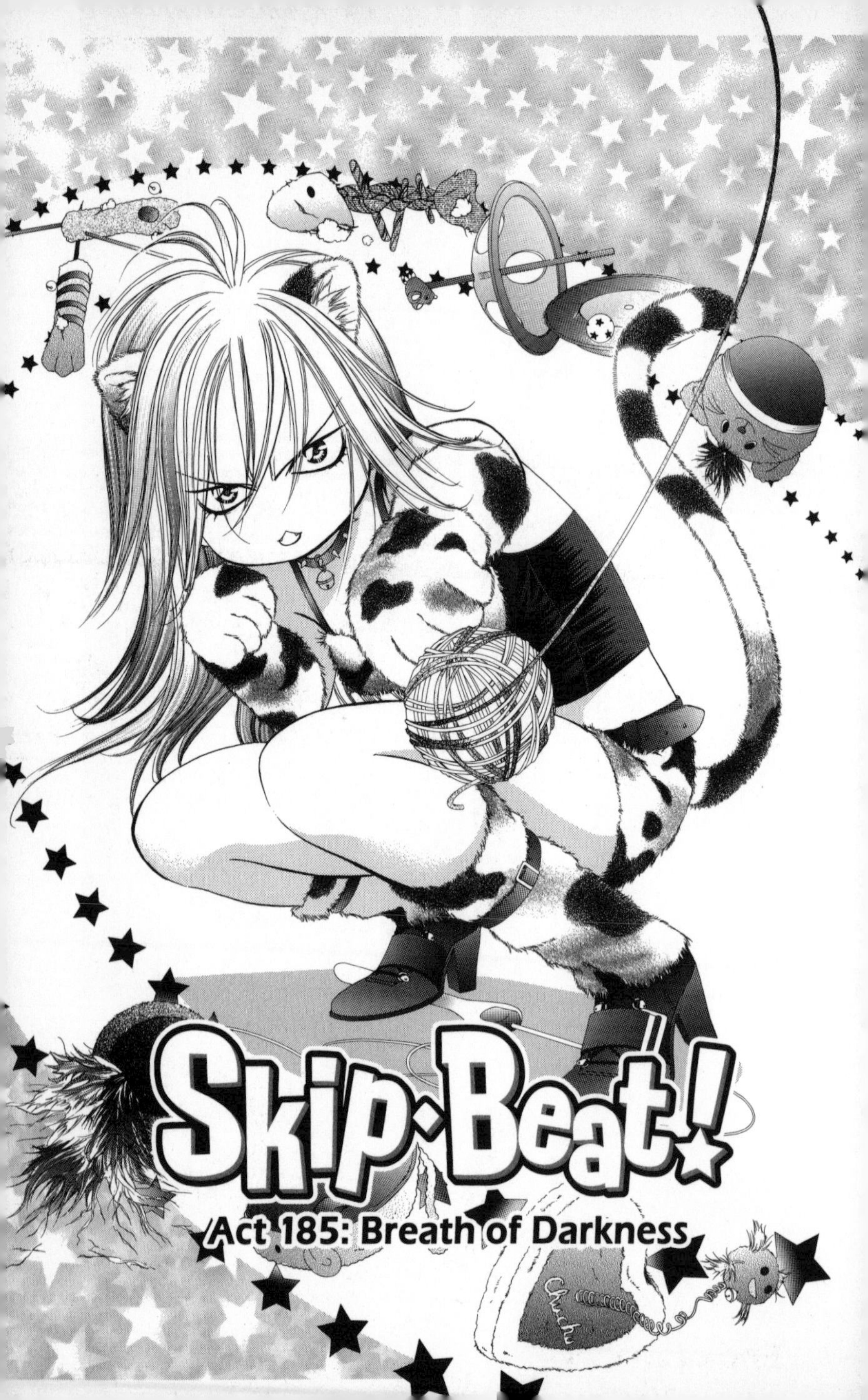
Skip·Beat!
Act 185: Breath of Darkness

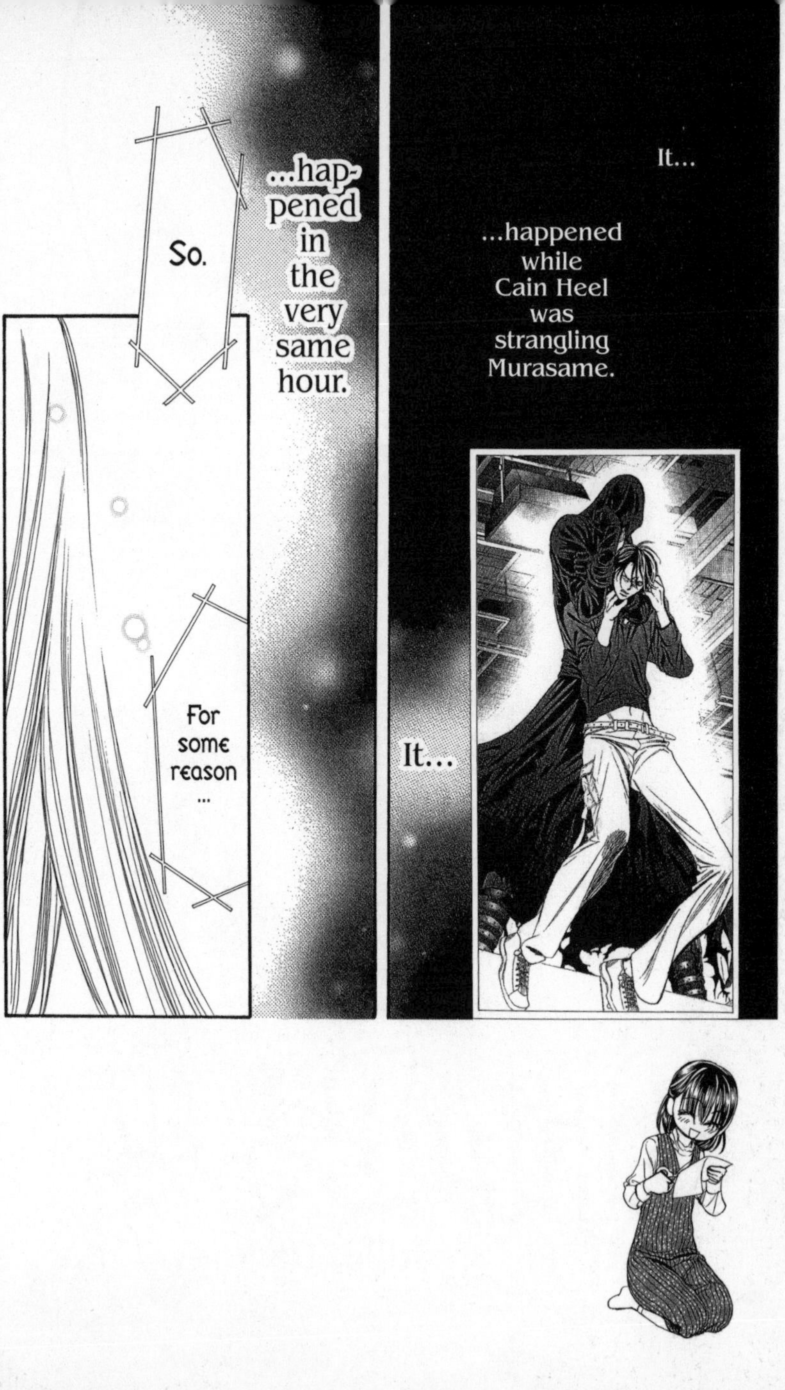
It...
...happened while Cain Heel was strangling Murasame.
It...
...hap-pened in the very same hour.
So.
For some reason ...

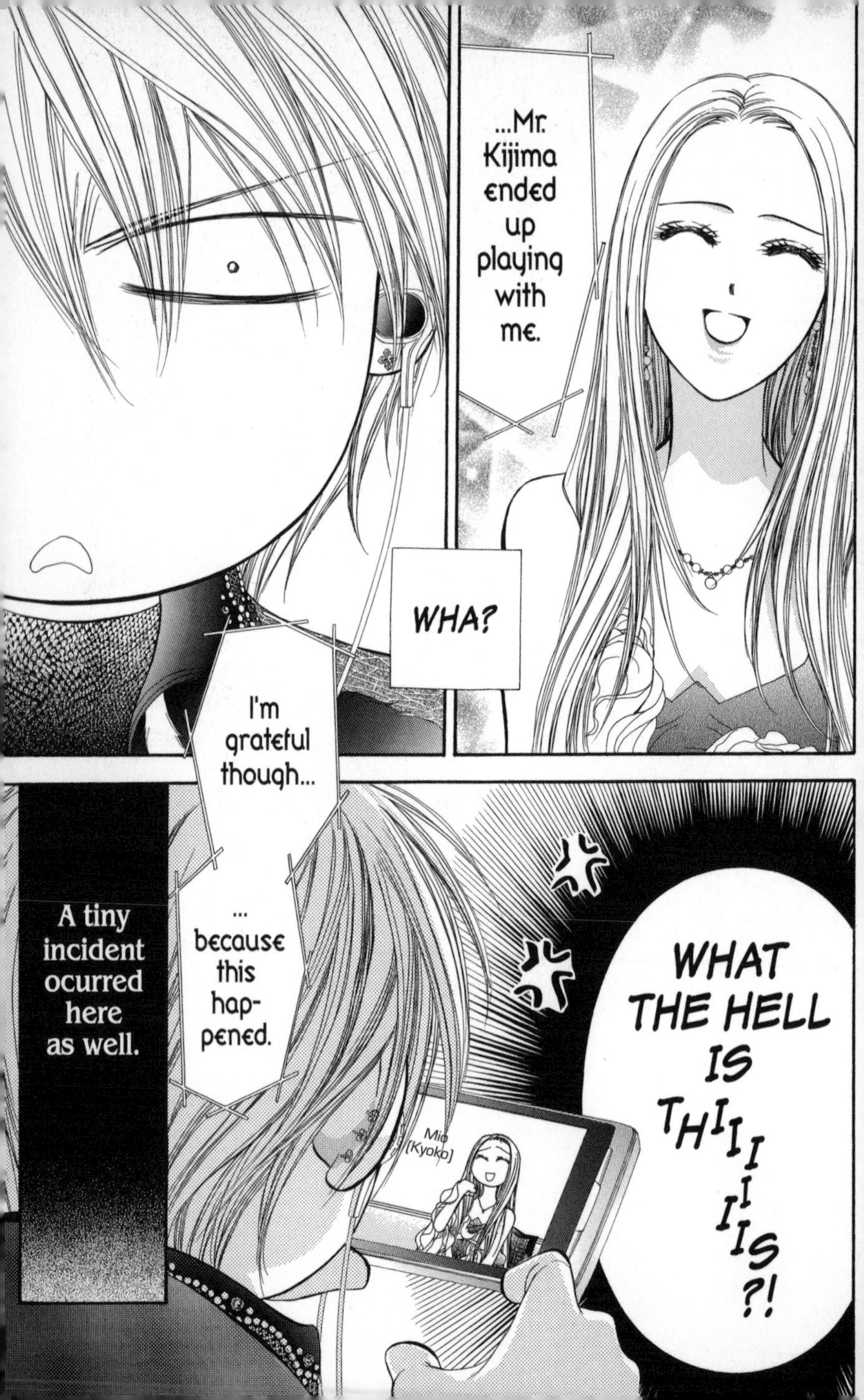
...Mr. Kijima ended up playing with me.
WHA?
I'm grateful though...
...because this hap-pened.
WHAT THE HELL IS THIIIIIS?!
Mio (Kyoko)
A tiny incident ocurred here as well.

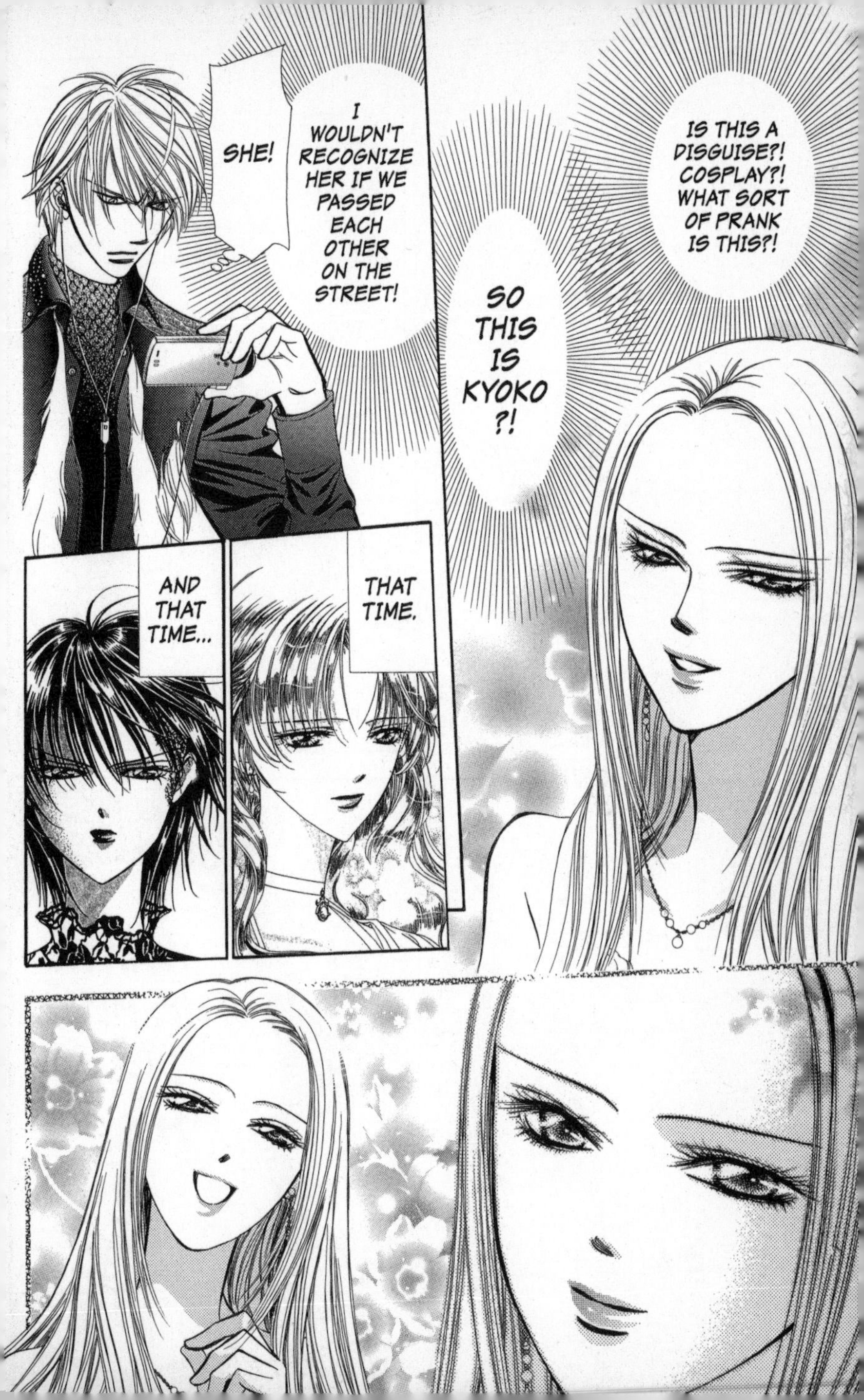
IS THIS A DISGUISE?! COSPLAY?! WHAT SORT OF PRANK IS THIS?!
SO THIS IS KYOKO ?!
I WOULDN'T RECOGNIZE HER IF WE PASSED EACH OTHER ON THE STREET!
SHE!
THAT TIME.
AND THAT TIME...

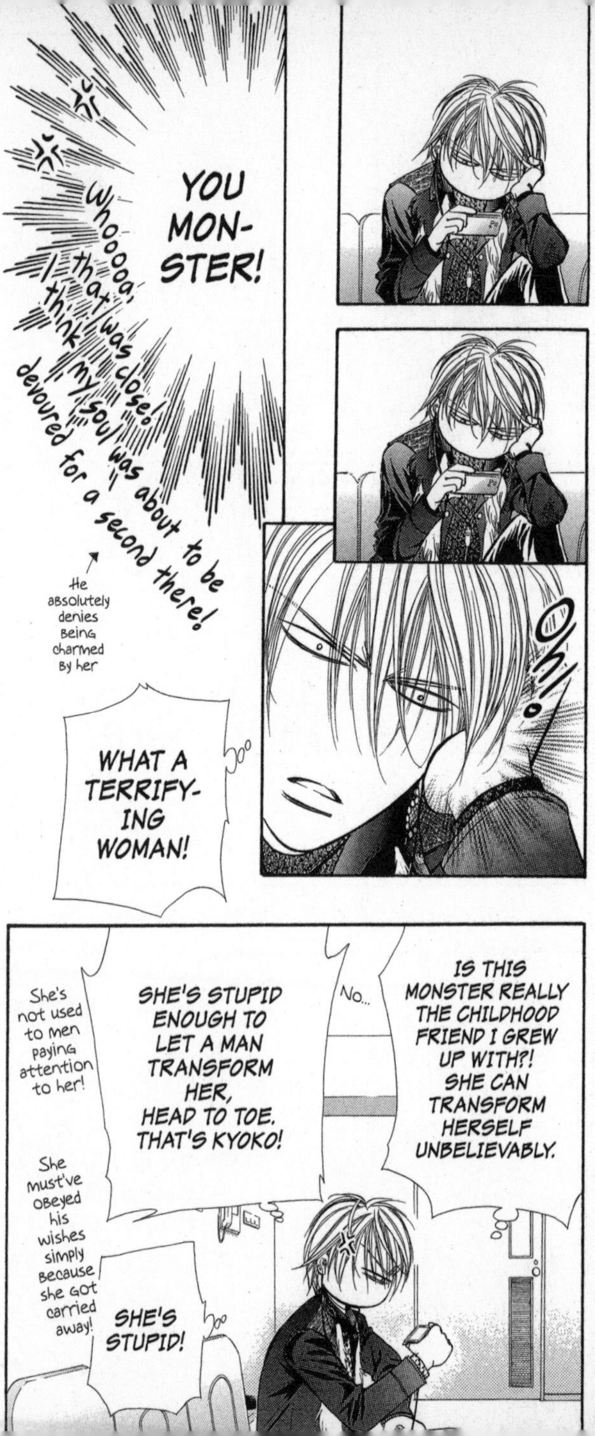
YOU MONSTER!
Whoooa, that was close! I think my soul was about to be devoured for a second there!
He absolutely denies being charmed by her
Oh!!
WHAT A TERRIFYING WOMAN!
IS THIS MONSTER REALLY THE CHILDHOOD FRIEND I GREW UP WITH?! SHE CAN TRANSFORM HERSELF UNBELIEVABLY.
No...
SHE'S STUPID ENOUGH TO LET A MAN TRANSFORM HER, HEAD TO TOE. THAT'S KYOKO!
She's not used to men paying attention to her!
SHE'S STUPID!
She must've obeyed his wishes simply because she got carried away!

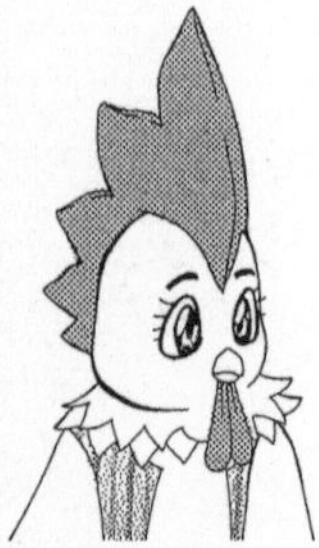

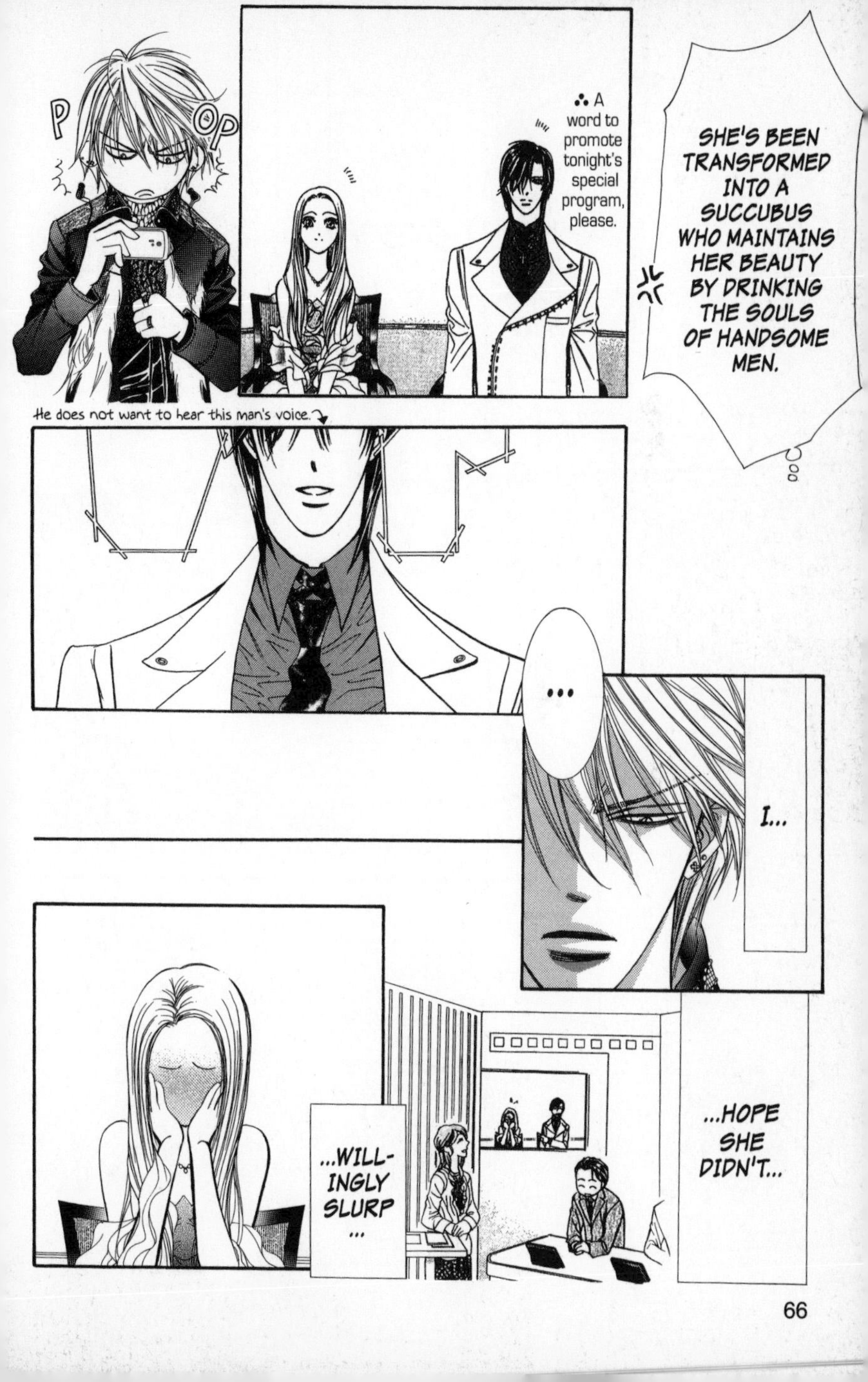
SHE'S BEEN TRANSFORMED INTO A SUCCUBUS WHO MAINTAINS HER BEAUTY BY DRINKING THE SOULS OF HANDSOME MEN.
A word to promote tonight's special program, please.
POP
...
I...
He does not want to hear this man's voice.
...HOPE SHE DIDN'T...
...WILL-INGLY SLURP ...

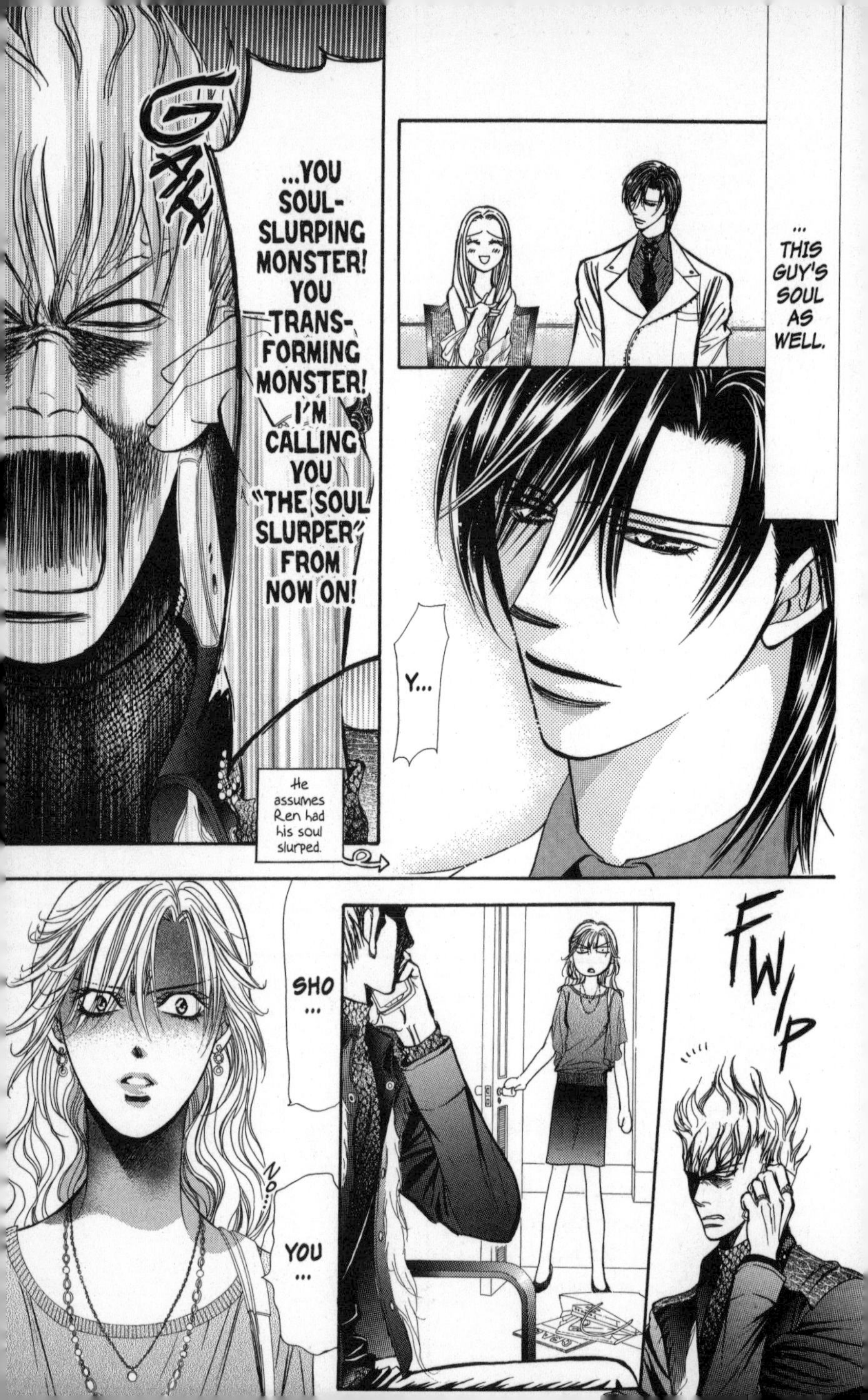
... THIS GUY'S SOUL AS WELL.
Y...
GAH
...YOU SOUL-SLURPING MONSTER! YOU TRANS-FORMING MONSTER! I'M CALLING YOU "THE SOUL SLURPER" FROM NOW ON!
He assumes Ren had his soul slurped.
FWIP
SHO ...
NO...
YOU ...

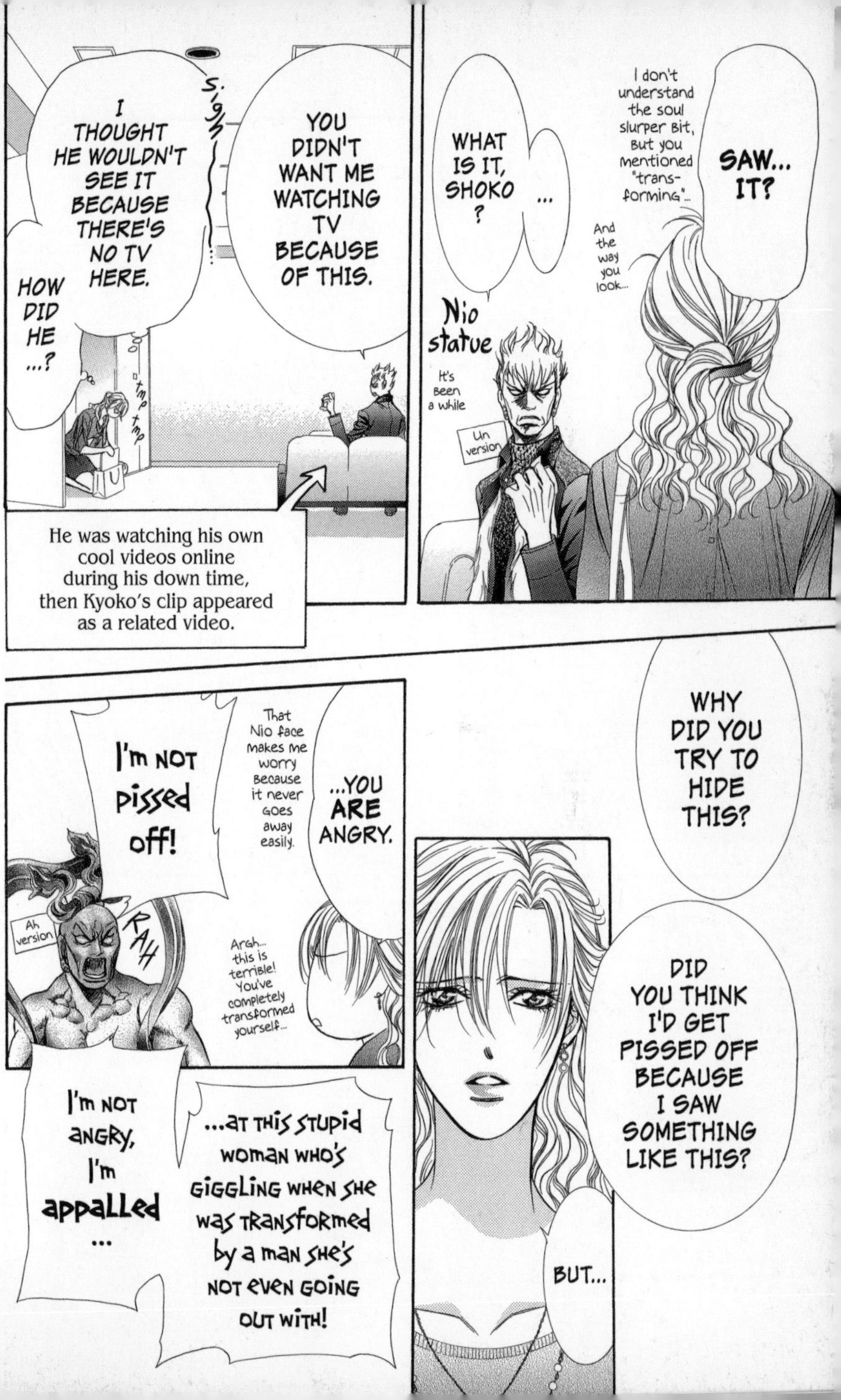
SAW... IT?
I don't understand the soul slurper bit, but you mentioned "trans-forming"...
And the way you look...
...
WHAT IS IT, SHOKO?
Nio statue
It's been a while
Un version
YOU DIDN'T WANT ME WATCHING TV BECAUSE OF THIS.
Sigh...
I THOUGHT HE WOULDN'T SEE IT BECAUSE THERE'S NO TV HERE.
HOW DID HE ...?
tmp tmp
He was watching his own cool videos online during his down time, then Kyoko's clip appeared as a related video.
WHY DID YOU TRY TO HIDE THIS?
DID YOU THINK I'D GET PISSED OFF BECAUSE I SAW SOMETHING LIKE THIS?
BUT...
...YOU ARE ANGRY.
That Nio face makes me worry because it never goes away easily.
I'm NOT pissed off!
RAH
Ah version
Argh... this is terrible! You've completely transformed yourself...
I'm NOT angry, I'm appalled ...
...at this stupid woman who's giggling when she was transformed by a man she's not even going out with!

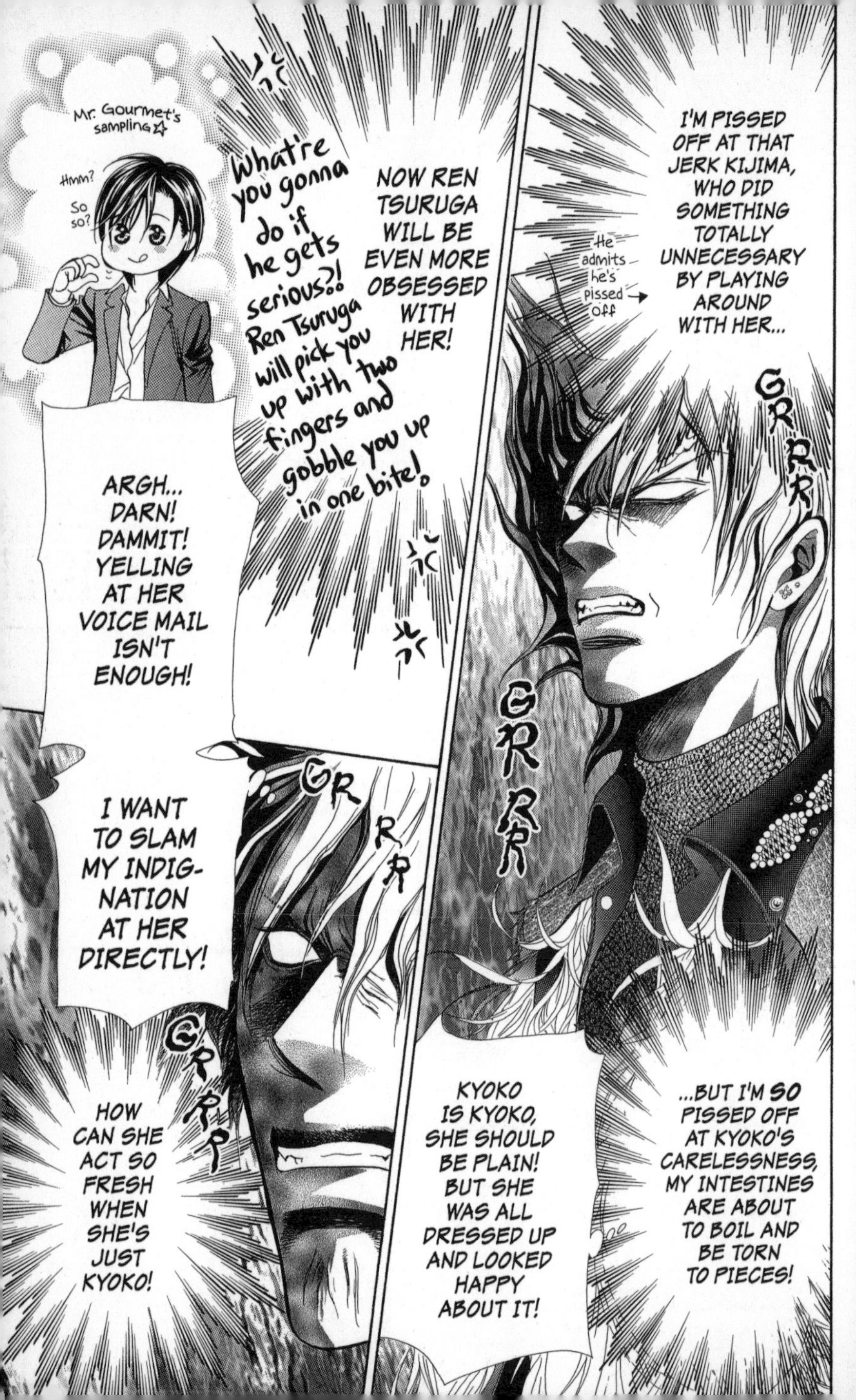
I'M PISSED OFF AT THAT JERK KIJIMA, WHO DID SOMETHING TOTALLY UNNECESSARY BY PLAYING AROUND WITH HER...
He admits he's pissed off
GRRR
NOW REN TSURUGA WILL BE EVEN MORE OBSESSED WITH HER!
What're you gonna do if he gets serious?! Ren Tsuruga will pick you up with two fingers and gobble you up in one bite!
Mr. Gourmet's sampling☆
Hmm?
So so?
ARGH... DARN! DAMMIT! YELLING AT HER VOICE MAIL ISN'T ENOUGH!
GRRR
GRRR
I WANT TO SLAM MY INDIG-NATION AT HER DIRECTLY!
...BUT I'M **SO** PISSED OFF AT KYOKO'S CARELESSNESS, MY INTESTINES ARE ABOUT TO BOIL AND BE TORN TO PIECES!
KYOKO IS KYOKO, SHE SHOULD BE PLAIN! BUT SHE WAS ALL DRESSED UP AND LOOKED HAPPY ABOUT IT!
GRRR
HOW CAN SHE ACT SO FRESH WHEN SHE'S JUST KYOKO!

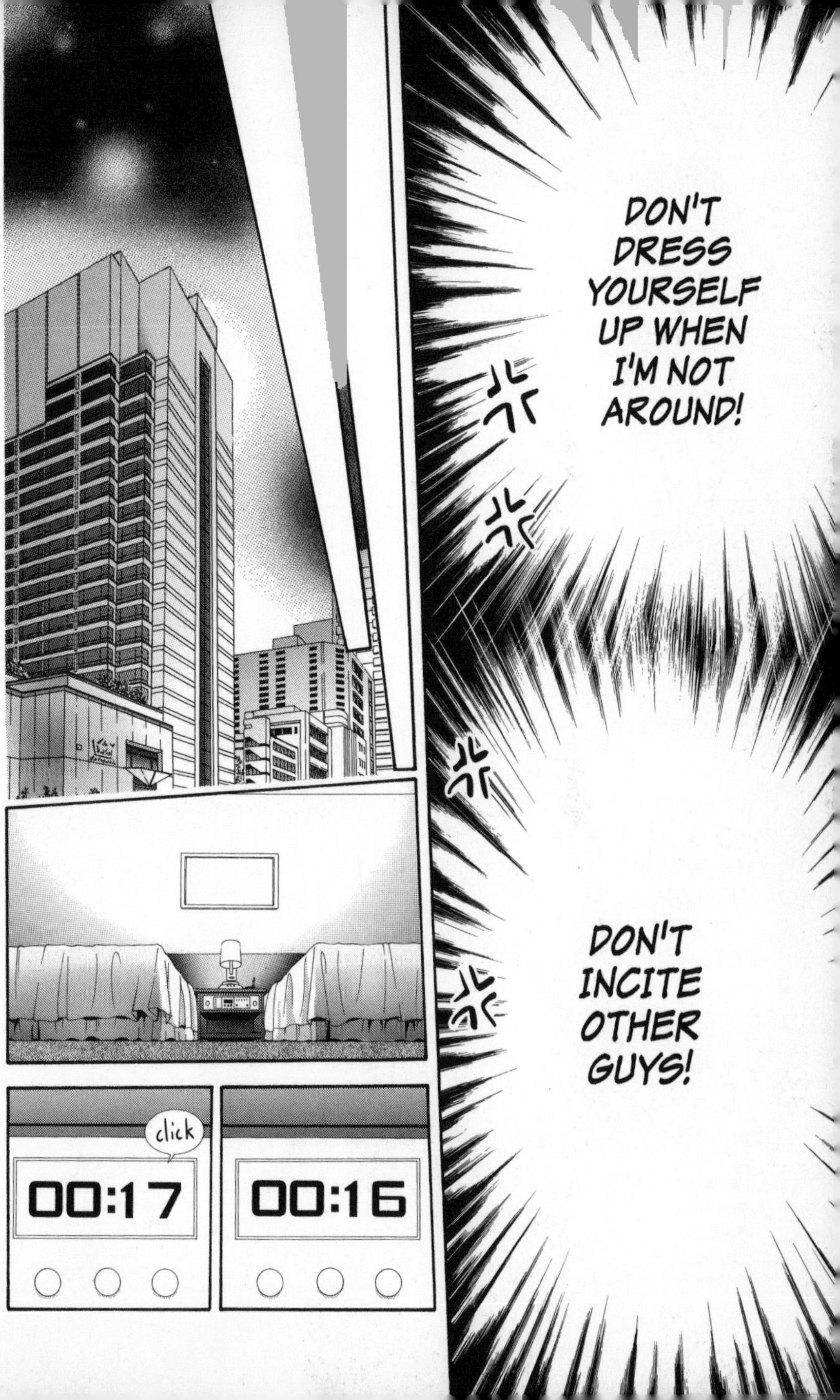
DON'T DRESS YOURSELF UP WHEN I'M NOT AROUND!
DON'T INCITE OTHER GUYS!
00:16
click
00:17

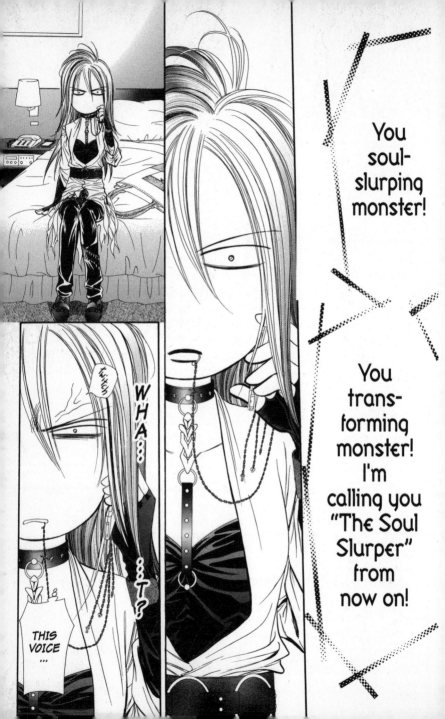

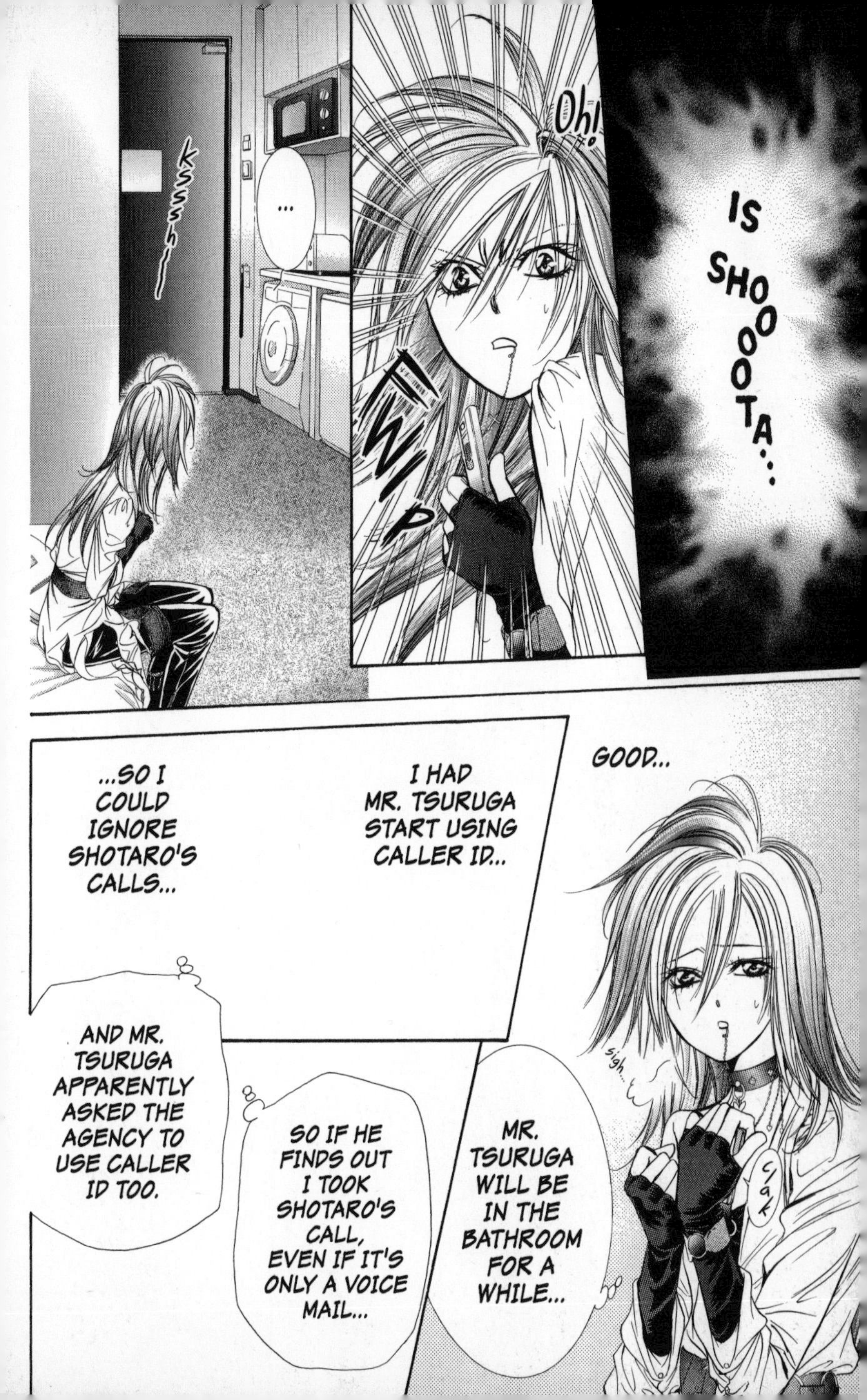
IS SHOOOOOTA...
Oh!
FWIP
...
KSSSHH
GOOD...
sigh...
clak
MR. TSURUGA WILL BE IN THE BATHROOM FOR A WHILE...
SO IF HE FINDS OUT I TOOK SHOTARO'S CALL, EVEN IF IT'S ONLY A VOICE MAIL...
I HAD MR. TSURUGA START USING CALLER ID...
...SO I COULD IGNORE SHOTARO'S CALLS...
AND MR. TSURUGA APPARENTLY ASKED THE AGENCY TO USE CALLER ID TOO.

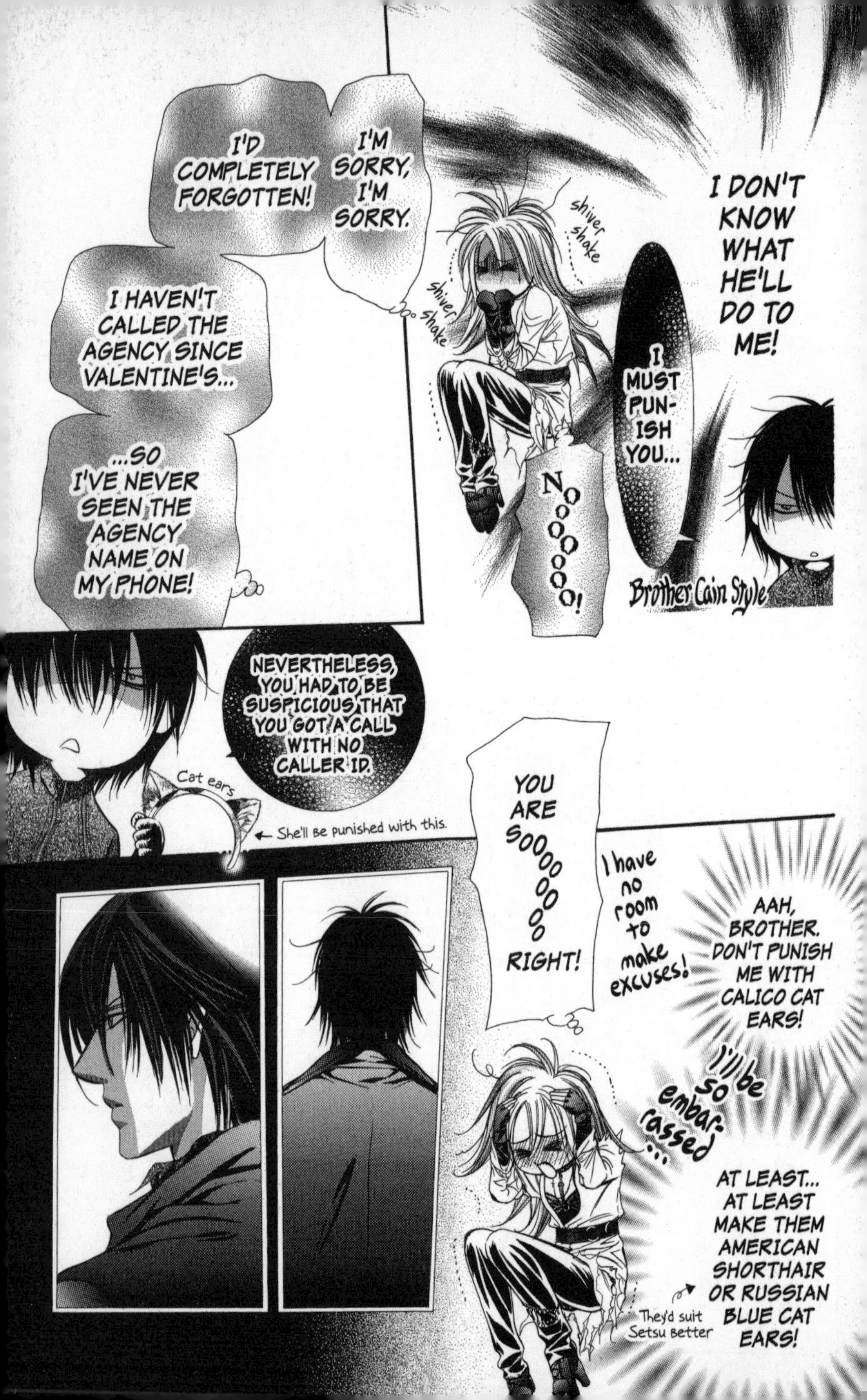
I DON'T KNOW WHAT HE'LL DO TO ME!
I MUST PUN-ISH YOU...
Brother Cain Style
shiver shake
shiver shake
NOOOOOOOOO!
I'M SORRY, I'M SORRY.
I'D COMPLETELY FORGOTTEN!
I HAVEN'T CALLED THE AGENCY SINCE VALENTINE'S...
...SO I'VE NEVER SEEN THE AGENCY NAME ON MY PHONE!
NEVERTHELESS, YOU HAD TO BE SUSPICIOUS THAT YOU GOT A CALL WITH NO CALLER ID.
Cat ears
She'll be punished with this.
AAH, BROTHER. DON'T PUNISH ME WITH CALICO CAT EARS!
I'll be so embar-rassed...
AT LEAST... AT LEAST MAKE THEM AMERICAN SHORTHAIR OR RUSSIAN BLUE CAT EARS!
They'd suit Setsu better
I have no room to make excuses!
YOU ARE SOOOOOOOOO RIGHT!

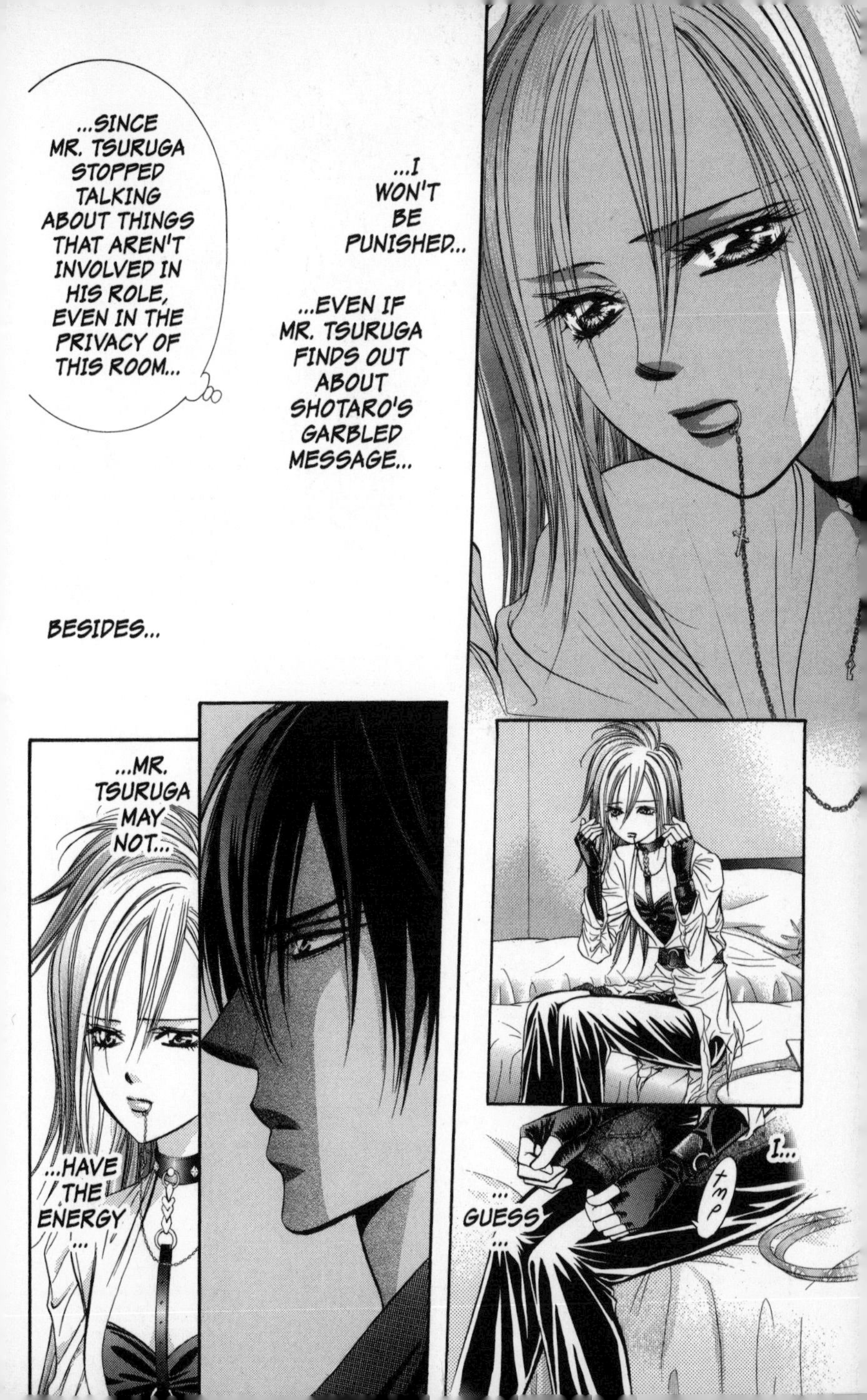
...I WON'T BE PUNISHED...
...EVEN IF MR. TSURUGA FINDS OUT ABOUT SHOTARO'S GARBLED MESSAGE...
...SINCE MR. TSURUGA STOPPED TALKING ABOUT THINGS THAT AREN'T INVOLVED IN HIS ROLE, EVEN IN THE PRIVACY OF THIS ROOM...
BESIDES...
I...
TMP
...GUESS...
...MR. TSURUGA MAY NOT...
...HAVE THE ENERGY...

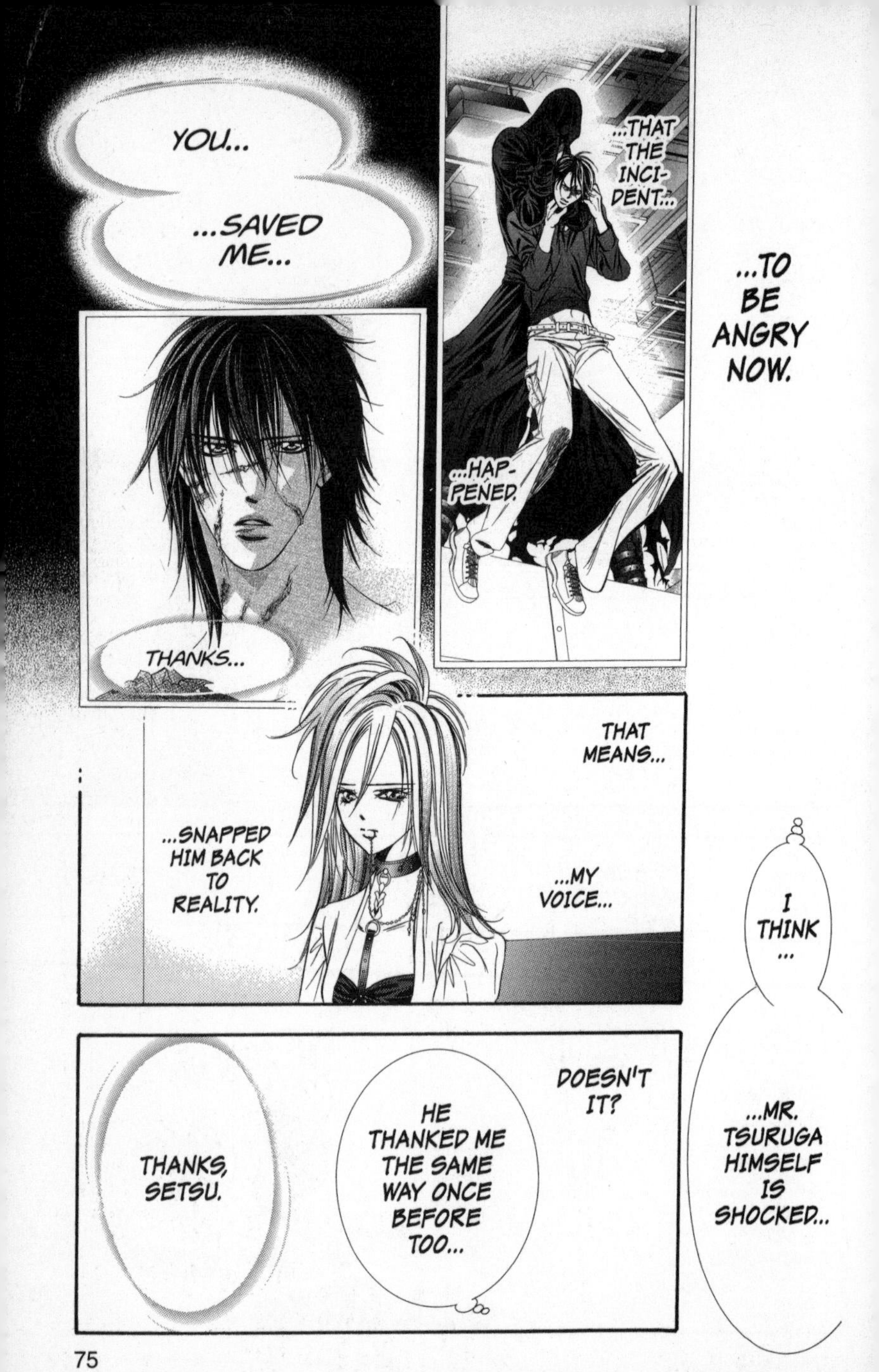
...TO BE ANGRY NOW.
...THAT THE INCIDENT...
...HAPPENED.
YOU...
...SAVED ME...
THANKS...
THAT MEANS...
...MY VOICE...
...SNAPPED HIM BACK TO REALITY.
I THINK...
...MR. TSURUGA HIMSELF IS SHOCKED...
DOESN'T IT?
HE THANKED ME THE SAME WAY ONCE BEFORE TOO...
THANKS, SETSU.

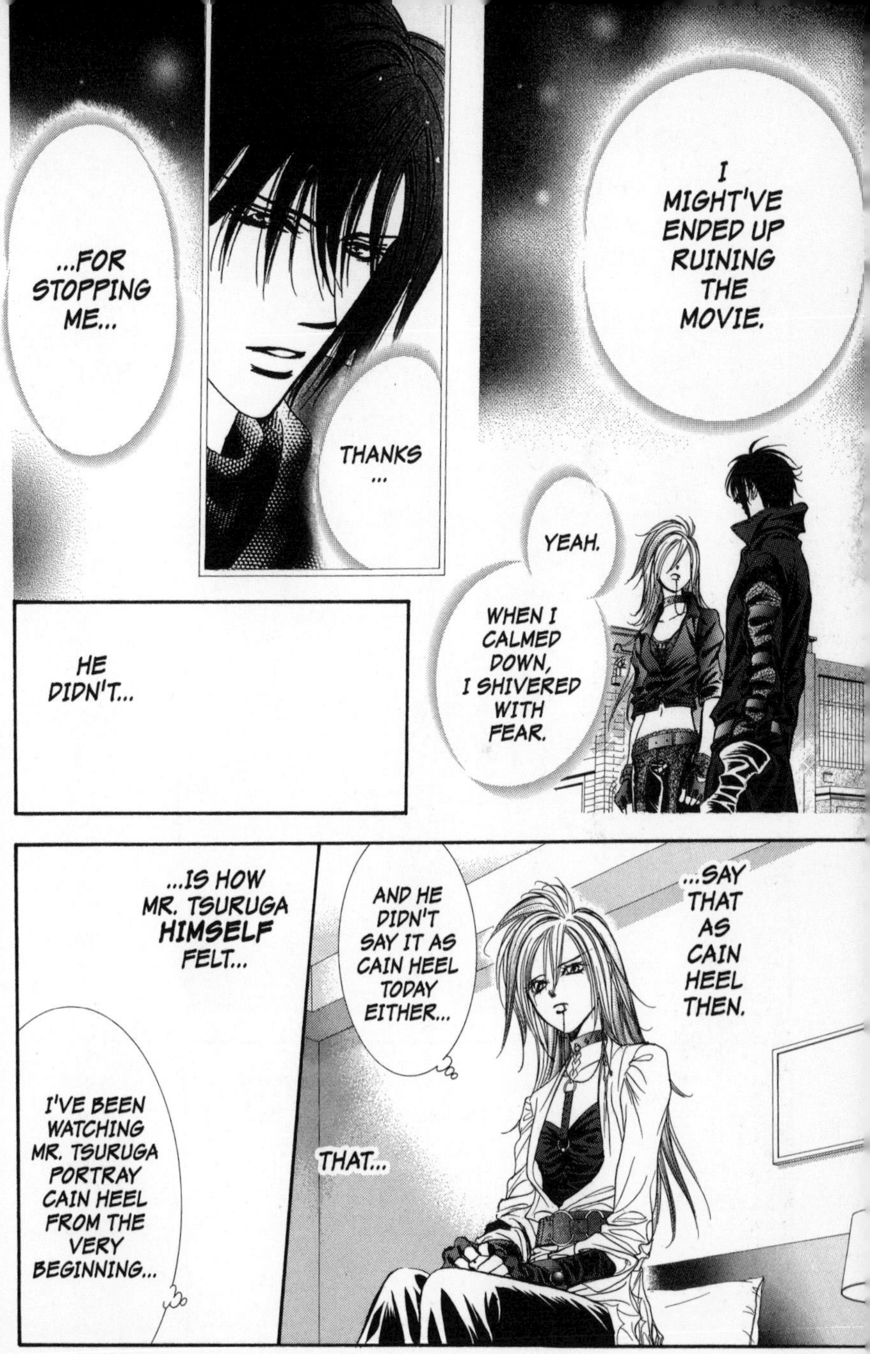
I MIGHT'VE ENDED UP RUINING THE MOVIE.
THANKS...
...FOR STOPPING ME...
YEAH.
WHEN I CALMED DOWN, I SHIVERED WITH FEAR.
HE DIDN'T...
...SAY THAT AS CAIN HEEL THEN.
AND HE DIDN'T SAY IT AS CAIN HEEL TODAY EITHER...
THAT...
...IS HOW MR. TSURUGA HIMSELF FELT...
I'VE BEEN WATCHING MR. TSURUGA PORTRAY CAIN HEEL FROM THE VERY BEGINNING...

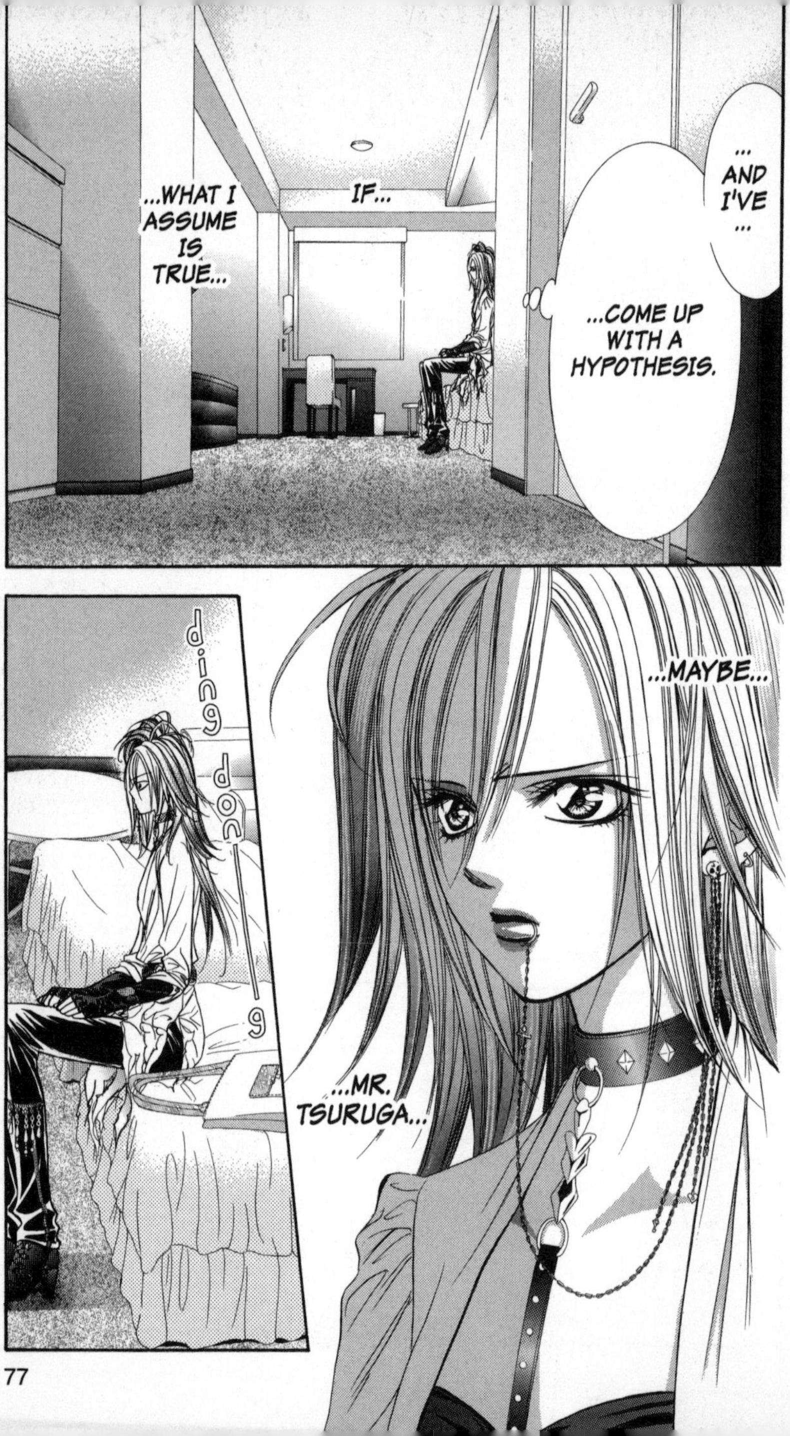
... AND I'VE ...
...COME UP WITH A HYPOTHESIS.
IF...
...WHAT I ASSUME IS TRUE...
...MAYBE...
...MR. TSURUGA...
ding dong

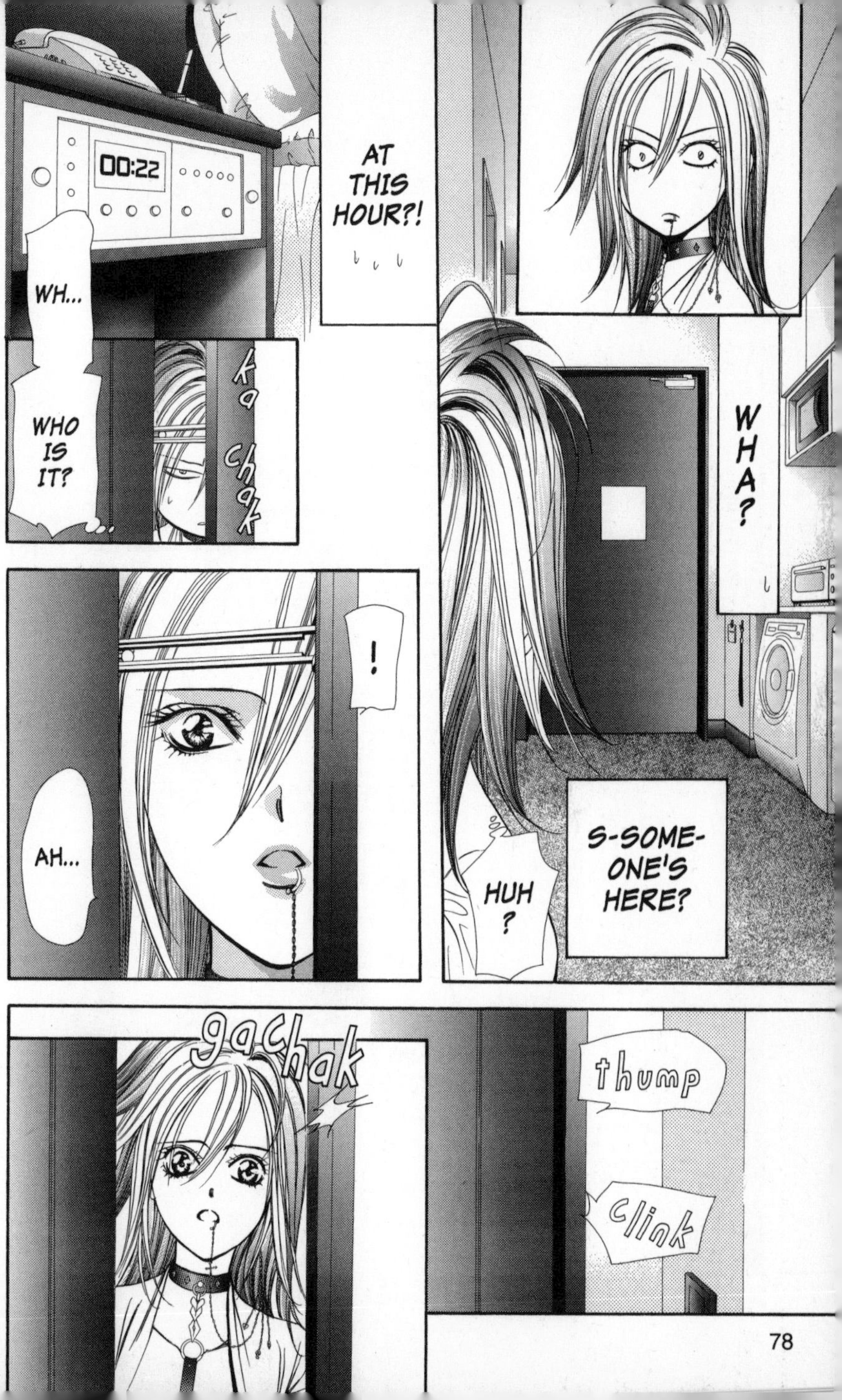
AT THIS HOUR?!
00:22
WH...
WHA?
S-SOME-ONE'S HERE?
HUH?
WHO IS IT?
ka chak
!
AH...
thump
clink
gachak

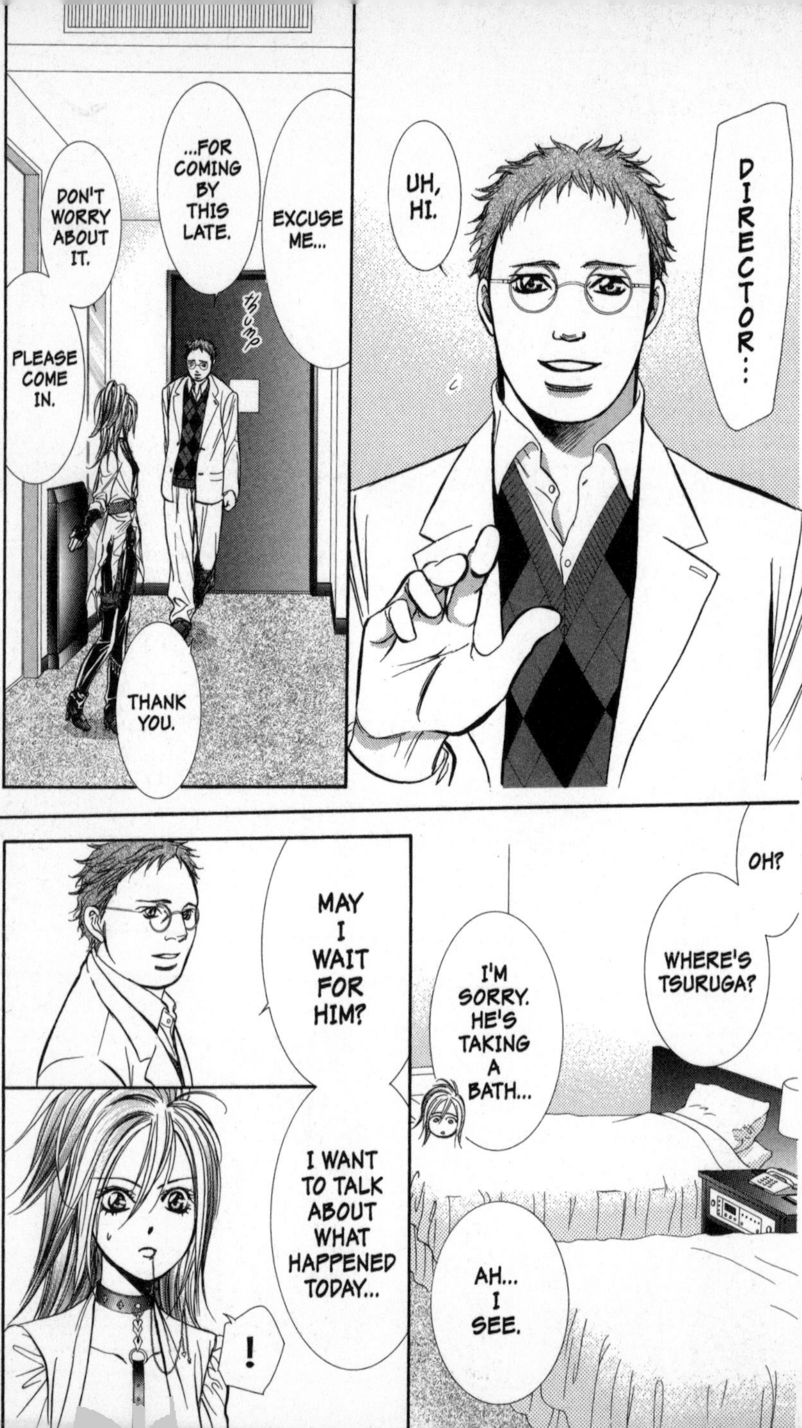
DIRECTOR...
UH, HI.
EXCUSE ME...
...FOR COMING BY THIS LATE.
thump
DON'T WORRY ABOUT IT.
PLEASE COME IN.
THANK YOU.
OH?
WHERE'S TSURUGA?
I'M SORRY. HE'S TAKING A BATH...
AH... I SEE.
MAY I WAIT FOR HIM?
I WANT TO TALK ABOUT WHAT HAPPENED TODAY...
!

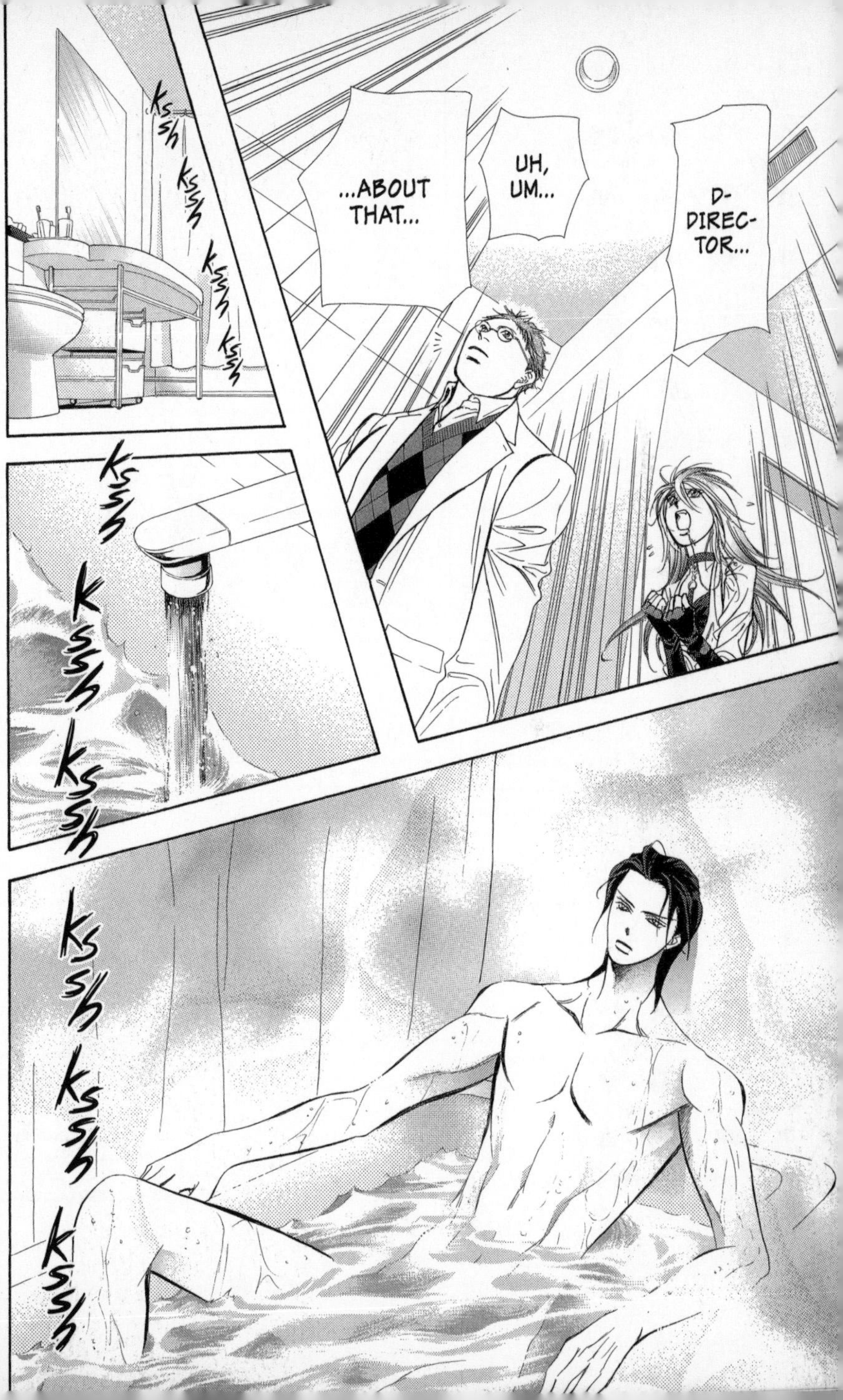
D-DIRECTOR...
UH, UM...
...ABOUT THAT...
KSSH
KSSSH
KSSSH
KSSH
KSSSH
KSSSH
KSSSH
KSSH
KSSSH
KSSH

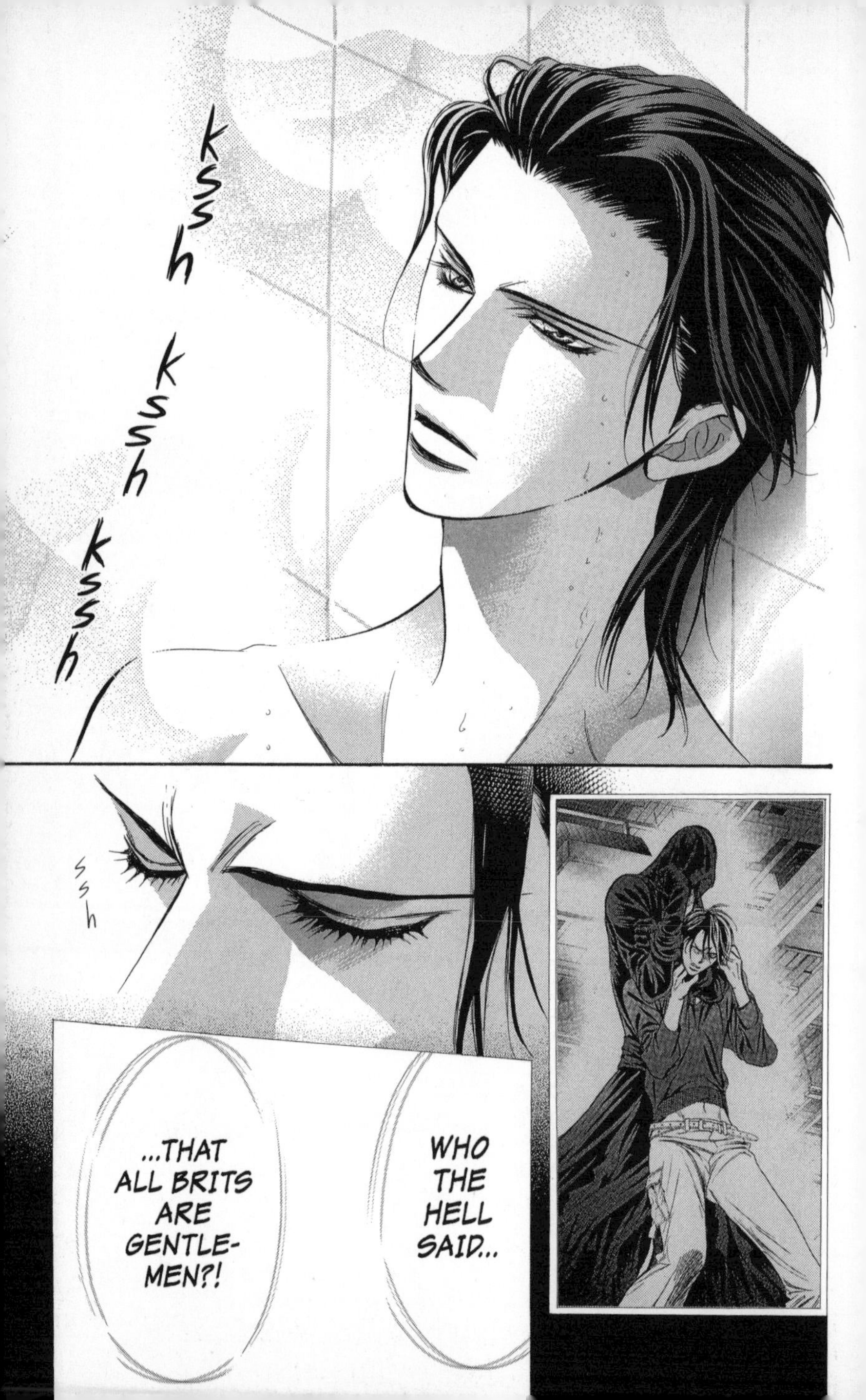
kssh kssh kssh
ssh
WHO THE HELL SAID...
...THAT ALL BRITS ARE GENTLE-MEN?!

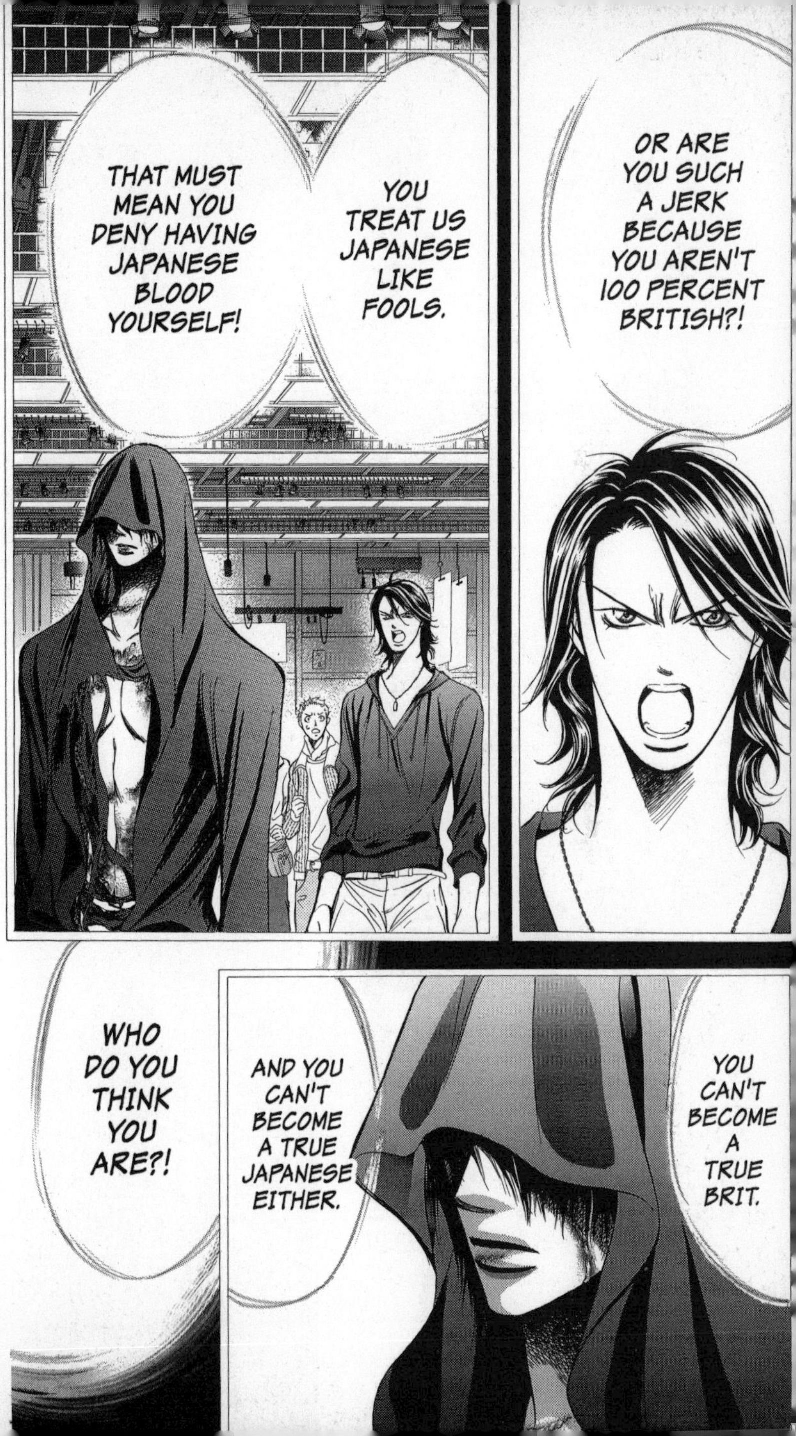
YOU TREAT US JAPANESE LIKE FOOLS.
THAT MUST MEAN YOU DENY HAVING JAPANESE BLOOD YOURSELF!
OR ARE YOU SUCH A JERK BECAUSE YOU AREN'T 100 PERCENT BRITISH?!
YOU CAN'T BECOME A TRUE BRIT.
AND YOU CAN'T BECOME A TRUE JAPANESE EITHER.
WHO DO YOU THINK YOU ARE?!

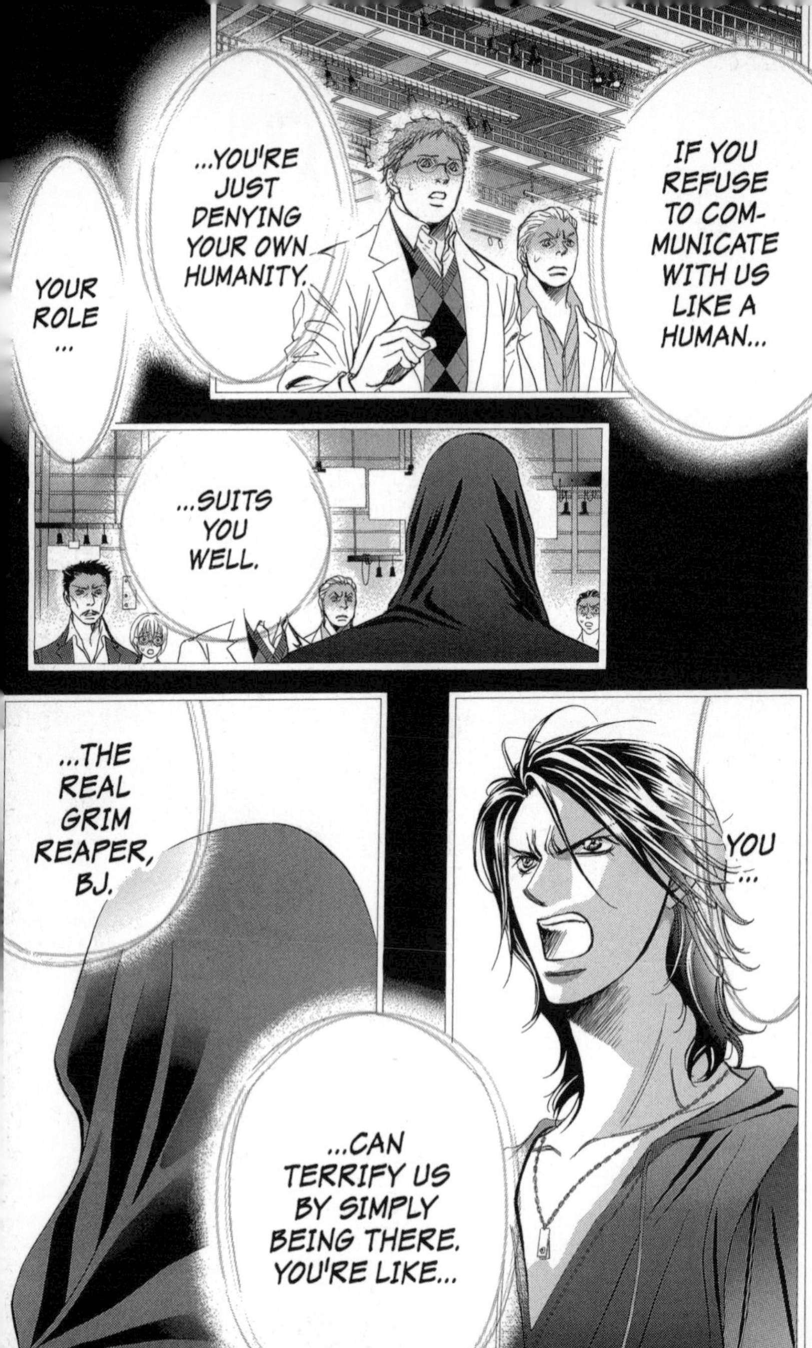
IF YOU REFUSE TO COM-MUNICATE WITH US LIKE A HUMAN...
...YOU'RE JUST DENYING YOUR OWN HUMANITY.
YOUR ROLE ...
...SUITS YOU WELL.
YOU ...
...CAN TERRIFY US BY SIMPLY BEING THERE. YOU'RE LIKE...
...THE REAL GRIM REAPER, BJ.

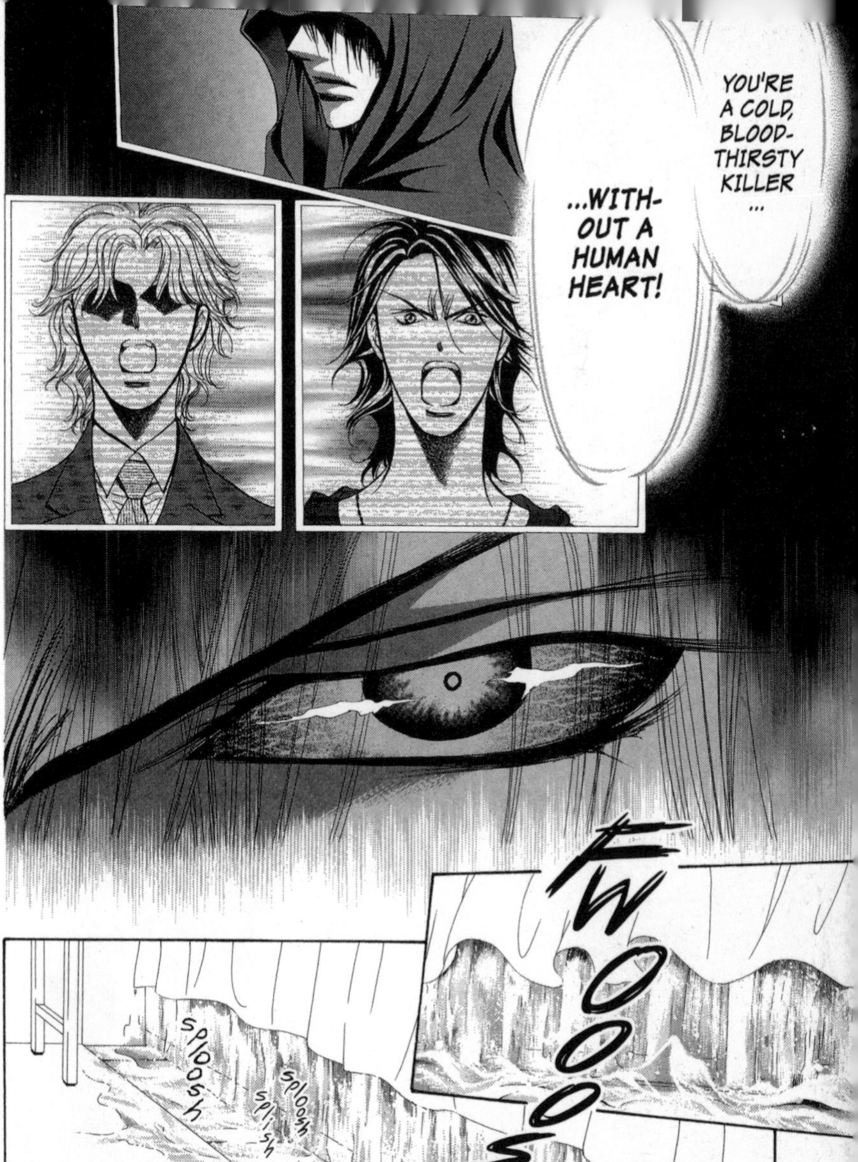
YOU'RE A COLD, BLOOD-THIRSTY KILLER ...
...WITH-OUT A HUMAN HEART!
FWOOOOSH
sploosh
splish
sploosh

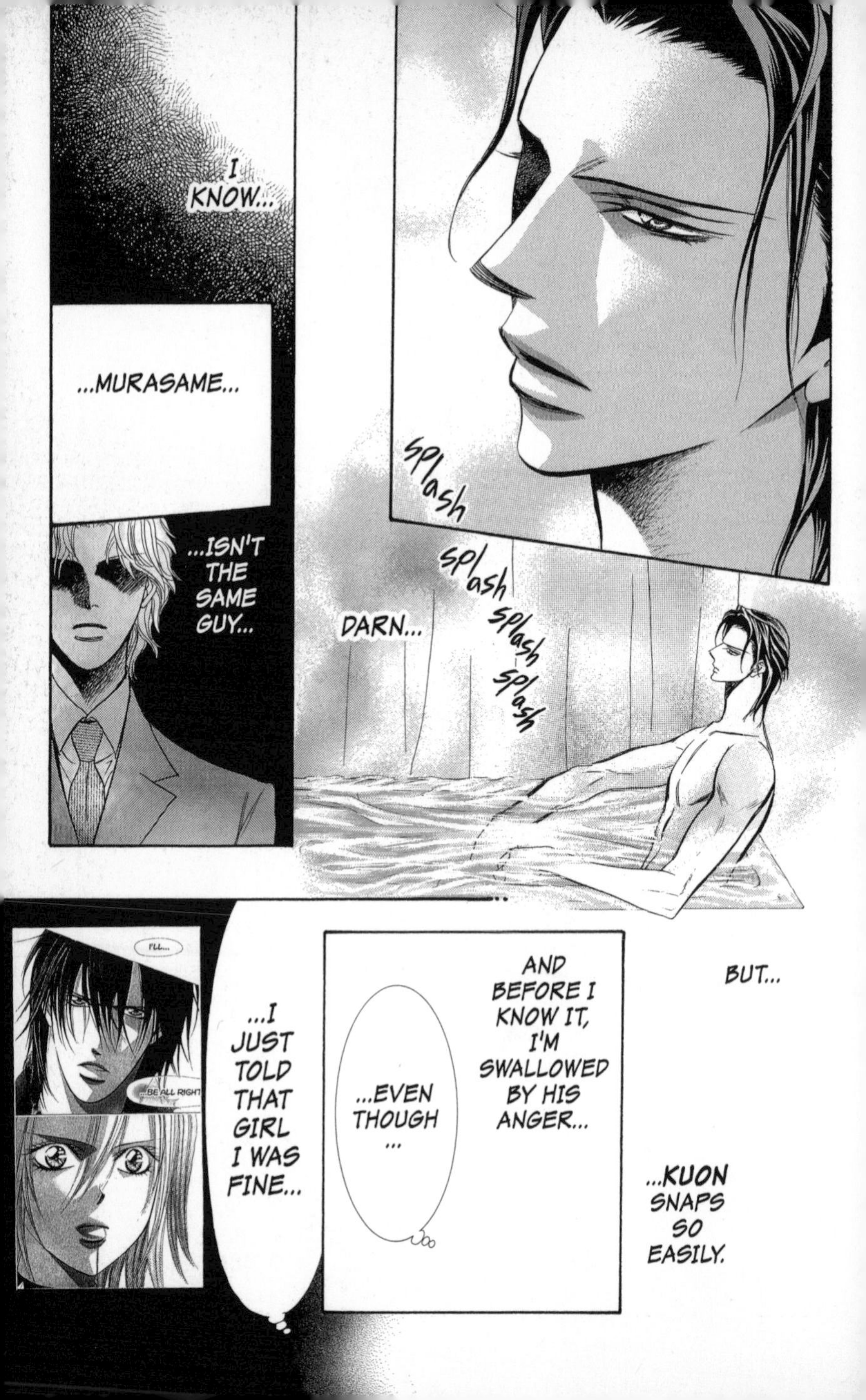
splash
splash
DARN...
splash
splash
I KNOW...
...MURASAME...
...ISN'T THE SAME GUY...
BUT...
...KUON SNAPS SO EASILY.
AND BEFORE I KNOW IT, I'M SWALLOWED BY HIS ANGER...
...EVEN THOUGH...
...I JUST TOLD THAT GIRL I WAS FINE...
I'LL...
...BE ALL RIGHT

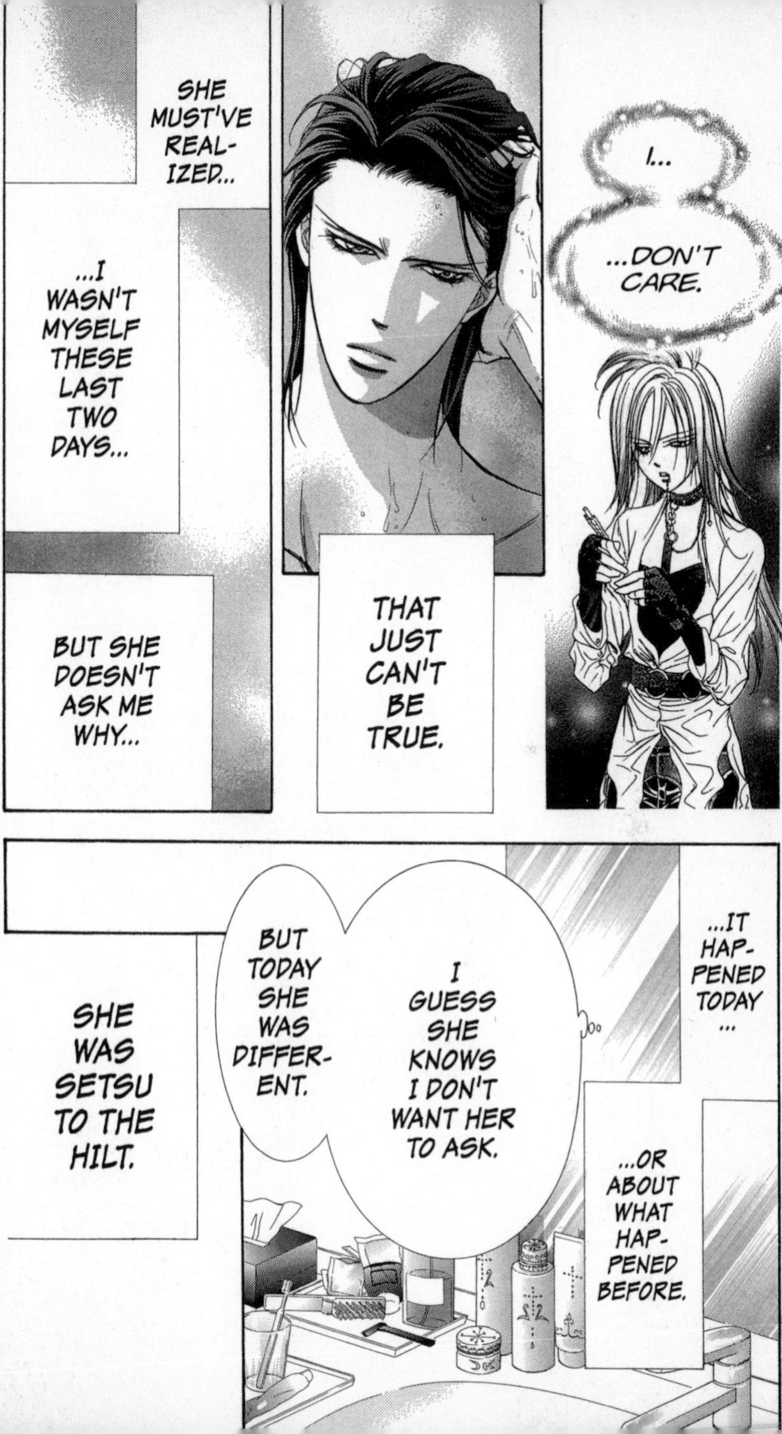
I...
...DON'T CARE.
THAT JUST CAN'T BE TRUE.
SHE MUST'VE REALIZED...
...I WASN'T MYSELF THESE LAST TWO DAYS...
BUT SHE DOESN'T ASK ME WHY...
...IT HAPPENED TODAY...
...OR ABOUT WHAT HAPPENED BEFORE.
I GUESS SHE KNOWS I DON'T WANT HER TO ASK.
BUT TODAY SHE WAS DIFFERENT.
SHE WAS SETSU TO THE HILT.

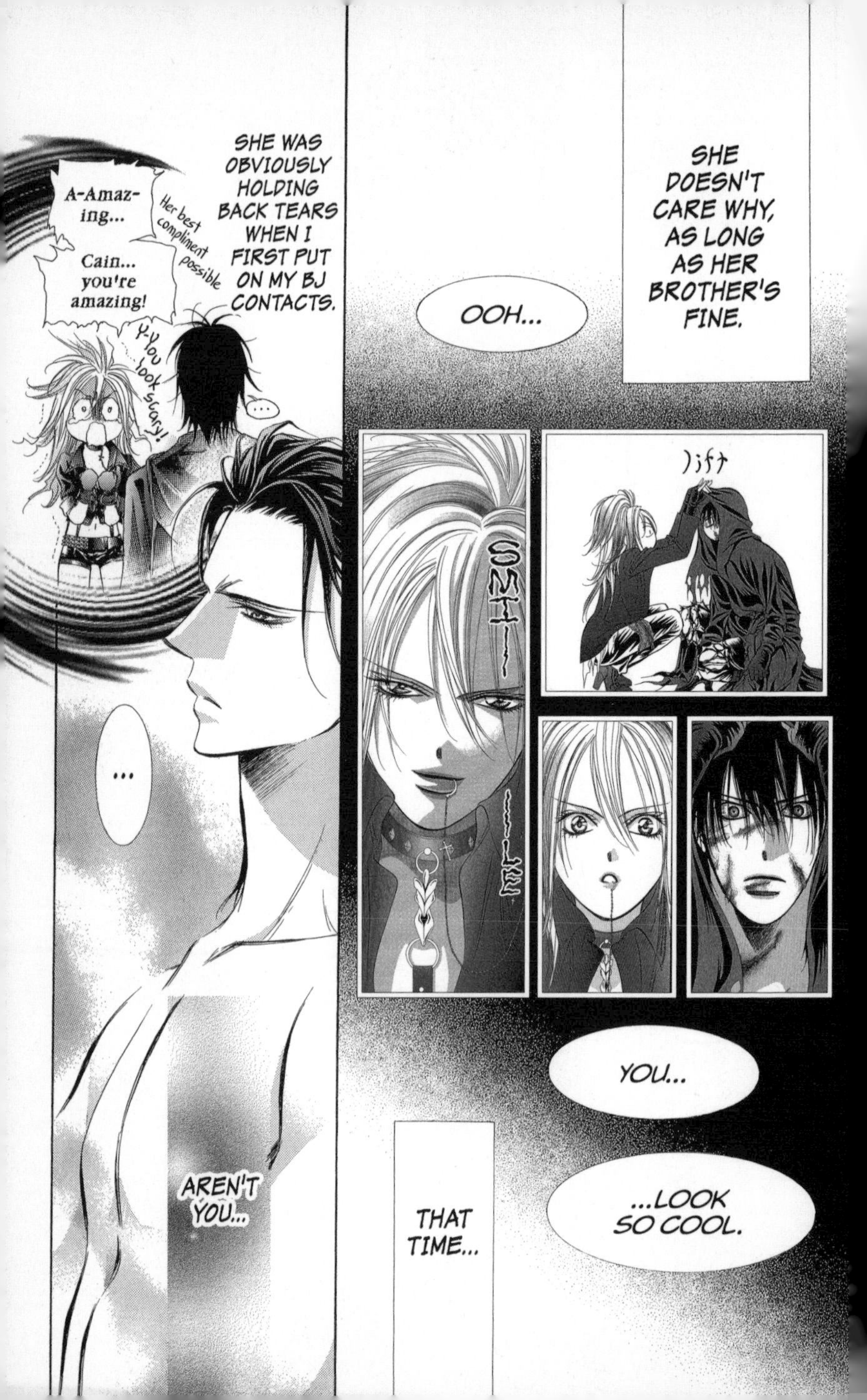
SHE DOESN'T CARE WHY, AS LONG AS HER BROTHER'S FINE.
OOH...
lift
SMIIILE
YOU...
...LOOK SO COOL.
THAT TIME...
SHE WAS OBVIOUSLY HOLDING BACK TEARS WHEN I FIRST PUT ON MY BJ CONTACTS.
A-Amazing...
Cain... you're amazing!
Her best compliment possible
...
Y-You look scary!
...
AREN'T YOU...

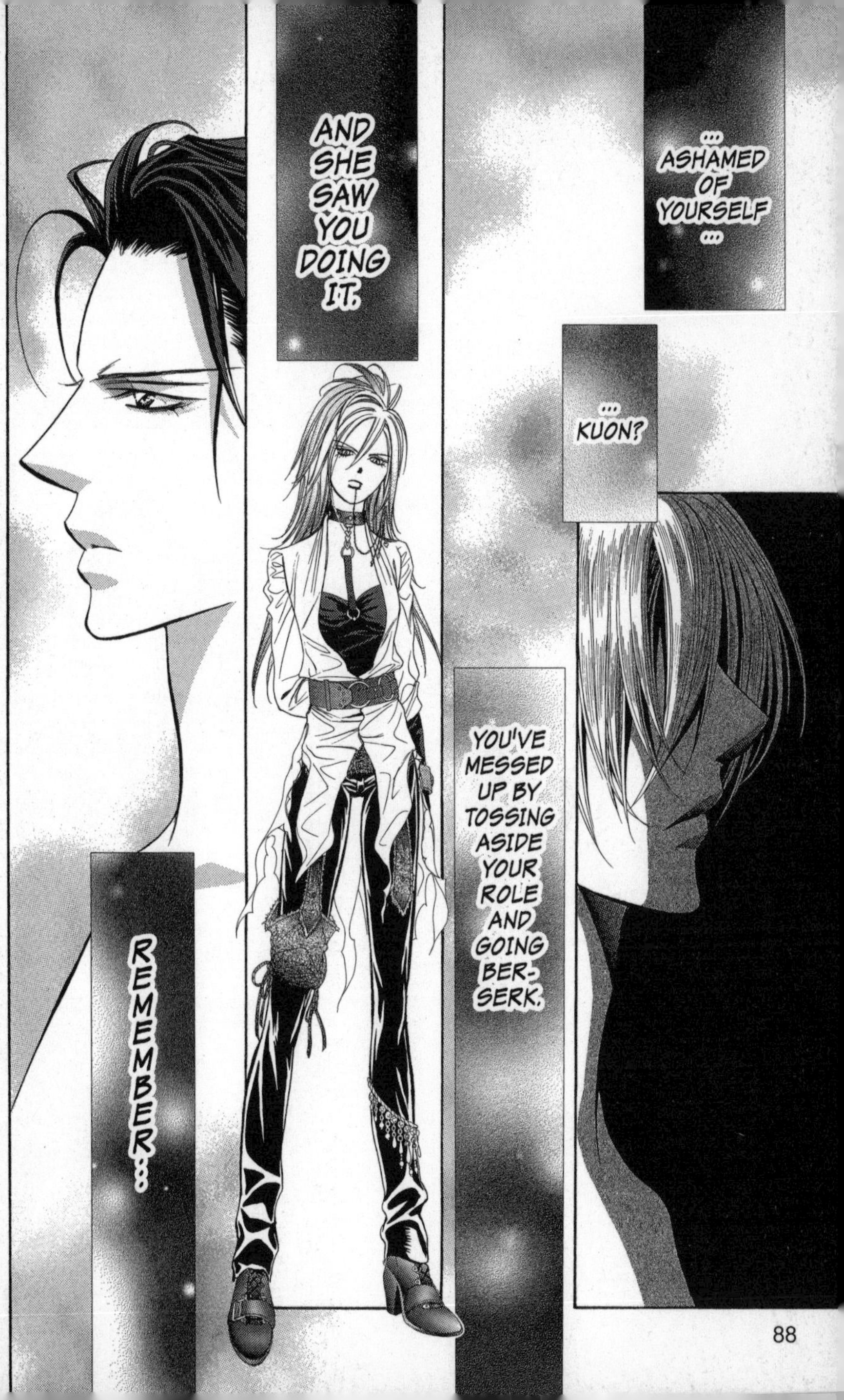
...ASHAMED OF YOURSELF...
...KUON?
YOU'VE MESSED UP BY TOSSING ASIDE YOUR ROLE AND GOING BER-SERK.
AND SHE SAW YOU DOING IT.
REMEMBER...

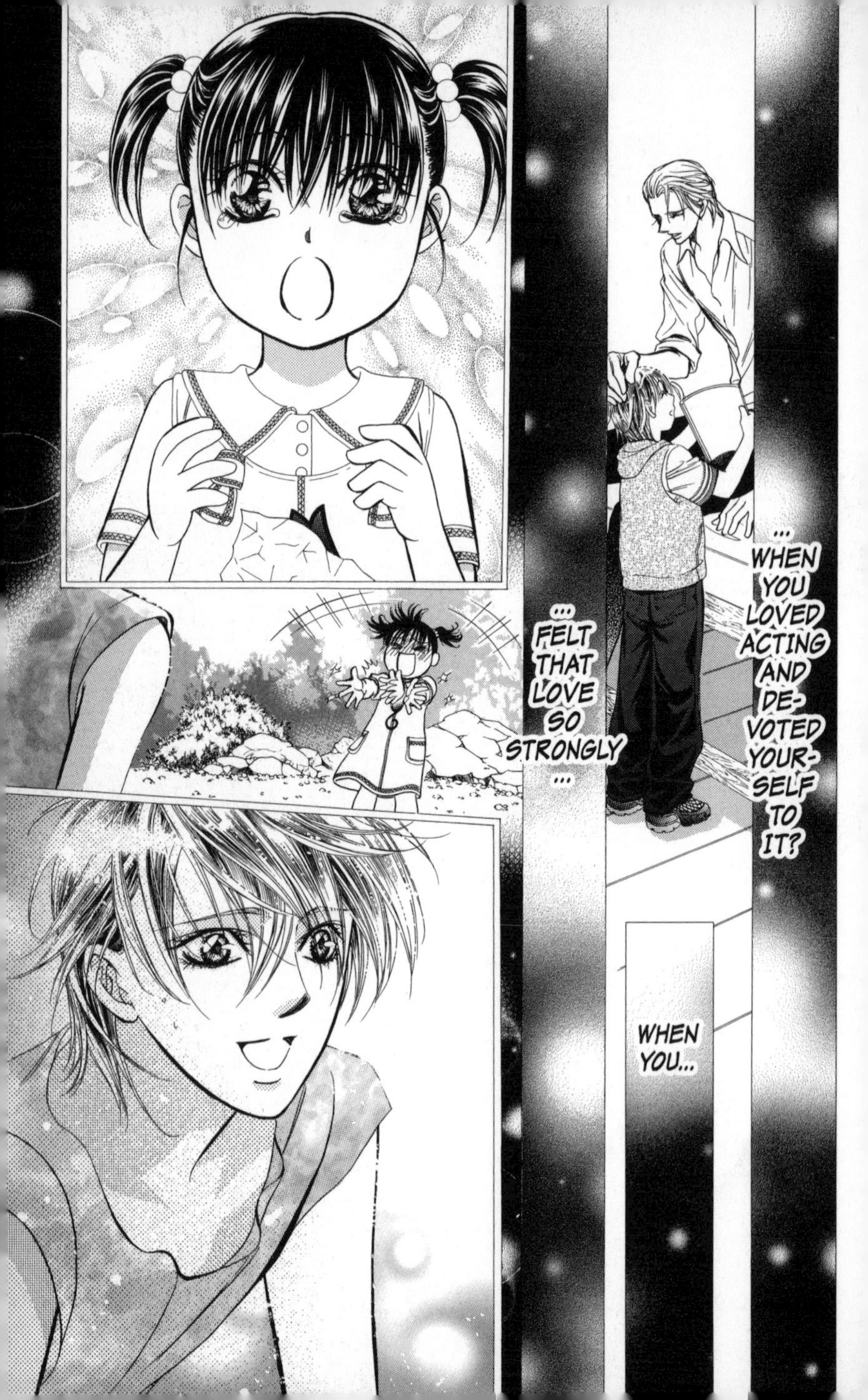
...WHEN YOU LOVED ACTING AND DE-VOTED YOUR-SELF TO IT?
WHEN YOU...
...FELT THAT LOVE SO STRONGLY...

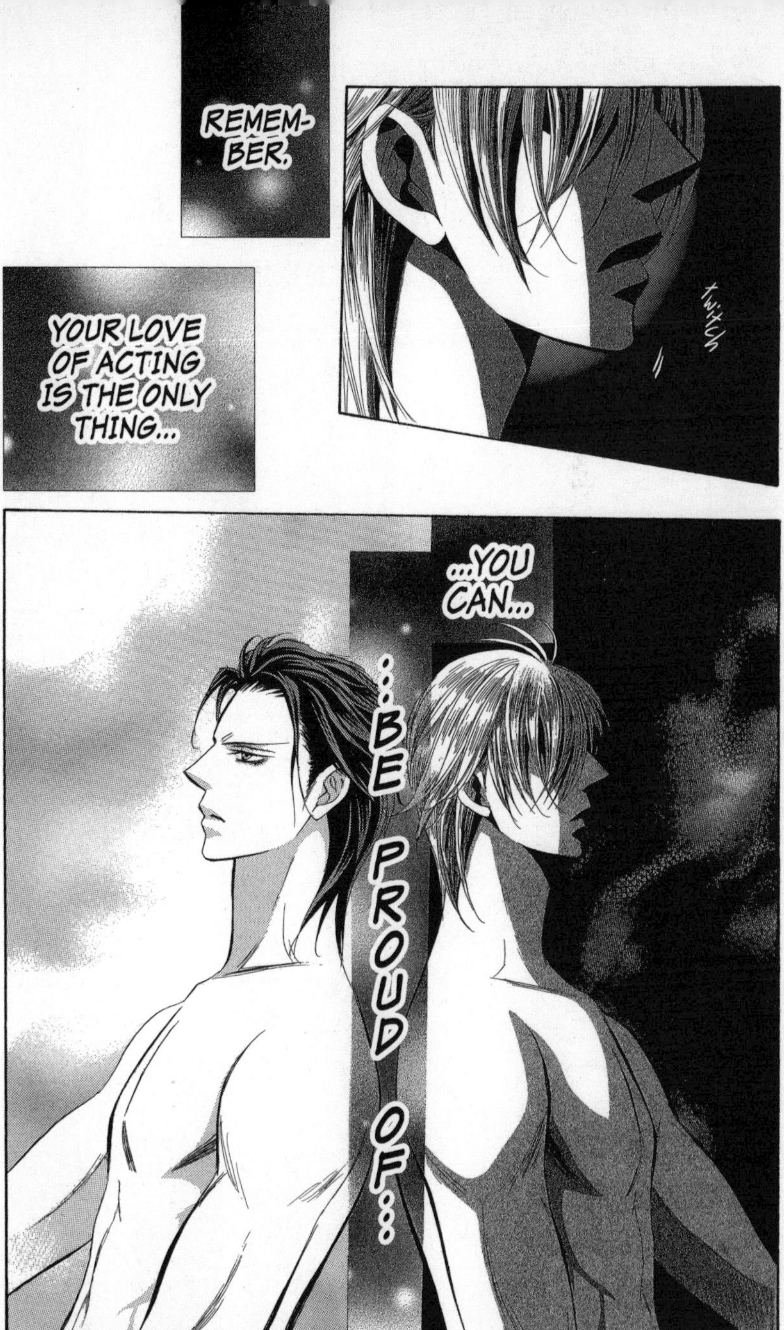
twitch
REMEM-BER.
YOUR LOVE OF ACTING IS THE ONLY THING...
...YOU CAN...
...BE PROUD OF...

End of Act 185

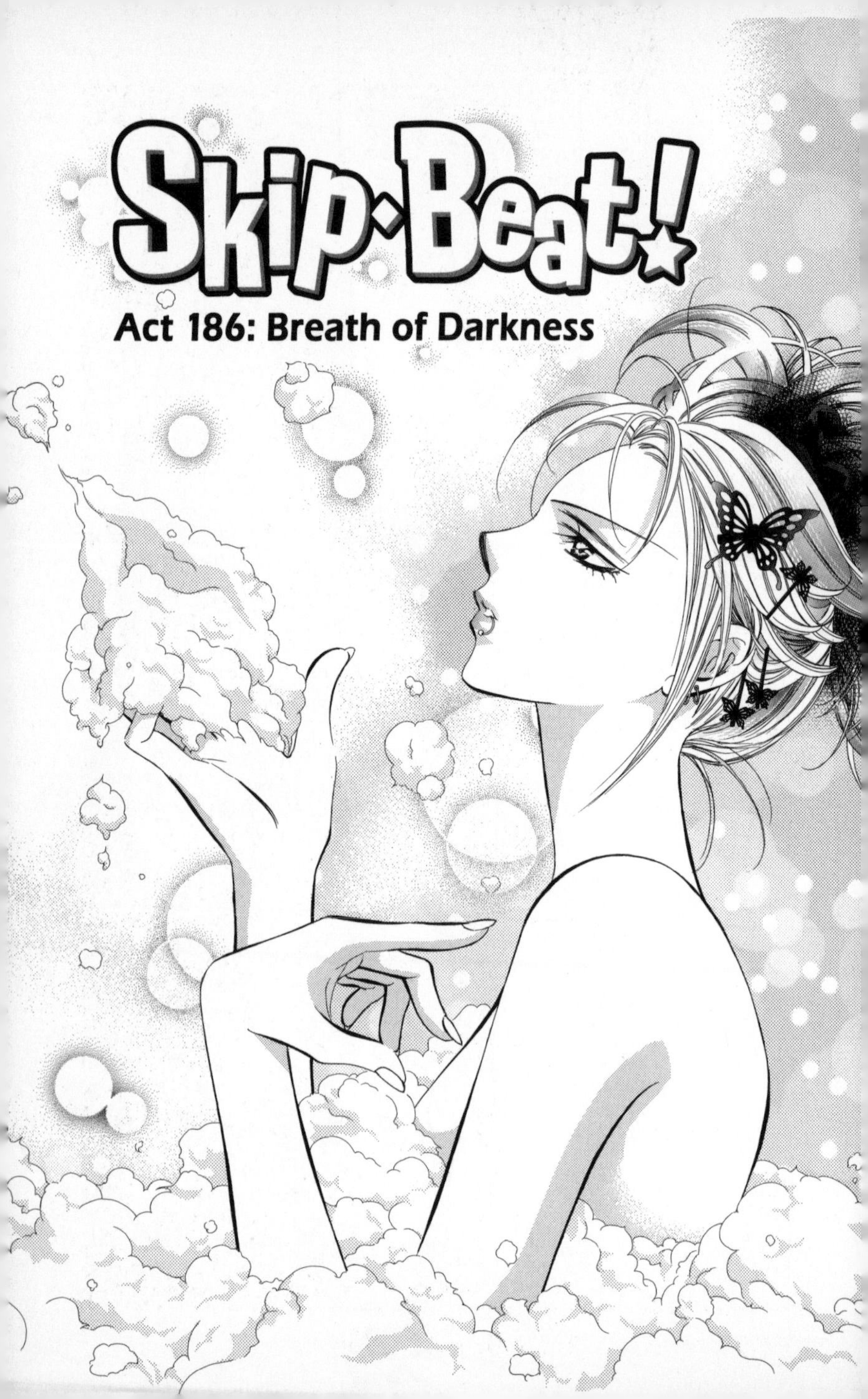
Skip·Beat!
Act 186: Breath of Darkness

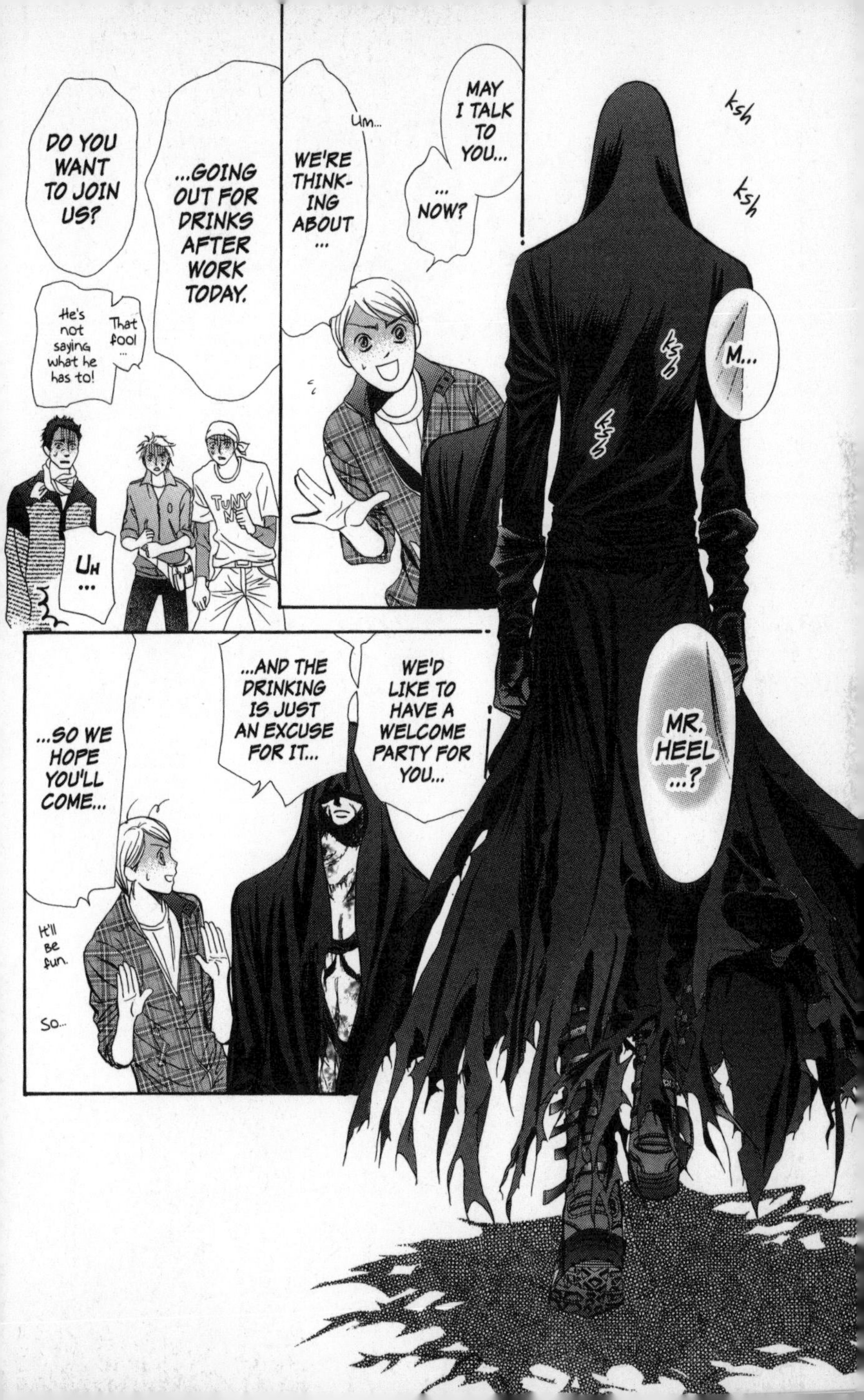
ksh
ksh
M...
ksh
ksh
MR. HEEL ...?
MAY I TALK TO YOU...
... NOW?
Um...
WE'RE THINKING ABOUT ...
...GOING OUT FOR DRINKS AFTER WORK TODAY.
DO YOU WANT TO JOIN US?
That fool ...
He's not saying what he has to!
UH ...
WE'D LIKE TO HAVE A WELCOME PARTY FOR YOU...
...AND THE DRINKING IS JUST AN EXCUSE FOR IT...
...SO WE HOPE YOU'LL COME...
It'll be fun.
So...

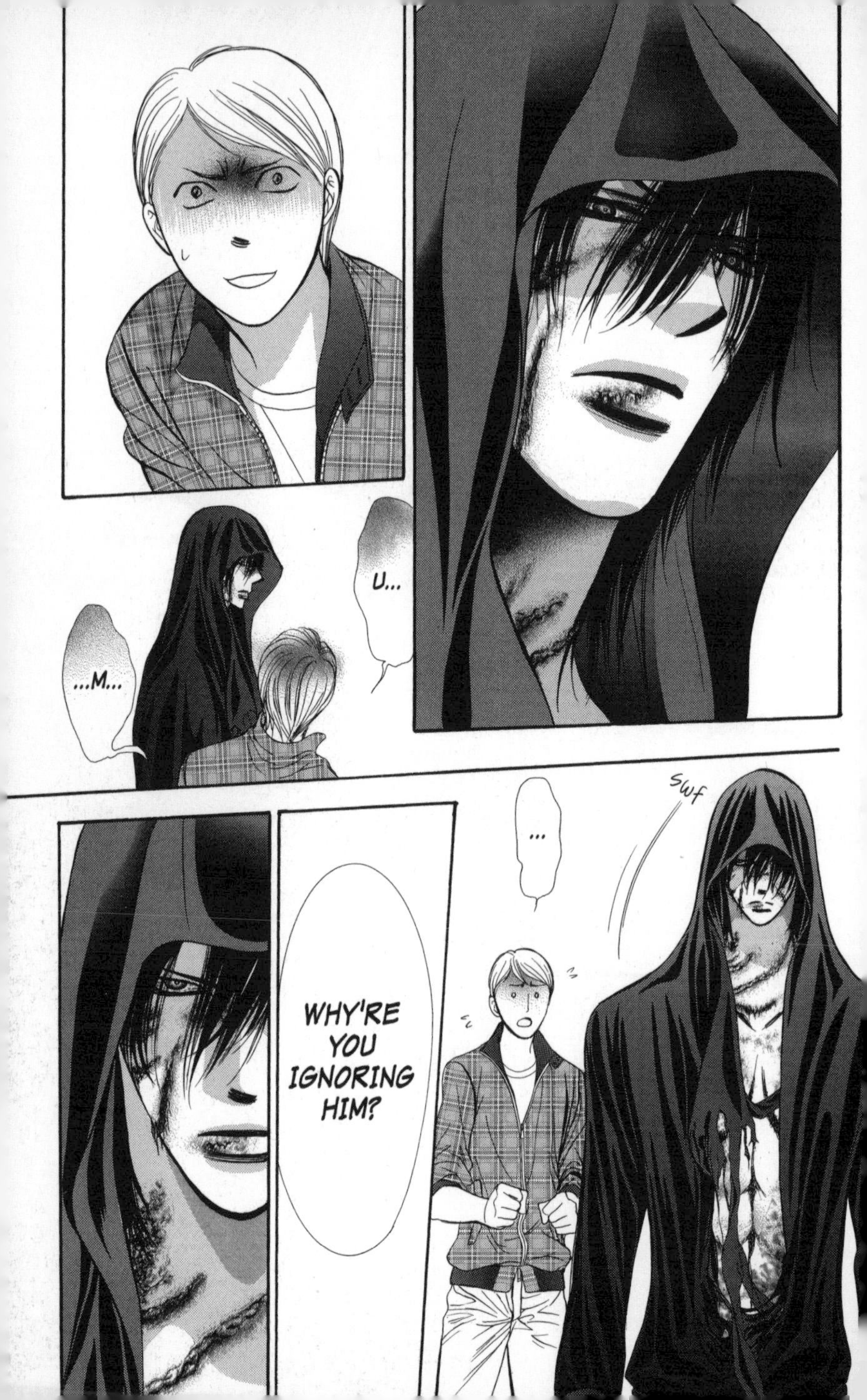
U...
...M...
SWF
...
WHY'RE YOU IGNORING HIM?

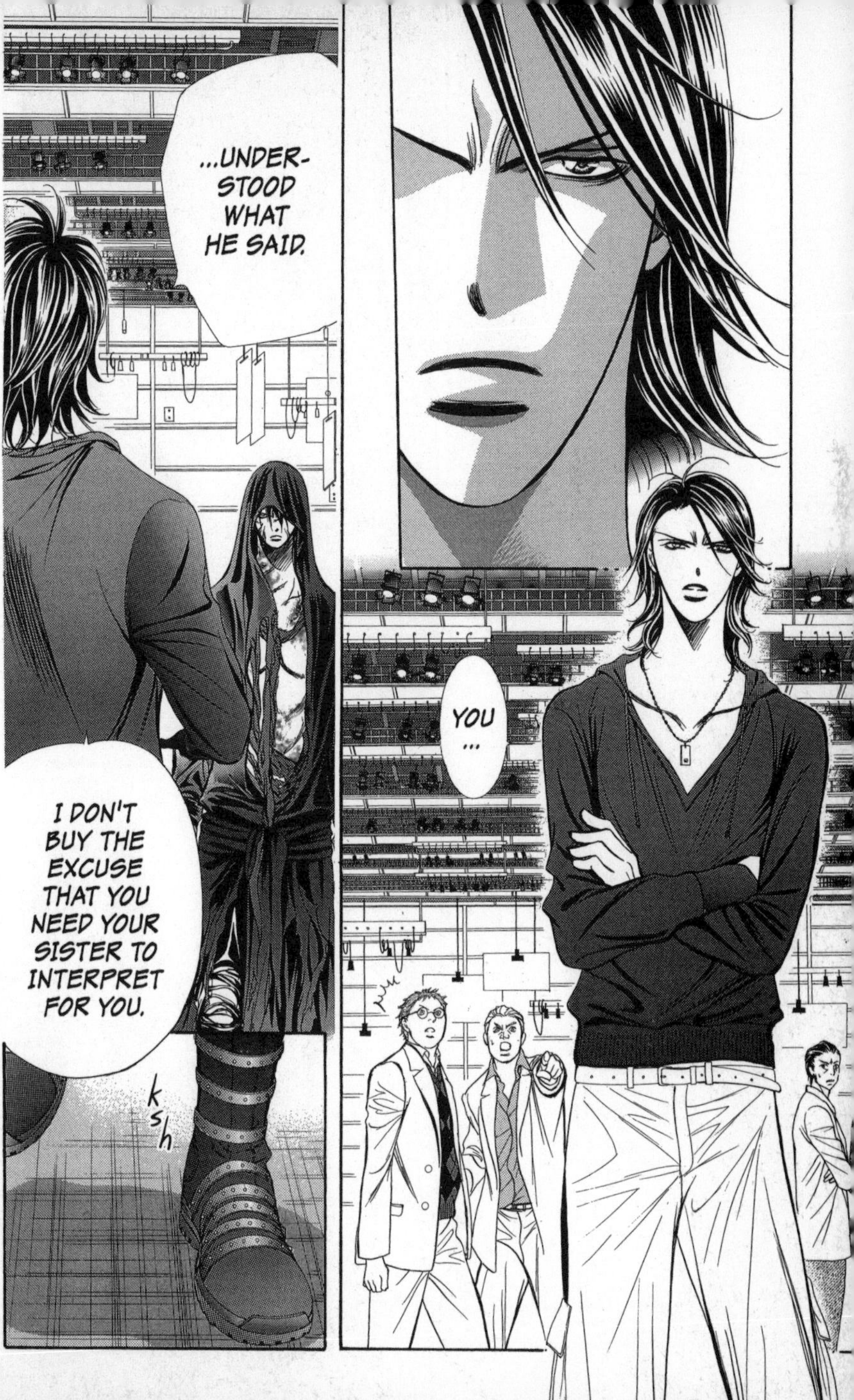
YOU ...
...UNDER-STOOD WHAT HE SAID.
I DON'T BUY THE EXCUSE THAT YOU NEED YOUR SISTER TO INTERPRET FOR YOU.
ksh

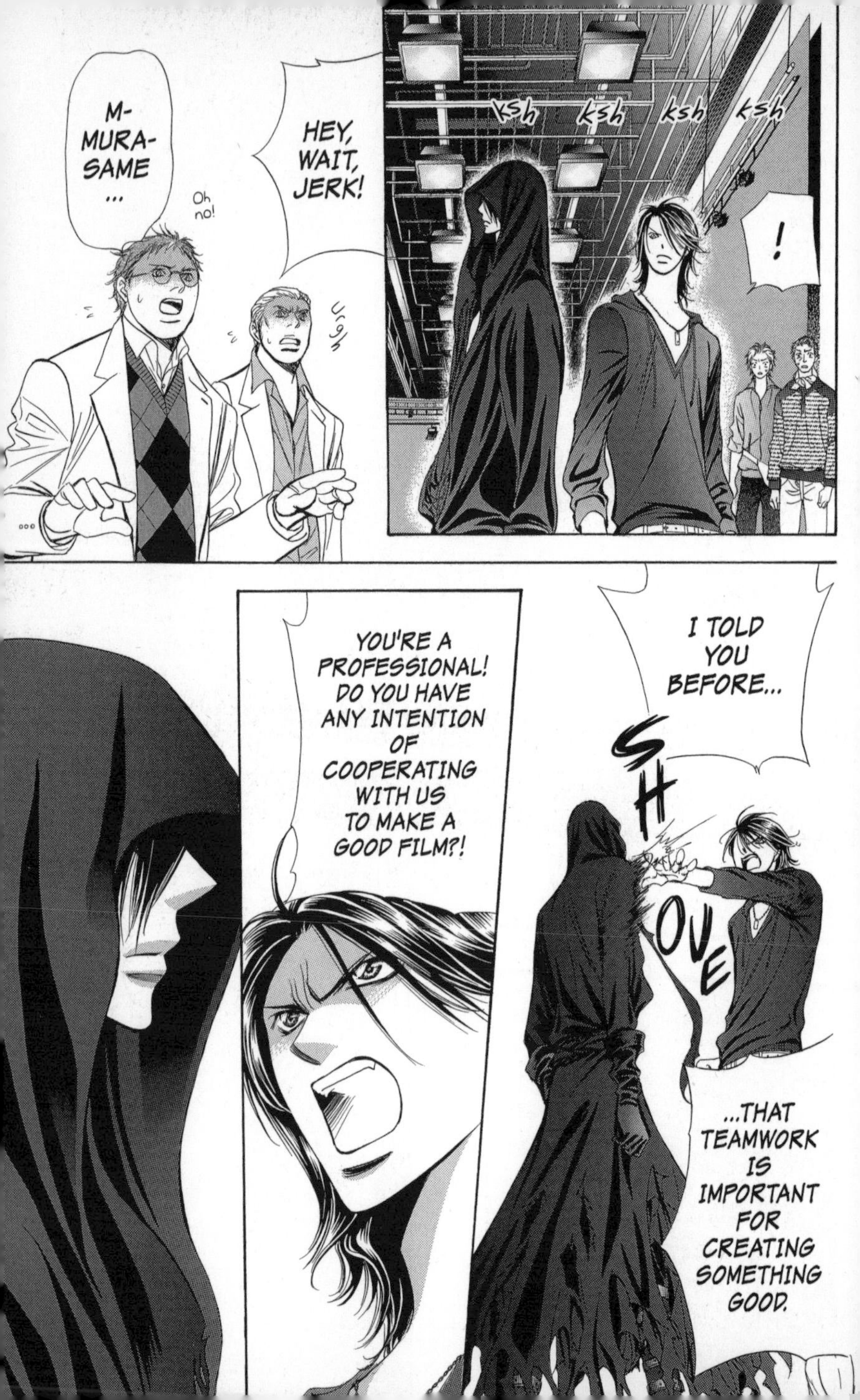

ksh ksh ksh ksh
!
HEY, WAIT, JERK!
M-MURASAME...
Oh no!
Urgh
I TOLD YOU BEFORE...
SHOVE
...THAT TEAMWORK IS IMPORTANT FOR CREATING SOMETHING GOOD.
YOU'RE A PROFESSIONAL! DO YOU HAVE ANY INTENTION OF COOPERATING WITH US TO MAKE A GOOD FILM?!

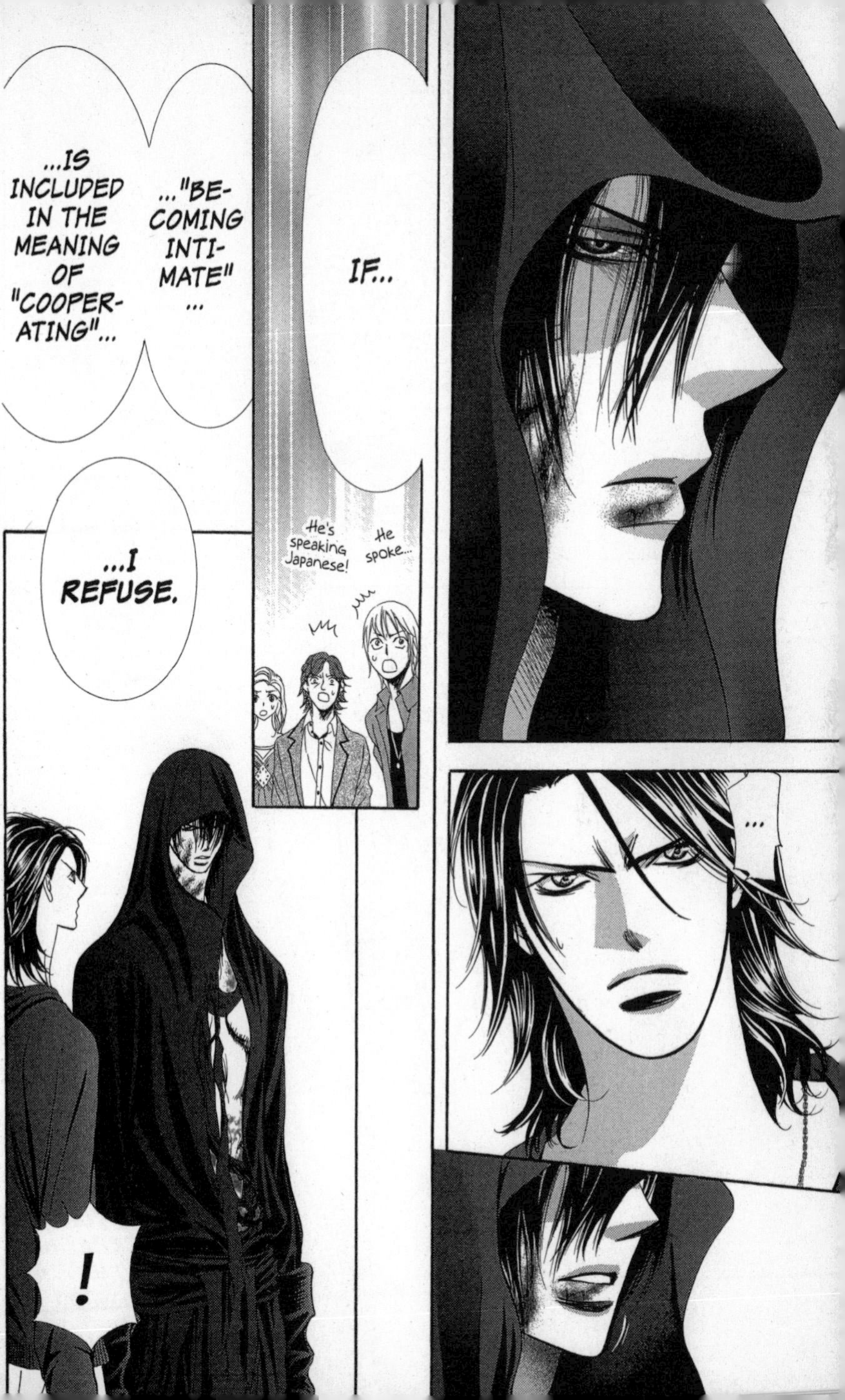
IF...
He spoke...
He's speaking Japanese!
..."BE-COMING INTI-MATE"...
...IS INCLUDED IN THE MEANING OF "COOPER-ATING"...
...I REFUSE.
...
!

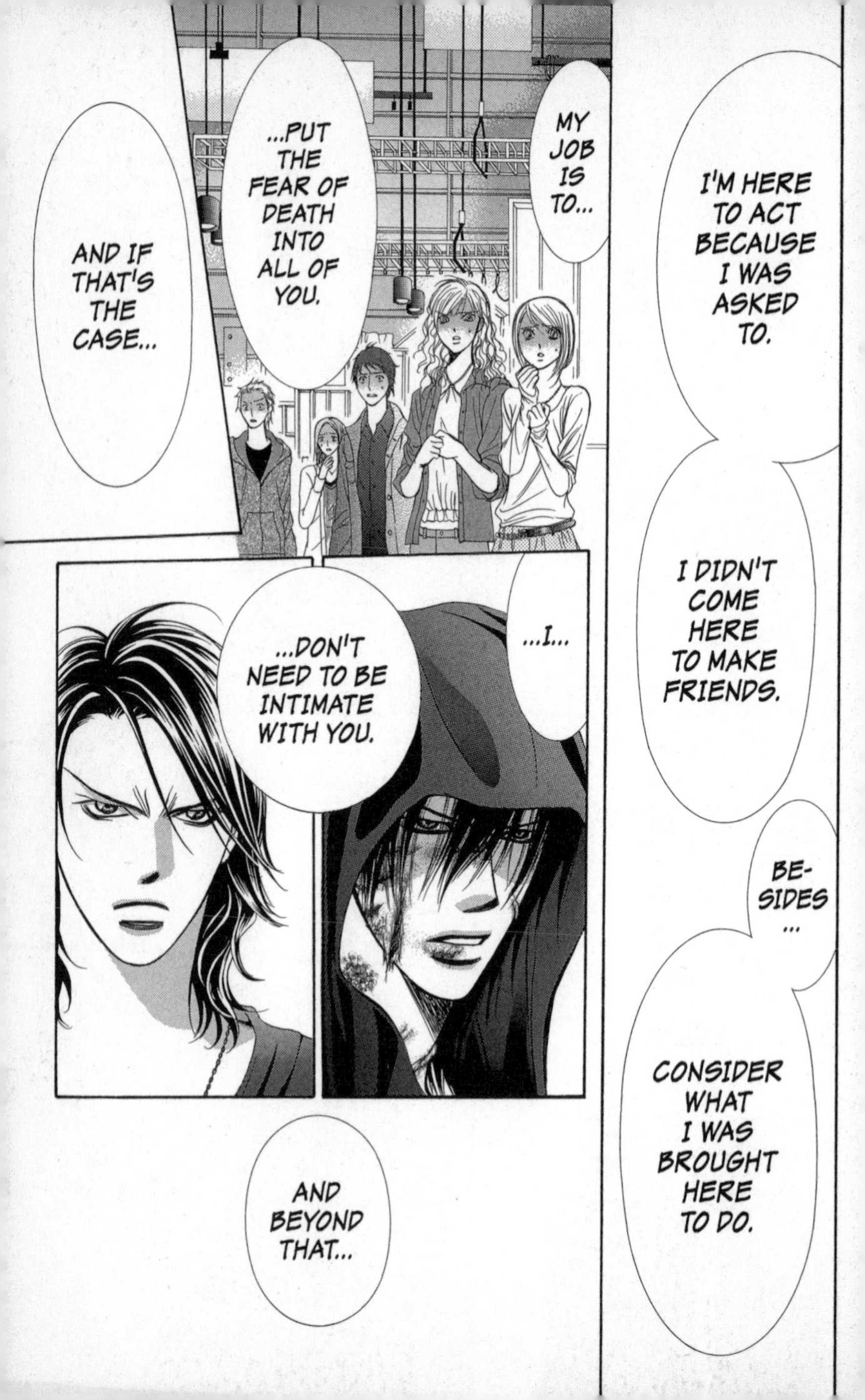
I'M HERE TO ACT BECAUSE I WAS ASKED TO.
I DIDN'T COME HERE TO MAKE FRIENDS.
BE-SIDES...
CONSIDER WHAT I WAS BROUGHT HERE TO DO.
MY JOB IS TO...
...PUT THE FEAR OF DEATH INTO ALL OF YOU.
AND IF THAT'S THE CASE...
...I...
...DON'T NEED TO BE INTIMATE WITH YOU.
AND BEYOND THAT...

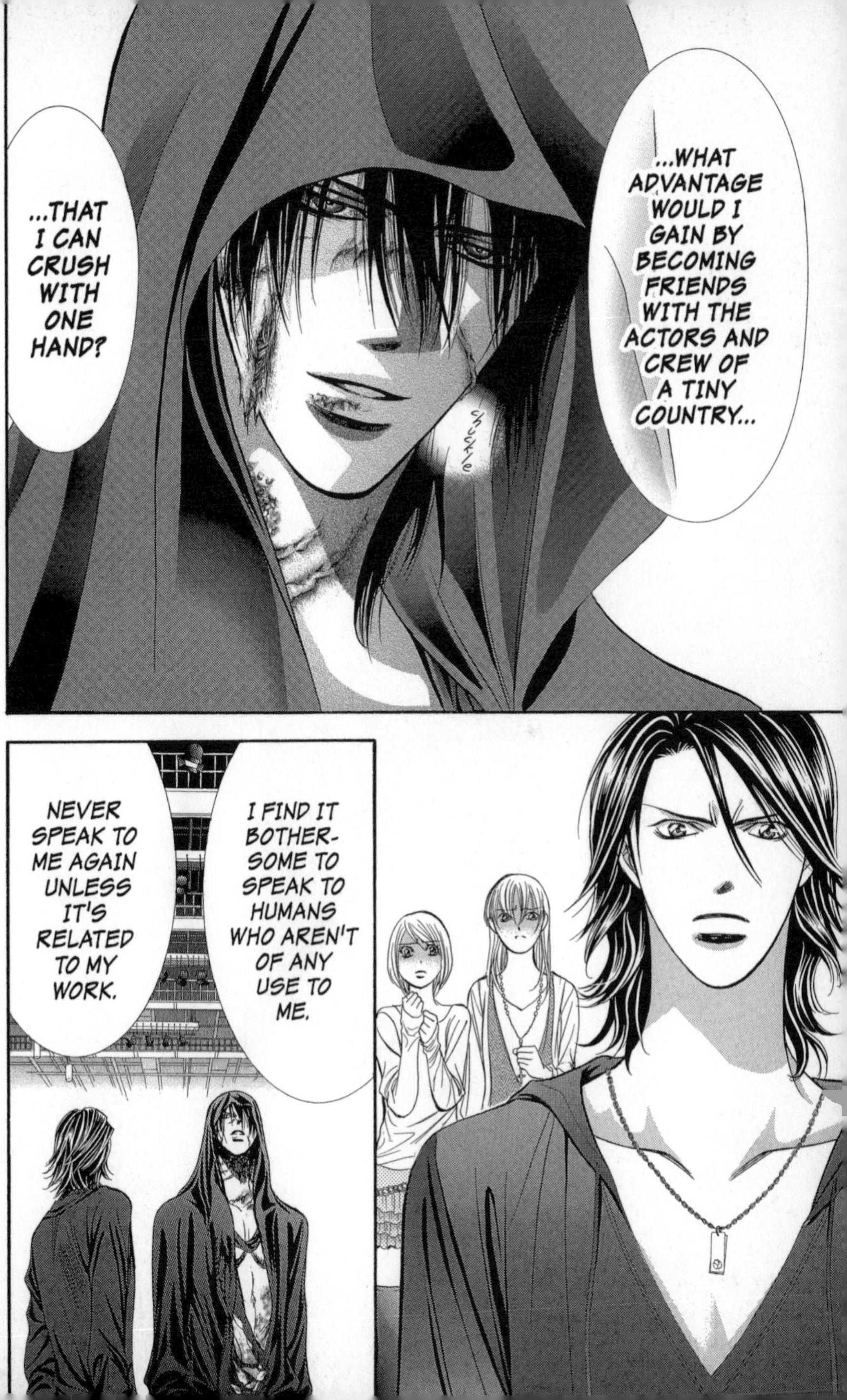
...WHAT ADVANTAGE WOULD I GAIN BY BECOMING FRIENDS WITH THE ACTORS AND CREW OF A TINY COUNTRY...
chuckle
...THAT I CAN CRUSH WITH ONE HAND?
I FIND IT BOTHER-SOME TO SPEAK TO HUMANS WHO AREN'T OF ANY USE TO ME.
NEVER SPEAK TO ME AGAIN UNLESS IT'S RELATED TO MY WORK.

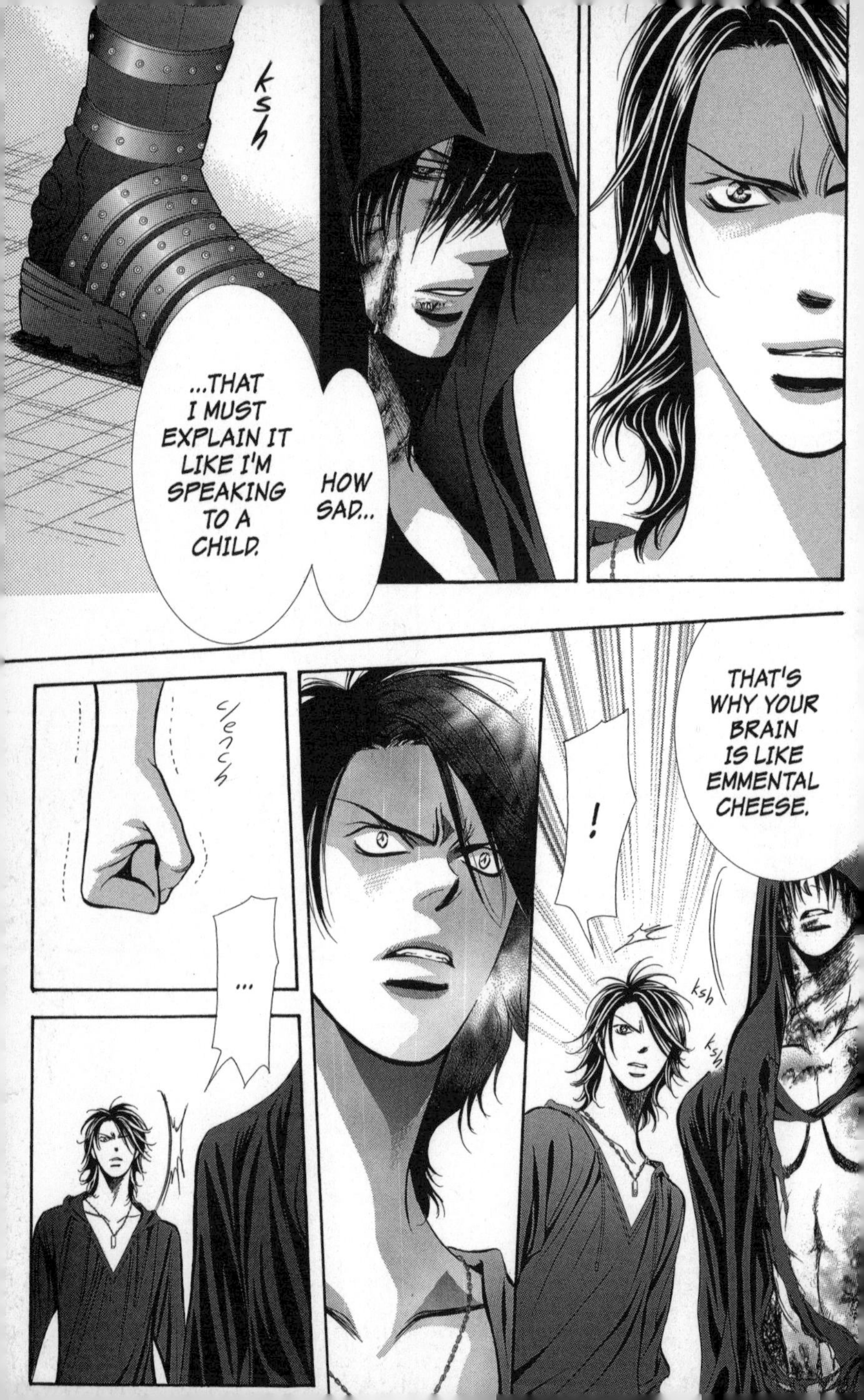
HOW SAD...
...THAT I MUST EXPLAIN IT LIKE I'M SPEAKING TO A CHILD.
ksh
THAT'S WHY YOUR BRAIN IS LIKE EMMENTAL CHEESE.
!
ksh
ksh
...
clench

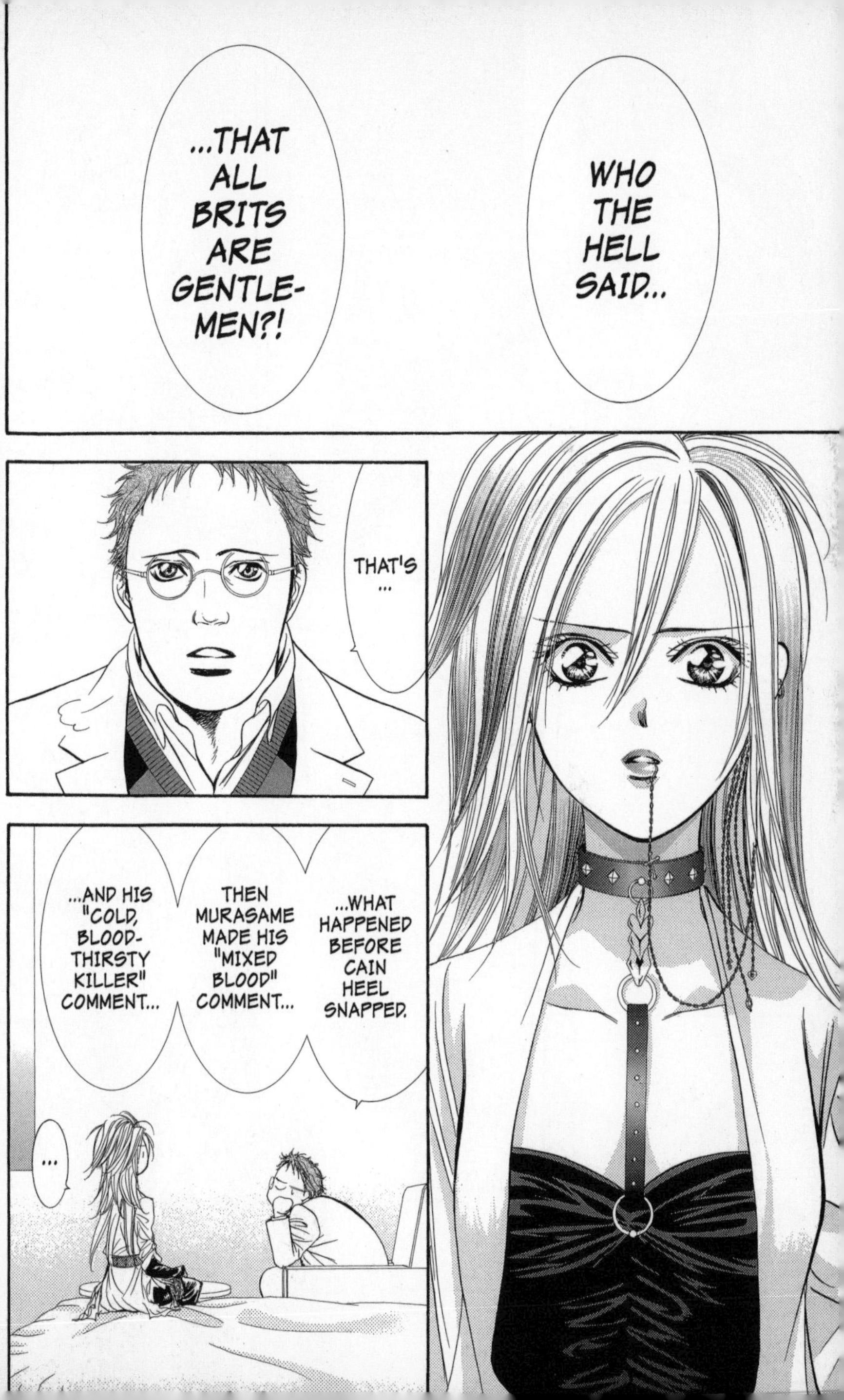
WHO THE HELL SAID...
...THAT ALL BRITS ARE GENTLE-MEN?!
THAT'S ...
...WHAT HAPPENED BEFORE CAIN HEEL SNAPPED.
THEN MURASAME MADE HIS "MIXED BLOOD" COMMENT...
...AND HIS "COLD, BLOOD-THIRSTY KILLER" COMMENT...
...

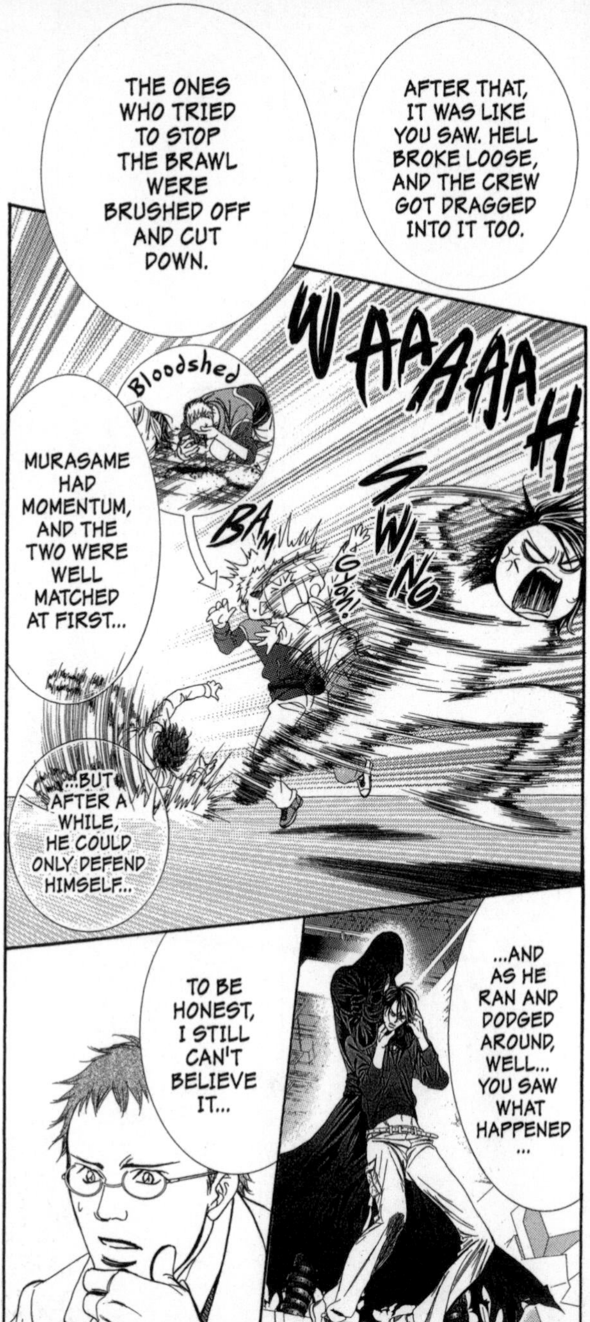
AFTER THAT, IT WAS LIKE YOU SAW. HELL BROKE LOOSE, AND THE CREW GOT DRAGGED INTO IT TOO.
THE ONES WHO TRIED TO STOP THE BRAWL WERE BRUSHED OFF AND CUT DOWN.
WAAAAAH
Bloodshed
MURASAME HAD MOMENTUM, AND THE TWO WERE WELL MATCHED AT FIRST...
SWING
BAM
...BUT AFTER A WHILE, HE COULD ONLY DEFEND HIMSELF...
...AND AS HE RAN AND DODGED AROUND, WELL... YOU SAW WHAT HAPPENED...
TO BE HONEST, I STILL CAN'T BELIEVE IT...
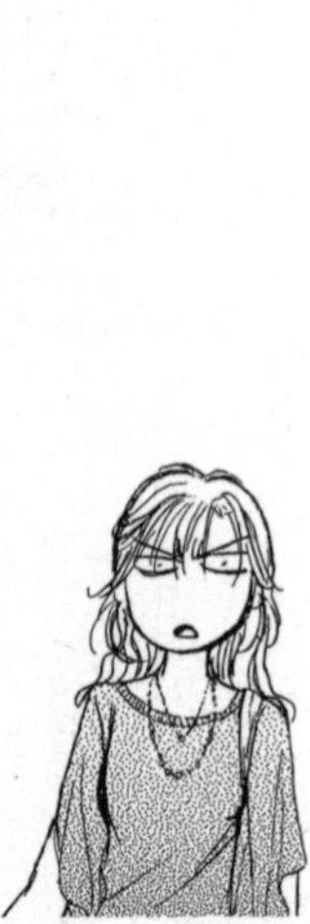

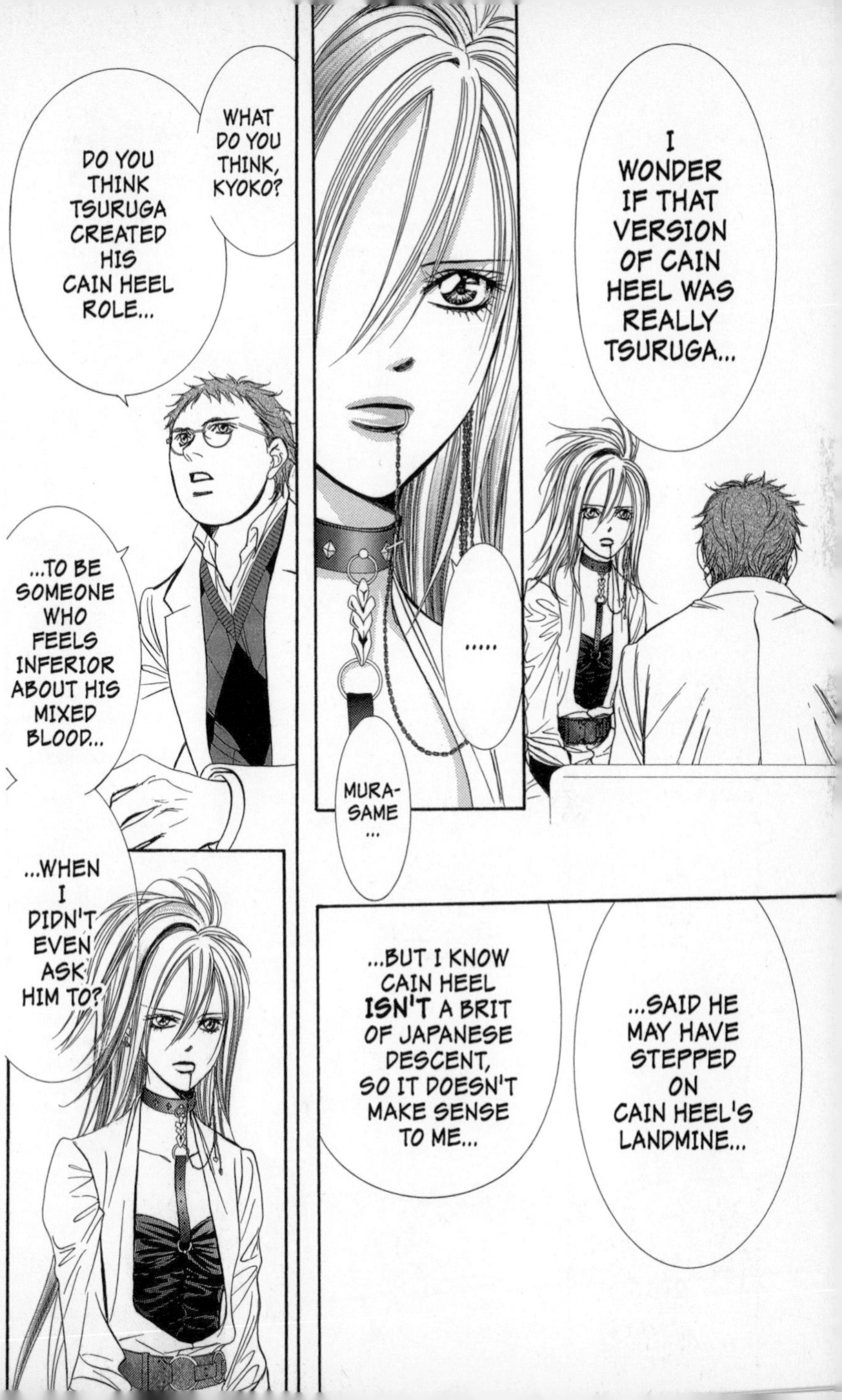
I WONDER IF THAT VERSION OF CAIN HEEL WAS REALLY TSURUGA...
.....
MURA-SAME...
...SAID HE MAY HAVE STEPPED ON CAIN HEEL'S LANDMINE...
...BUT I KNOW CAIN HEEL **ISN'T** A BRIT OF JAPANESE DESCENT, SO IT DOESN'T MAKE SENSE TO ME...
WHAT DO YOU THINK, KYOKO?
DO YOU THINK TSURUGA CREATED HIS CAIN HEEL ROLE...
...TO BE SOMEONE WHO FEELS INFERIOR ABOUT HIS MIXED BLOOD...
...WHEN I DIDN'T EVEN ASK HIM TO?

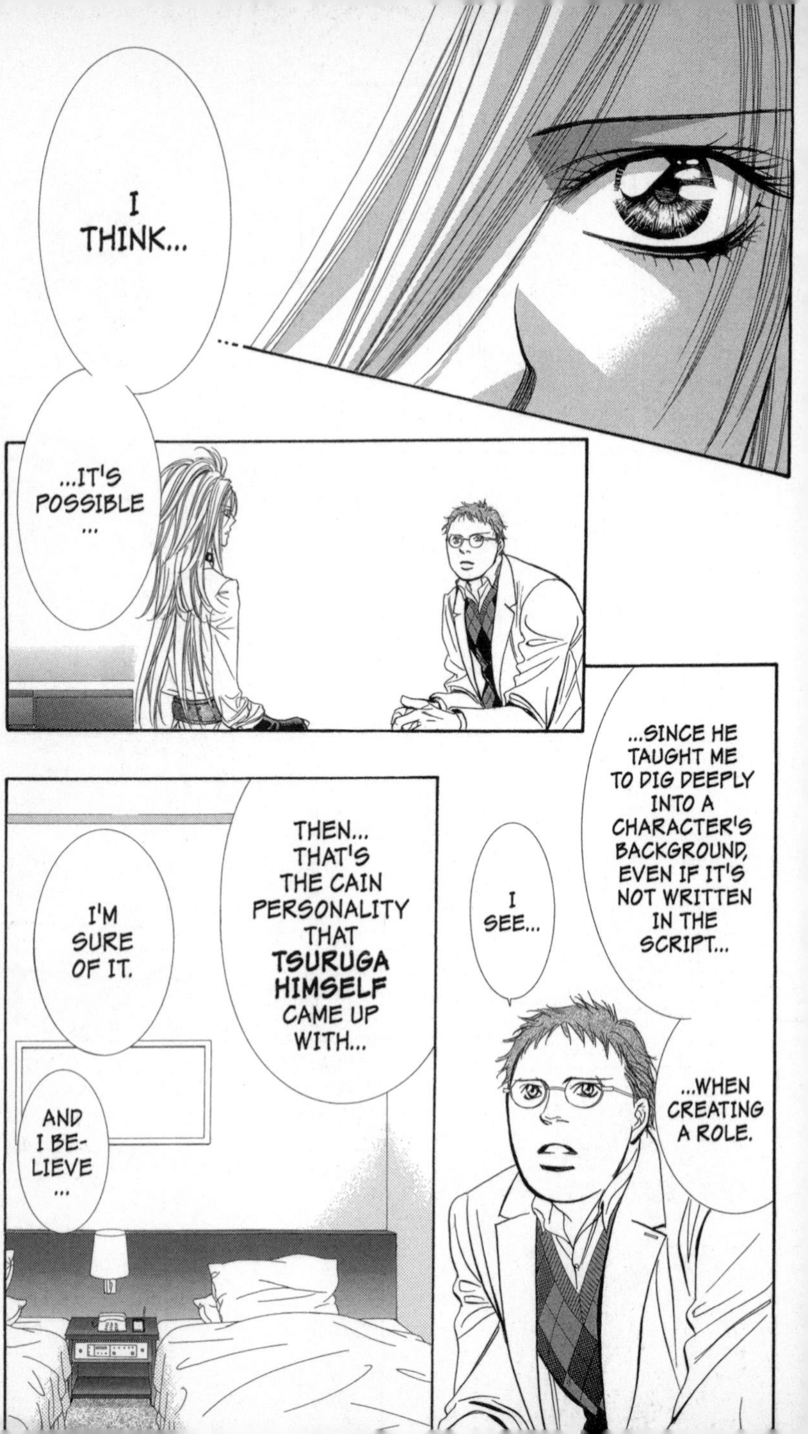
I THINK...
...IT'S POSSIBLE...
THEN... THAT'S THE CAIN PERSONALITY THAT **TSURUGA HIMSELF** CAME UP WITH...
I'M SURE OF IT.
AND I BE-LIEVE...
...SINCE HE TAUGHT ME TO DIG DEEPLY INTO A CHARACTER'S BACKGROUND, EVEN IF IT'S NOT WRITTEN IN THE SCRIPT...
...WHEN CREATING A ROLE.
I SEE...

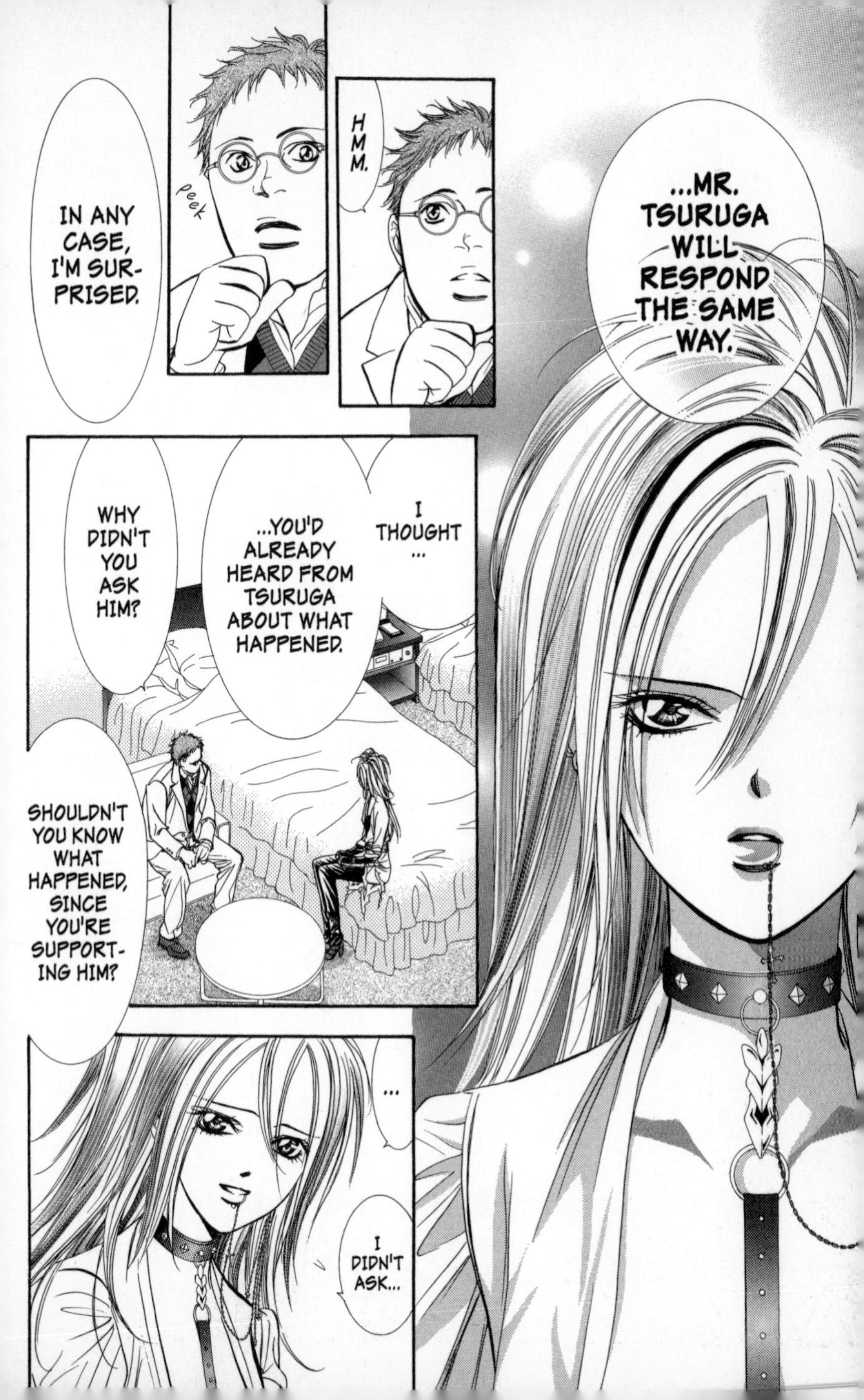
...MR. TSURUGA WILL RESPOND THE SAME WAY.
HMM.
peek
IN ANY CASE, I'M SUR-PRISED.
I THOUGHT...
...YOU'D ALREADY HEARD FROM TSURUGA ABOUT WHAT HAPPENED.
WHY DIDN'T YOU ASK HIM?
SHOULDN'T YOU KNOW WHAT HAPPENED, SINCE YOU'RE SUPPORT-ING HIM?
...
I DIDN'T ASK...

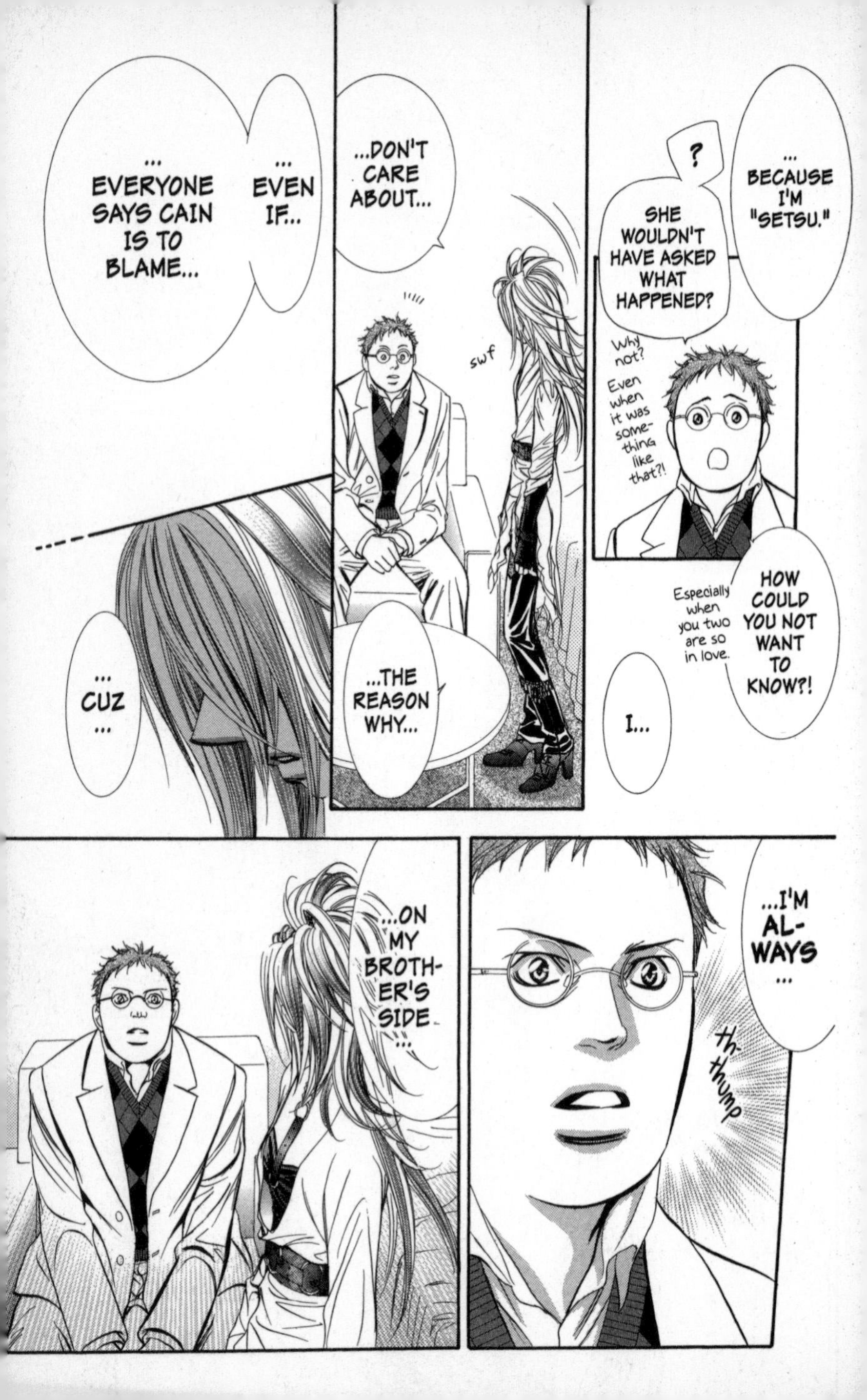
... BECAUSE I'M "SETSU."
?
SHE WOULDN'T HAVE ASKED WHAT HAPPENED?
Why not? Even when it was something like that?!
HOW COULD YOU NOT WANT TO KNOW?!
Especially when you two are so in love.
I...
...DON'T CARE ABOUT...
swf
...THE REASON WHY...
... EVEN IF...
... EVERYONE SAYS CAIN IS TO BLAME...
... CUZ ...
...I'M AL-WAYS ...
th-thump
...ON MY BROTH-ER'S SIDE...

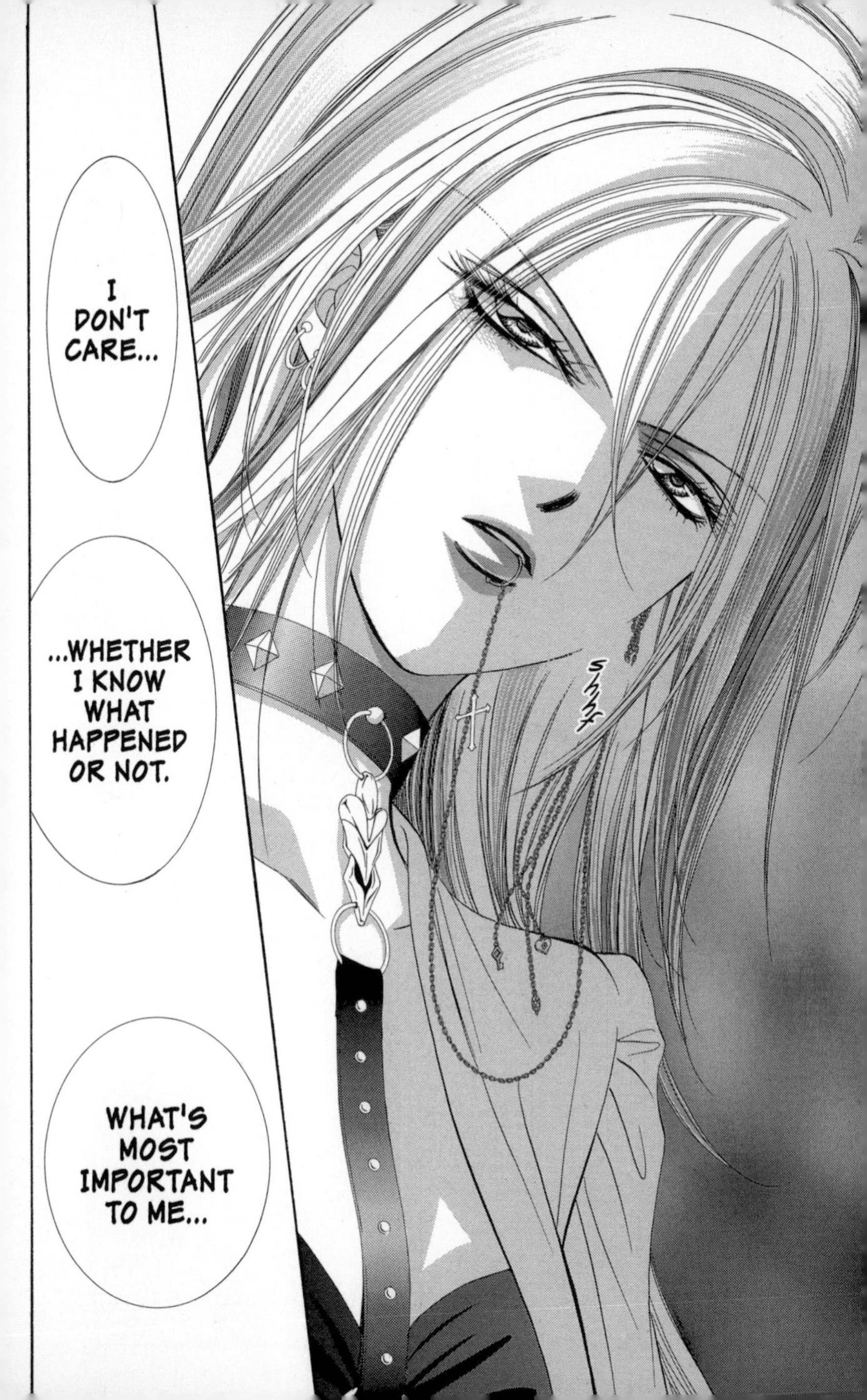

I DON'T CARE...
...WHETHER I KNOW WHAT HAPPENED OR NOT.
shhf
WHAT'S MOST IMPORTANT TO ME...

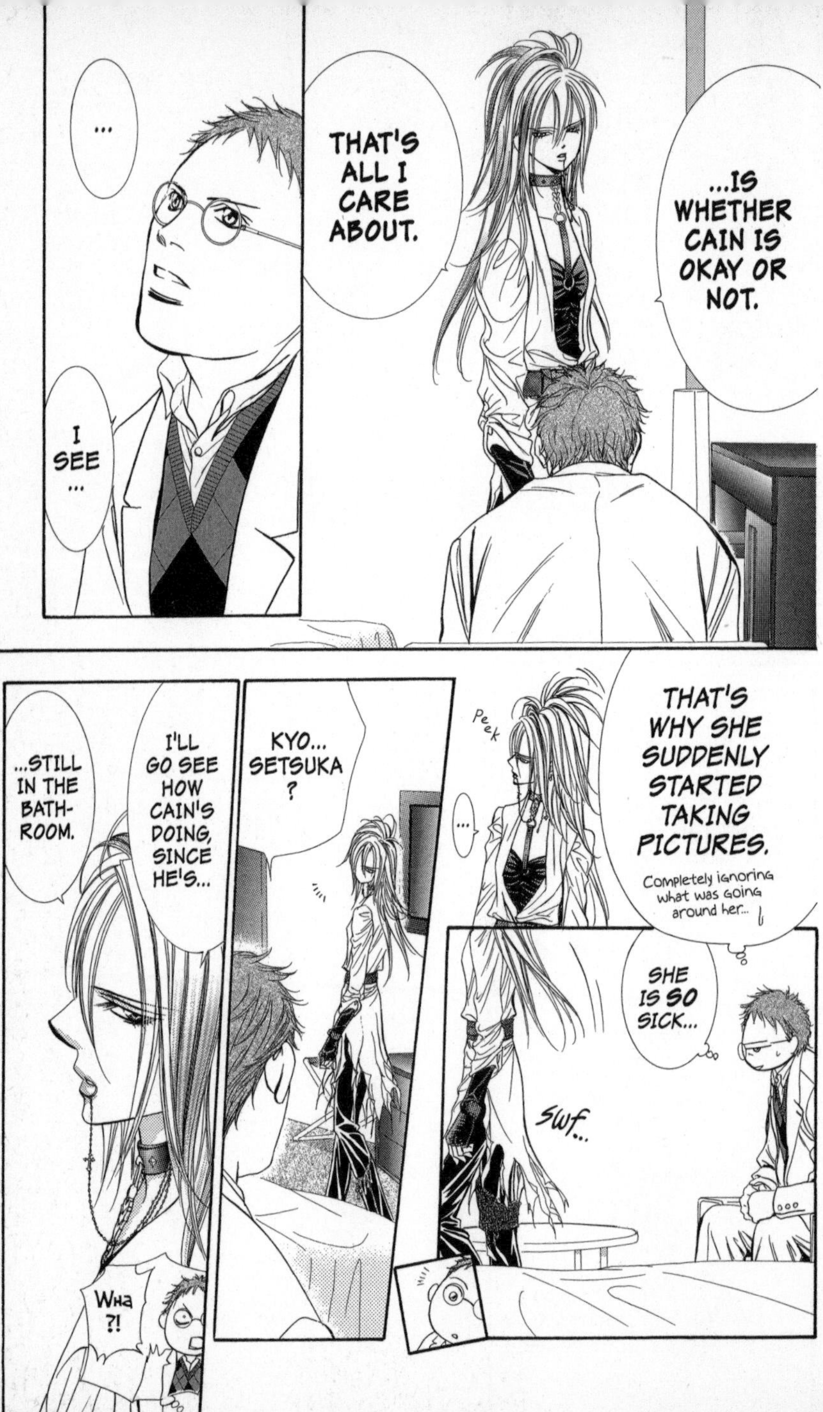
...IS WHETHER CAIN IS OKAY OR NOT.
THAT'S ALL I CARE ABOUT.
...
I SEE...
THAT'S WHY SHE SUDDENLY STARTED TAKING PICTURES.
Completely ignoring what was going around her...
Peek
...
SHE IS SO SICK...
Swf...
KYO... SETSUKA?
I'LL GO SEE HOW CAIN'S DOING, SINCE HE'S...
...STILL IN THE BATHROOM.
Wha?!

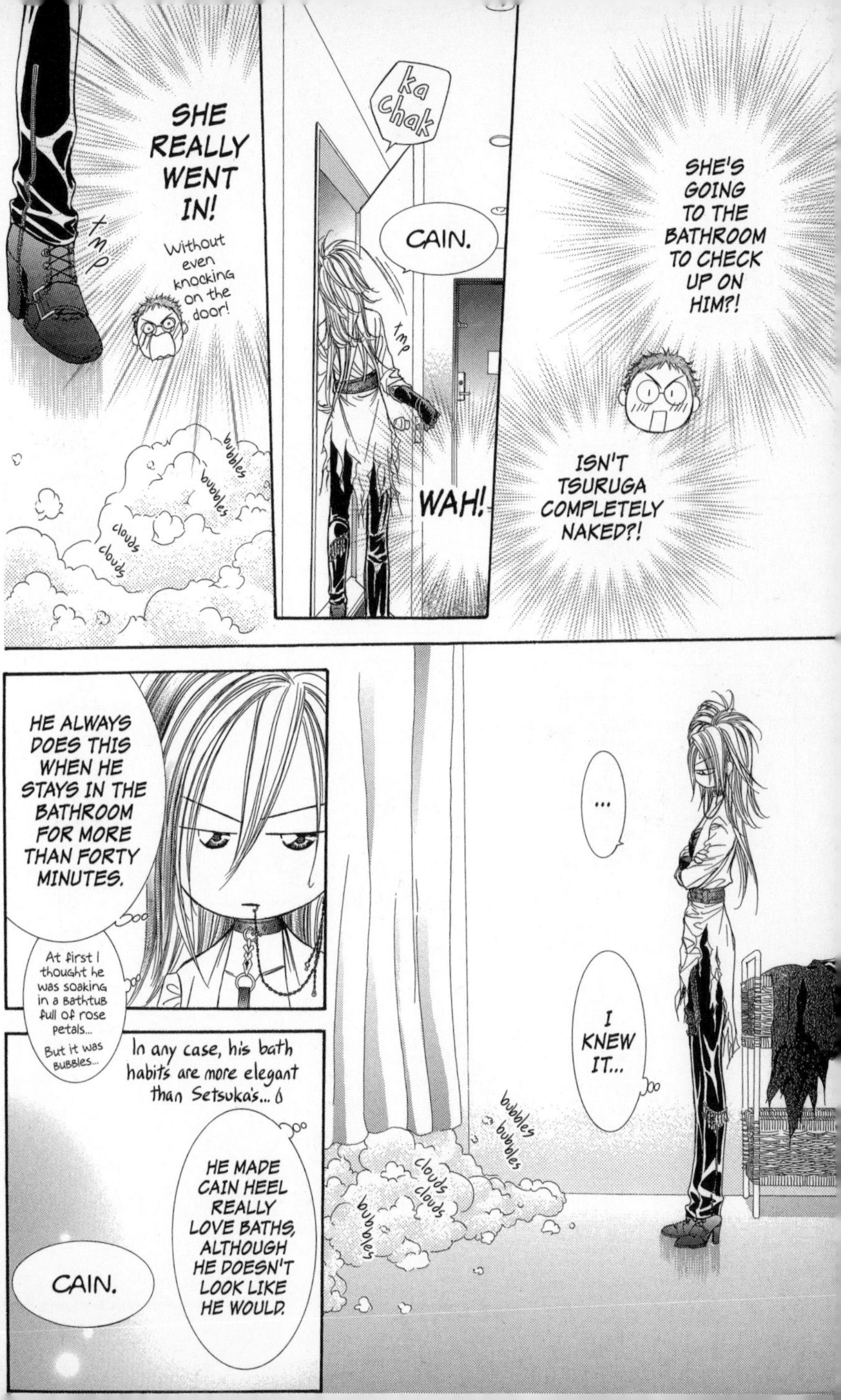
SHE'S GOING TO THE BATHROOM TO CHECK UP ON HIM?!
ISN'T TSURUGA COMPLETELY NAKED?!
ka chak
CAIN.
tmp
WAH!
SHE REALLY WENT IN!
Without even knocking on the door!
tmp
bubbles
bubbles
clouds
clouds
...
I KNEW IT...
bubbles
bubbles
clouds
clouds
bubbles
HE ALWAYS DOES THIS WHEN HE STAYS IN THE BATHROOM FOR MORE THAN FORTY MINUTES.
At first I thought he was soaking in a bathtub full of rose petals... But it was bubbles...
In any case, his bath habits are more elegant than Setsuka's...
HE MADE CAIN HEEL REALLY LOVE BATHS, ALTHOUGH HE DOESN'T LOOK LIKE HE WOULD.
CAIN.

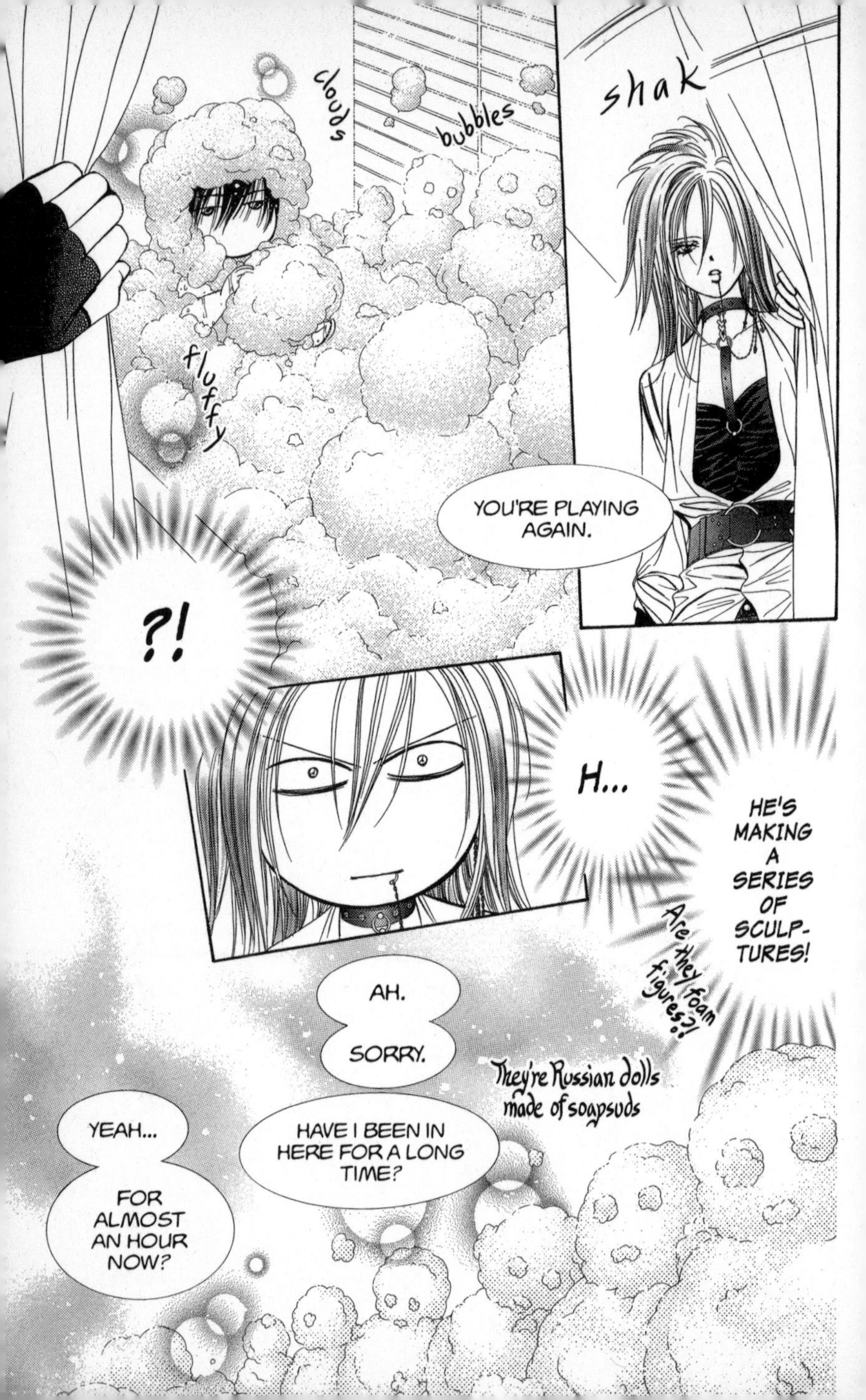

shak
YOU'RE PLAYING AGAIN.
bubbles
clouds
fluffy
?!
H...
HE'S MAKING A SERIES OF SCULP-TURES!
Are they foam figures?!
They're Russian dolls made of soapsuds
AH. SORRY.
HAVE I BEEN IN HERE FOR A LONG TIME?
YEAH... FOR ALMOST AN HOUR NOW?

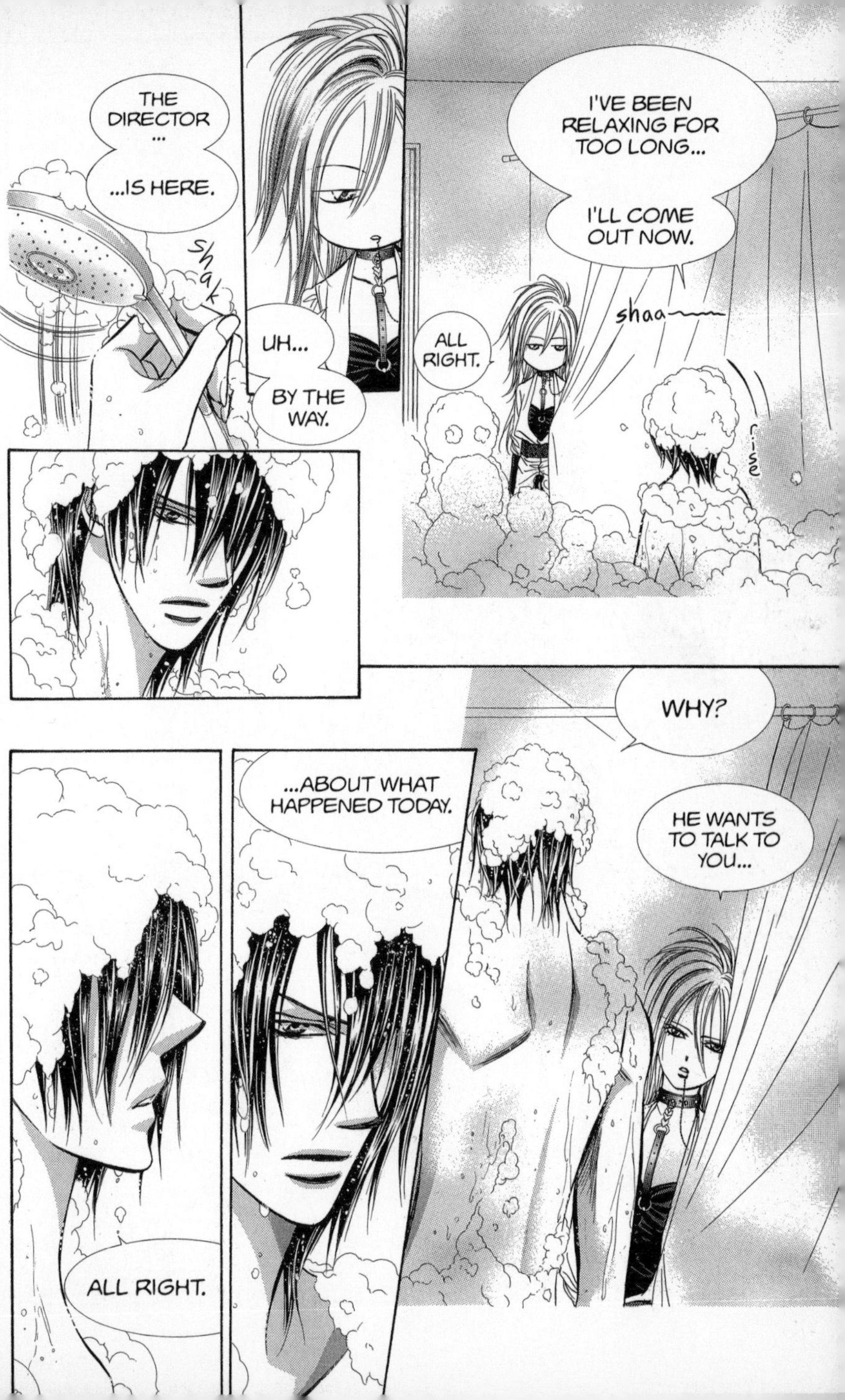
I'VE BEEN RELAXING FOR TOO LONG...
I'LL COME OUT NOW.
shaa
ALL RIGHT.
rise
UH...
BY THE WAY.
THE DIRECTOR ...
...IS HERE.
shak
WHY?
HE WANTS TO TALK TO YOU...
...ABOUT WHAT HAPPENED TODAY.
ALL RIGHT.

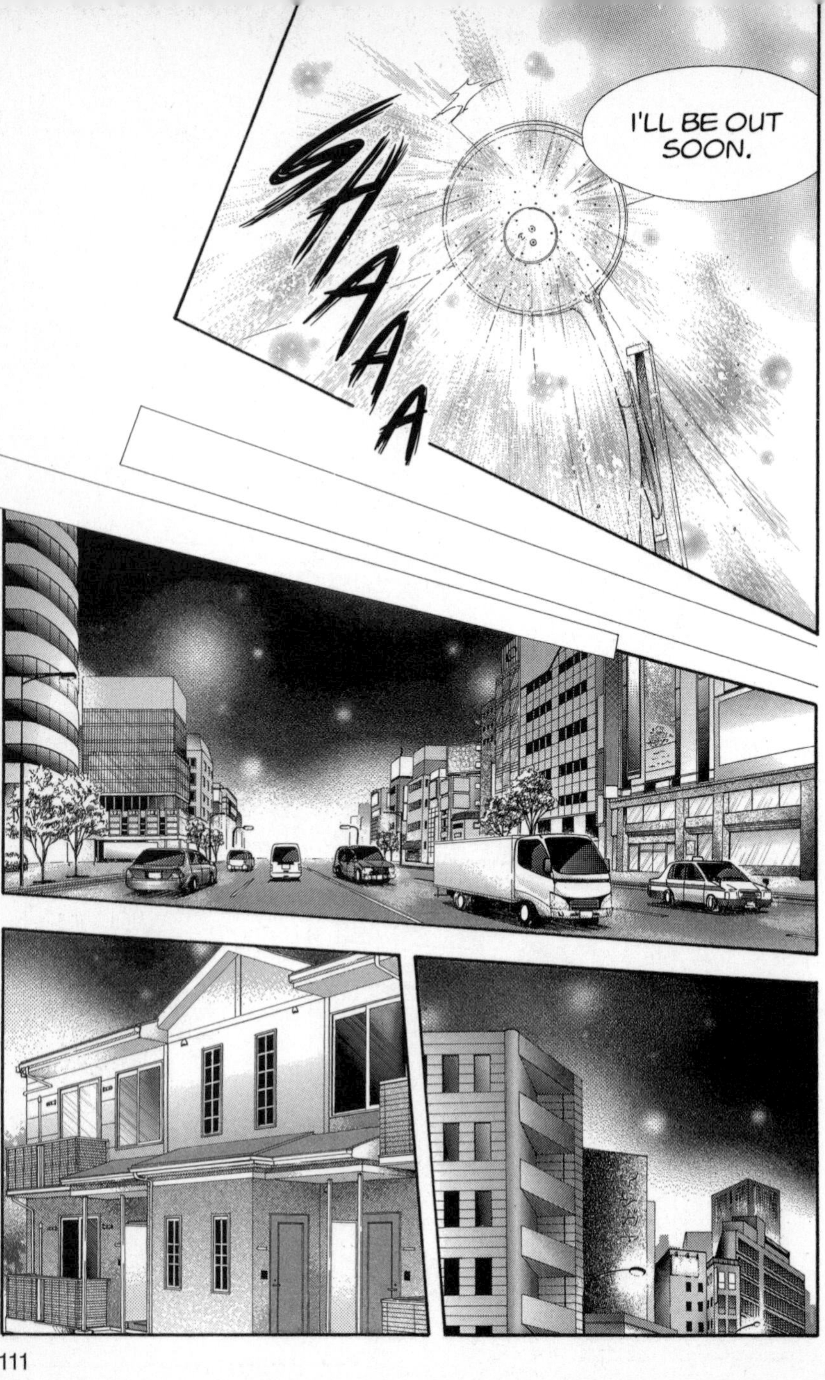
I'LL BE OUT SOON.
SHAAAA

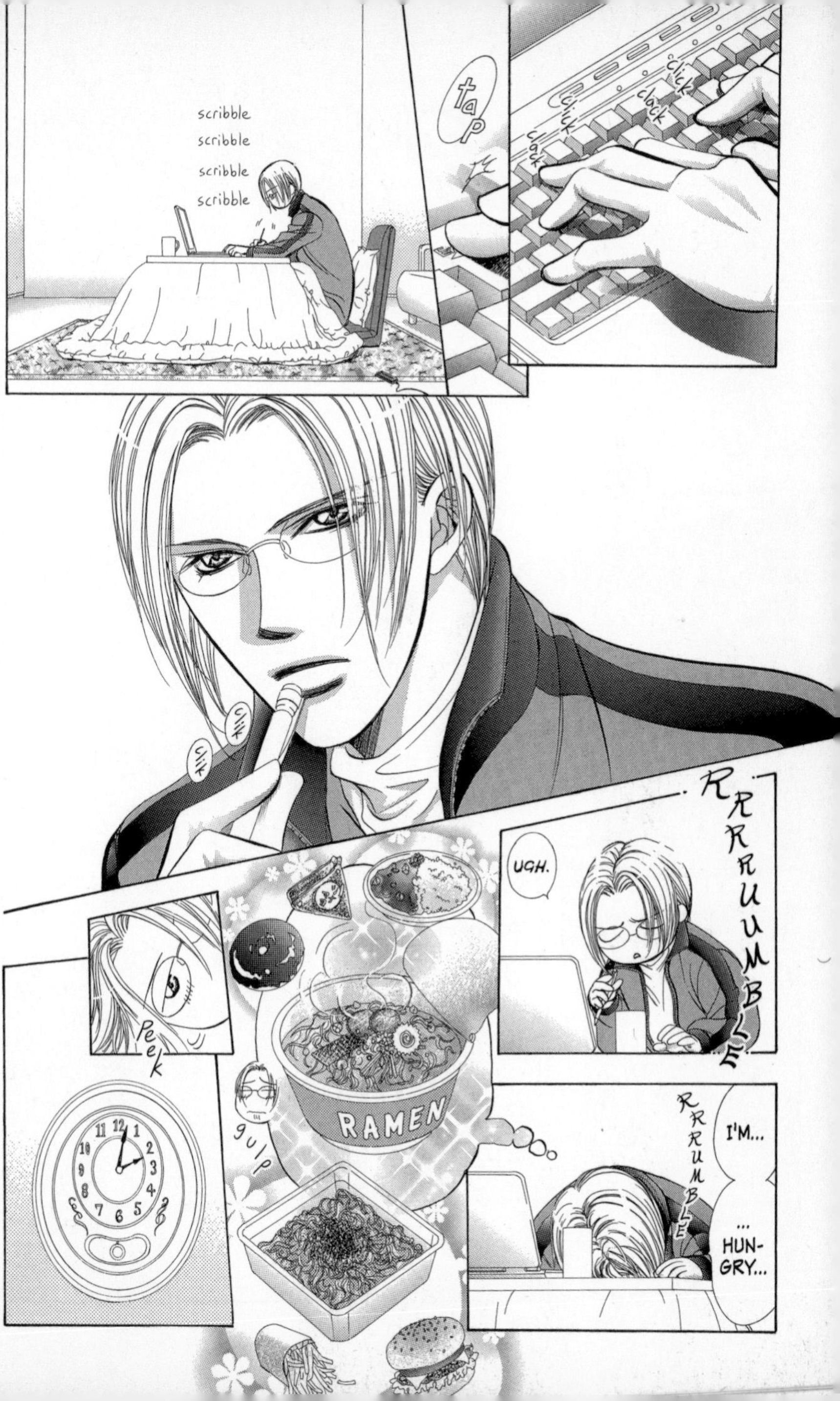
click
clack
click
clack
tap
scribble
scribble
scribble
scribble
clik
clik
RRRRUMBLE...
UGH.
Peek
RAMEN
gulp
RRRUMBLE
I'M...
...HUNGRY...

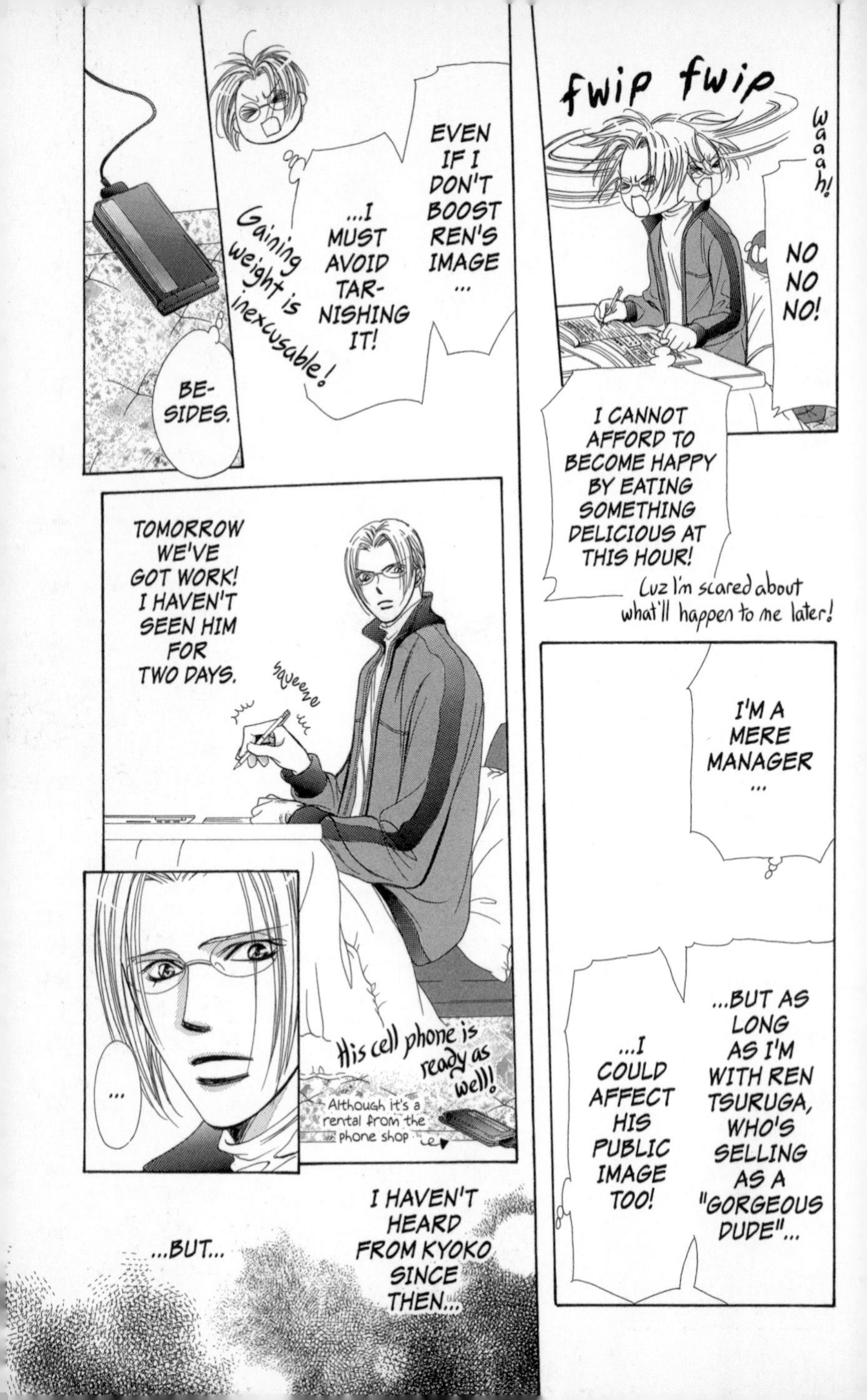
fwip fwip
Waaaah!
NO NO NO!
I CANNOT AFFORD TO BECOME HAPPY BY EATING SOMETHING DELICIOUS AT THIS HOUR!
Cuz I'm scared about what'll happen to me later!
I'M A MERE MANAGER...
...BUT AS LONG AS I'M WITH REN TSURUGA, WHO'S SELLING AS A "GORGEOUS DUDE"...
...I COULD AFFECT HIS PUBLIC IMAGE TOO!
EVEN IF I DON'T BOOST REN'S IMAGE...
...I MUST AVOID TARNISHING IT!
Gaining weight is inexcusable!
BESIDES.
TOMORROW WE'VE GOT WORK! I HAVEN'T SEEN HIM FOR TWO DAYS.
squeeze
His cell phone is ready as well!
Although it's a rental from the phone shop
...
I HAVEN'T HEARD FROM KYOKO SINCE THEN...
...BUT...

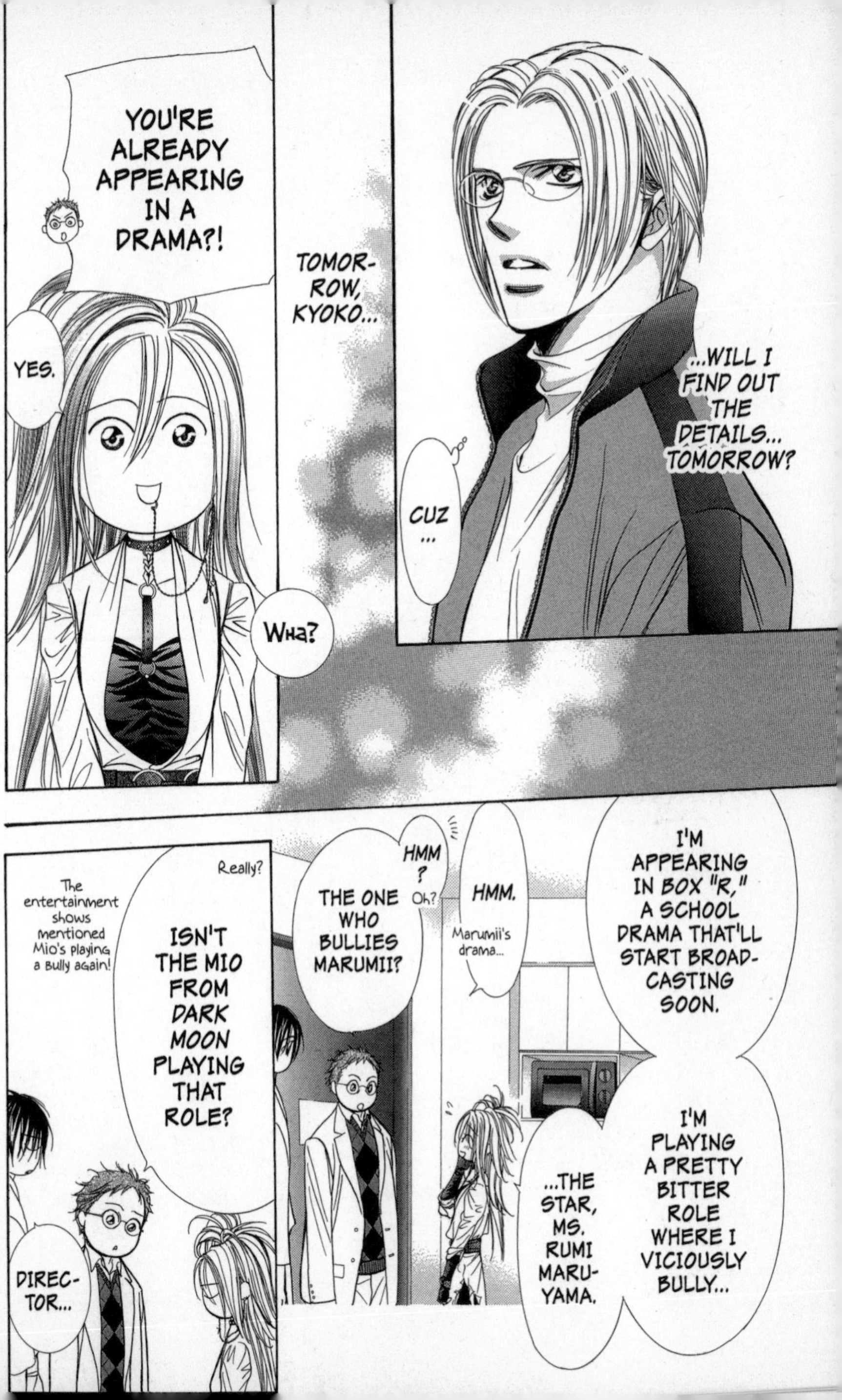
...WILL I FIND OUT THE DETAILS... TOMORROW?
CUZ ...
TOMORROW, KYOKO...
YOU'RE ALREADY APPEARING IN A DRAMA?!
YES.
Wha?
I'M APPEARING IN BOX "R," A SCHOOL DRAMA THAT'LL START BROADCASTING SOON.
I'M PLAYING A PRETTY BITTER ROLE WHERE I VICIOUSLY BULLY...
...THE STAR, MS. RUMI MARUYAMA.
HMM.
Marumii's drama...
HMM?
Oh?
THE ONE WHO BULLIES MARUMII?
Really?
ISN'T THE MIO FROM DARK MOON PLAYING THAT ROLE?
The entertainment shows mentioned Mio's playing a bully again!
DIRECTOR...

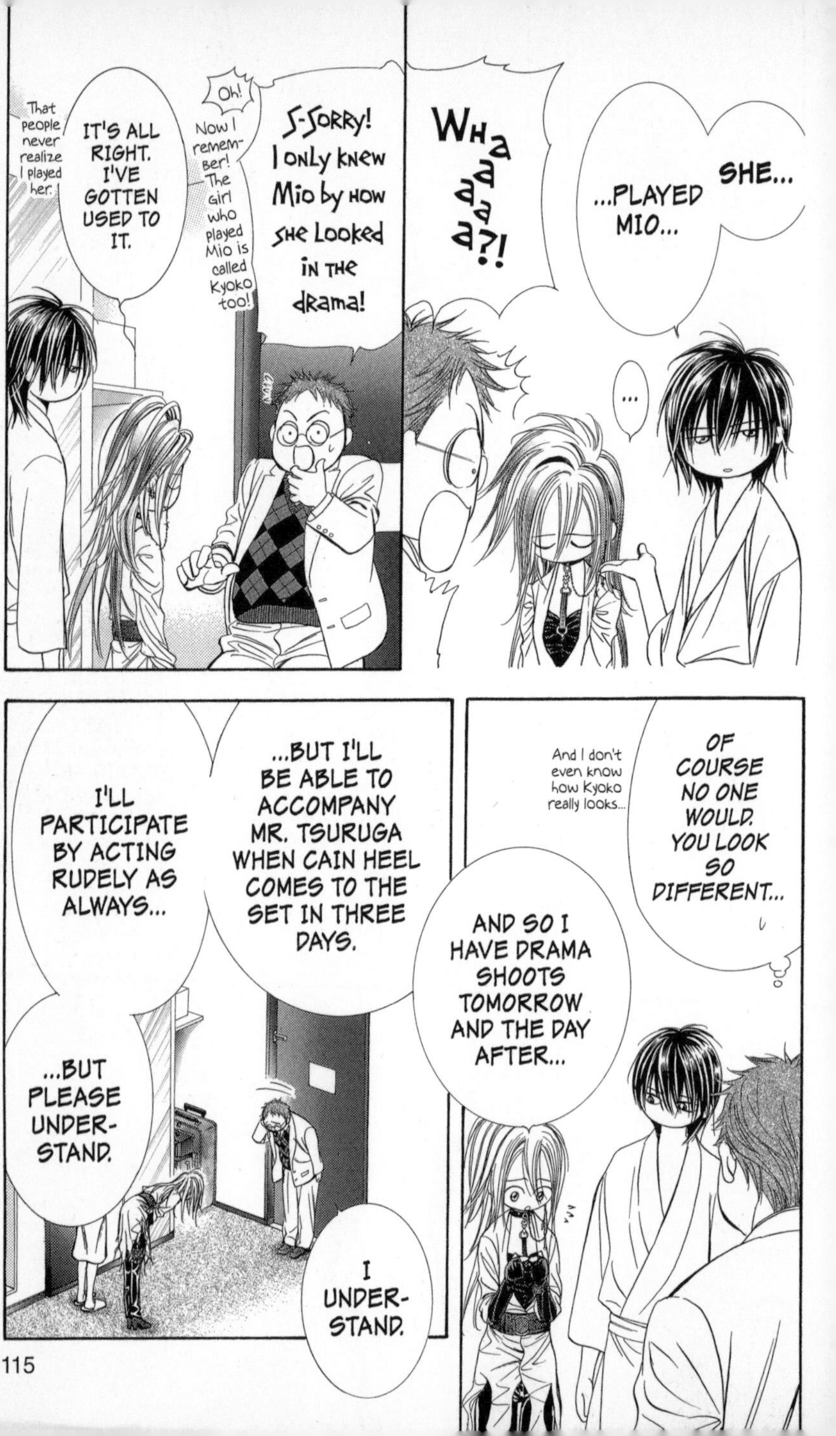
SHE...
...PLAYED MIO...
WHAaaaa?!
...
Oh!
S-SORRY! I ONLY KNEW MIO BY HOW SHE LOOKED IN THE DRAMA!
Now I remember! The girl who played Mio is called Kyoko too!
IT'S ALL RIGHT. I'VE GOTTEN USED TO IT.
That people never realize I played her.
OF COURSE NO ONE WOULD. YOU LOOK SO DIFFERENT...
And I don't even know how Kyoko really looks...
AND SO I HAVE DRAMA SHOOTS TOMORROW AND THE DAY AFTER...
...BUT I'LL BE ABLE TO ACCOMPANY MR. TSURUGA WHEN CAIN HEEL COMES TO THE SET IN THREE DAYS.
I'LL PARTICIPATE BY ACTING RUDELY AS ALWAYS...
...BUT PLEASE UNDERSTAND.
I UNDERSTAND.

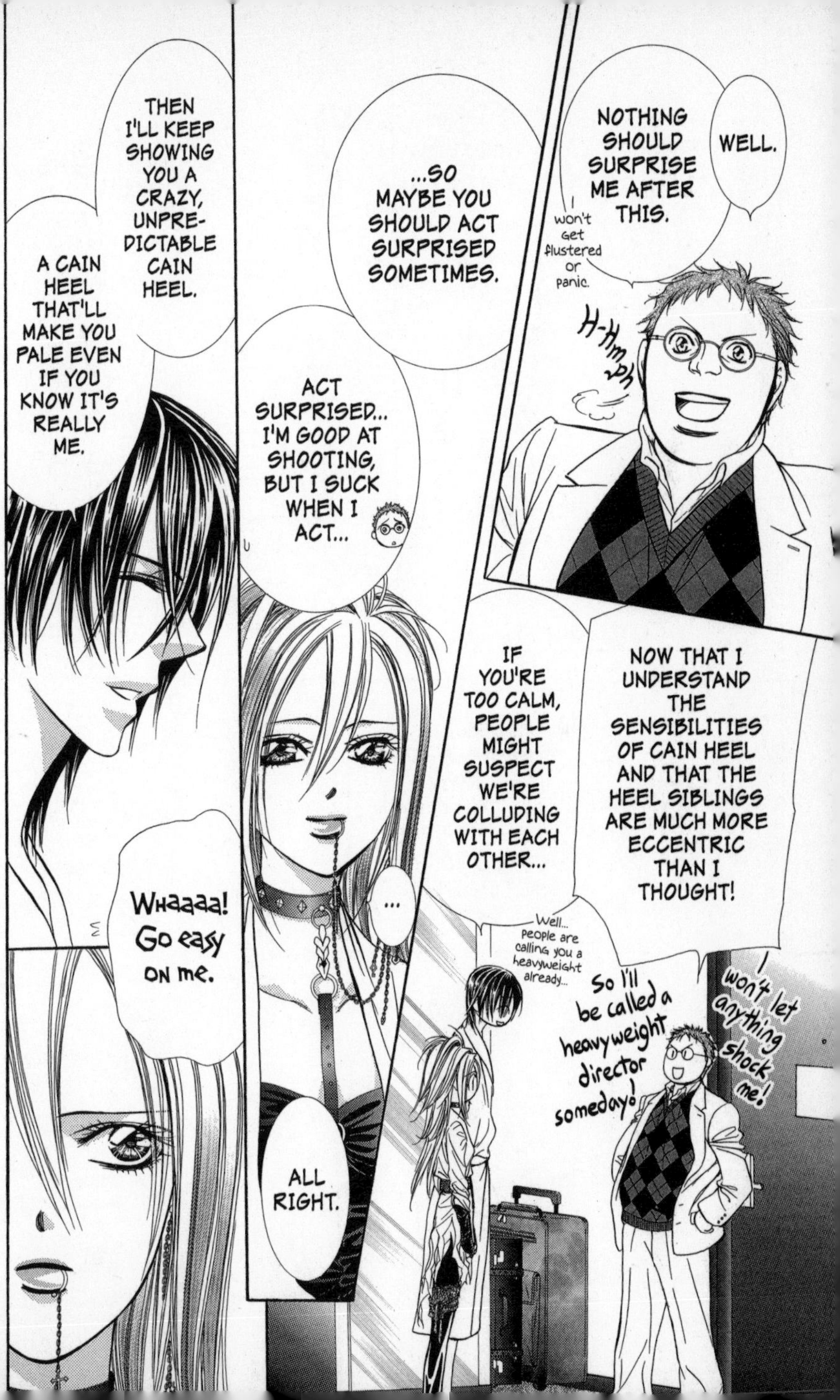
WELL.
NOTHING SHOULD SURPRISE ME AFTER THIS.
I won't get flustered or panic.
H-Hmph
NOW THAT I UNDERSTAND THE SENSIBILITIES OF CAIN HEEL AND THAT THE HEEL SIBLINGS ARE MUCH MORE ECCENTRIC THAN I THOUGHT!
IF YOU'RE TOO CALM, PEOPLE MIGHT SUSPECT WE'RE COLLUDING WITH EACH OTHER...
I won't let anything shock me!
So I'll be called a heavyweight director someday!
Well... People are calling you a heavyweight already...
...SO MAYBE YOU SHOULD ACT SURPRISED SOMETIMES.
ACT SURPRISED... I'M GOOD AT SHOOTING, BUT I SUCK WHEN I ACT...
...
ALL RIGHT.
THEN I'LL KEEP SHOWING YOU A CRAZY, UNPRE-DICTABLE CAIN HEEL.
A CAIN HEEL THAT'LL MAKE YOU PALE EVEN IF YOU KNOW IT'S REALLY ME.
Whaaaa! Go easy on me.

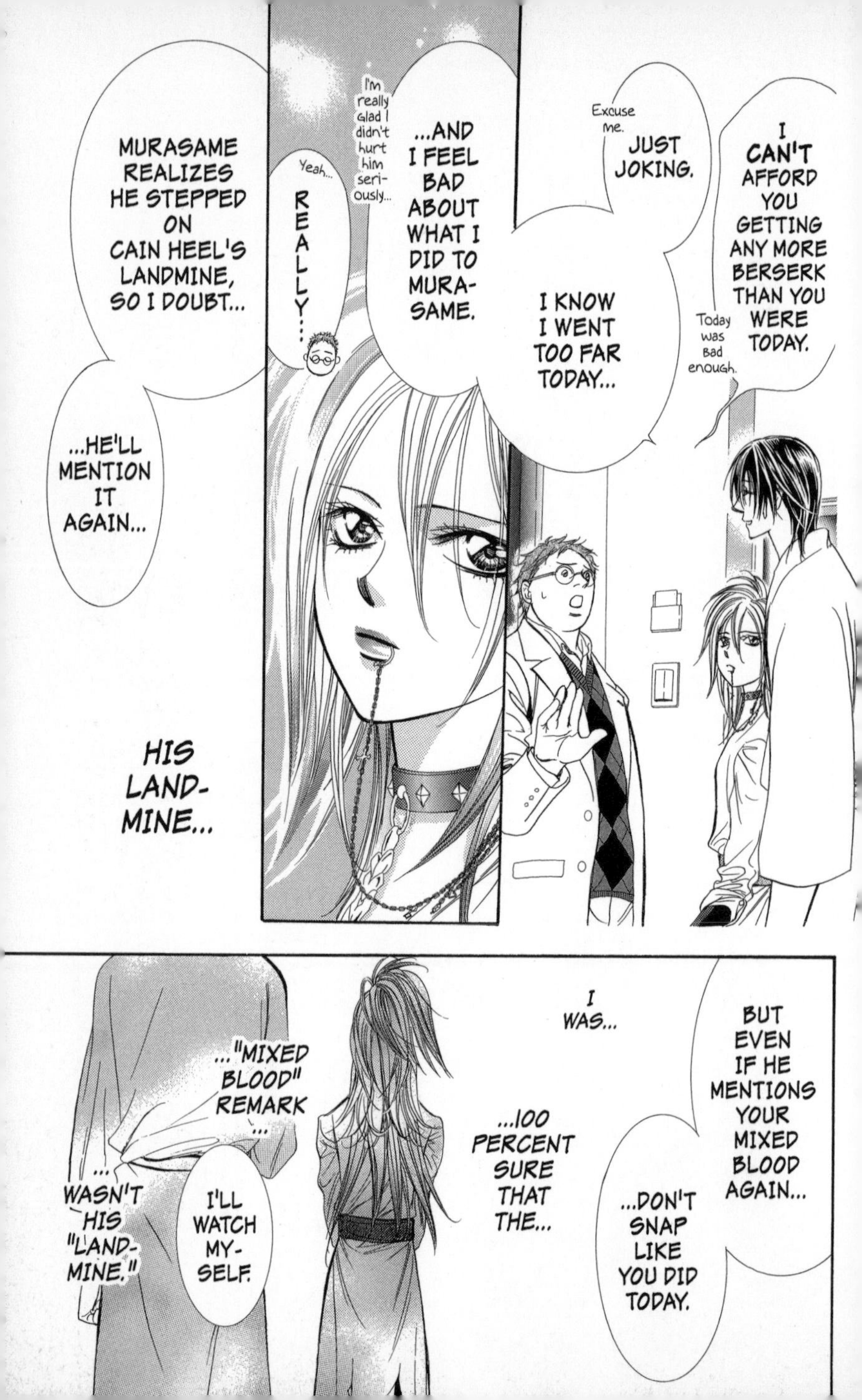
I CAN'T AFFORD YOU GETTING ANY MORE BERSERK THAN YOU WERE TODAY.
Today was Bad enough.
JUST JOKING.
Excuse me.
I KNOW I WENT TOO FAR TODAY...
...AND I FEEL BAD ABOUT WHAT I DID TO MURA-SAME.
I'm really Glad I didn't hurt him seri-ously...
REALLY...
Yeah...
MURASAME REALIZES HE STEPPED ON CAIN HEEL'S LANDMINE, SO I DOUBT...
...HE'LL MENTION IT AGAIN...
HIS LAND-MINE...
BUT EVEN IF HE MENTIONS YOUR MIXED BLOOD AGAIN...
...DON'T SNAP LIKE YOU DID TODAY.
I WAS...
...100 PERCENT SURE THAT THE...
..."MIXED BLOOD" REMARK...
I'LL WATCH MY-SELF.
...WASN'T HIS "LAND-MINE."

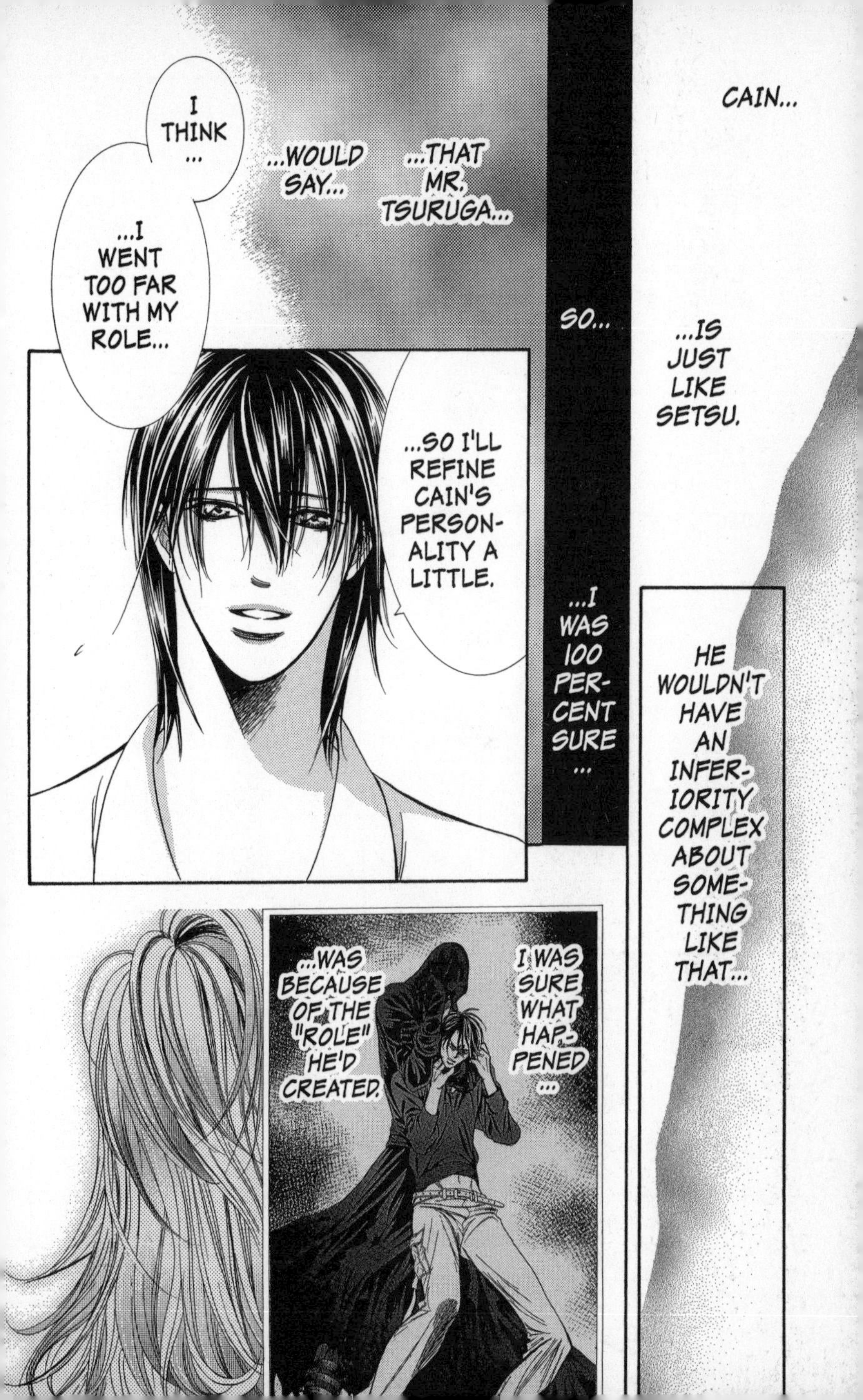
CAIN...
...IS JUST LIKE SETSU.
HE WOULDN'T HAVE AN INFERIORITY COMPLEX ABOUT SOMETHING LIKE THAT...
SO...
...I WAS 100 PERCENT SURE...
...THAT MR. TSURUGA...
...WOULD SAY...
I THINK...
...I WENT TOO FAR WITH MY ROLE...
...SO I'LL REFINE CAIN'S PERSONALITY A LITTLE.
I WAS SURE WHAT HAPPENED...
...WAS BECAUSE OF THE "ROLE" HE'D CREATED.

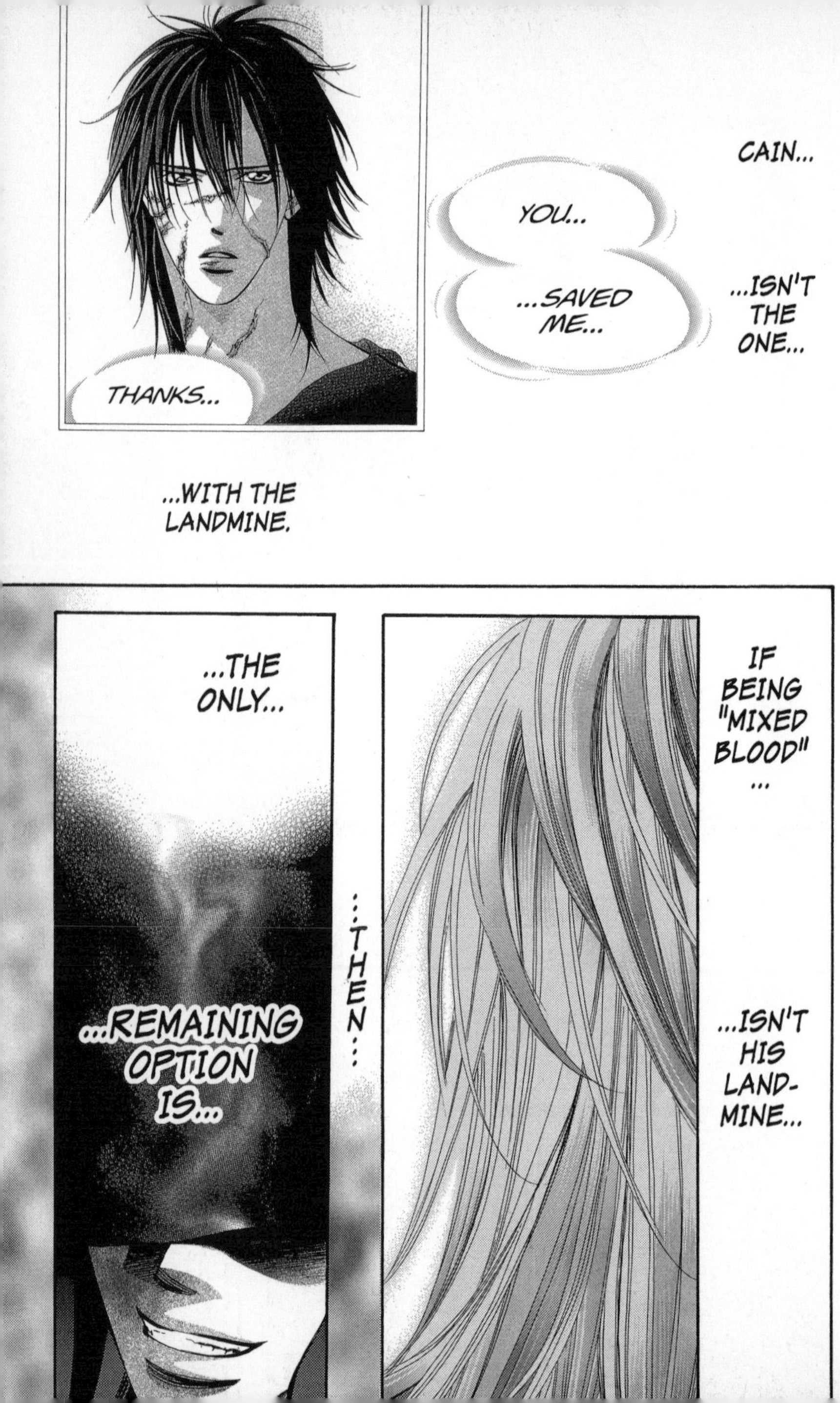
CAIN...
...ISN'T THE ONE...
YOU...
...SAVED ME...
THANKS...
...WITH THE LANDMINE.
IF BEING "MIXED BLOOD"...
...ISN'T HIS LANDMINE...
...THEN...
...THE ONLY...
...REMAINING OPTION IS...

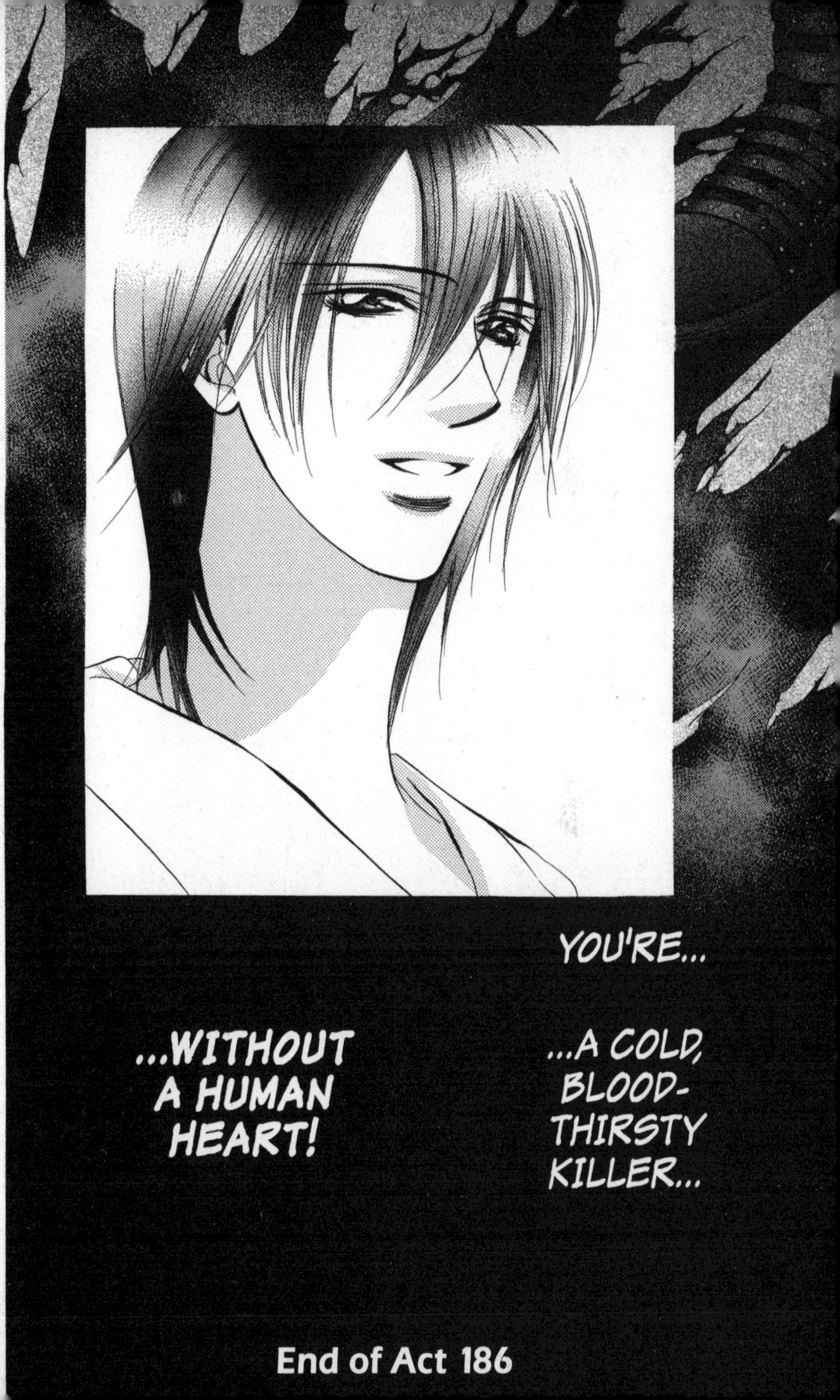
YOU'RE...
...A COLD, BLOOD-THIRSTY KILLER...
...WITHOUT A HUMAN HEART!
End of Act 186

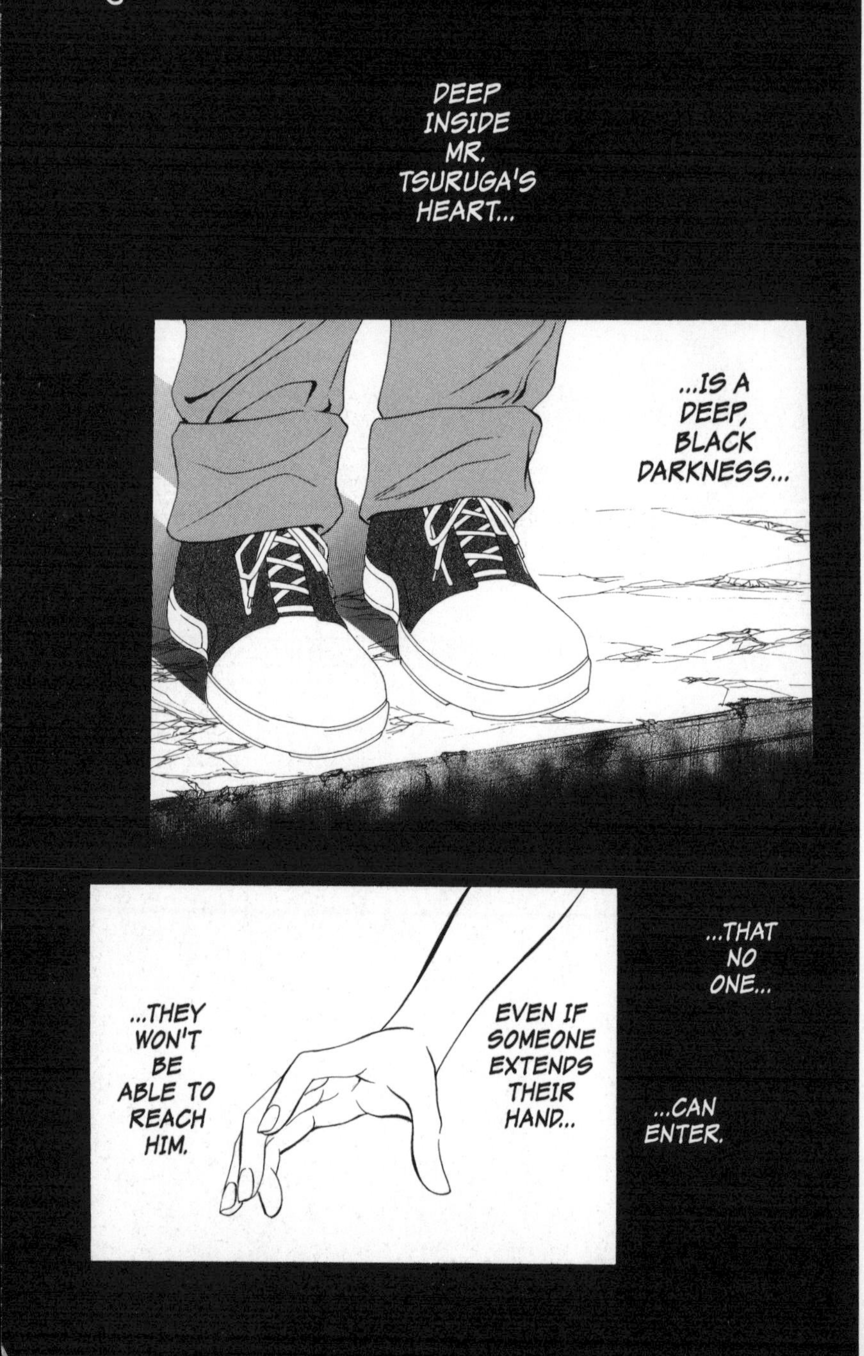
DEEP INSIDE MR. TSURUGA'S HEART...
...IS A DEEP, BLACK DARKNESS...
...THAT NO ONE...
...CAN ENTER.
EVEN IF SOMEONE EXTENDS THEIR HAND...
...THEY WON'T BE ABLE TO REACH HIM.

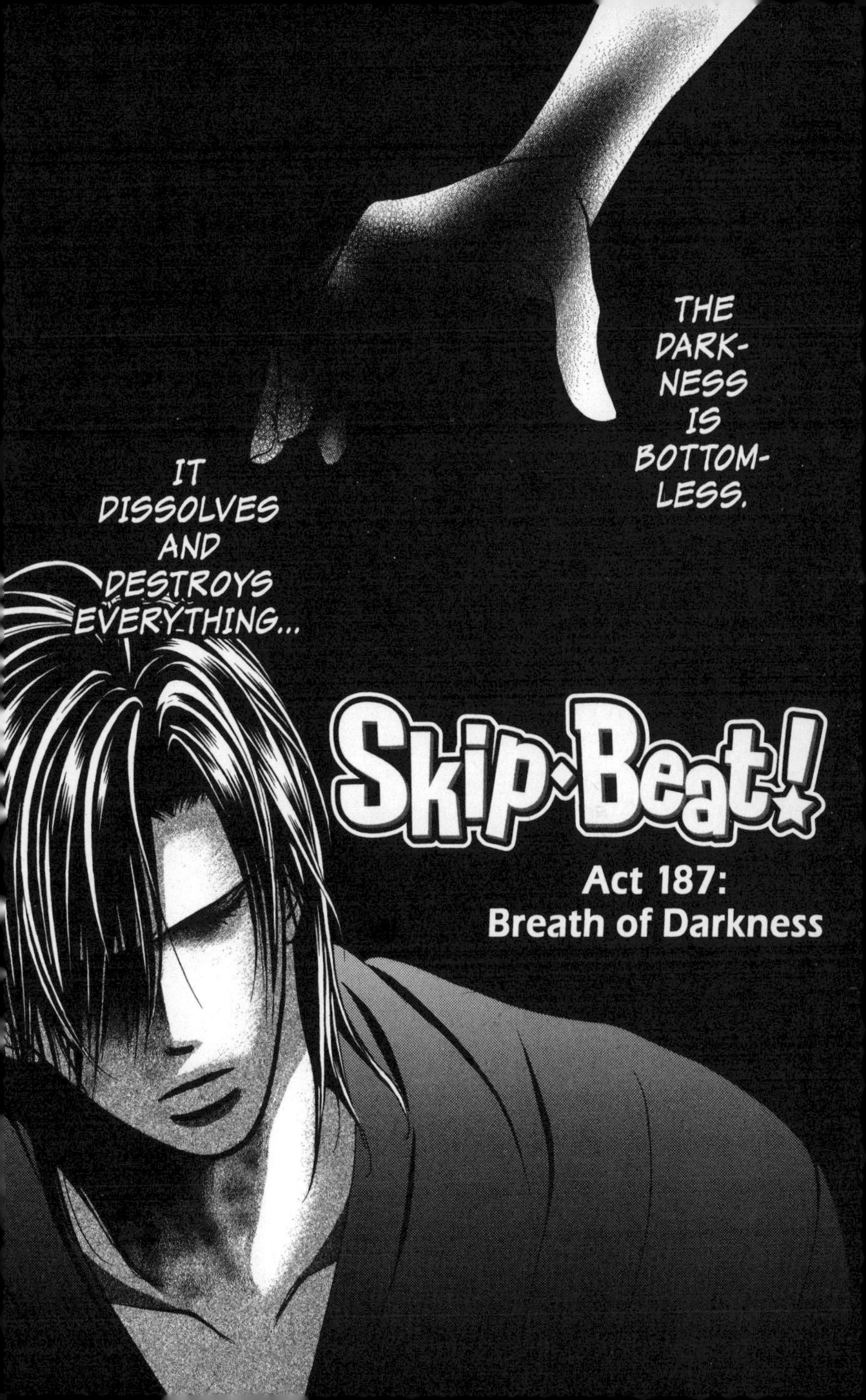
THE DARKNESS IS BOTTOMLESS.
IT DISSOLVES AND DESTROYS EVERYTHING...
Skip·Beat!
Act 187: Breath of Darkness

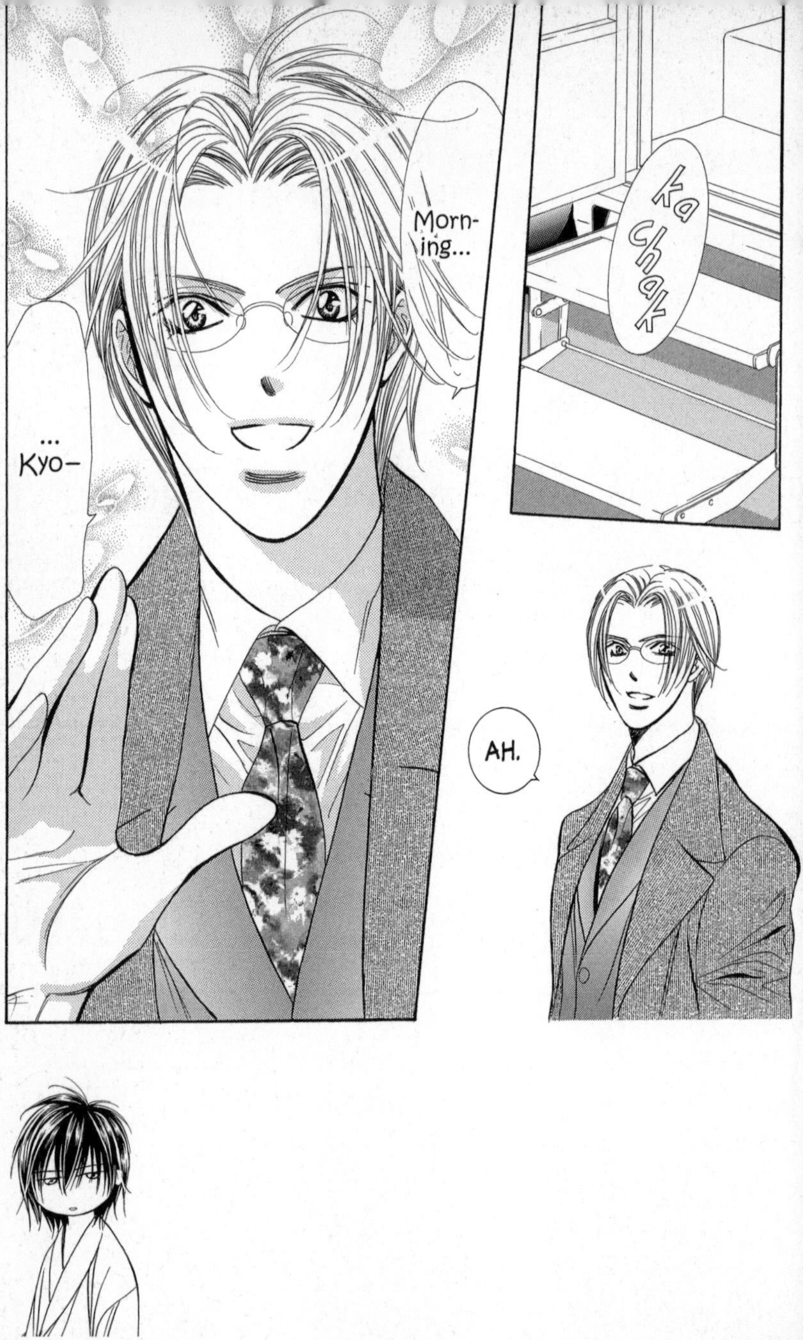
ka chak
AH.
Morning...
... Kyo-

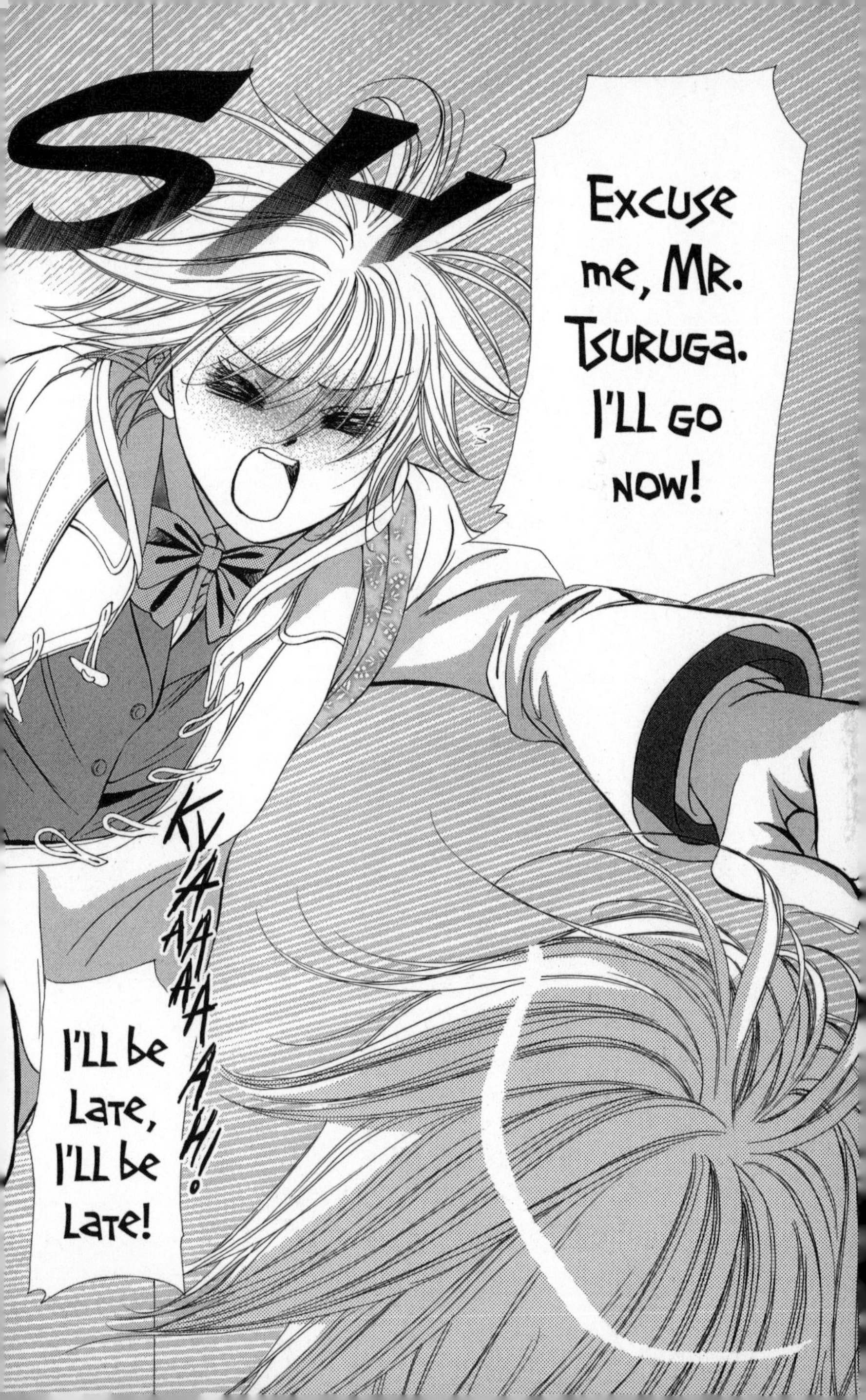
SHH
Excuse me, Mr. Tsuruga. I'll go now!
KYAAAAAAAAH!
I'll be late, I'll be late!

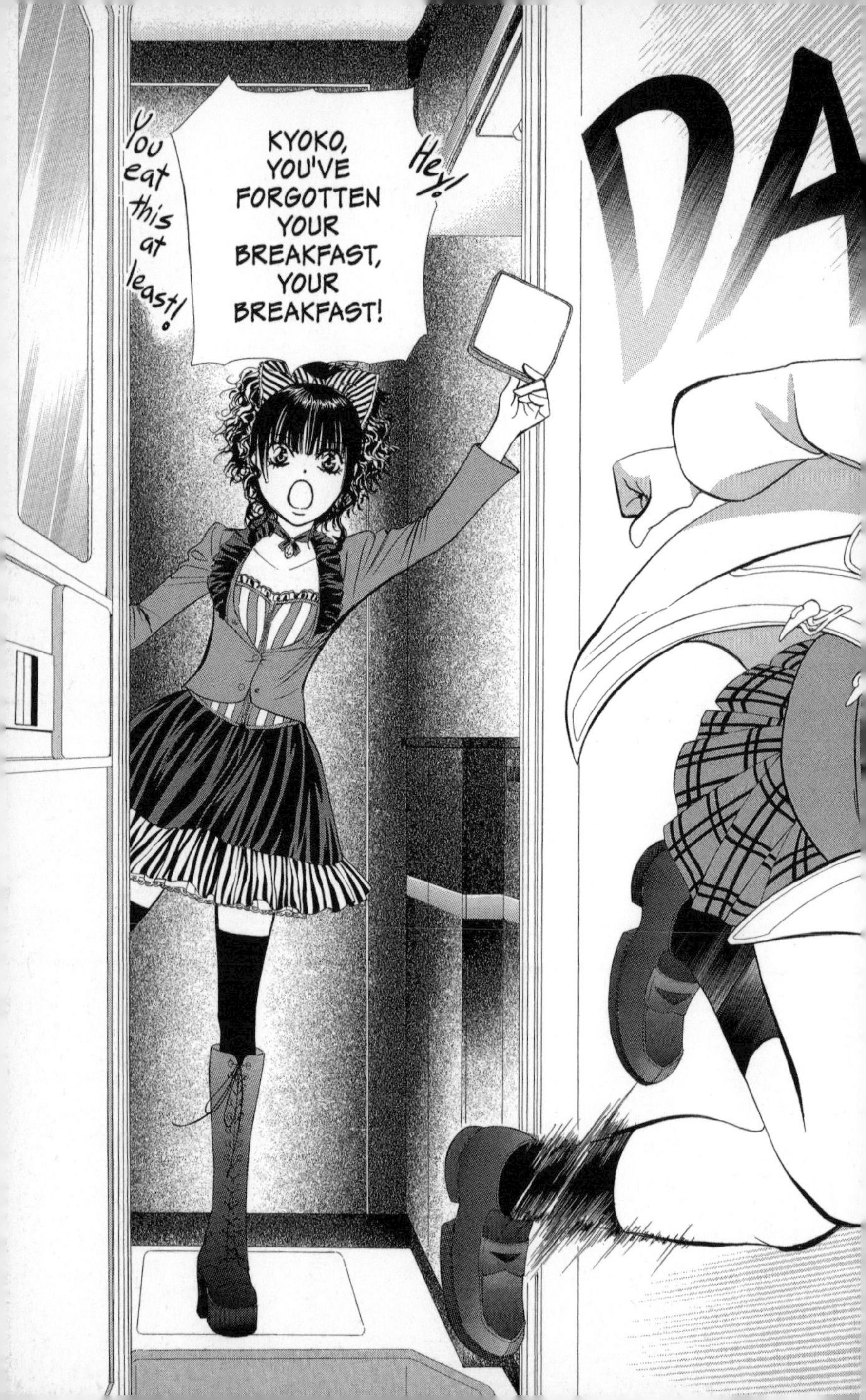
DA
Hey!
KYOKO, YOU'VE FORGOTTEN YOUR BREAKFAST, YOUR BREAKFAST!
You eat this at least!

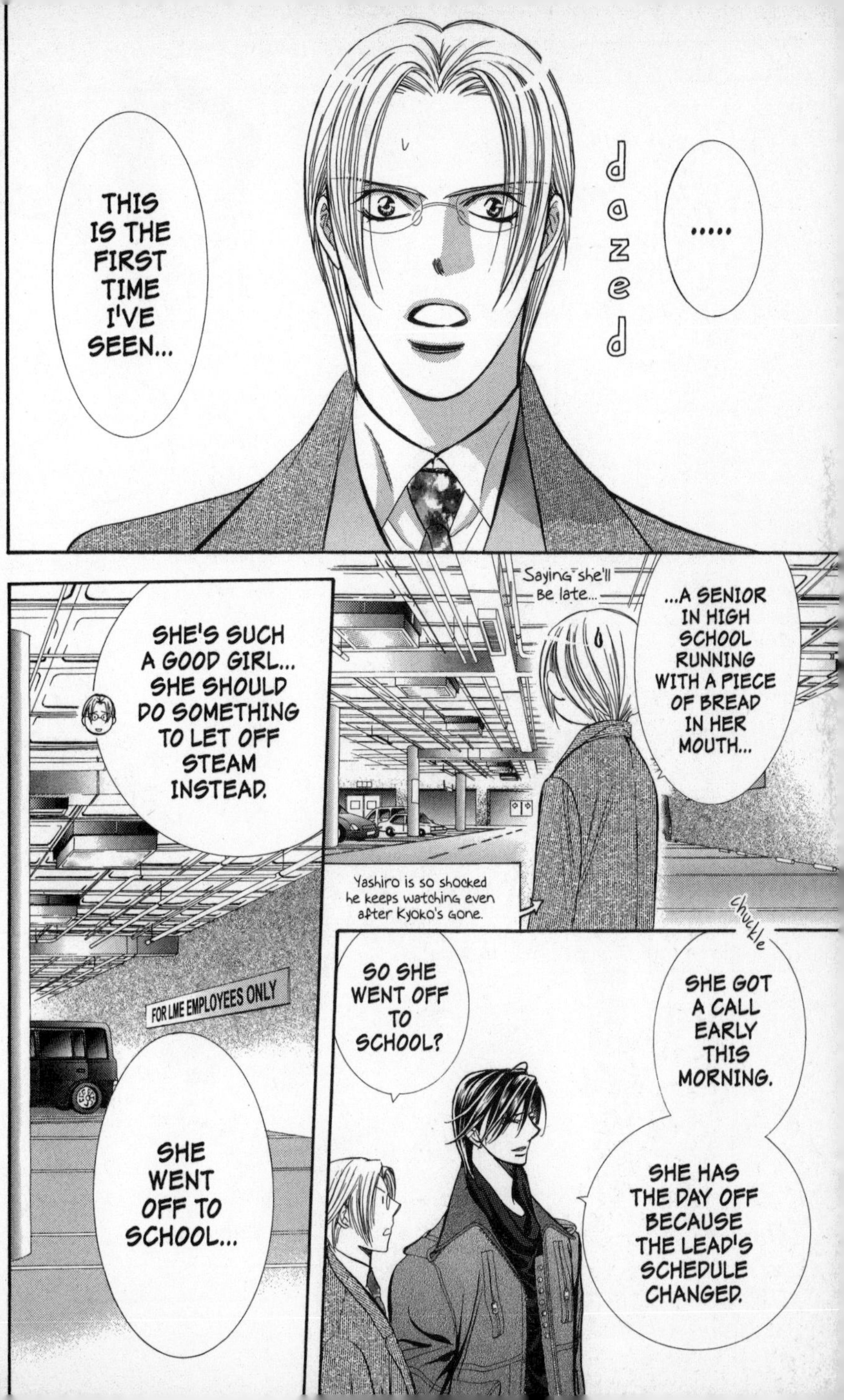

......
dazed
THIS IS THE FIRST TIME I'VE SEEN...
Saying she'll be late...
...A SENIOR IN HIGH SCHOOL RUNNING WITH A PIECE OF BREAD IN HER MOUTH...
Yashiro is so shocked he keeps watching even after Kyoko's gone.
chuckle
SHE GOT A CALL EARLY THIS MORNING.
SO SHE WENT OFF TO SCHOOL?
SHE HAS THE DAY OFF BECAUSE THE LEAD'S SCHEDULE CHANGED.
SHE'S SUCH A GOOD GIRL... SHE SHOULD DO SOMETHING TO LET OFF STEAM INSTEAD.
FOR LME EMPLOYEES ONLY
SHE WENT OFF TO SCHOOL...

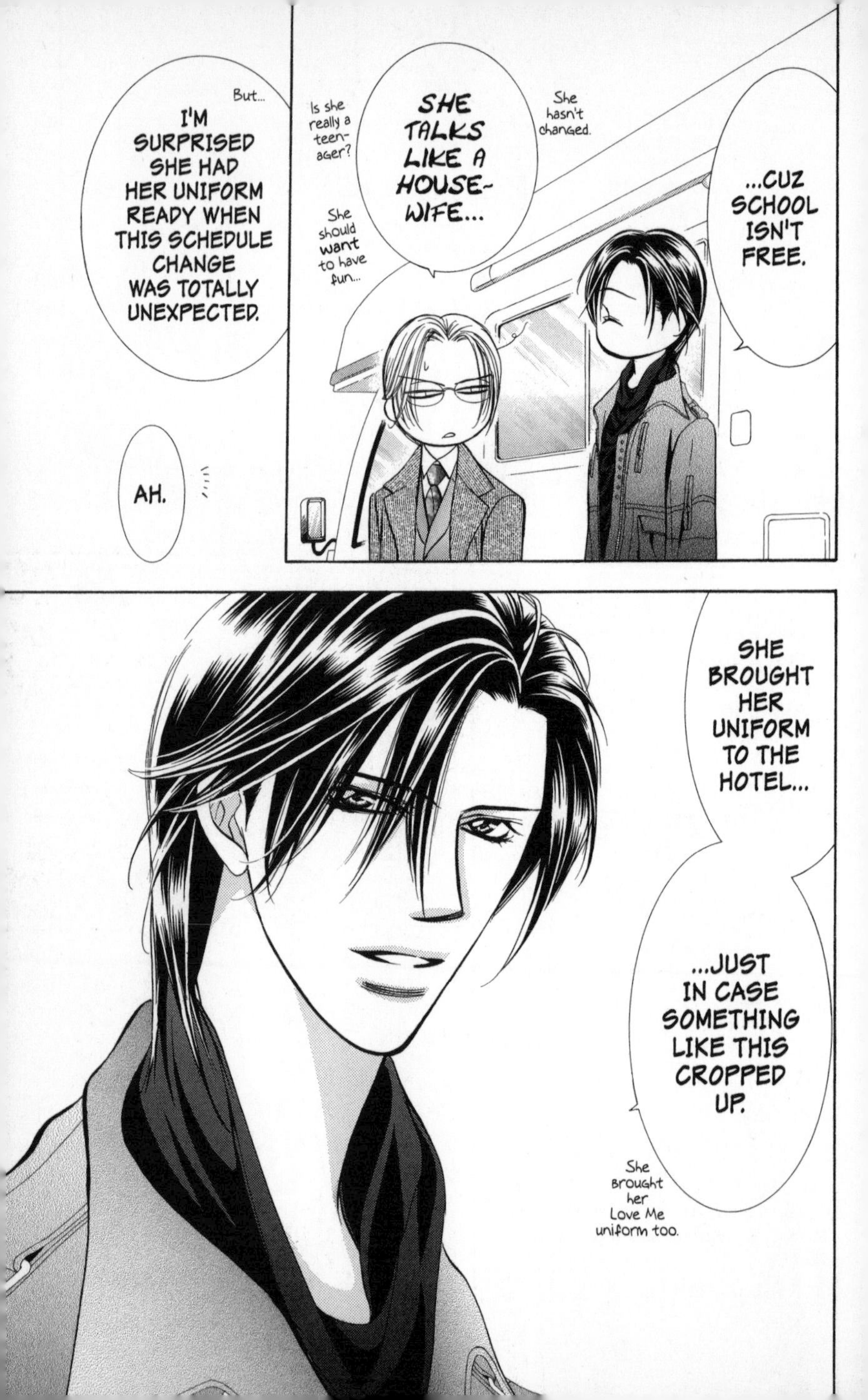
...CUZ SCHOOL ISN'T FREE.
She hasn't changed.
SHE TALKS LIKE A HOUSE-WIFE...
Is she really a teen-ager?
She should want to have fun...
But...
I'M SURPRISED SHE HAD HER UNIFORM READY WHEN THIS SCHEDULE CHANGE WAS TOTALLY UNEXPECTED.
AH.
SHE BROUGHT HER UNIFORM TO THE HOTEL...
...JUST IN CASE SOMETHING LIKE THIS CROPPED UP.
She brought her Love Me uniform too.

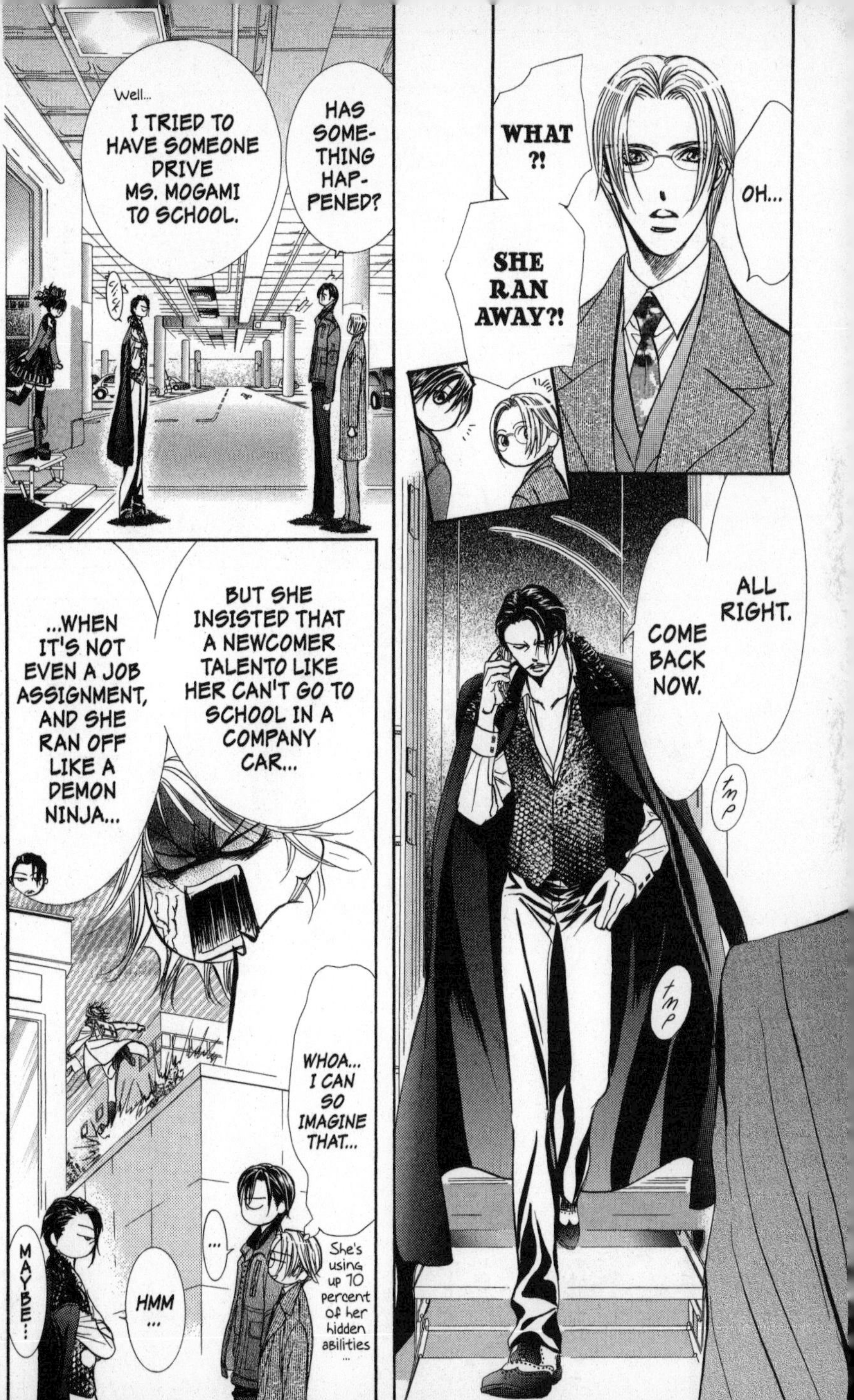
OH...
WHAT?!
SHE RAN AWAY?!
ALL RIGHT.
COME BACK NOW.
tmp
tmp
HAS SOMETHING HAPPENED?
Well...
I TRIED TO HAVE SOMEONE DRIVE MS. MOGAMI TO SCHOOL.
click
BUT SHE INSISTED THAT A NEWCOMER TALENTO LIKE HER CAN'T GO TO SCHOOL IN A COMPANY CAR...
...WHEN IT'S NOT EVEN A JOB ASSIGNMENT, AND SHE RAN OFF LIKE A DEMON NINJA...
WHOA... I CAN SO IMAGINE THAT...
She's using up 10 percent of her hidden abilities...
...
HMM ...
MAYBE...

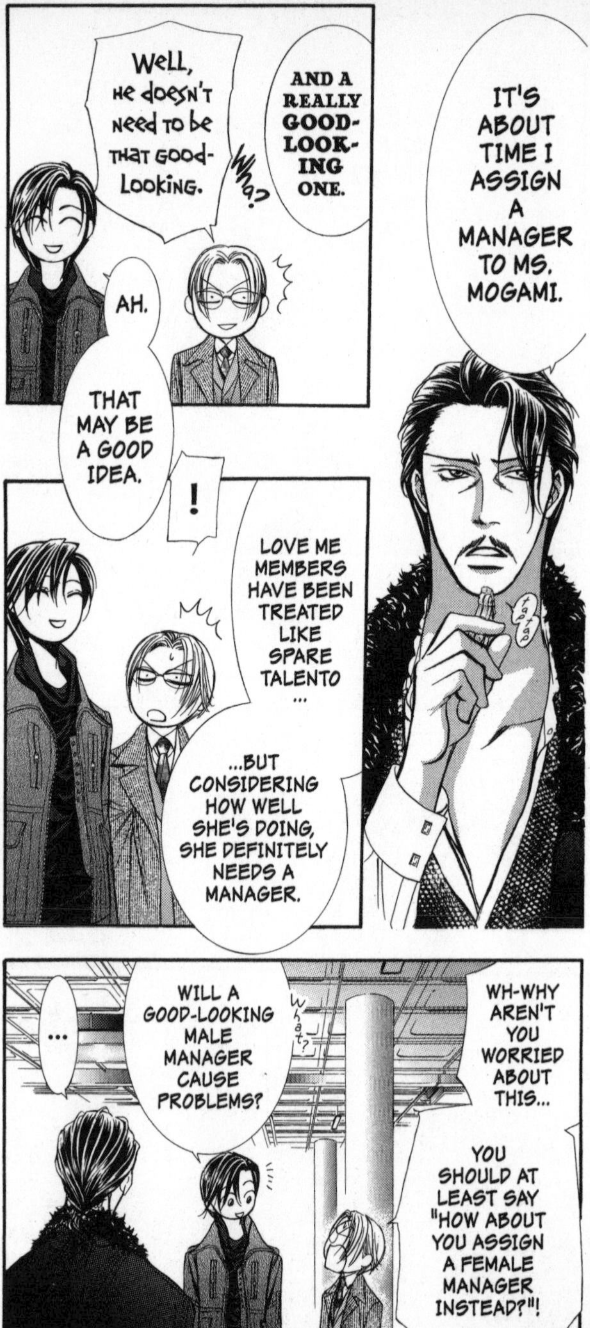
IT'S ABOUT TIME I ASSIGN A MANAGER TO MS. MOGAMI.
tap tap
AND A REALLY GOOD-LOOKING ONE.
Wha?
Well, he doesn't need to be that good-looking.
AH.
THAT MAY BE A GOOD IDEA.
!
LOVE ME MEMBERS HAVE BEEN TREATED LIKE SPARE TALENTO ...
...BUT CONSIDERING HOW WELL SHE'S DOING, SHE DEFINITELY NEEDS A MANAGER.
WH-WHY AREN'T YOU WORRIED ABOUT THIS...
YOU SHOULD AT LEAST SAY "HOW ABOUT YOU ASSIGN A FEMALE MANAGER INSTEAD?"!
WILL A GOOD-LOOKING MALE MANAGER CAUSE PROBLEMS?
What?
...
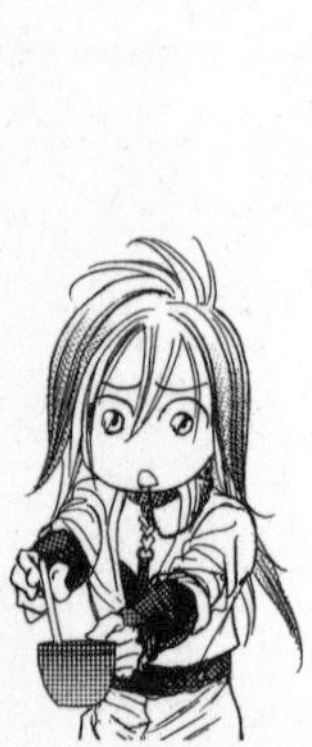

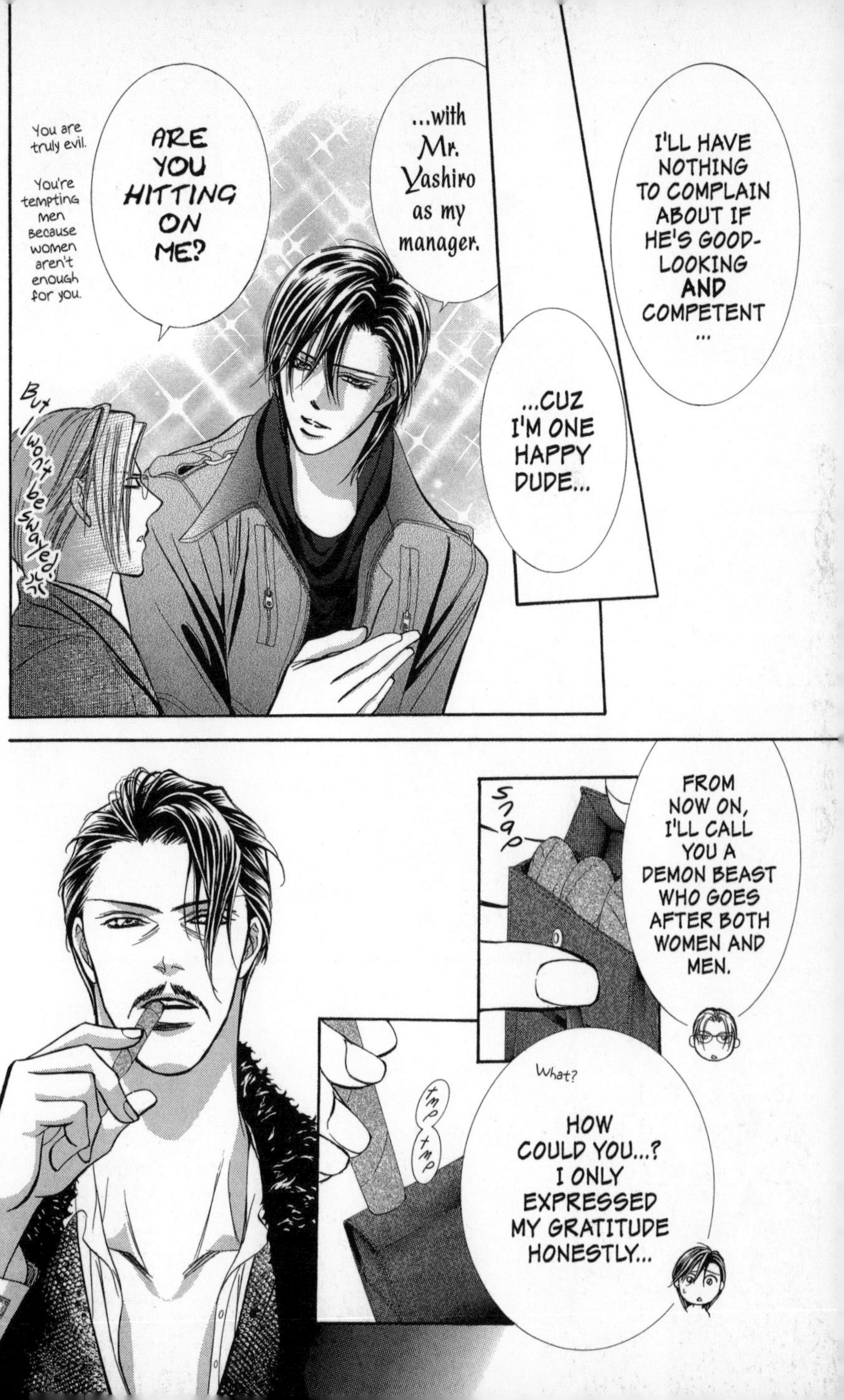
I'LL HAVE NOTHING TO COMPLAIN ABOUT IF HE'S GOOD-LOOKING AND COMPETENT ...
...CUZ I'M ONE HAPPY DUDE...
...with Mr. Yashiro as my manager.
ARE YOU HITTING ON ME?
You are truly evil.
You're tempting men because women aren't enough for you.
But I won't be swayed.
FROM NOW ON, I'LL CALL YOU A DEMON BEAST WHO GOES AFTER BOTH WOMEN AND MEN.
snap
What?
HOW COULD YOU...? I ONLY EXPRESSED MY GRATITUDE HONESTLY...
tmp tmp

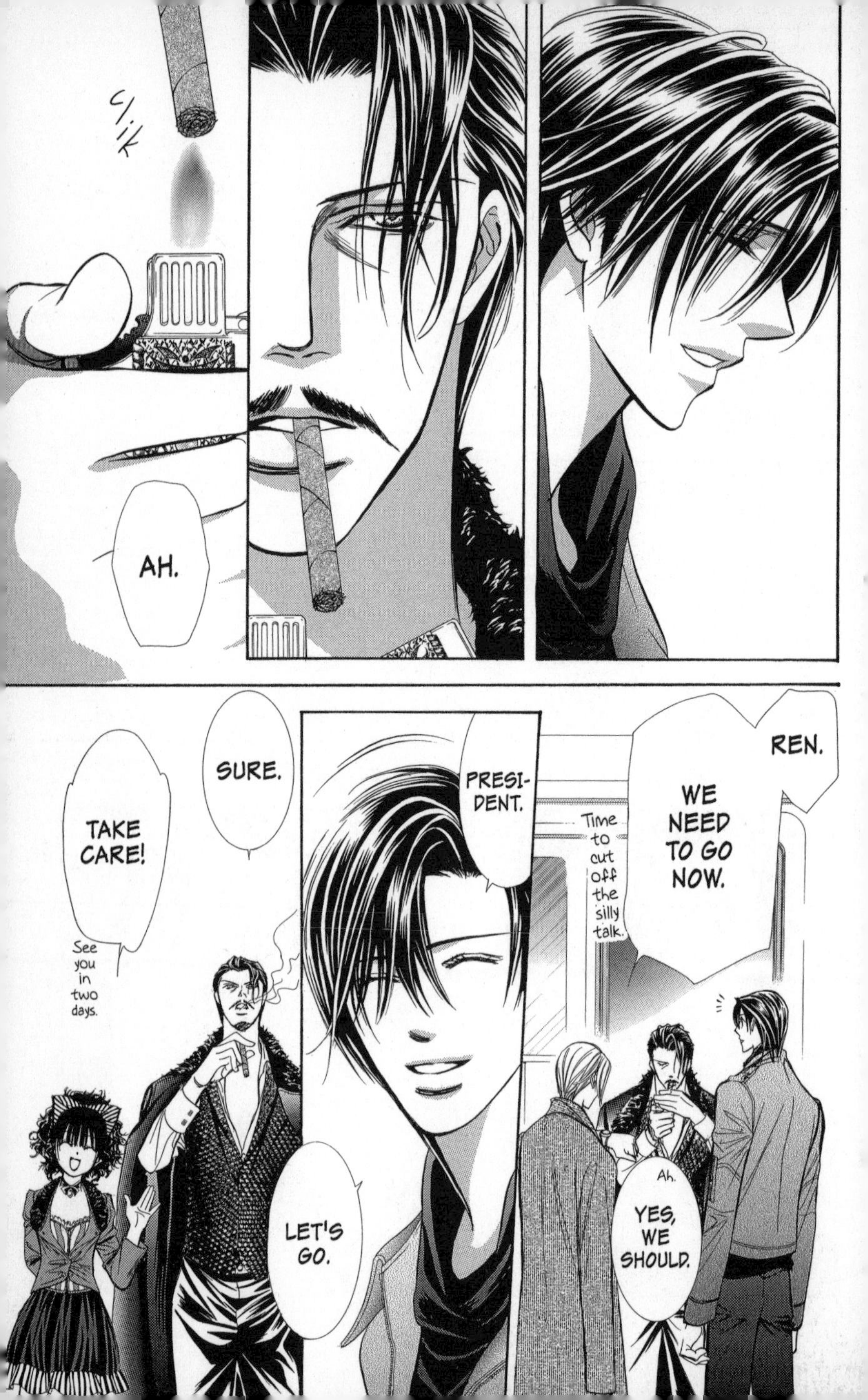

clik
AH.
REN.
WE NEED TO GO NOW.
Time to cut off the silly talk.
PRESI-DENT.
SURE.
TAKE CARE!
See you in two days.
Ah.
YES, WE SHOULD.
LET'S GO.

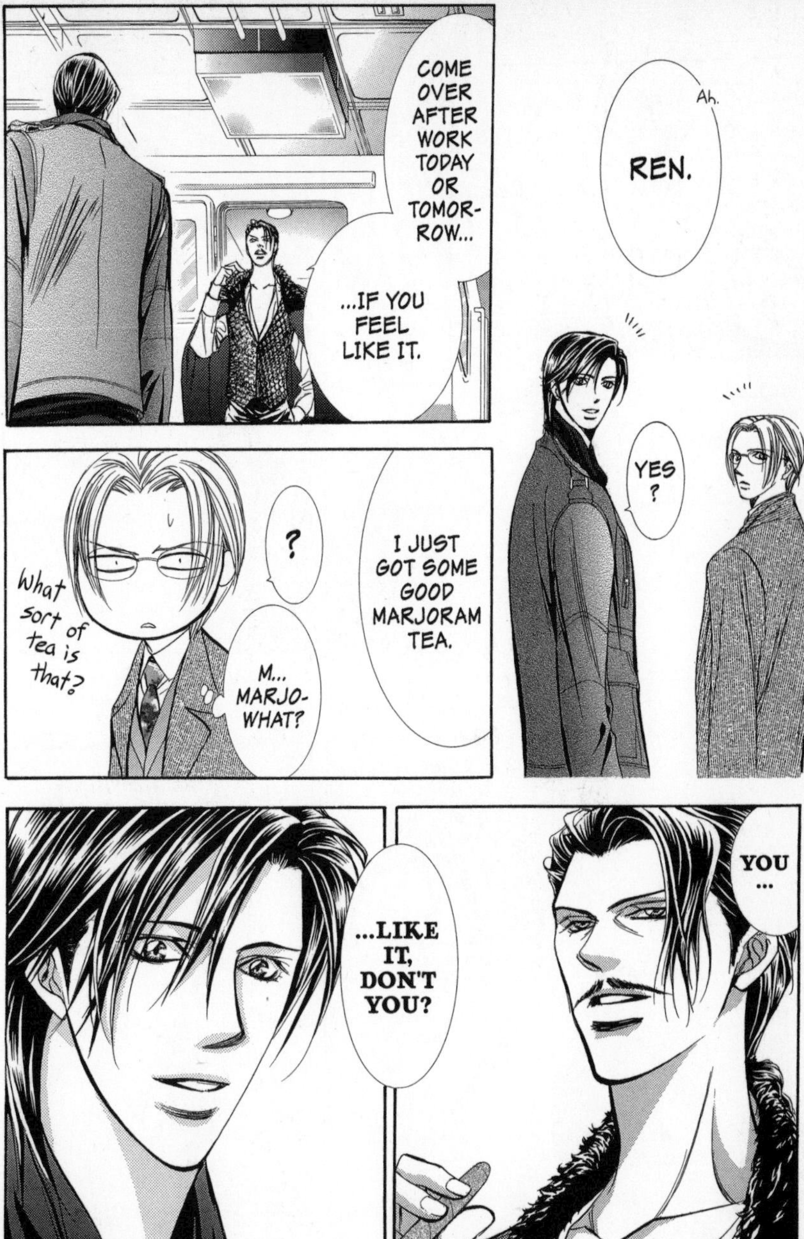
Ah.
REN.
YES?
COME OVER AFTER WORK TODAY OR TOMORROW...
...IF YOU FEEL LIKE IT.
I JUST GOT SOME GOOD MARJORAM TEA.
?
M... MARJO-WHAT?
What sort of tea is that?
YOU...
...LIKE IT, DON'T YOU?

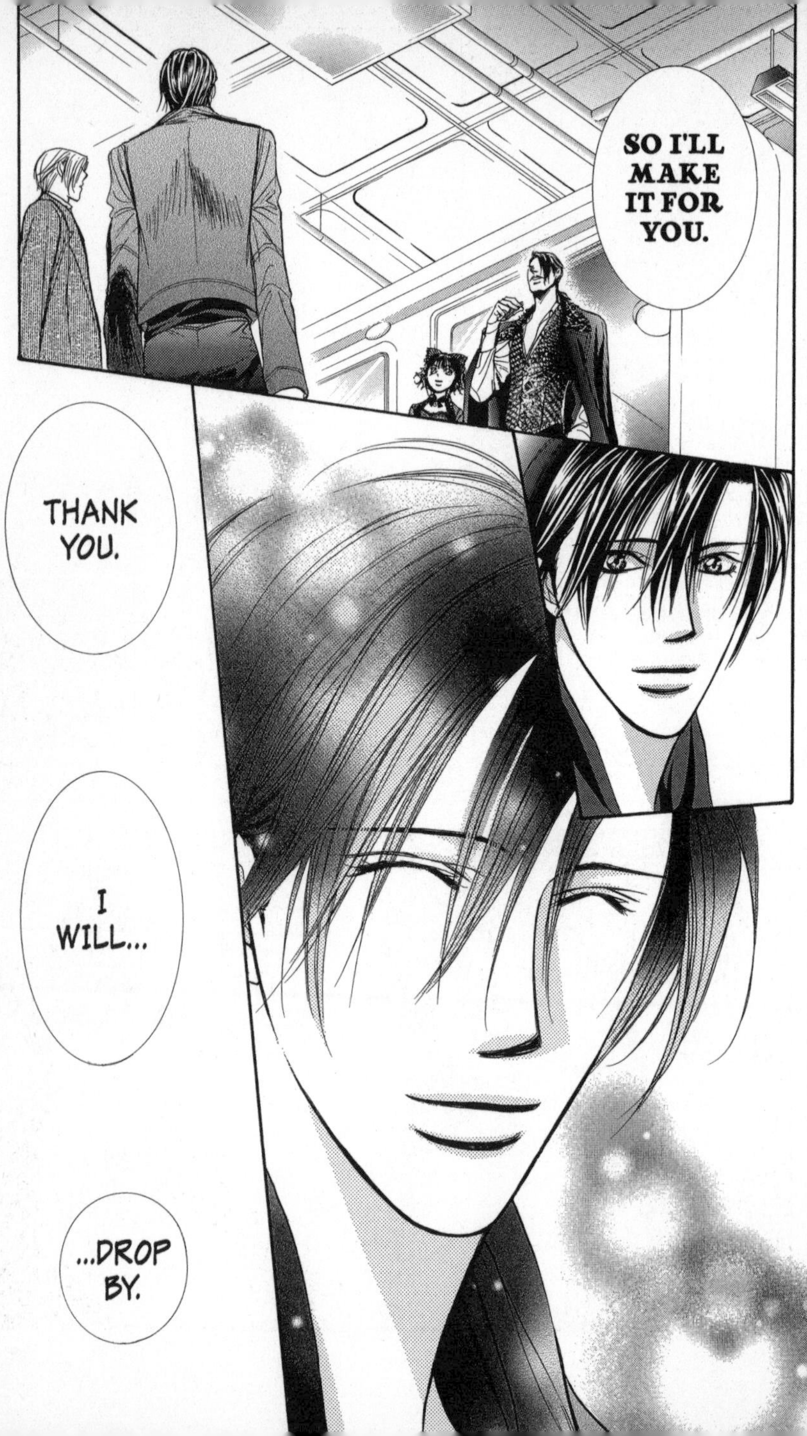
SO I'LL MAKE IT FOR YOU.
THANK YOU.
I WILL...
...DROP BY.

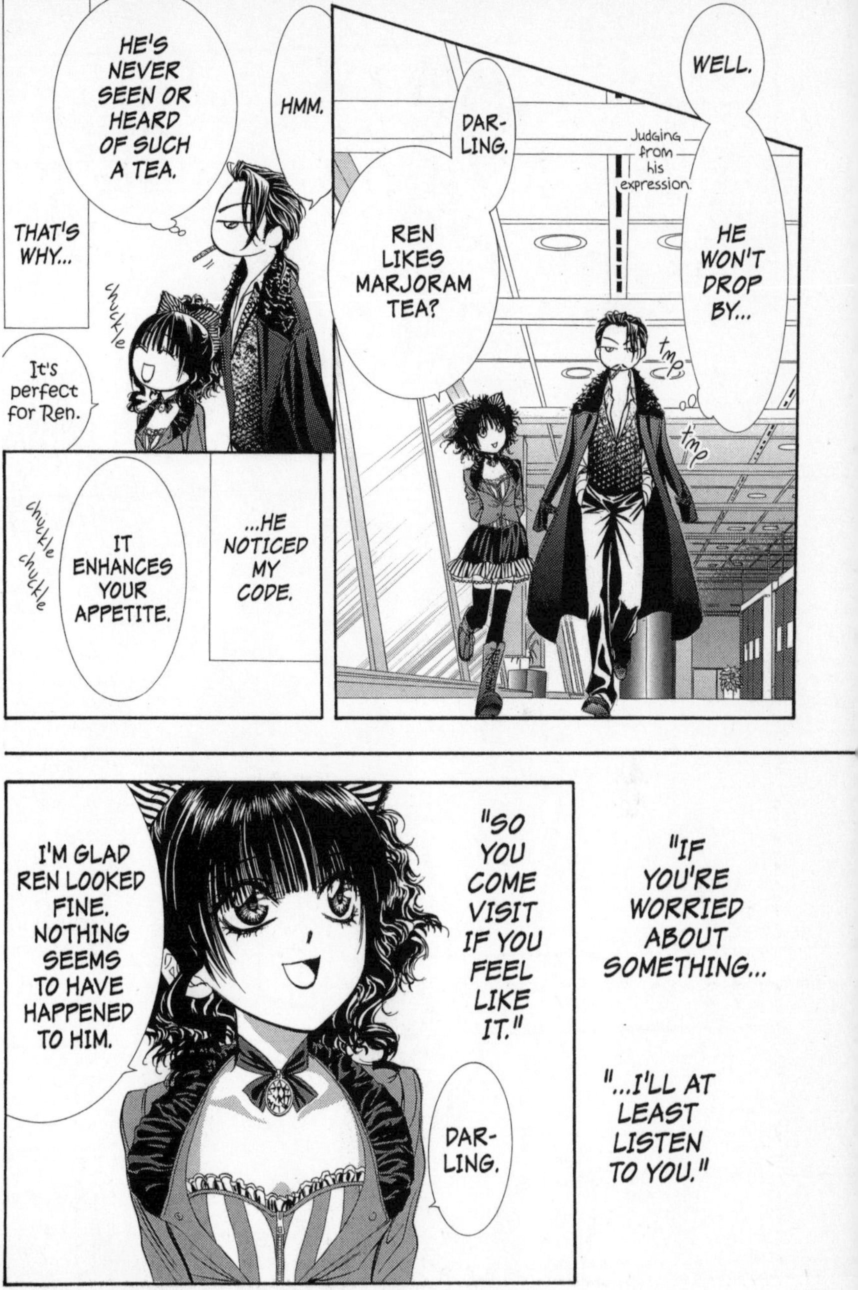
WELL.
Judging from his expression.
HE WON'T DROP BY...
tmp
tmp
DAR-LING.
REN LIKES MARJORAM TEA?
HMM.
HE'S NEVER SEEN OR HEARD OF SUCH A TEA.
THAT'S WHY...
chuckle
It's perfect for Ren.
...HE NOTICED MY CODE.
IT ENHANCES YOUR APPETITE.
chuckle chuckle
"IF YOU'RE WORRIED ABOUT SOMETHING...
"...I'LL AT LEAST LISTEN TO YOU."
"SO YOU COME VISIT IF YOU FEEL LIKE IT."
DAR-LING.
I'M GLAD REN LOOKED FINE. NOTHING SEEMS TO HAVE HAPPENED TO HIM.

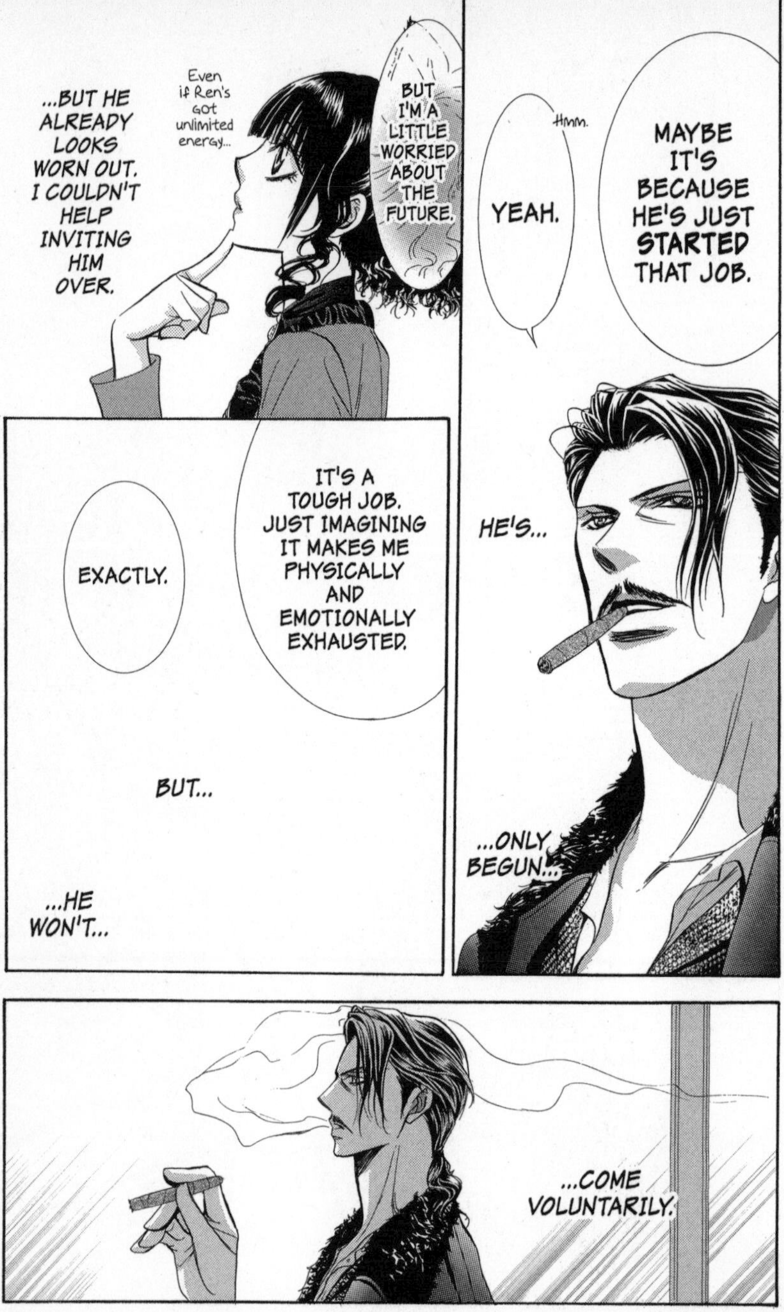
MAYBE IT'S BECAUSE HE'S JUST STARTED THAT JOB.
Hmm.
YEAH.
HE'S...
...ONLY BEGUN...
BUT I'M A LITTLE WORRIED ABOUT THE FUTURE.
Even if Ren's got unlimited energy...
...BUT HE ALREADY LOOKS WORN OUT. I COULDN'T HELP INVITING HIM OVER.
IT'S A TOUGH JOB. JUST IMAGINING IT MAKES ME PHYSICALLY AND EMOTIONALLY EXHAUSTED.
EXACTLY.
BUT...
...HE WON'T...
...COME VOLUNTARILY.

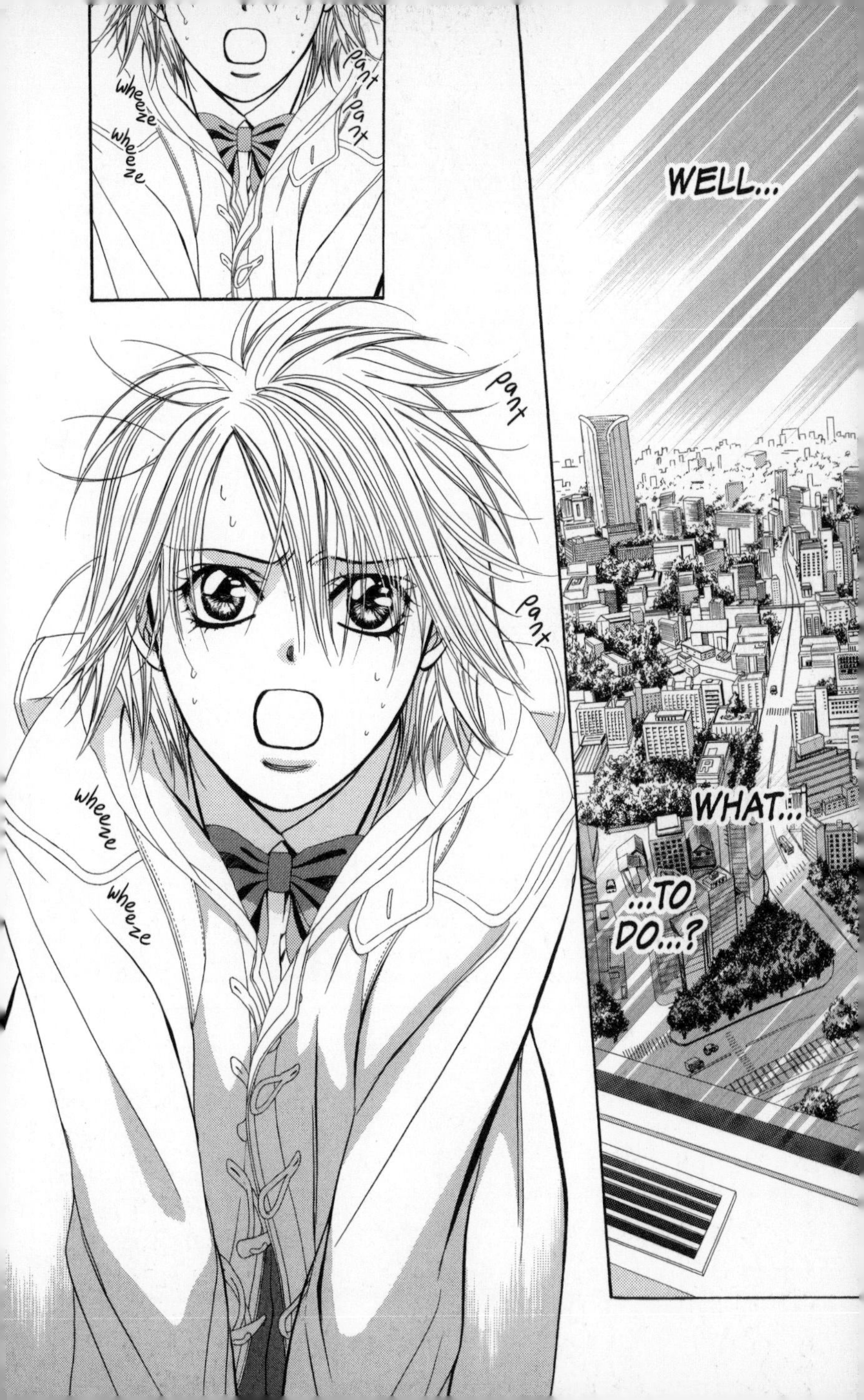
WELL...
WHAT...
...TO DO...?
pant pant
wheeze wheeze
pant
pant
wheeze
wheeze

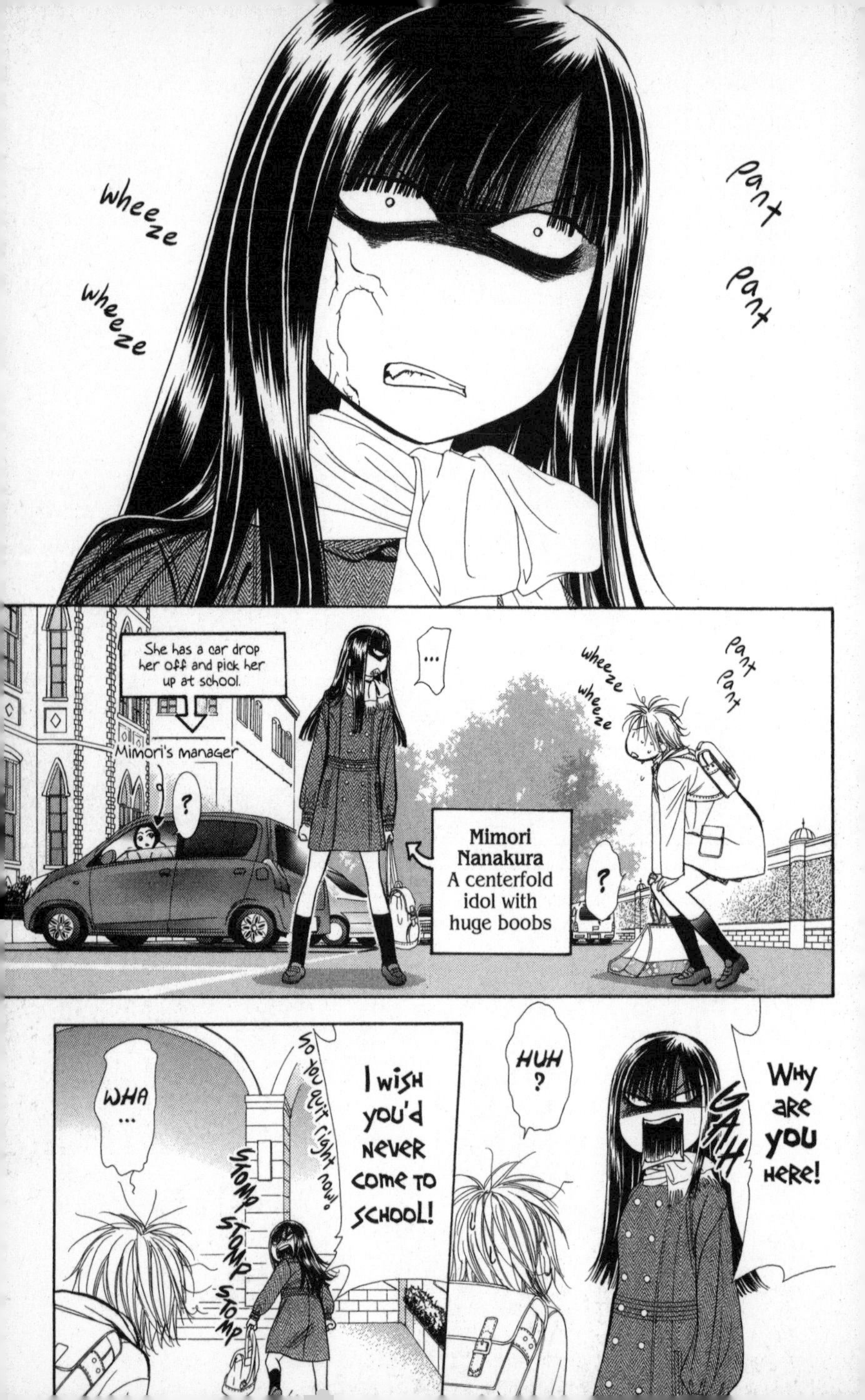
pant
pant
wheeze
wheeze
pant
pant
wheeze
wheeze
...
?
Mimori Nanakura A centerfold idol with huge boobs
She has a car drop her off and pick her up at school.
Mimori's manager
?
Why are you here!
GAH
HUH?
I wish you'd never come to school!
So you quit right now!
STOMP STOMP STOMP STOMP
WHA...

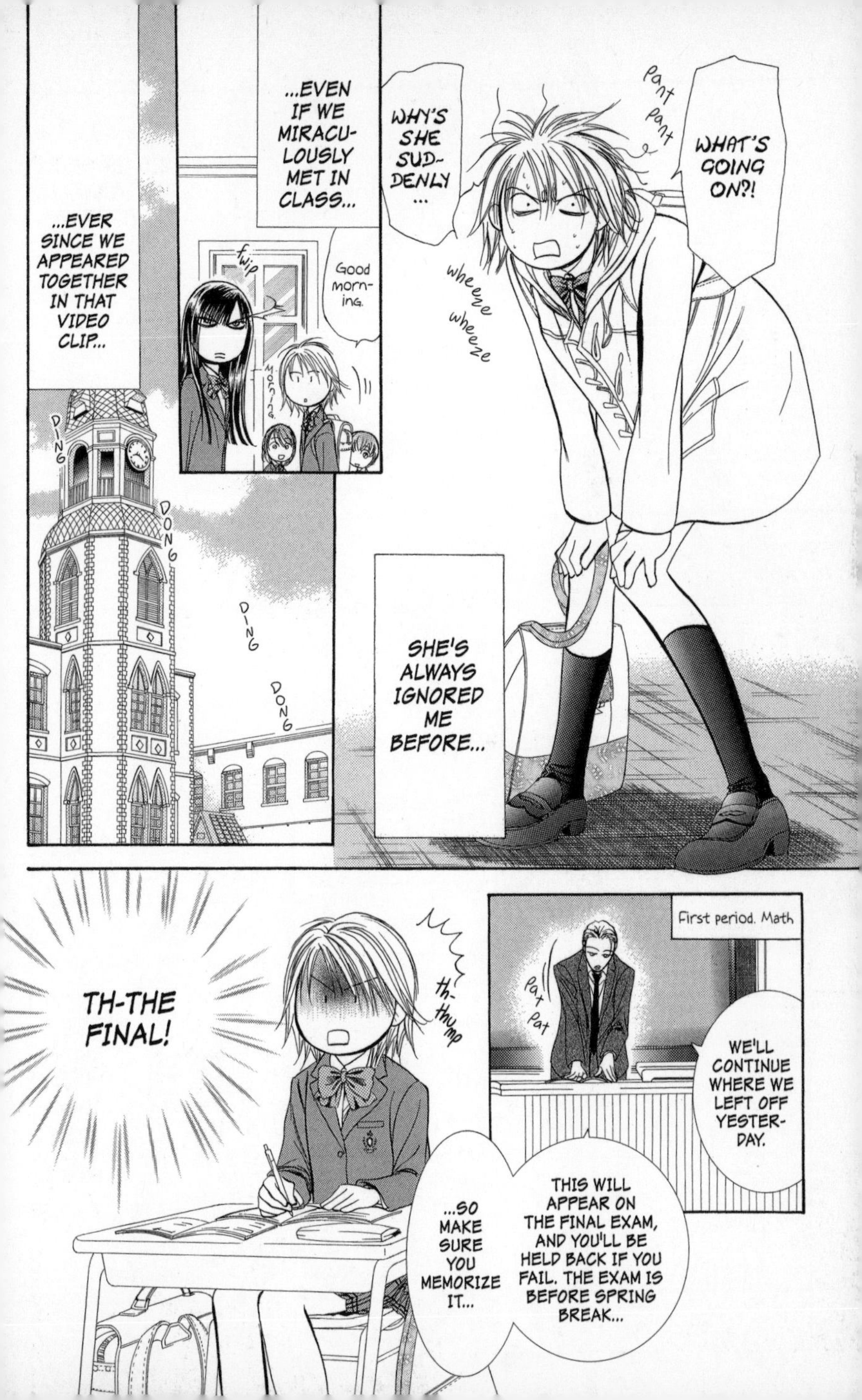
WHAT'S GOING ON?!
Pant pant
WHY'S SHE SUD-DENLY...
wheeze wheeze
SHE'S ALWAYS IGNORED ME BEFORE...
...EVEN IF WE MIRACU-LOUSLY MET IN CLASS...
Good morn-ing.
fwip
Morning.
...EVER SINCE WE APPEARED TOGETHER IN THAT VIDEO CLIP...
DING DONG DING DONG
First period. Math
Pat Pat
WE'LL CONTINUE WHERE WE LEFT OFF YESTER-DAY.
THIS WILL APPEAR ON THE FINAL EXAM, AND YOU'LL BE HELD BACK IF YOU FAIL. THE EXAM IS BEFORE SPRING BREAK...
...SO MAKE SURE YOU MEMORIZE IT...
th-thump
TH-THE FINAL!

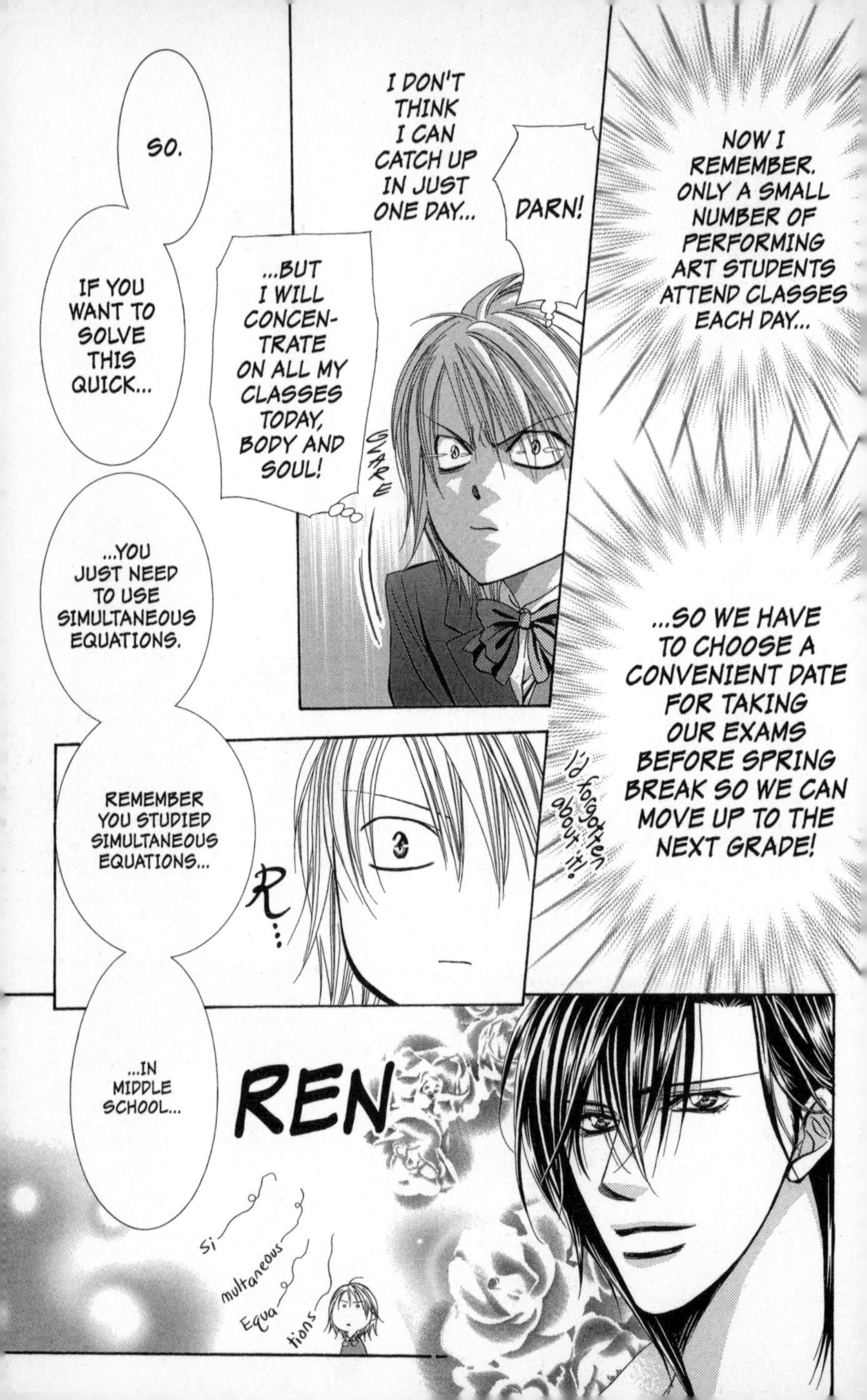
NOW I REMEMBER. ONLY A SMALL NUMBER OF PERFORMING ART STUDENTS ATTEND CLASSES EACH DAY...
...SO WE HAVE TO CHOOSE A CONVENIENT DATE FOR TAKING OUR EXAMS BEFORE SPRING BREAK SO WE CAN MOVE UP TO THE NEXT GRADE!
DARN!
I DON'T THINK I CAN CATCH UP IN JUST ONE DAY...
...BUT I WILL CONCENTRATE ON ALL MY CLASSES TODAY, BODY AND SOUL!
GLARE
SO.
IF YOU WANT TO SOLVE THIS QUICK...
...YOU JUST NEED TO USE SIMULTANEOUS EQUATIONS.
I'd forgotten about it!!
R...
REMEMBER YOU STUDIED SIMULTANEOUS EQUATIONS...
...IN MIDDLE SCHOOL...
REN
Si multaneous Equa tions

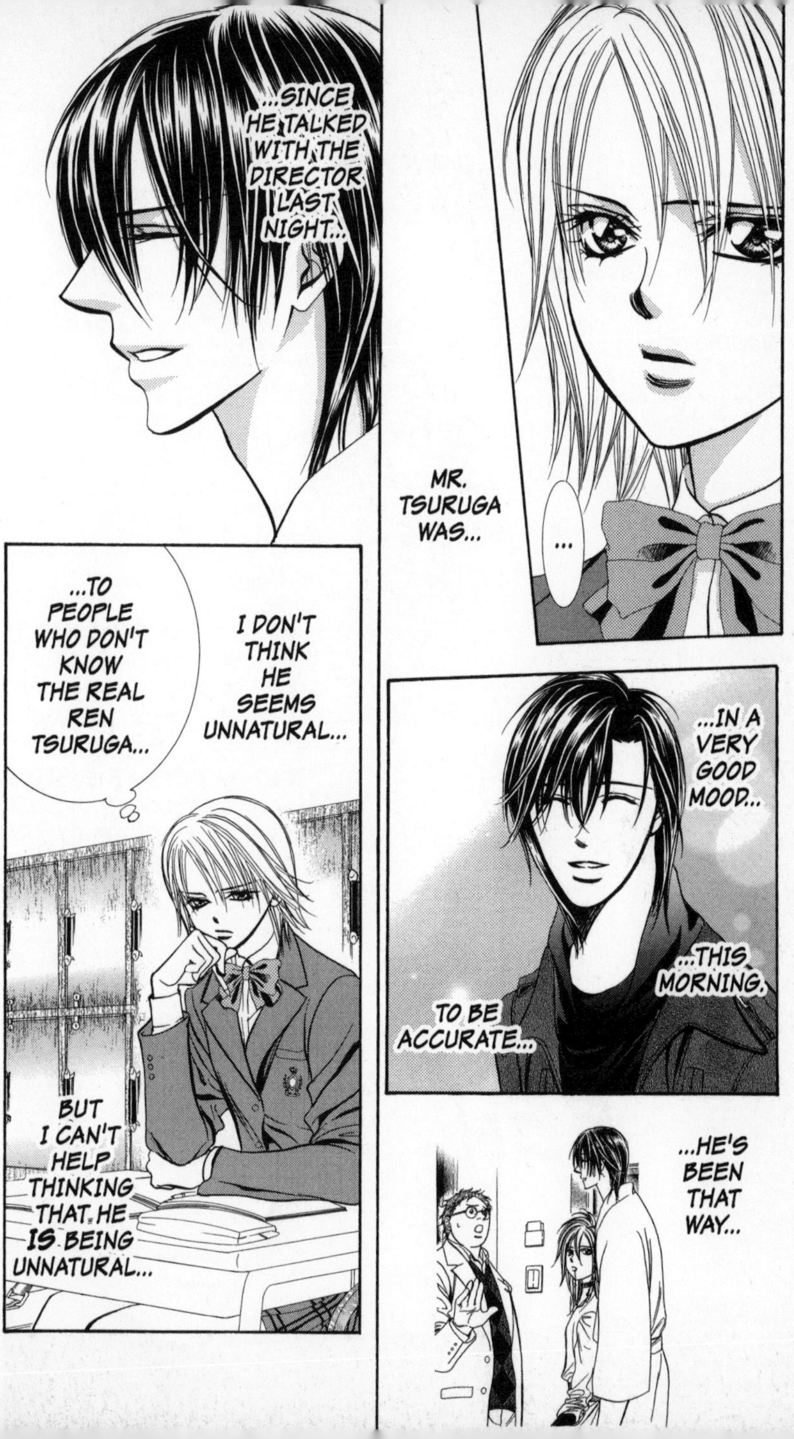
...
MR. TSURUGA WAS...
...SINCE HE TALKED WITH THE DIRECTOR LAST NIGHT...
...IN A VERY GOOD MOOD...
TO BE ACCURATE...
...THIS MORNING.
...HE'S BEEN THAT WAY...
I DON'T THINK HE SEEMS UNNATURAL...
...TO PEOPLE WHO DON'T KNOW THE REAL REN TSURUGA...
BUT I CAN'T HELP THINKING THAT HE **IS** BEING UNNATURAL...

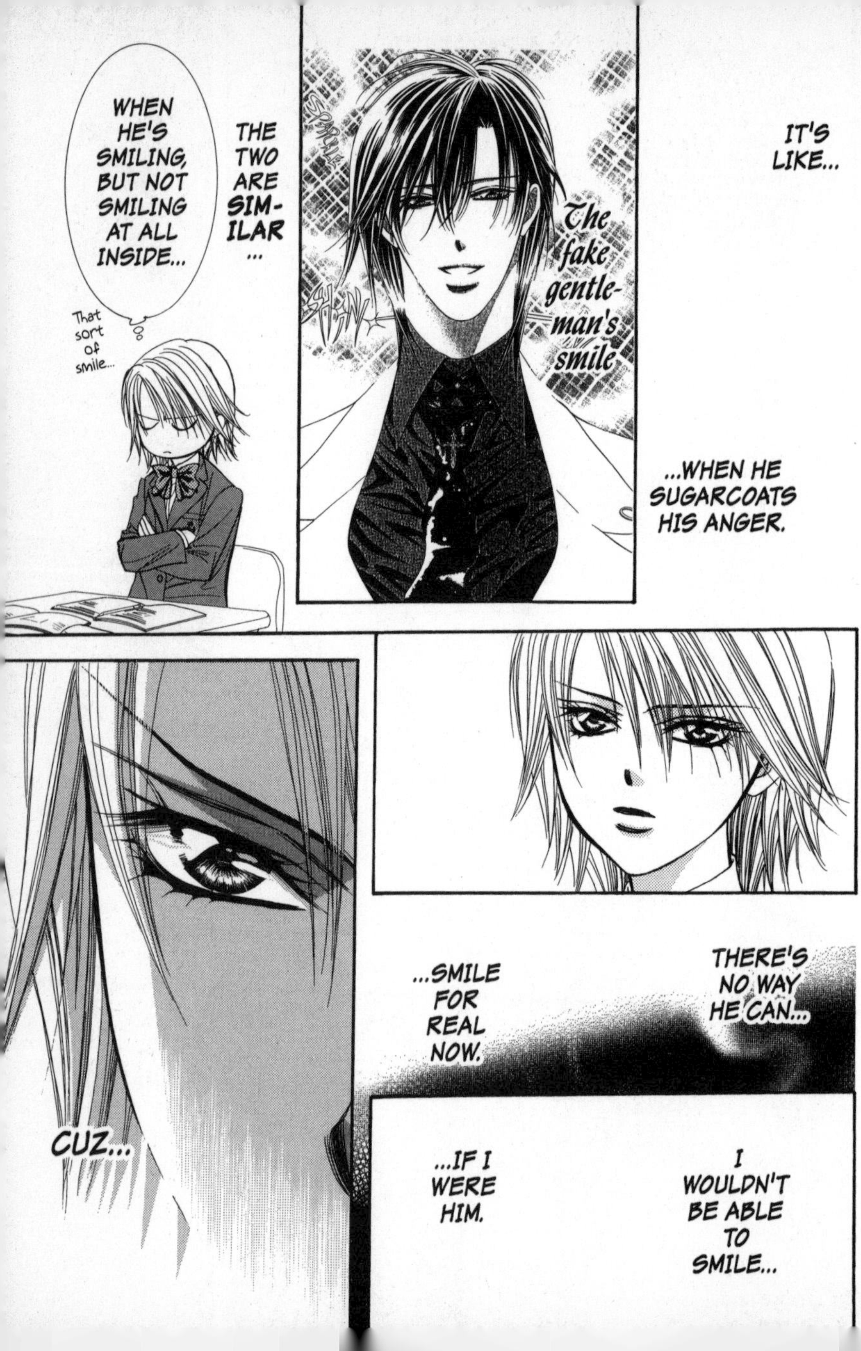
IT'S LIKE...
...WHEN HE SUGARCOATS HIS ANGER.
The fake gentle-man's smile
THE TWO ARE SIM-ILAR...
WHEN HE'S SMILING, BUT NOT SMILING AT ALL INSIDE...
That sort of smile...
THERE'S NO WAY HE CAN...
...SMILE FOR REAL NOW.
I WOULDN'T BE ABLE TO SMILE...
...IF I WERE HIM.
CUZ...

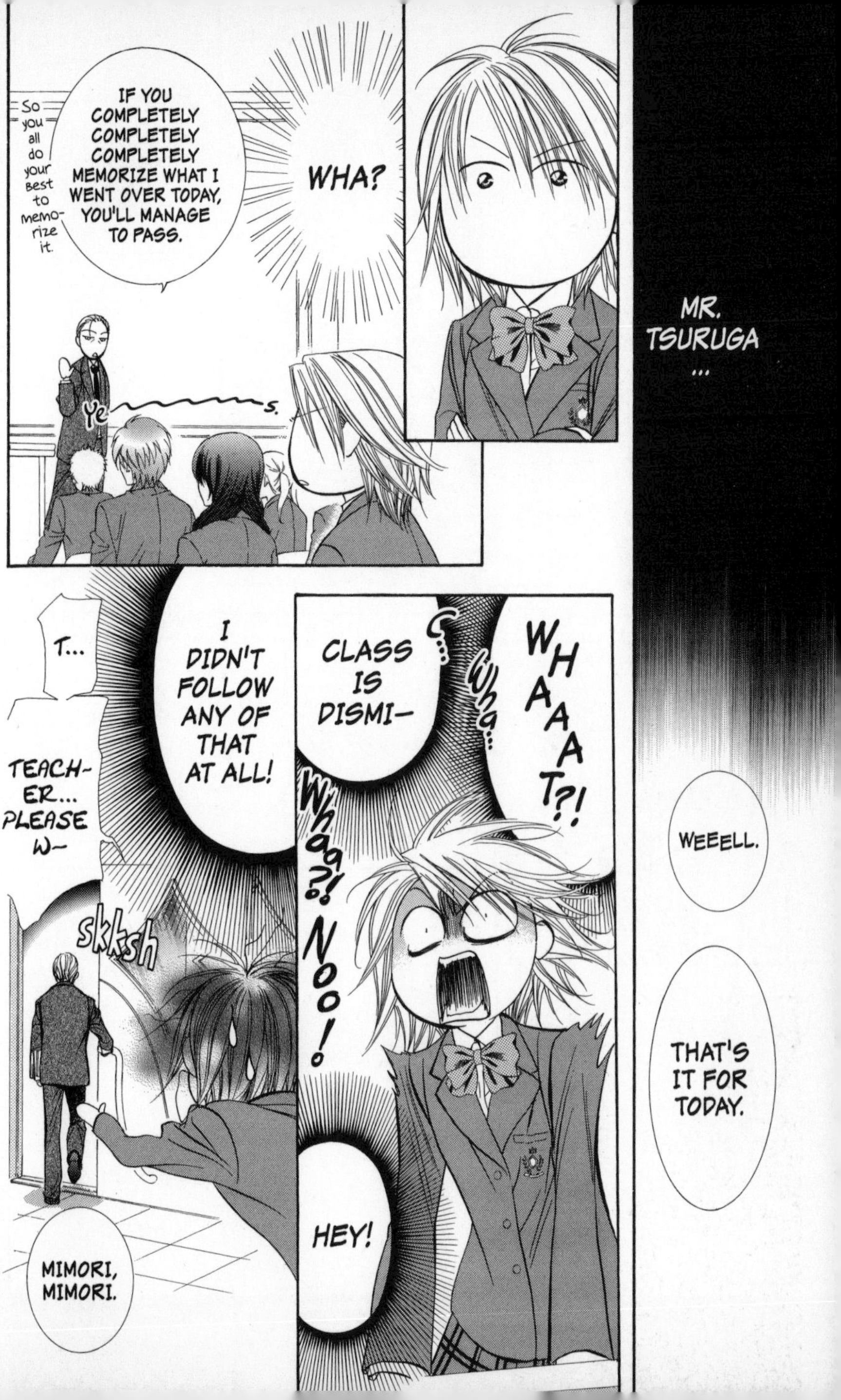
MR. TSURUGA ...
WEEELL.
THAT'S IT FOR TODAY.
WHA?
IF YOU COMPLETELY COMPLETELY COMPLETELY MEMORIZE WHAT I WENT OVER TODAY, YOU'LL MANAGE TO PASS.
So you all do your best to memorize it.
Ye~~s.
WHAAAT?!
CLASS IS DISMI-
Wha..
Whaa?!
Nooo!
HEY!
I DIDN'T FOLLOW ANY OF THAT AT ALL!
T...
TEACHER... PLEASE W-
skksh
MIMORI, MIMORI.

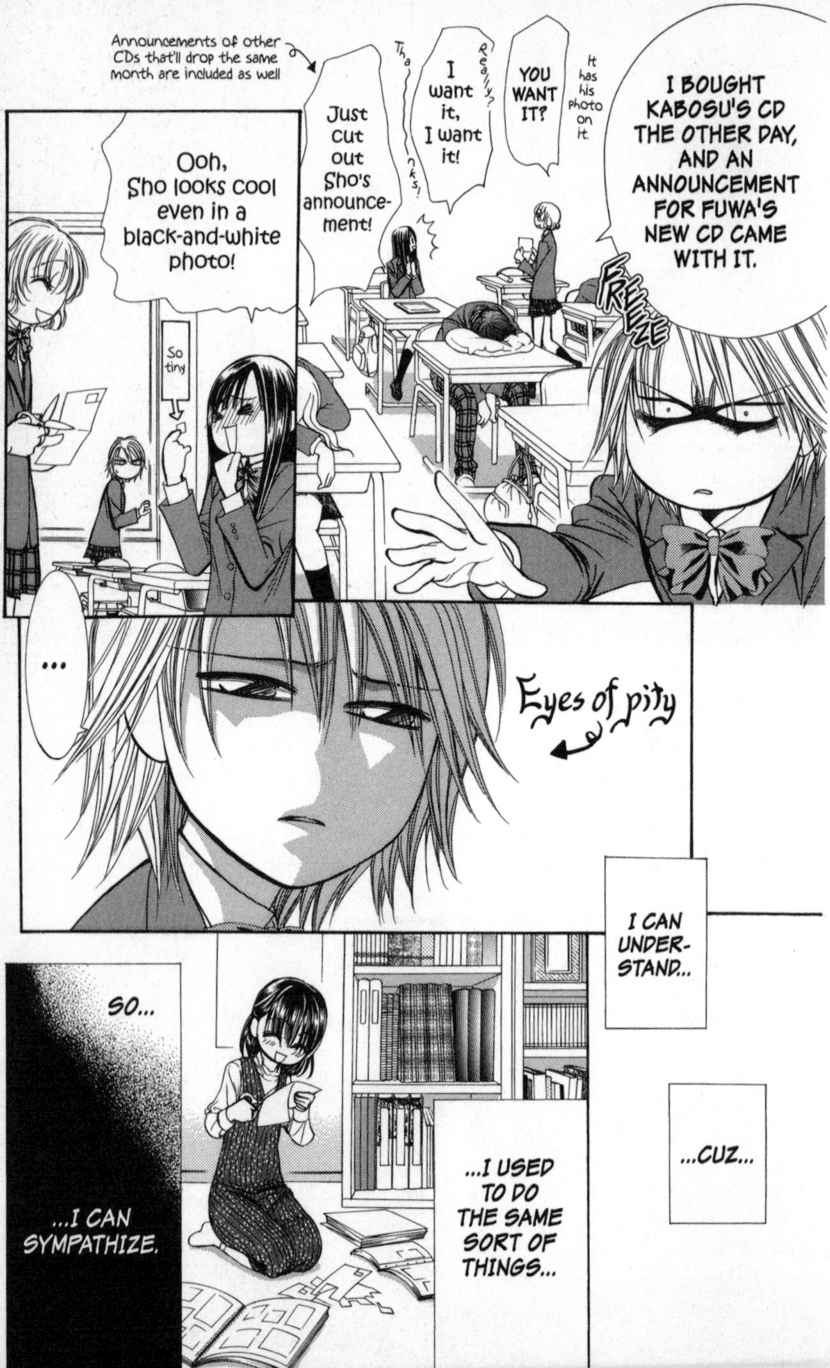
I BOUGHT KABOSU'S CD THE OTHER DAY, AND AN ANNOUNCEMENT FOR FUWA'S NEW CD CAME WITH IT.
FREEZE
It has his photo on it.
YOU WANT IT?
Really?
I want it, I want it!
Thanks!
Just cut out Sho's announcement!
Announcements of other CDs that'll drop the same month are included as well
Ooh, Sho looks cool even in a black-and-white photo!
So tiny
...
Eyes of pity
I CAN UNDERSTAND...
...CUZ...
...I USED TO DO THE SAME SORT OF THINGS...
SO...
...I CAN SYMPATHIZE.

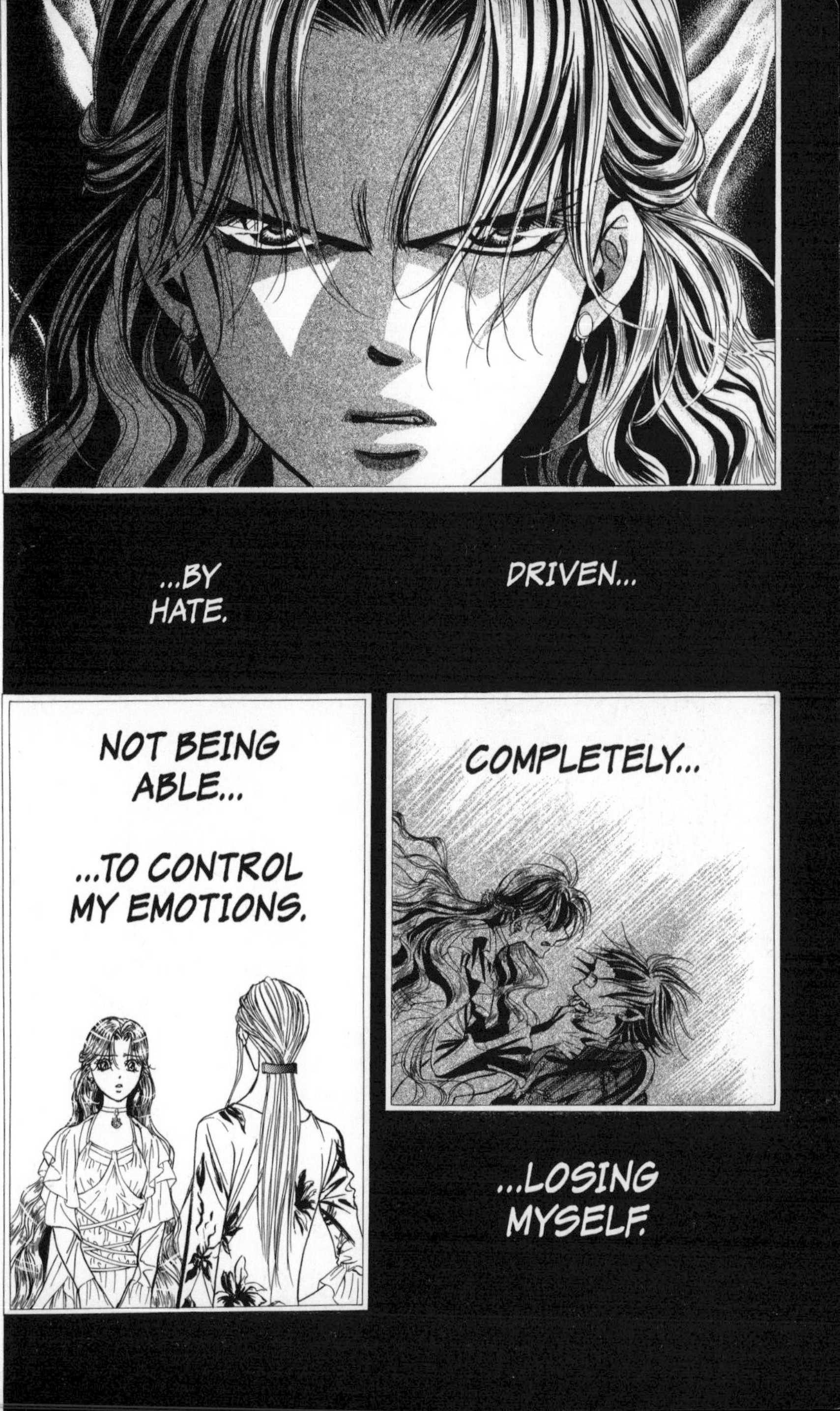
DRIVEN...
...BY HATE.
COMPLETELY...
...LOSING MYSELF.
NOT BEING ABLE...
...TO CONTROL MY EMOTIONS.

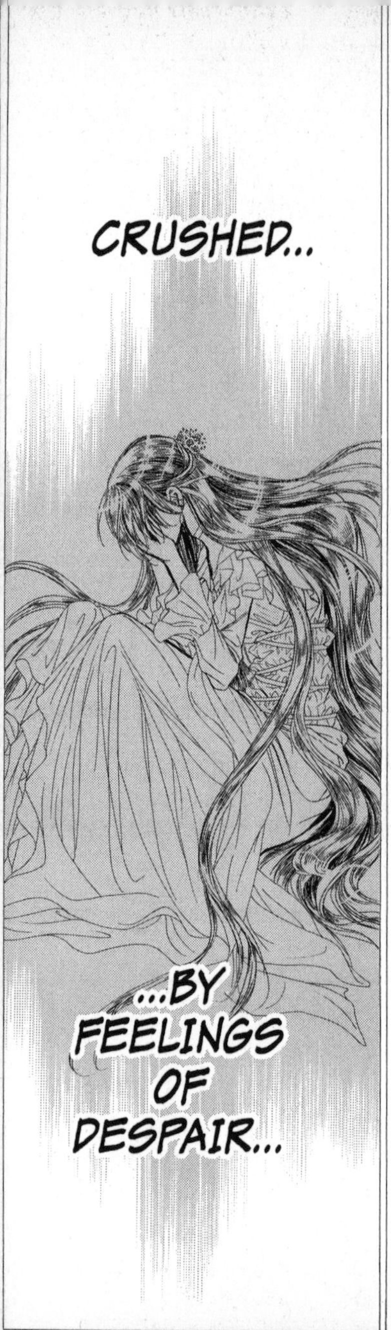
CRUSHED...
...BY FEELINGS OF DESPAIR...

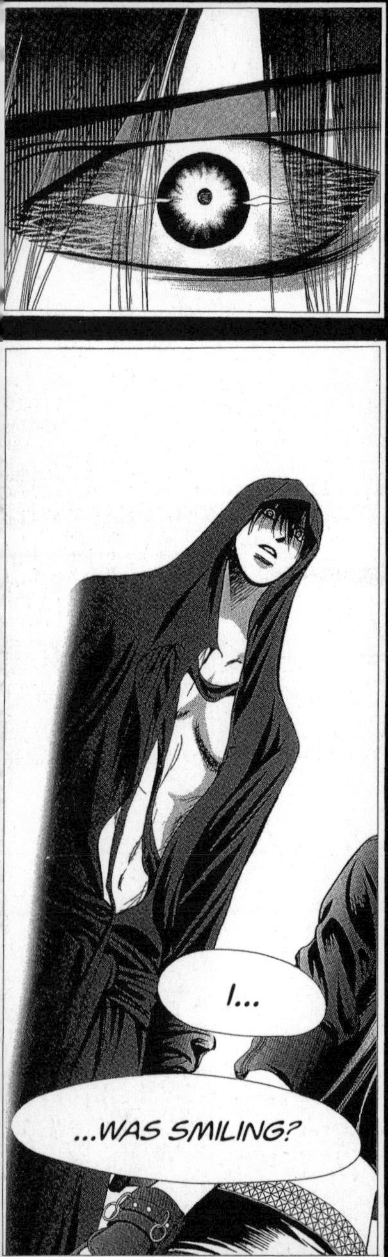
I...
...WAS SMILING?

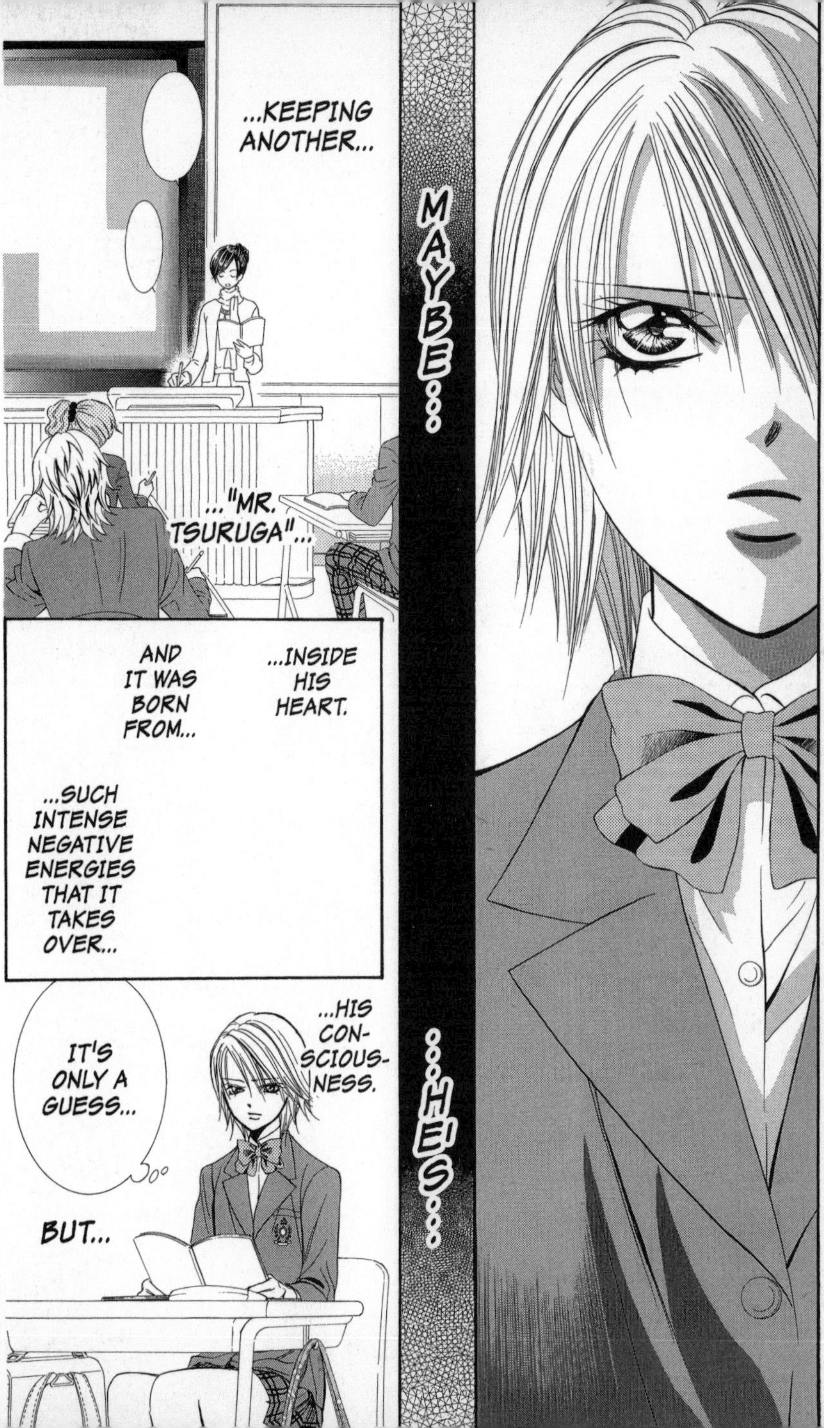
MAYBE...
...HE'S...
...KEEPING ANOTHER...
..."MR. TSURUGA"...
...INSIDE HIS HEART.
AND IT WAS BORN FROM...
...SUCH INTENSE NEGATIVE ENERGIES THAT IT TAKES OVER...
...HIS CON-SCIOUS-NESS.
IT'S ONLY A GUESS...
BUT...

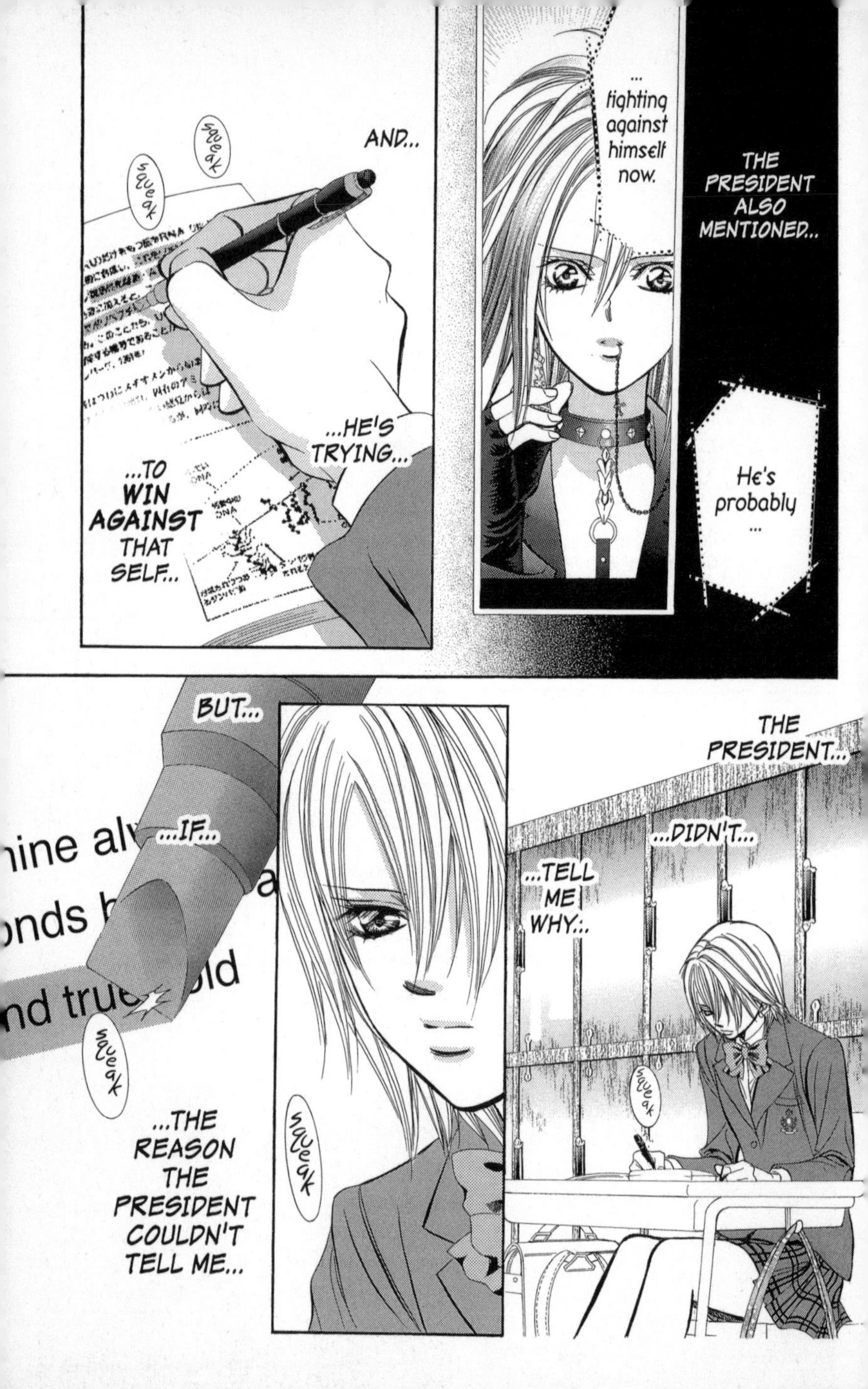
THE PRESIDENT ALSO MENTIONED...
He's probably ...
... fighting against himself now.
AND...
squeak
squeak
...HE'S TRYING...
...TO WIN AGAINST THAT SELF...
THE PRESIDENT...
...DIDN'T...
...TELL ME WHY...
squeak
squeak
BUT...
...IF...
squeak
...THE REASON THE PRESIDENT COULDN'T TELL ME...

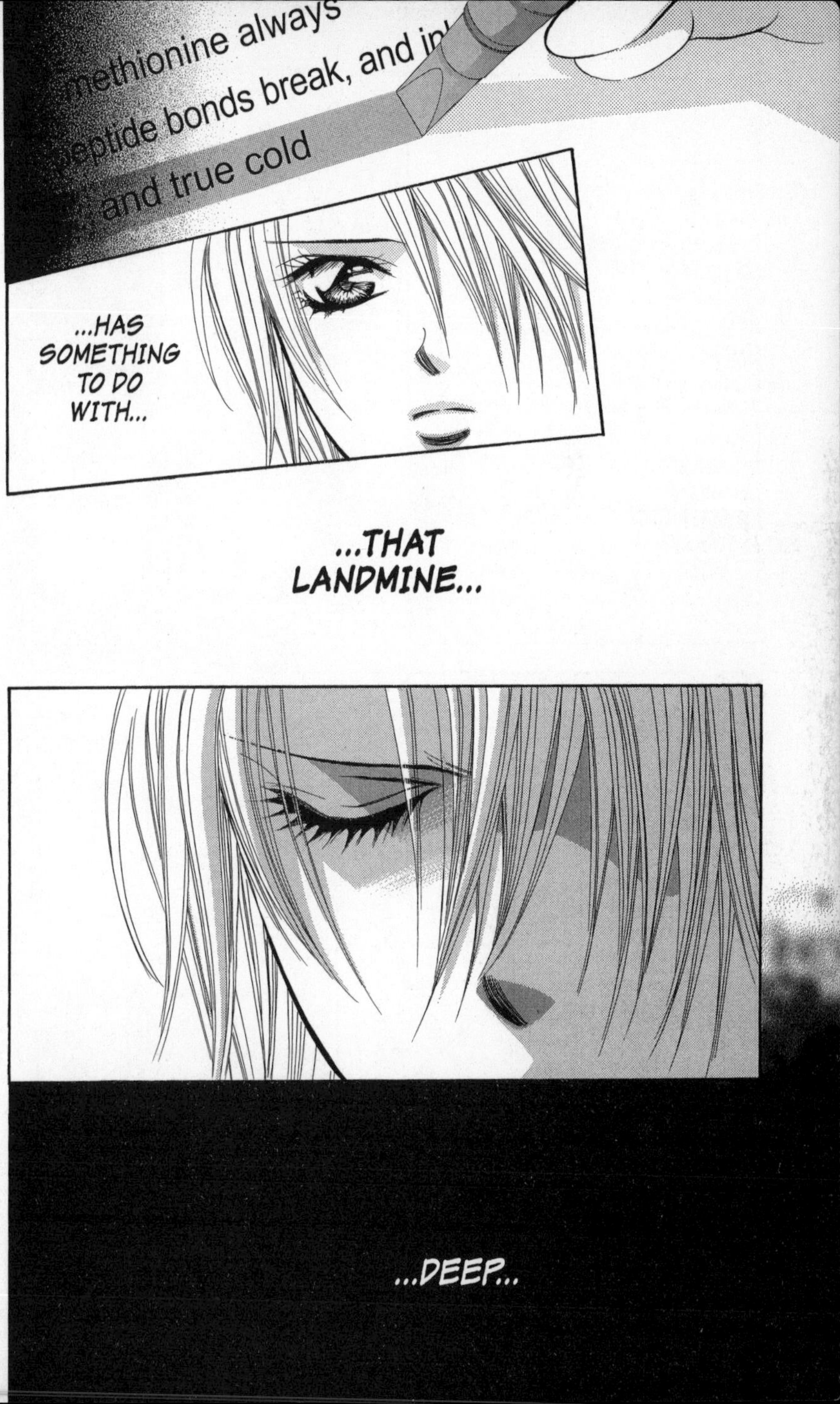
methionine always
peptide bonds break, and in
and true cold
...HAS SOMETHING TO DO WITH...
...THAT LANDMINE...
...DEEP...

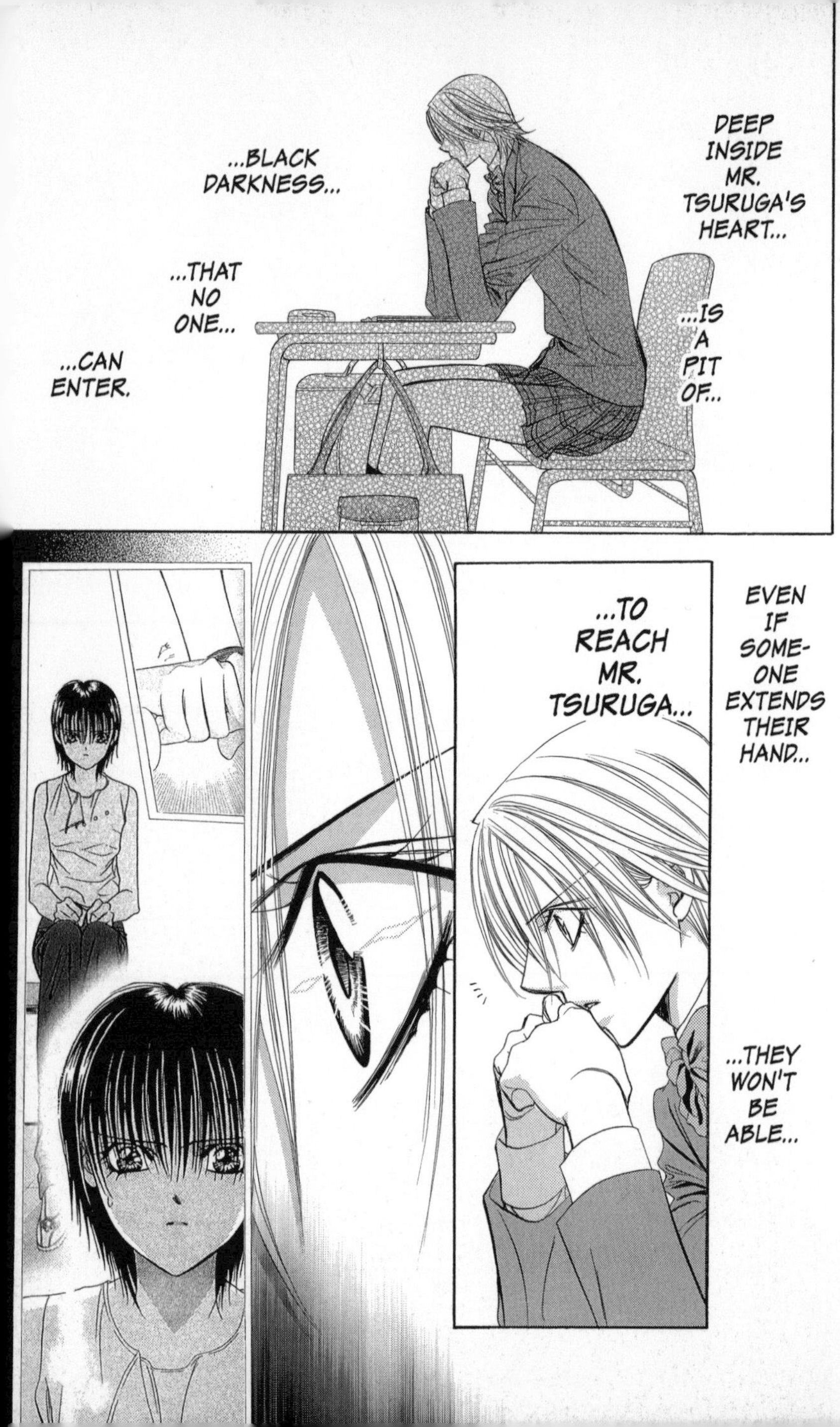
DEEP INSIDE MR. TSURUGA'S HEART...
...IS A PIT OF...
...BLACK DARKNESS...
...THAT NO ONE...
...CAN ENTER.
EVEN IF SOME-ONE EXTENDS THEIR HAND...
...THEY WON'T BE ABLE...
...TO REACH MR. TSURUGA...

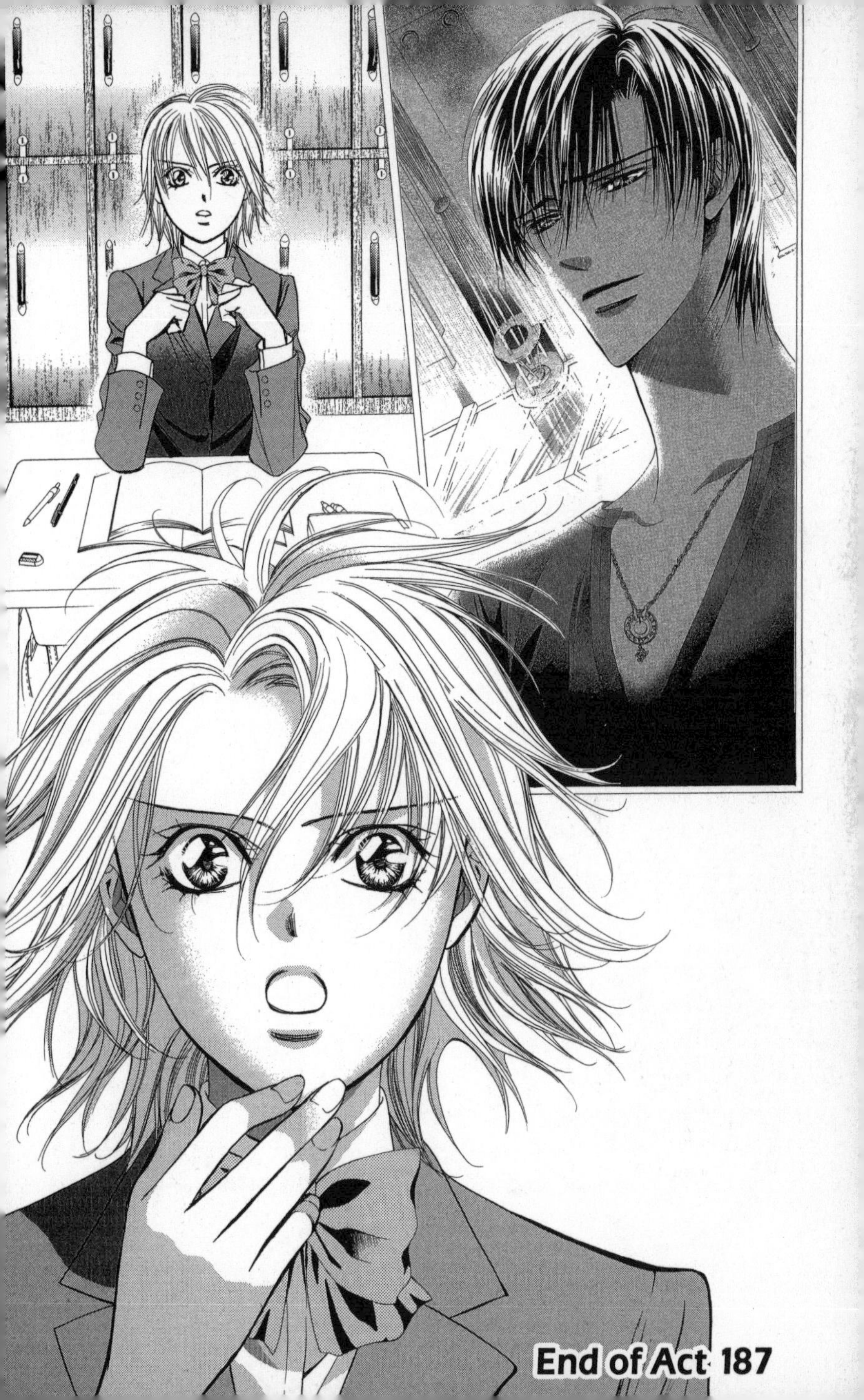
End of Act 187

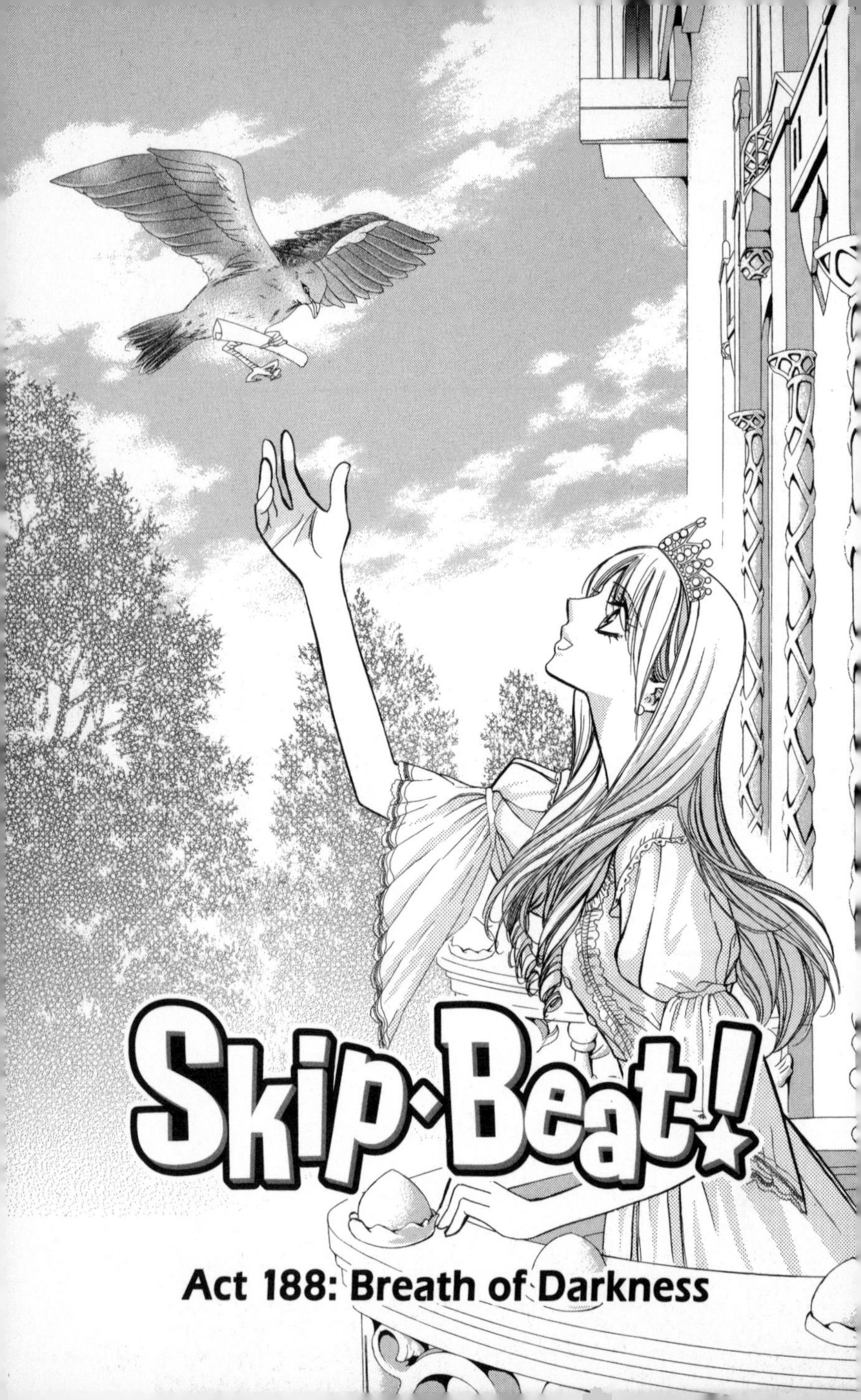
Skip·Beat!
Act 188: Breath of Darkness

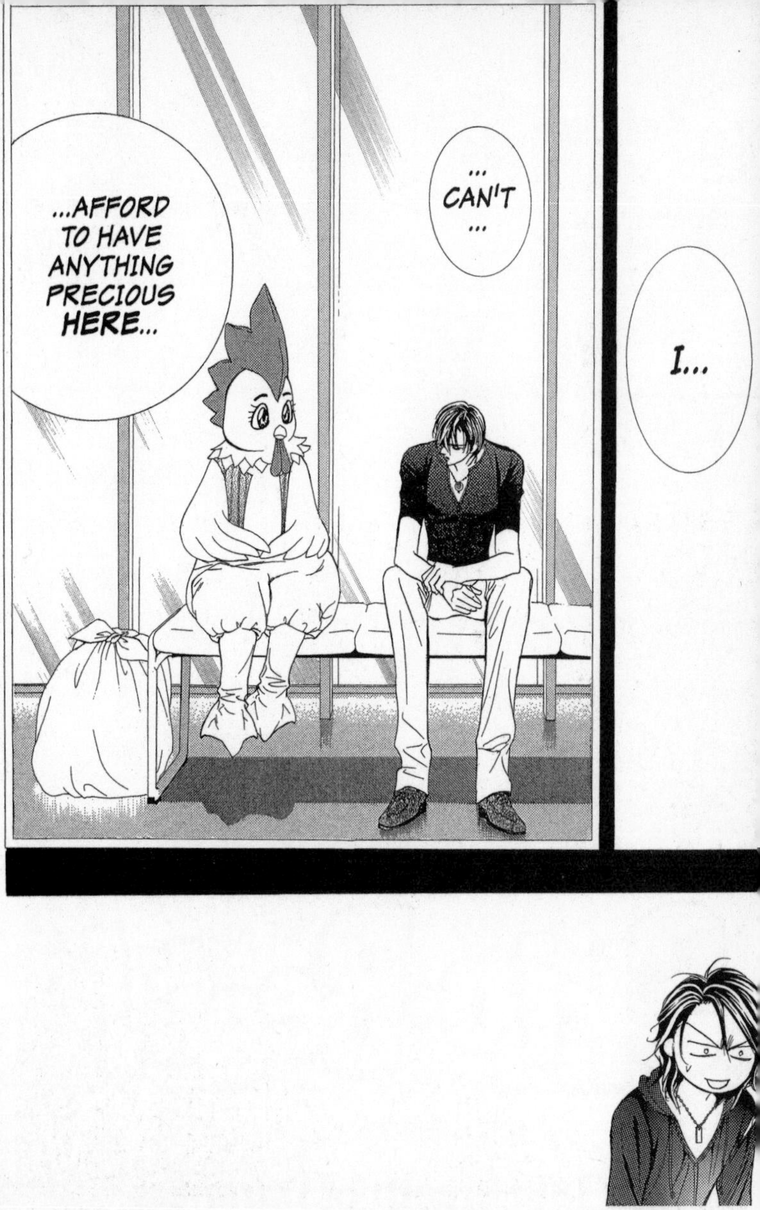
I...
...CAN'T...
...AFFORD TO HAVE ANYTHING PRECIOUS HERE...

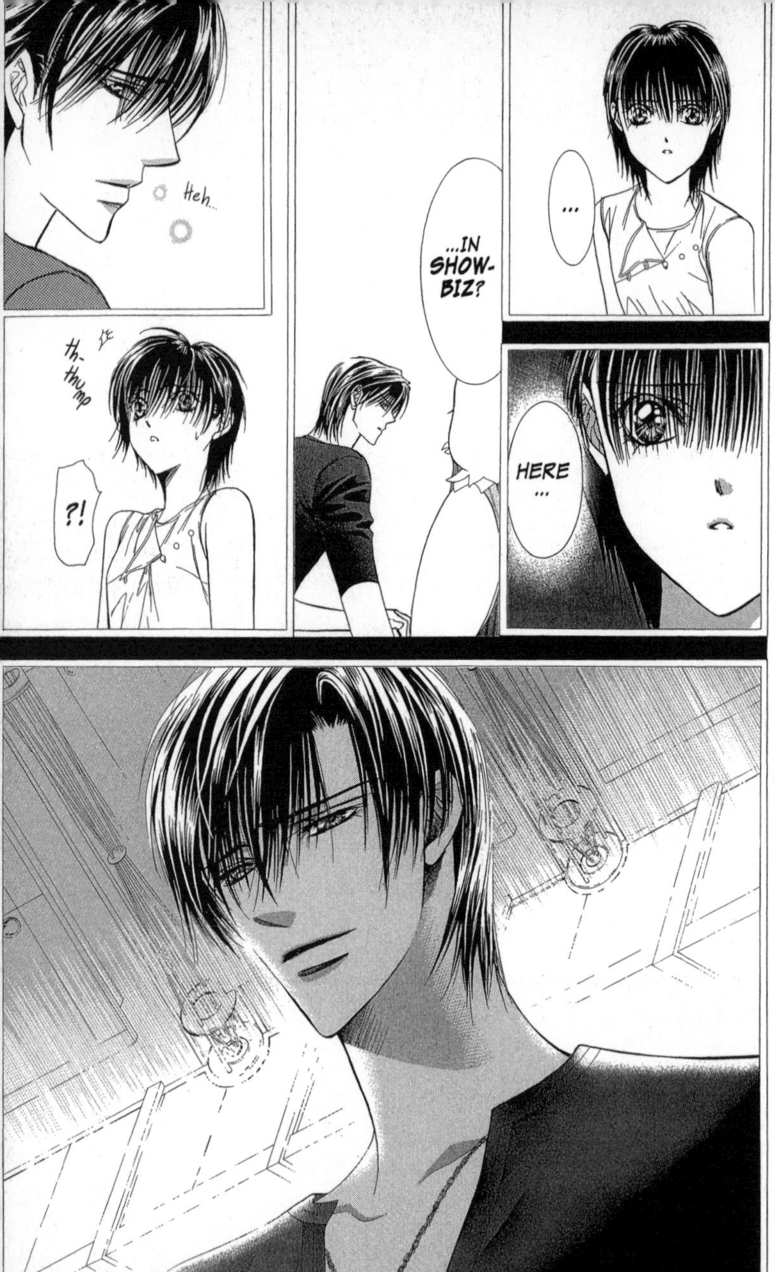
...
HERE ...
...IN SHOW-BIZ?
Heh...
Th-thump
?!

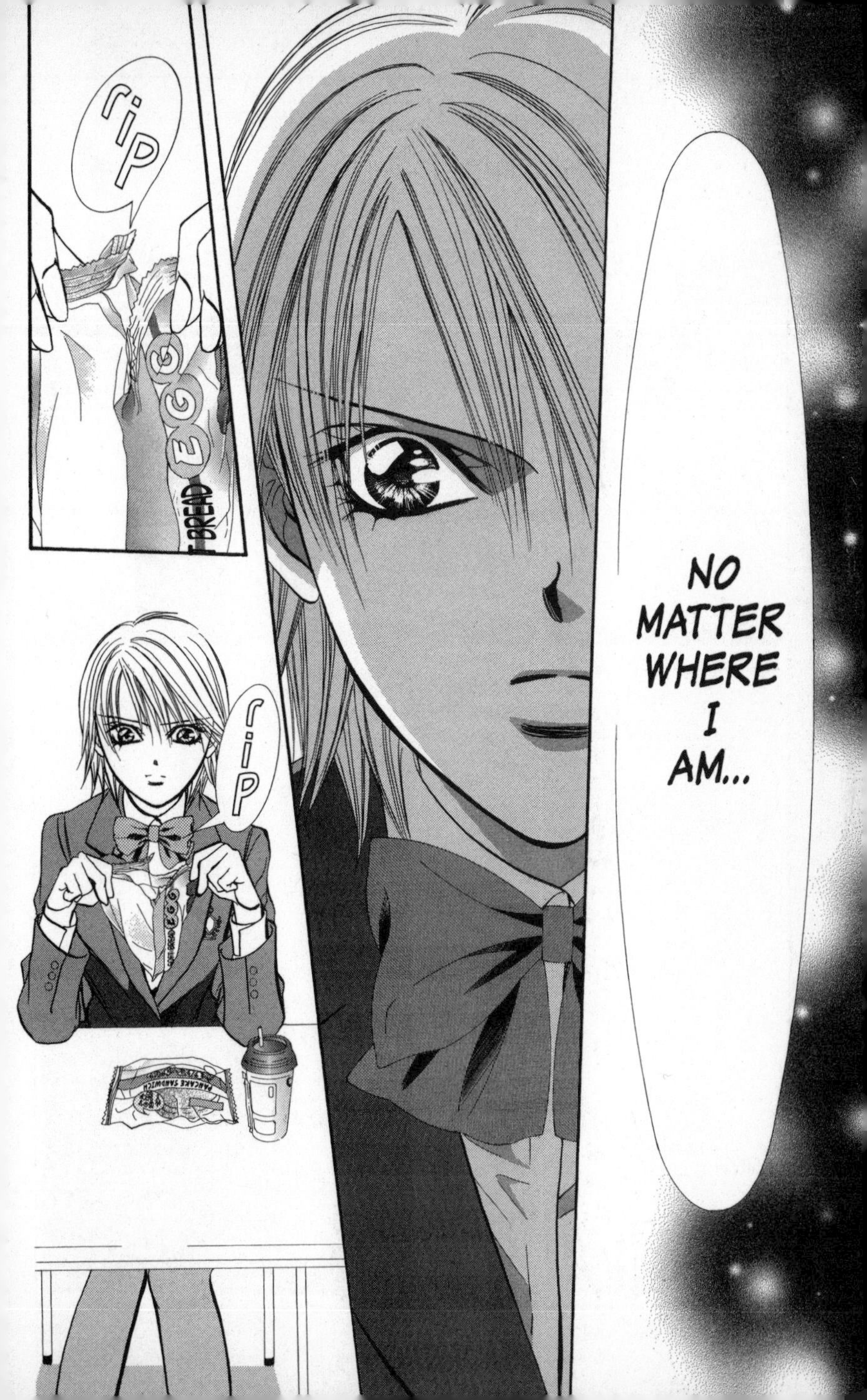
NO MATTER WHERE I AM...
rip
EGG
BREAD
rip

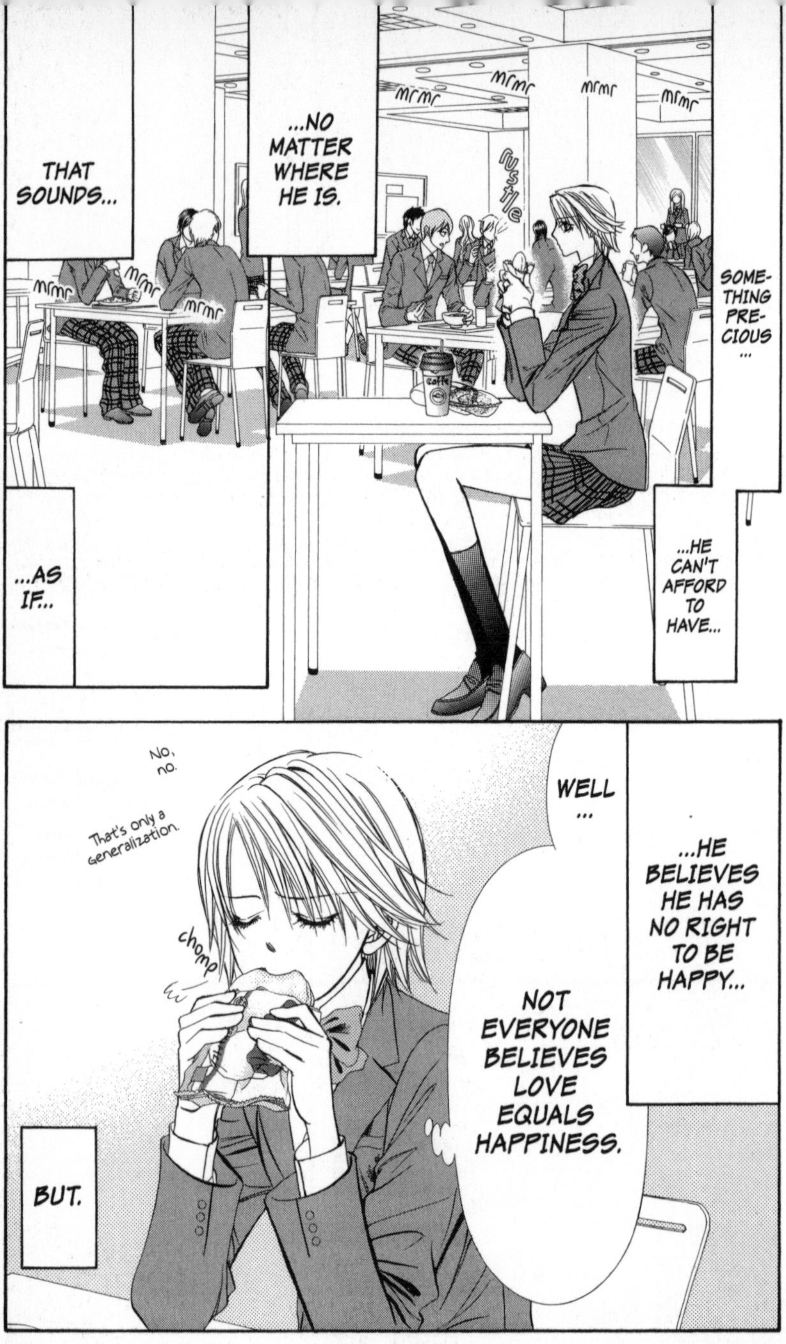
SOME-THING PRE-CIOUS...
...HE CAN'T AFFORD TO HAVE...
mrmr
mrmr
mrmr
rustle
...NO MATTER WHERE HE IS.
mrmr
THAT SOUNDS...
mrmr
mrmr
...AS IF...
...HE BELIEVES HE HAS NO RIGHT TO BE HAPPY...
WELL...
NOT EVERYONE BELIEVES LOVE EQUALS HAPPINESS.
No, no.
That's only a generalization.
chomp
BUT.

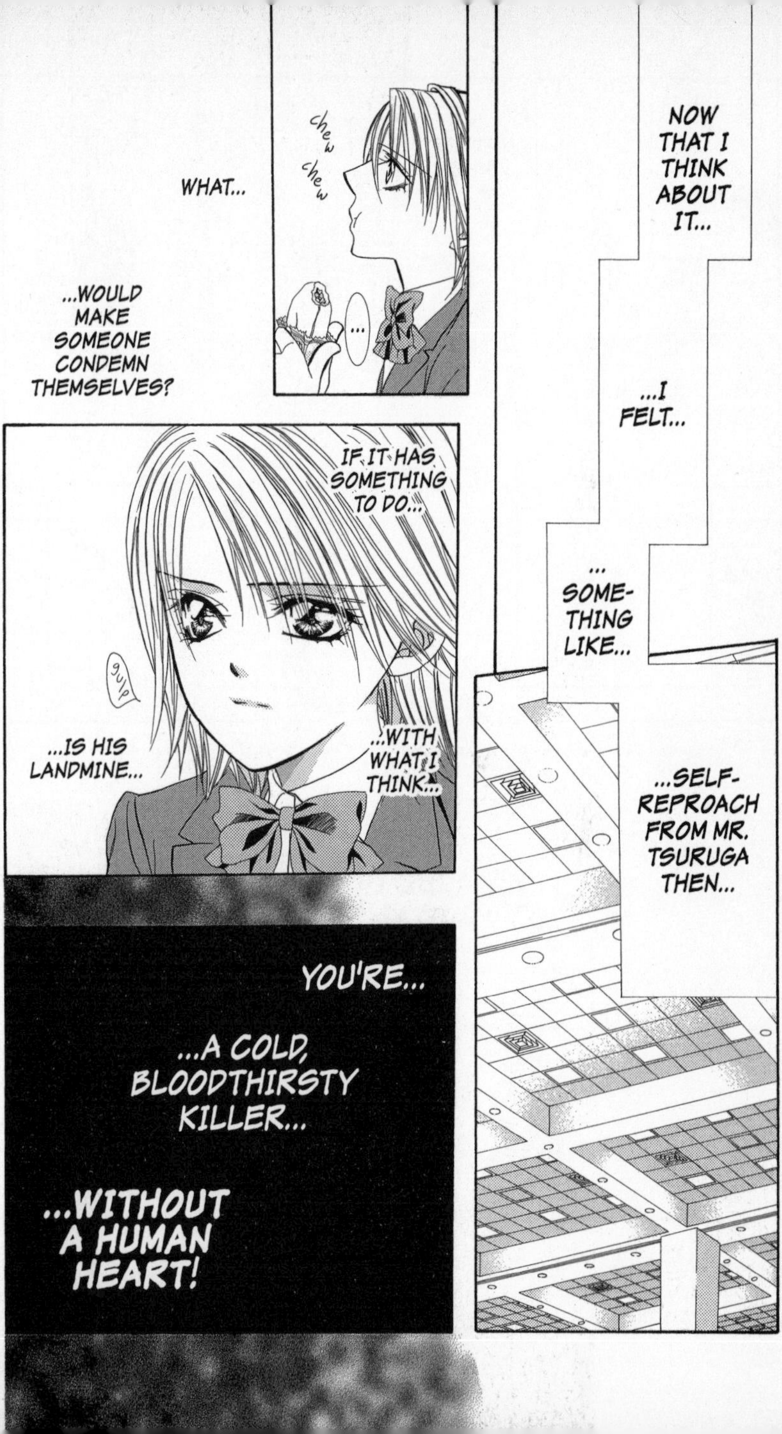
NOW THAT I THINK ABOUT IT...
...I FELT...
...SOMETHING-LIKE...
...SELF-REPROACH FROM MR. TSURUGA THEN...
chew chew
...
WHAT...
...WOULD MAKE SOMEONE CONDEMN THEMSELVES?
IF IT HAS SOMETHING TO DO...
...WITH WHAT I THINK...
gulp
...IS HIS LANDMINE...
YOU'RE...
...A COLD, BLOODTHIRSTY KILLER...
...WITHOUT A HUMAN HEART!

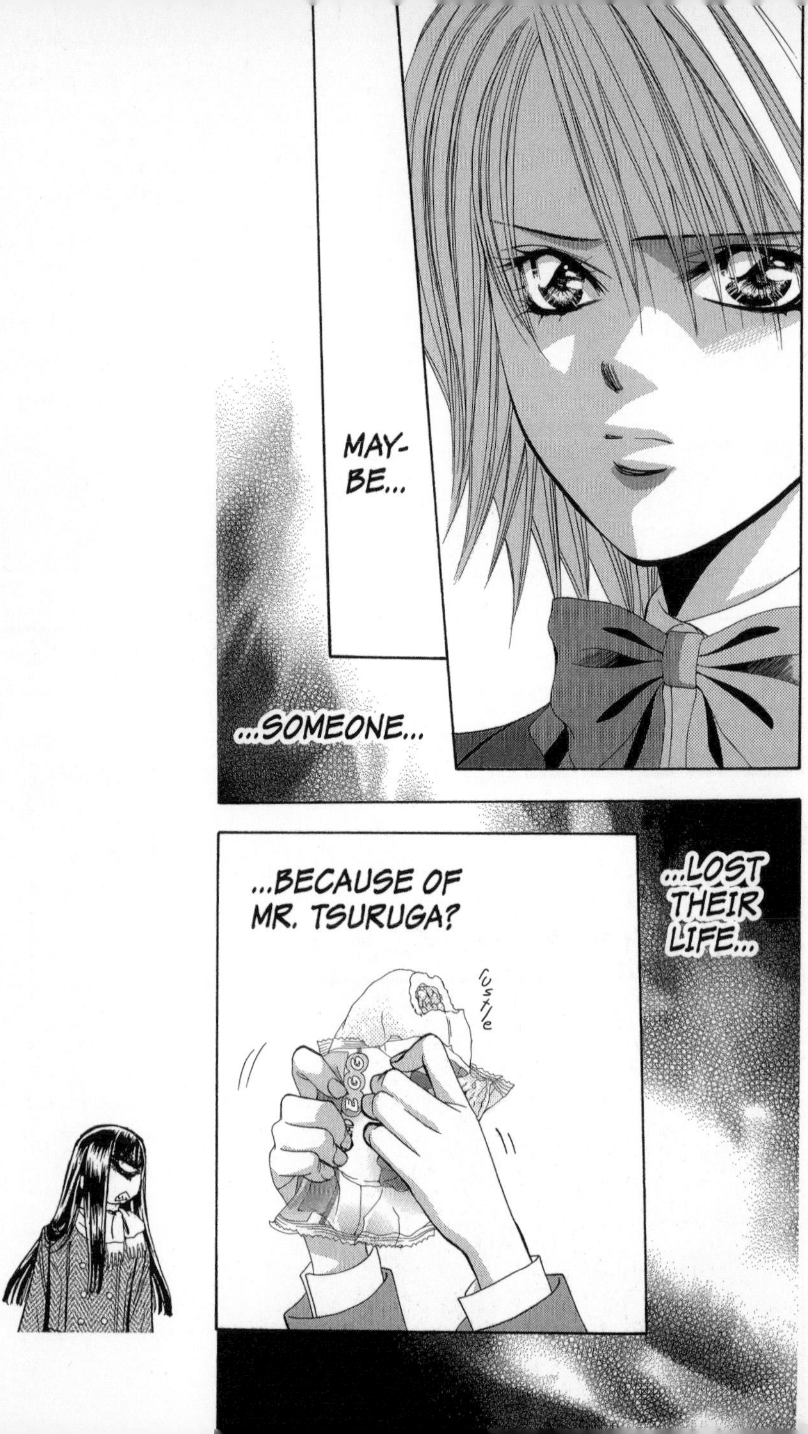
MAY-BE...
...SOMEONE...
...LOST THEIR LIFE...
...BECAUSE OF MR. TSURUGA?
rustle

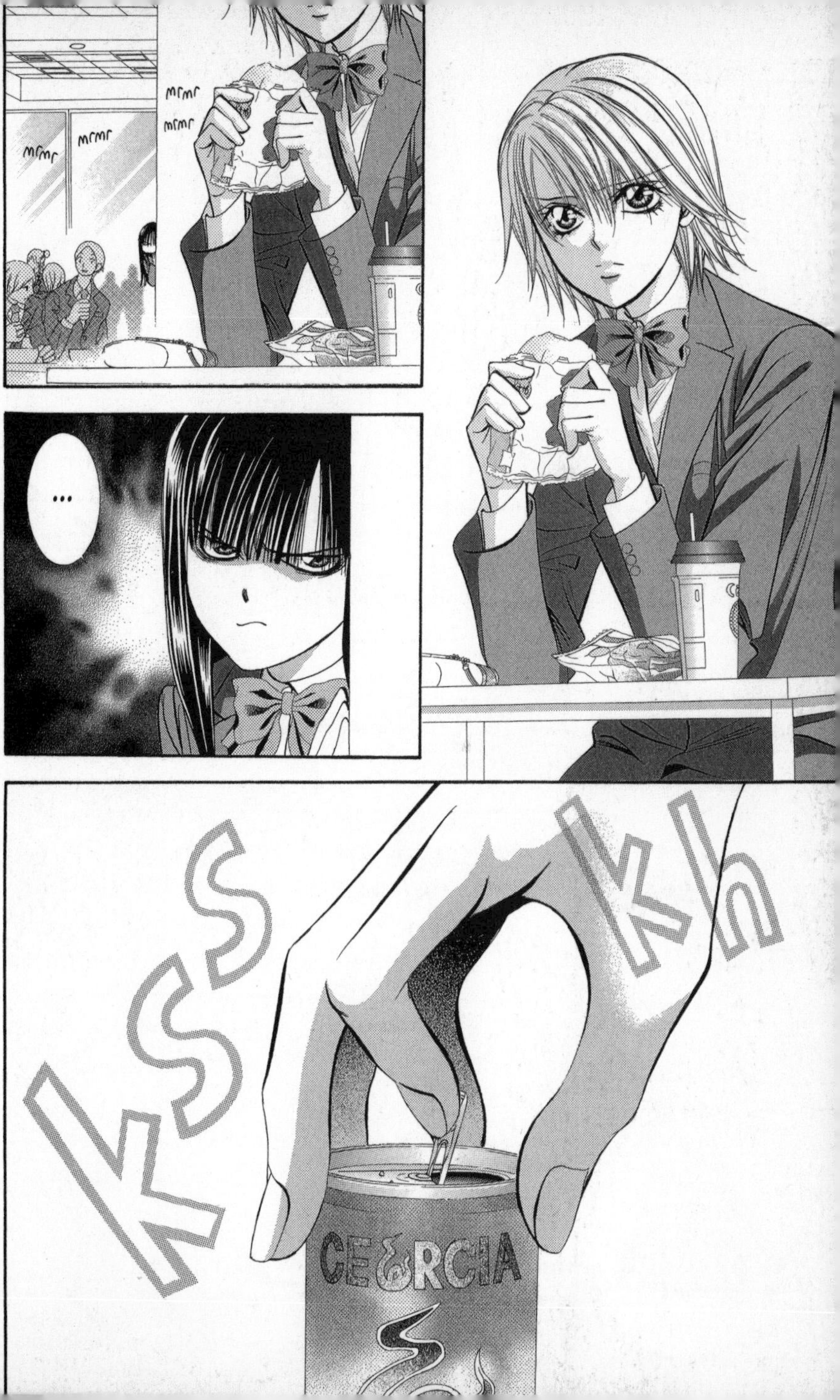
mrmr
mrmr
mrmr
mrmr
...
KSSKH

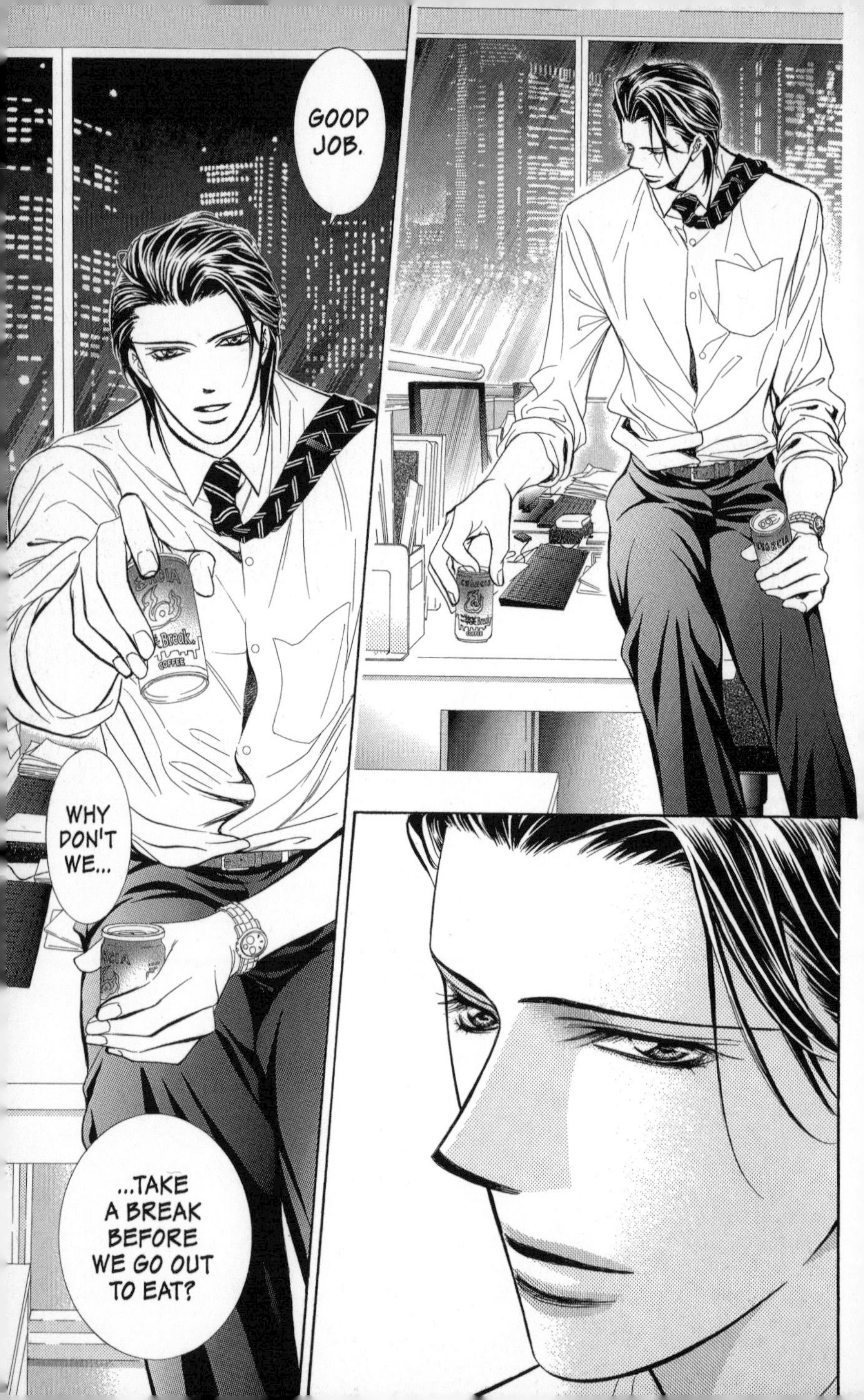
GOOD JOB.
WHY DON'T WE...
...TAKE A BREAK BEFORE WE GO OUT TO EAT?

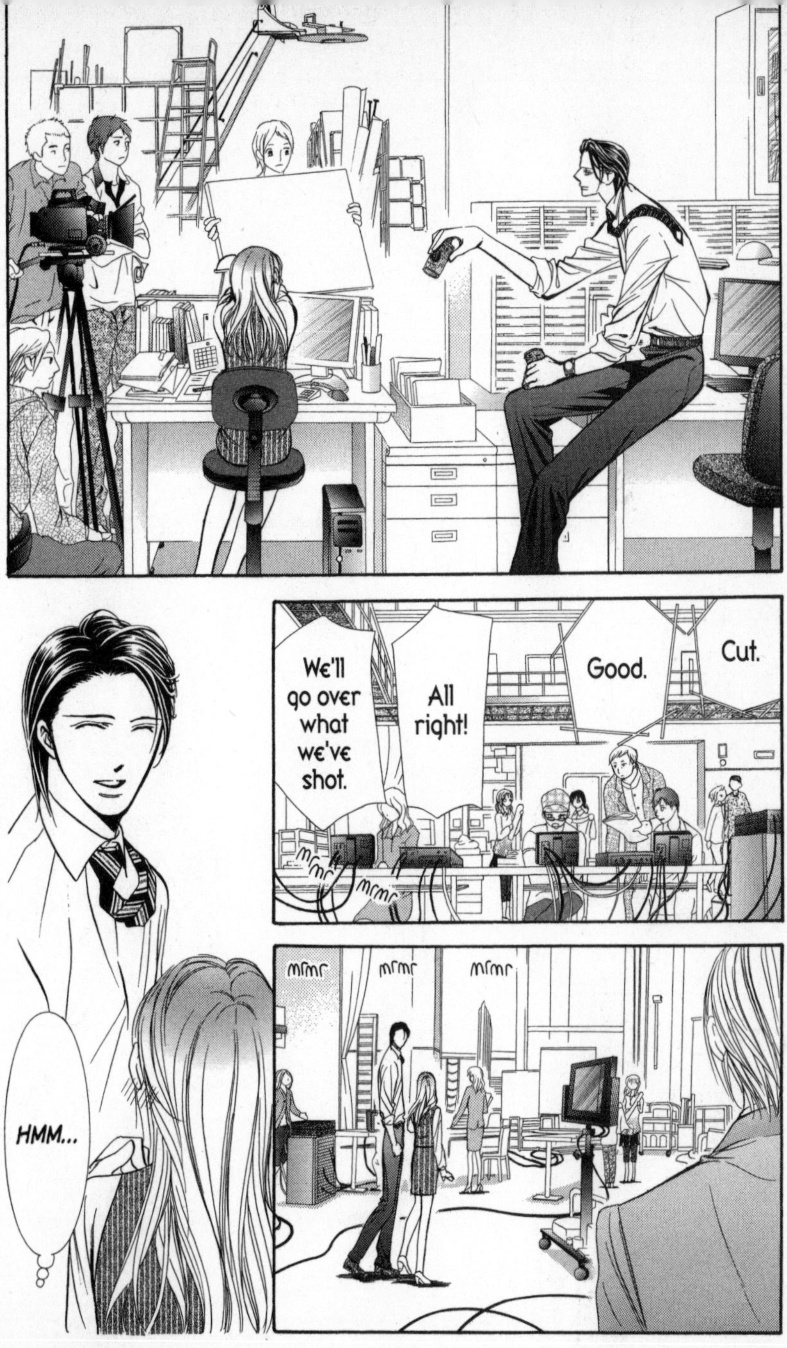
Cut.
Good.
All right!
We'll go over what we've shot.
mrmr
mrmr
mrmr
mrmr
mrmr
HMM...

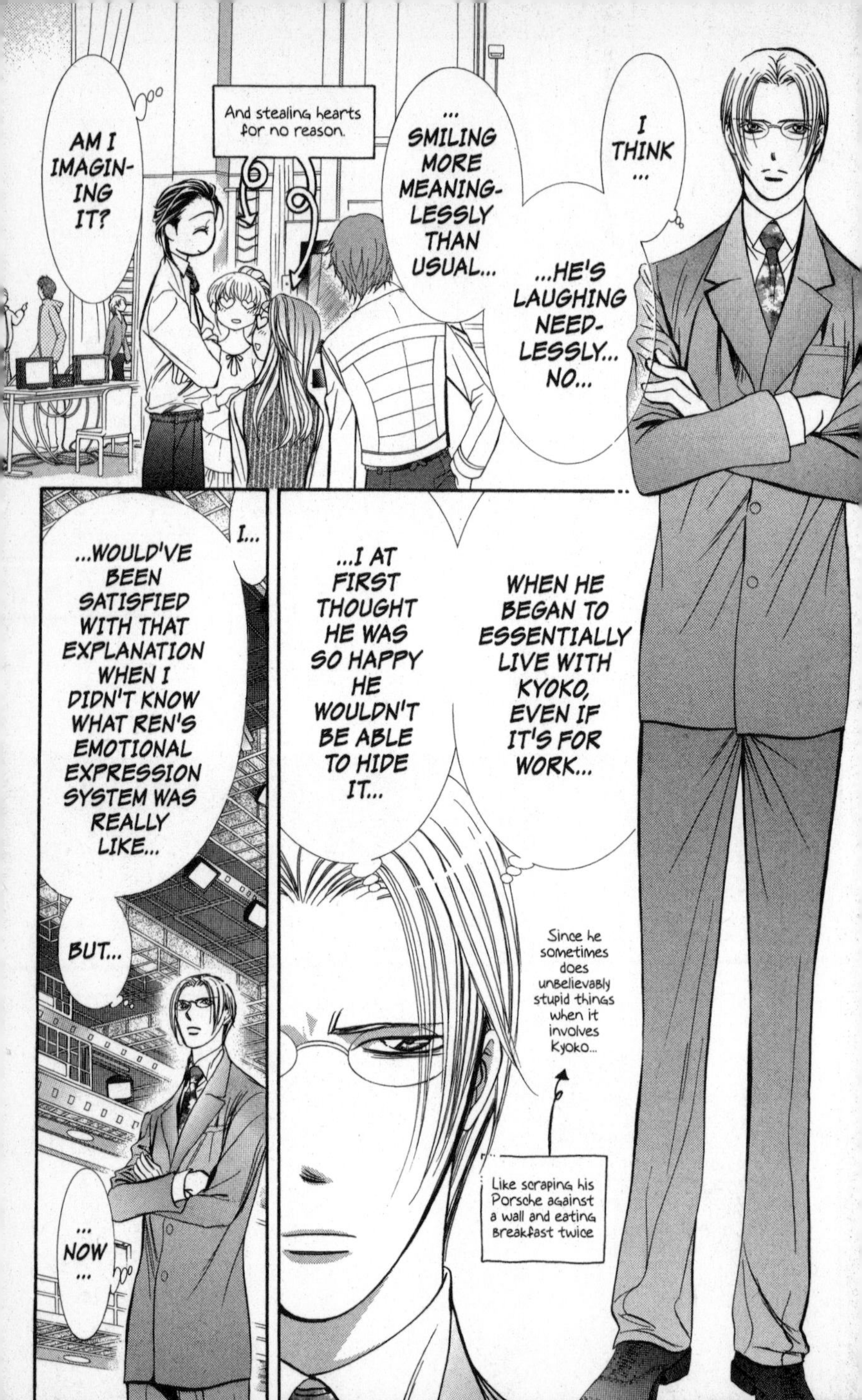
I THINK ...
...HE'S LAUGHING NEEDLESSLY... NO...
... SMILING MORE MEANINGLESSLY THAN USUAL...
And stealing hearts for no reason.
AM I IMAGINING IT?
WHEN HE BEGAN TO ESSENTIALLY LIVE WITH KYOKO, EVEN IF IT'S FOR WORK...
...I AT FIRST THOUGHT HE WAS SO HAPPY HE WOULDN'T BE ABLE TO HIDE IT...
Since he sometimes does unbelievably stupid things when it involves Kyoko...
Like scraping his Porsche against a wall and eating breakfast twice
I...
...WOULD'VE BEEN SATISFIED WITH THAT EXPLANATION WHEN I DIDN'T KNOW WHAT REN'S EMOTIONAL EXPRESSION SYSTEM WAS REALLY LIKE...
BUT...
... NOW ...

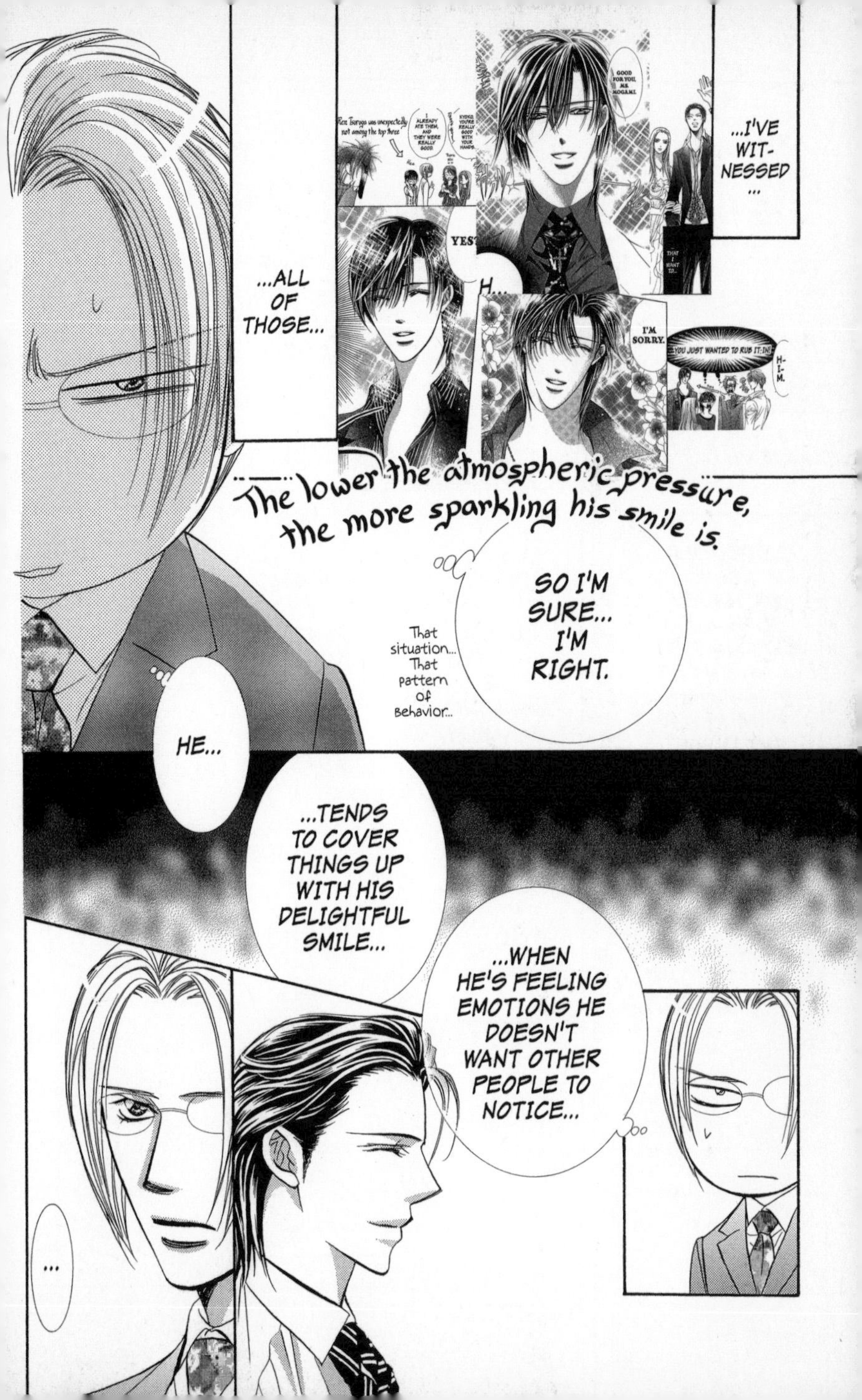
...I'VE WIT-NESSED...
GOOD FOR YOU, MS. MOGAMI.
THAT I WANT TO...
KYOKO, YOU'RE REALLY GOOD WITH YOUR HANDS.
I ALREADY ATE THEM, AND THEY WERE REALLY GOOD.
Ren Tsuruga was unexpectedly not among the top three
YES!
H...
H-I-M.
YOU JUST WANTED TO RUB IT IN!
I'M SORRY.
...ALL OF THOSE...
The lower the atmospheric pressure, the more sparkling his smile is.
SO I'M SURE... I'M RIGHT.
That situation... That pattern of Behavior...
HE...
...TENDS TO COVER THINGS UP WITH HIS DELIGHTFUL SMILE...
...WHEN HE'S FEELING EMOTIONS HE DOESN'T WANT OTHER PEOPLE TO NOTICE...
...

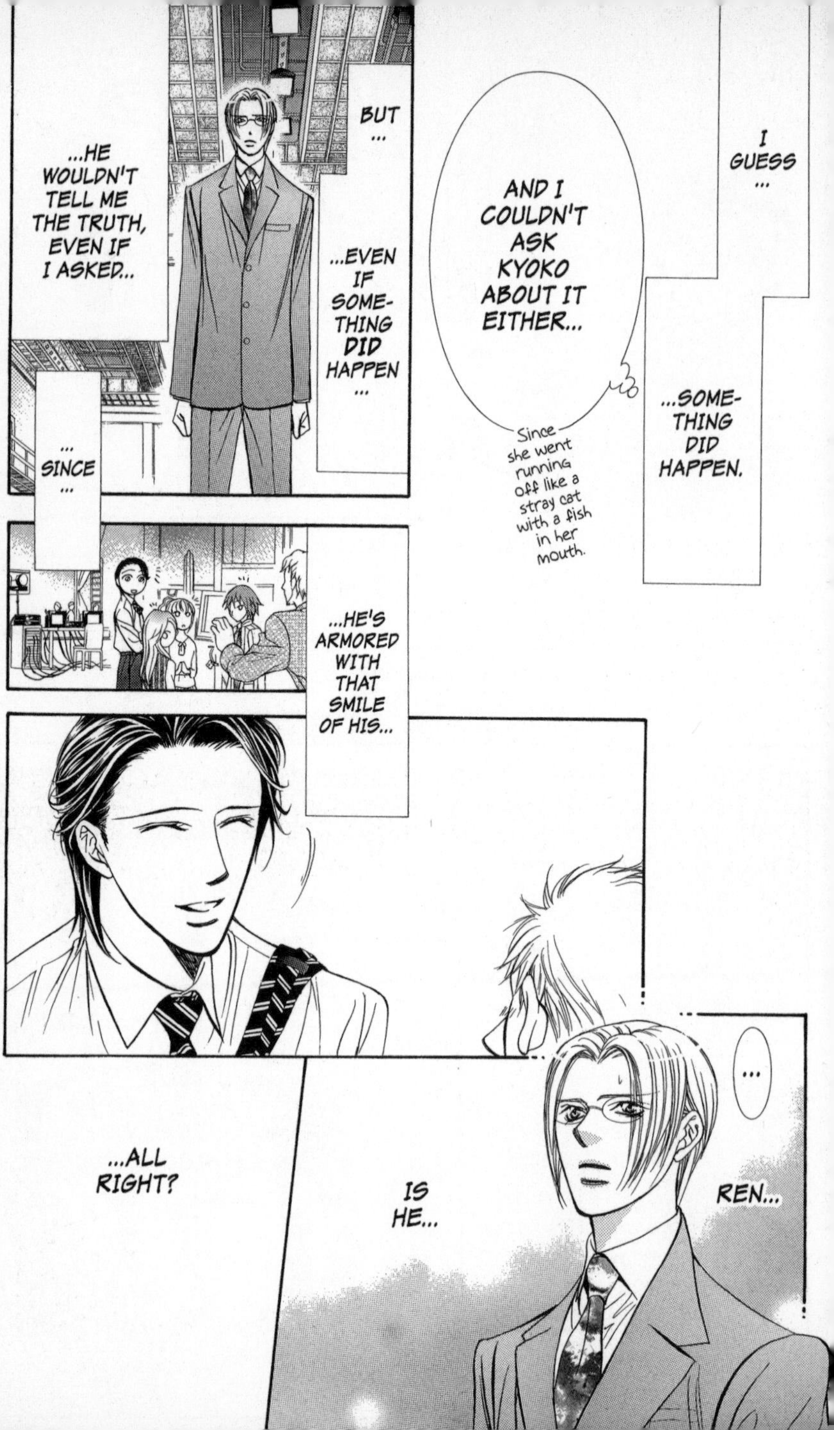
I GUESS...
...SOMETHING DID HAPPEN.
AND I COULDN'T ASK KYOKO ABOUT IT EITHER...
Since she went running off like a stray cat with a fish in her mouth.
BUT...
...EVEN IF SOMETHING DID HAPPEN...
...HE WOULDN'T TELL ME THE TRUTH, EVEN IF I ASKED...
...SINCE...
...HE'S ARMORED WITH THAT SMILE OF HIS...
...
REN...
IS HE...
...ALL RIGHT?

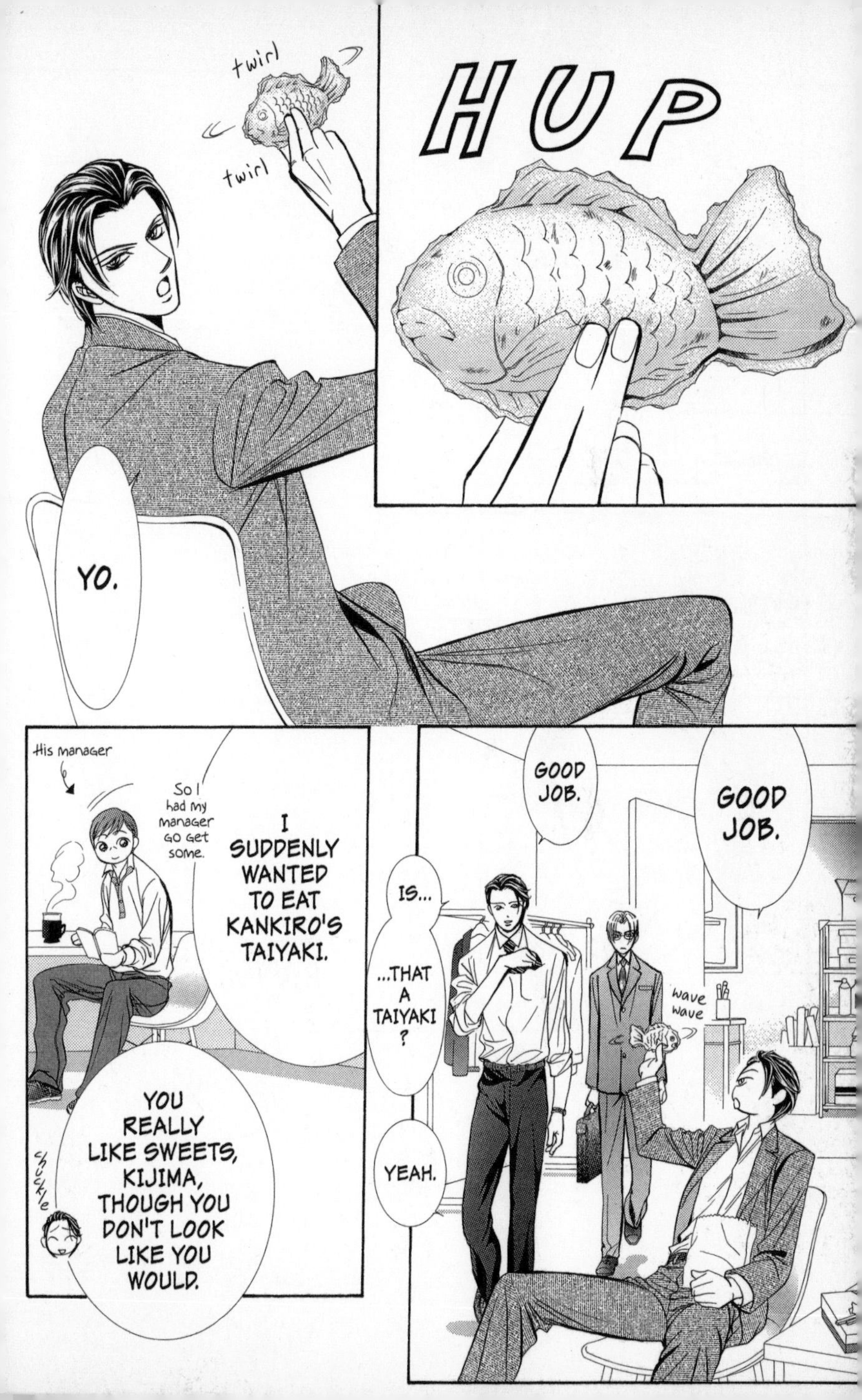
HUP
twirl
twirl
YO.
GOOD JOB.
GOOD JOB.
IS...
...THAT A TAIYAKI?
wave wave
YEAH.
I SUDDENLY WANTED TO EAT KANKIRO'S TAIYAKI.
So I had my manager go get some.
His manager
YOU REALLY LIKE SWEETS, KIJIMA, THOUGH YOU DON'T LOOK LIKE YOU WOULD.
chuckle

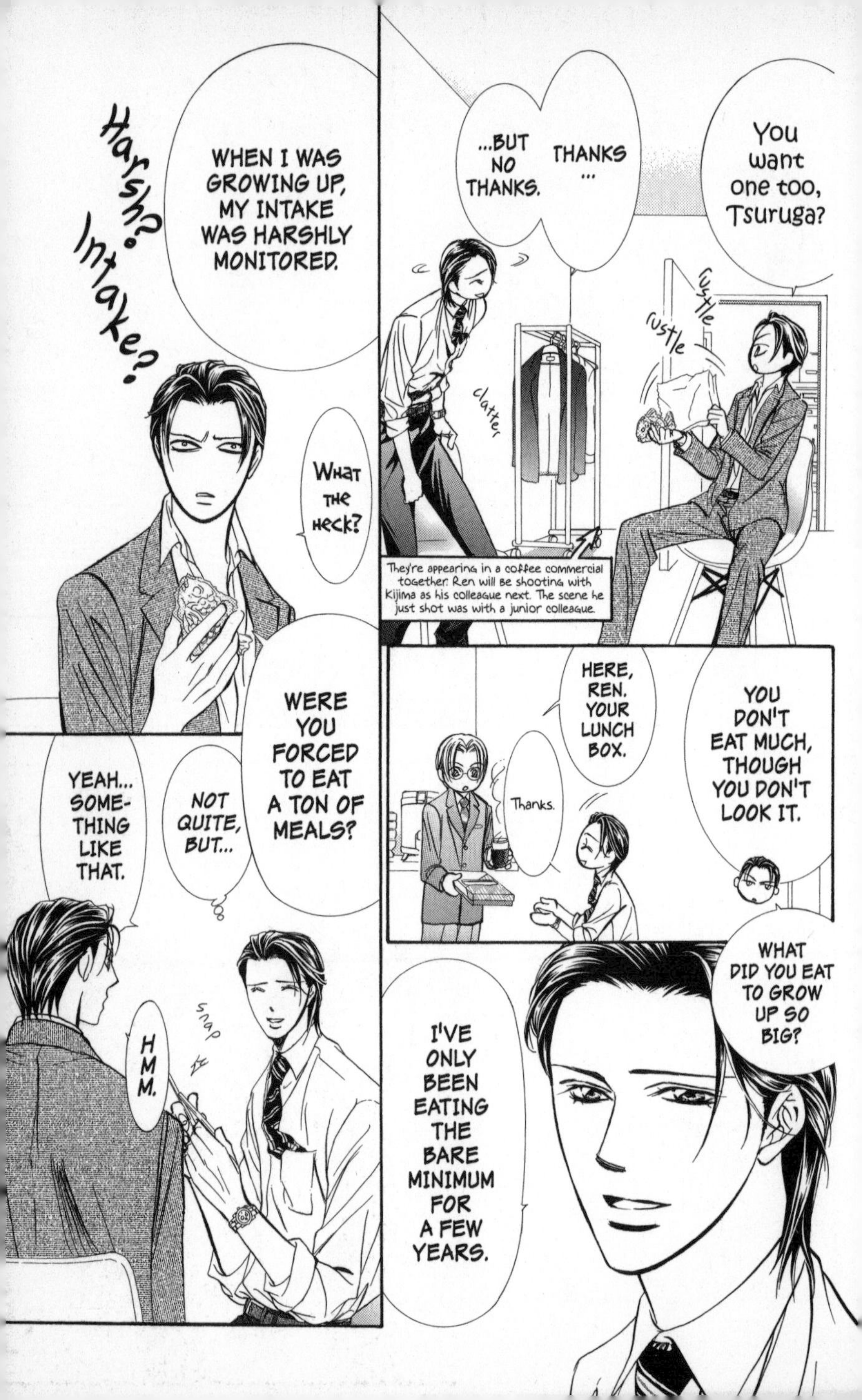
You want one too, Tsuruga?
THANKS ...
...BUT NO THANKS.
rustle
rustle
clatter
They're appearing in a coffee commercial together. Ren will be shooting with Kijima as his colleague next. The scene he just shot was with a junior colleague.
YOU DON'T EAT MUCH, THOUGH YOU DON'T LOOK IT.
HERE, REN. YOUR LUNCH BOX.
Thanks.
WHAT DID YOU EAT TO GROW UP SO BIG?
I'VE ONLY BEEN EATING THE BARE MINIMUM FOR A FEW YEARS.
WHEN I WAS GROWING UP, MY INTAKE WAS HARSHLY MONITORED.
Harsh? Intake?
What the heck?
WERE YOU FORCED TO EAT A TON OF MEALS?
NOT QUITE, BUT...
YEAH... SOMETHING LIKE THAT.
HMM.
snap

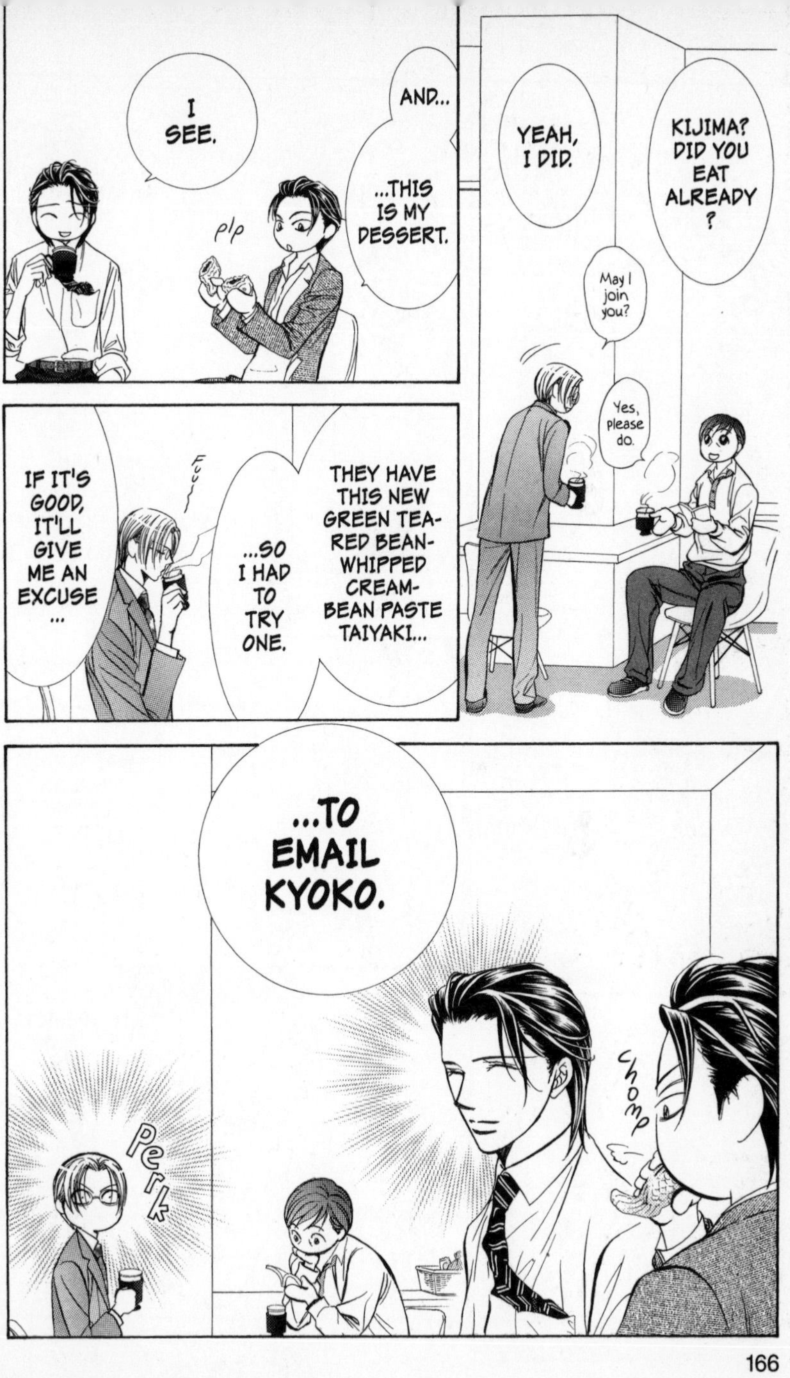
KIJIMA? DID YOU EAT ALREADY?
YEAH, I DID.
May I join you?
Yes, please do.
AND...
...THIS IS MY DESSERT.
plp
I SEE.
THEY HAVE THIS NEW GREEN TEA-RED BEAN-WHIPPED CREAM-BEAN PASTE TAIYAKI...
...SO I HAD TO TRY ONE.
IF IT'S GOOD, IT'LL GIVE ME AN EXCUSE...
...TO EMAIL KYOKO.
Chomp
Perk

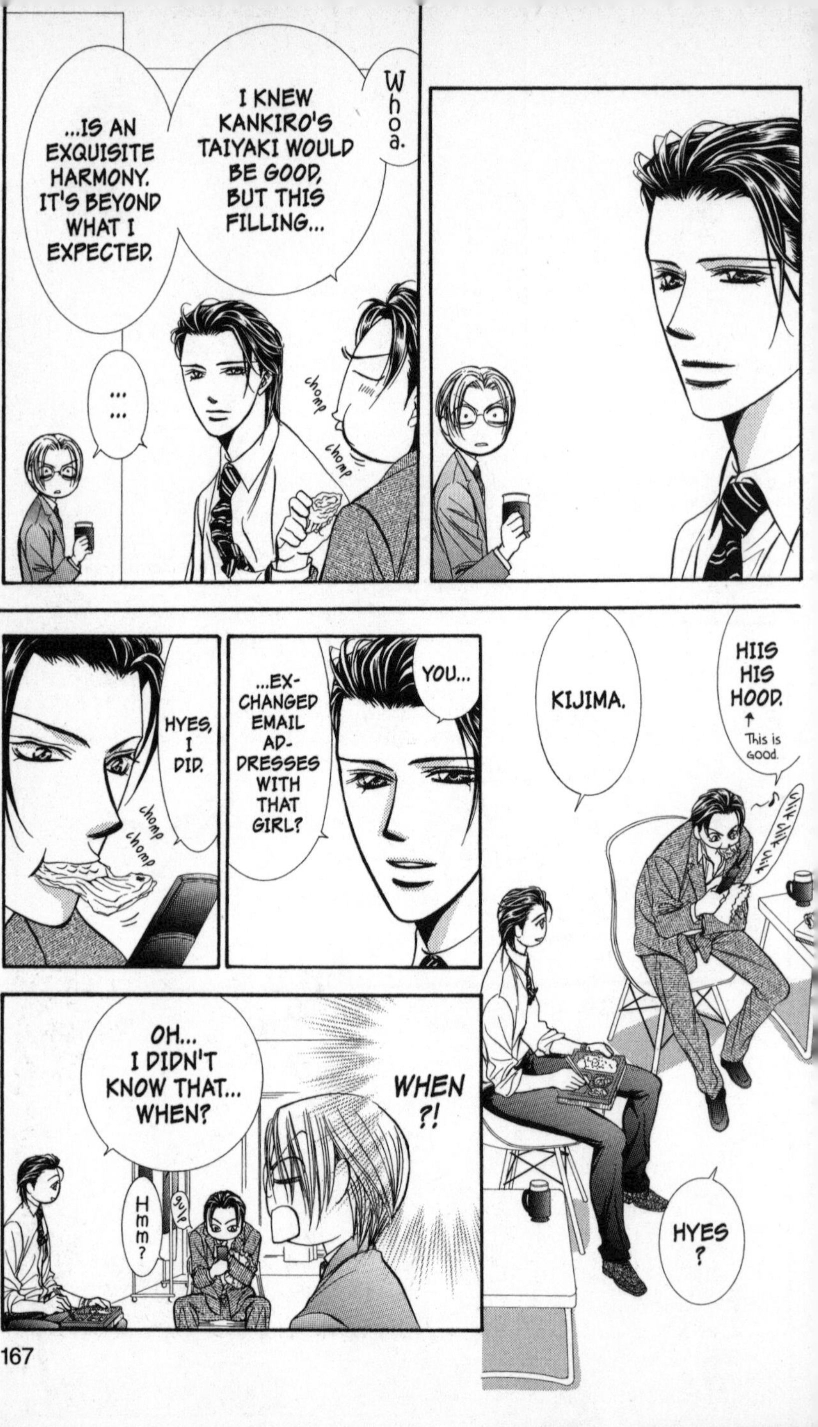
Whoa.
I KNEW KANKIRO'S TAIYAKI WOULD BE GOOD, BUT THIS FILLING...
...IS AN EXQUISITE HARMONY. IT'S BEYOND WHAT I EXPECTED.
chomp chomp
......
HIIS HIS HOOD.
This is good.
KIJIMA.
HYES?
YOU...
...EX-CHANGED EMAIL AD-DRESSES WITH THAT GIRL?
HYES, I DID.
chomp chomp
WHEN?!
OH... I DIDN'T KNOW THAT... WHEN?
gulp
Hmm?

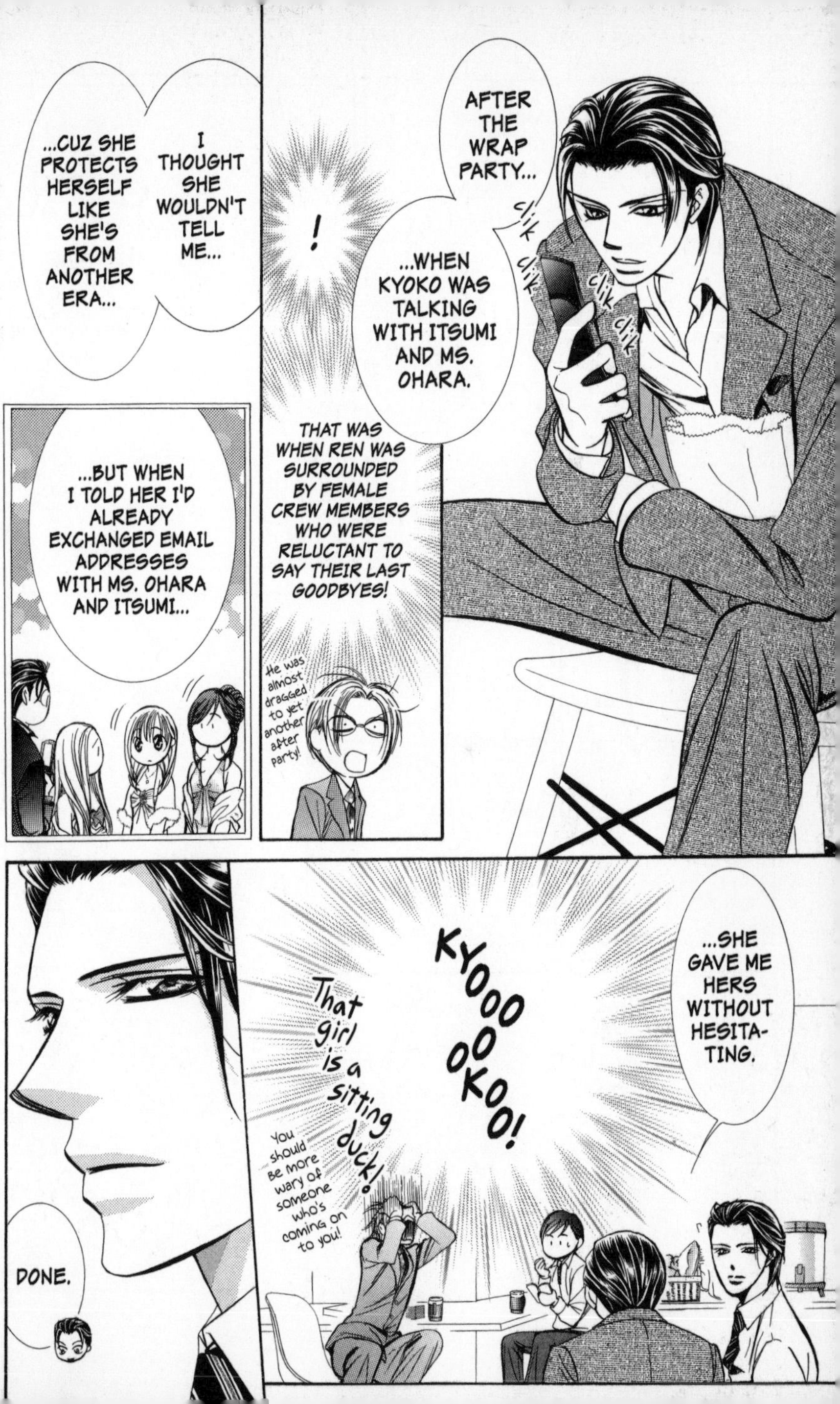
AFTER THE WRAP PARTY...
clik clik clik clik
...WHEN KYOKO WAS TALKING WITH ITSUMI AND MS. OHARA.
!
THAT WAS WHEN REN WAS SURROUNDED BY FEMALE CREW MEMBERS WHO WERE RELUCTANT TO SAY THEIR LAST GOODBYES!
He was almost dragged to yet another after party!
I THOUGHT SHE WOULDN'T TELL ME...
...CUZ SHE PROTECTS HERSELF LIKE SHE'S FROM ANOTHER ERA...
...BUT WHEN I TOLD HER I'D ALREADY EXCHANGED EMAIL ADDRESSES WITH MS. OHARA AND ITSUMI...
...SHE GAVE ME HERS WITHOUT HESITA-TING.
KYOOOOOOKOO!
That girl is a sitting duck!
You should be more wary of someone who's coming on to you!
DONE.

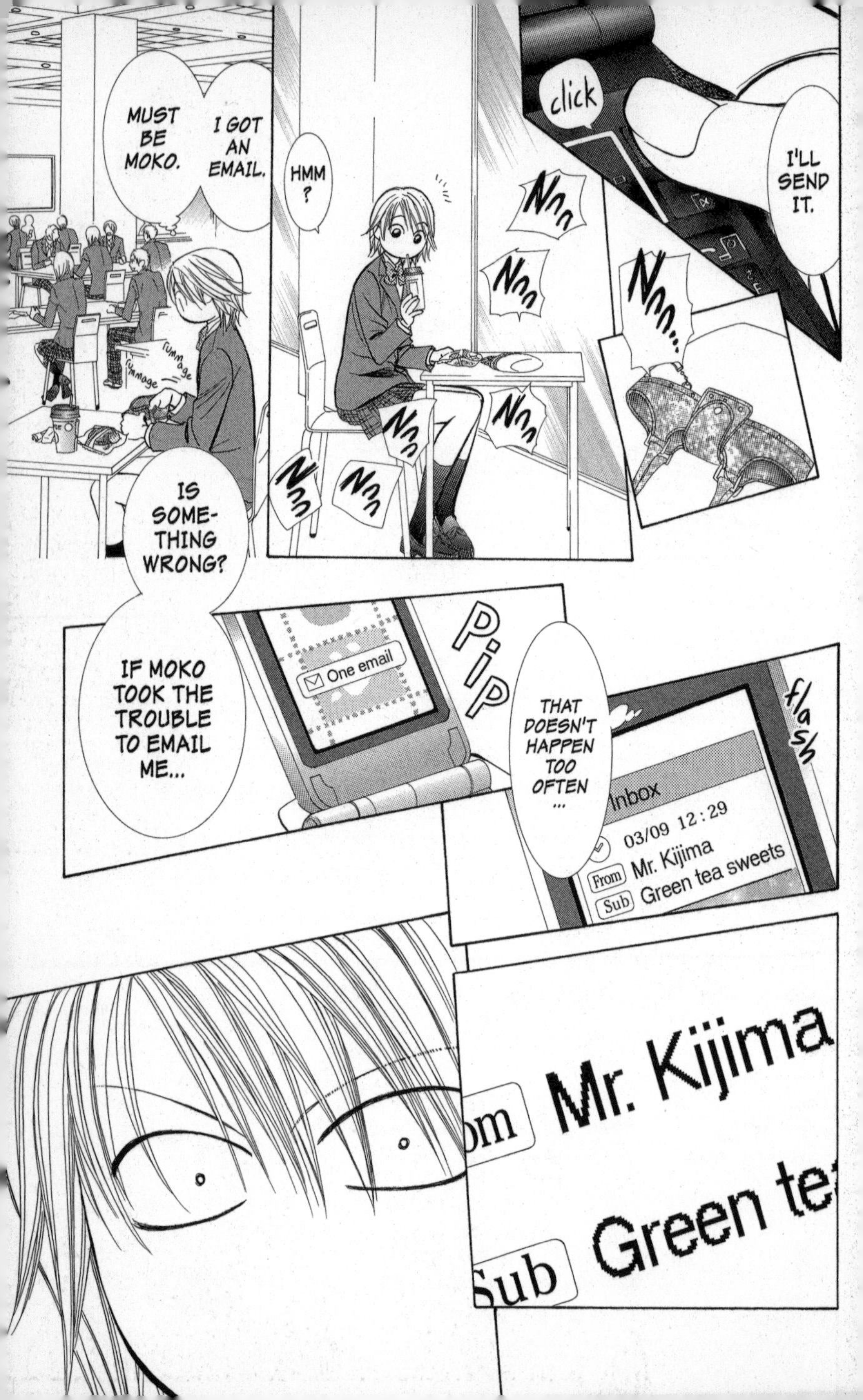
click
I'LL SEND IT.
Nnn...
HMM ?
Nnn
Nnn
Nnn
Nnn
Nnn
Nnn
I GOT AN EMAIL.
MUST BE MOKO.
rummage
rummage
IS SOMETHING WRONG?
Pip
One email
IF MOKO TOOK THE TROUBLE TO EMAIL ME...
flash
THAT DOESN'T HAPPEN TOO OFTEN ...
Inbox
03/09 12 : 29
From Mr. Kijima
Sub Green tea sweets
om Mr. Kijima
Sub Green te

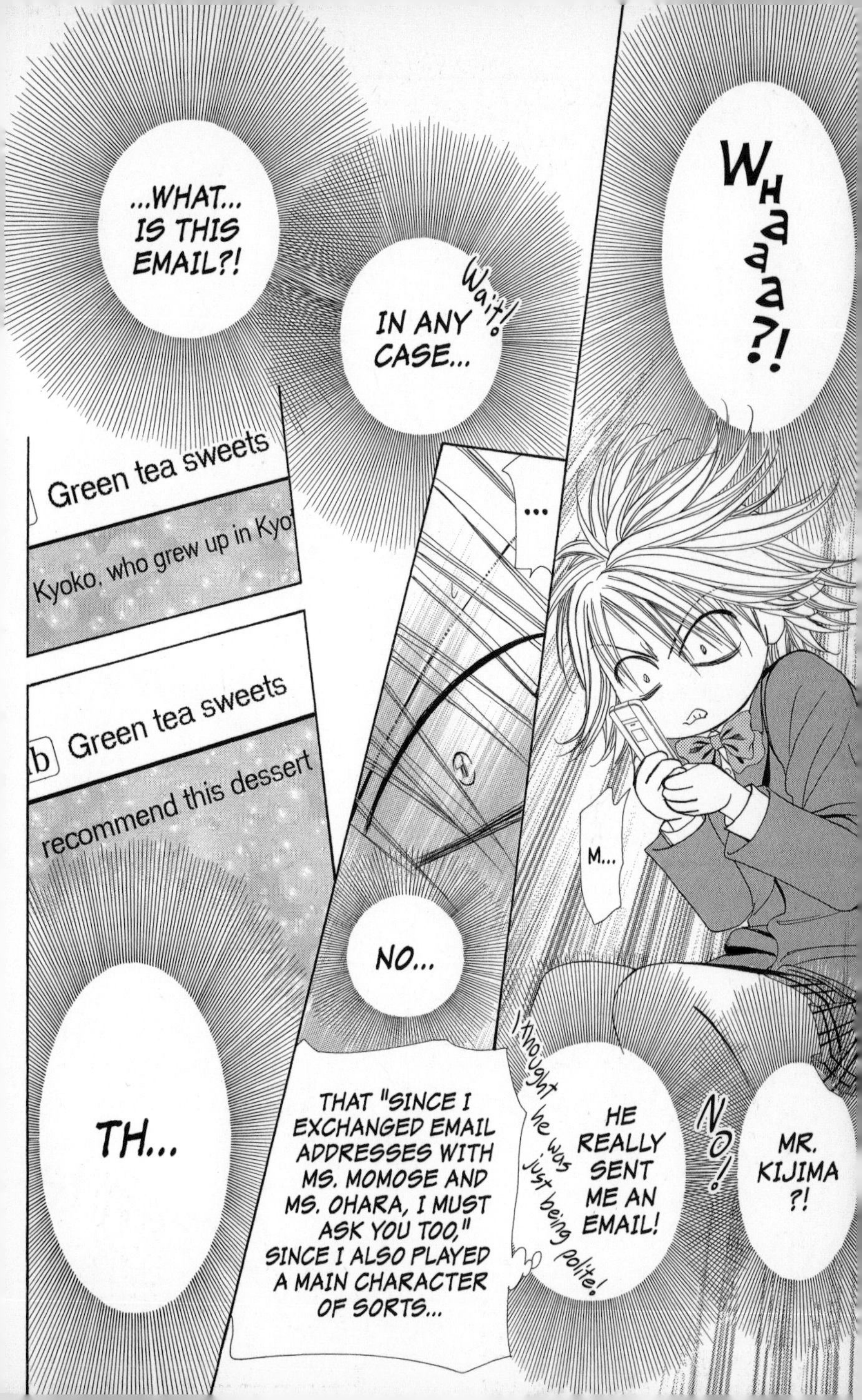
Whaaaa?!
M...
MR. KIJIMA?!
NO!
HE REALLY SENT ME AN EMAIL!
I thought he was just being polite!
...
NO...
THAT "SINCE I EXCHANGED EMAIL ADDRESSES WITH MS. MOMOSE AND MS. OHARA, I MUST ASK YOU TOO," SINCE I ALSO PLAYED A MAIN CHARACTER OF SORTS...
...WHAT... IS THIS EMAIL?!
Wait!
IN ANY CASE...
Green tea sweets
Kyoko, who grew up in Kyo
Green tea sweets
recommend this dessert
TH...

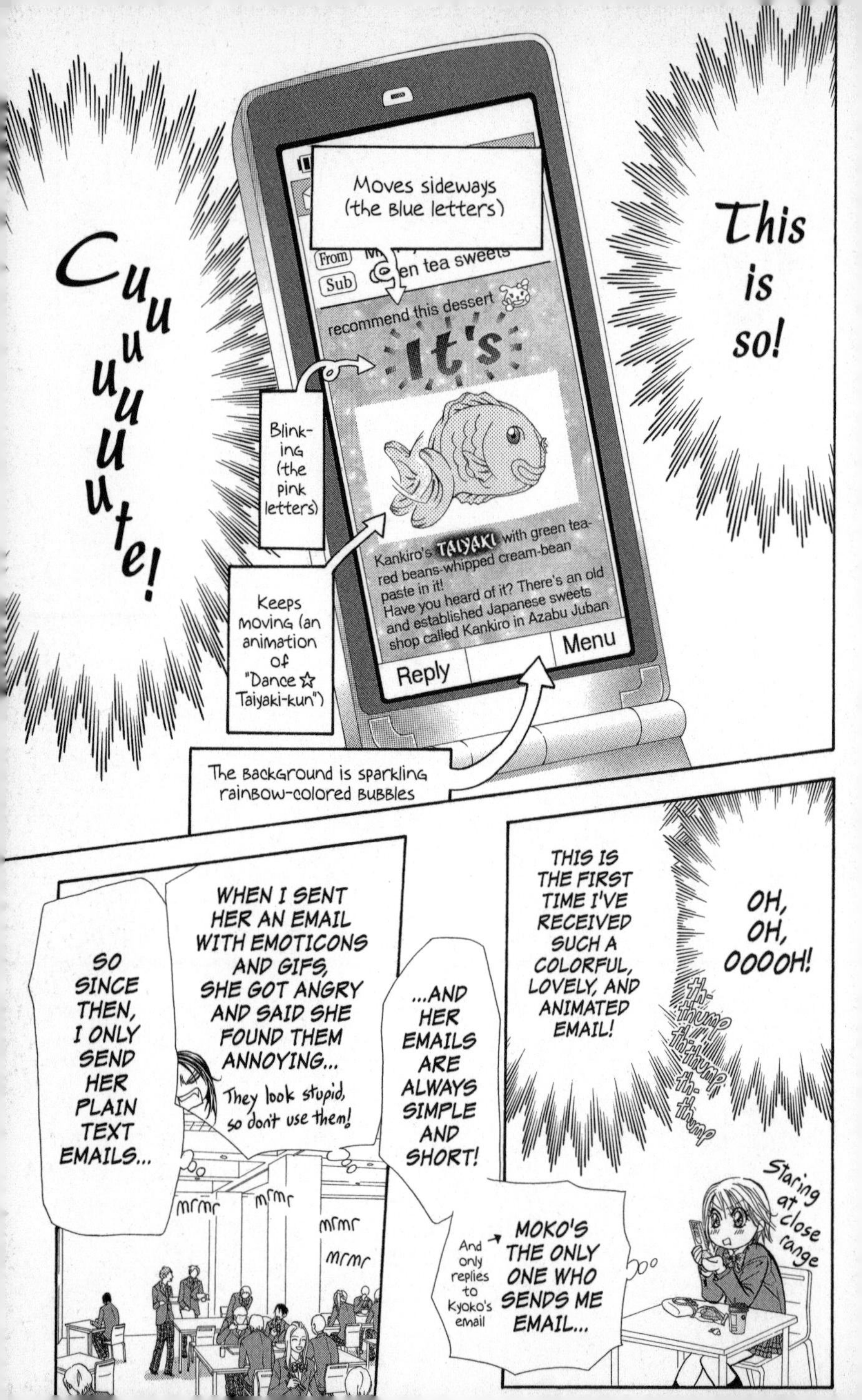
This is so!
Moves sideways (the Blue letters)
From
Sub
recommend this dessert
It's
Blink-ing (the pink letters)
Kankiro's TAIYAKI with green tea-red beans-whipped cream-bean paste in it!
Have you heard of it? There's an old and established Japanese sweets shop called Kankiro in Azabu Juban
Menu
Reply
Keeps moving (an animation of "Dance ☆ Taiyaki-kun")
Cuuuuuuute!
The Background is sparkling rainbow-colored Bubbles
OH, OH, OOOOH!
THIS IS THE FIRST TIME I'VE RECEIVED SUCH A COLORFUL, LOVELY, AND ANIMATED EMAIL!
th-thump th-thump th-thump
Staring at close range
MOKO'S THE ONLY ONE WHO SENDS ME EMAIL...
And only replies to Kyoko's email
...AND HER EMAILS ARE ALWAYS SIMPLE AND SHORT!
WHEN I SENT HER AN EMAIL WITH EMOTICONS AND GIFS, SHE GOT ANGRY AND SAID SHE FOUND THEM ANNOYING...
They look stupid, so don't use them!
SO SINCE THEN, I ONLY SEND HER PLAIN TEXT EMAILS...
mrmr
mrmr
mrmr
mrmr

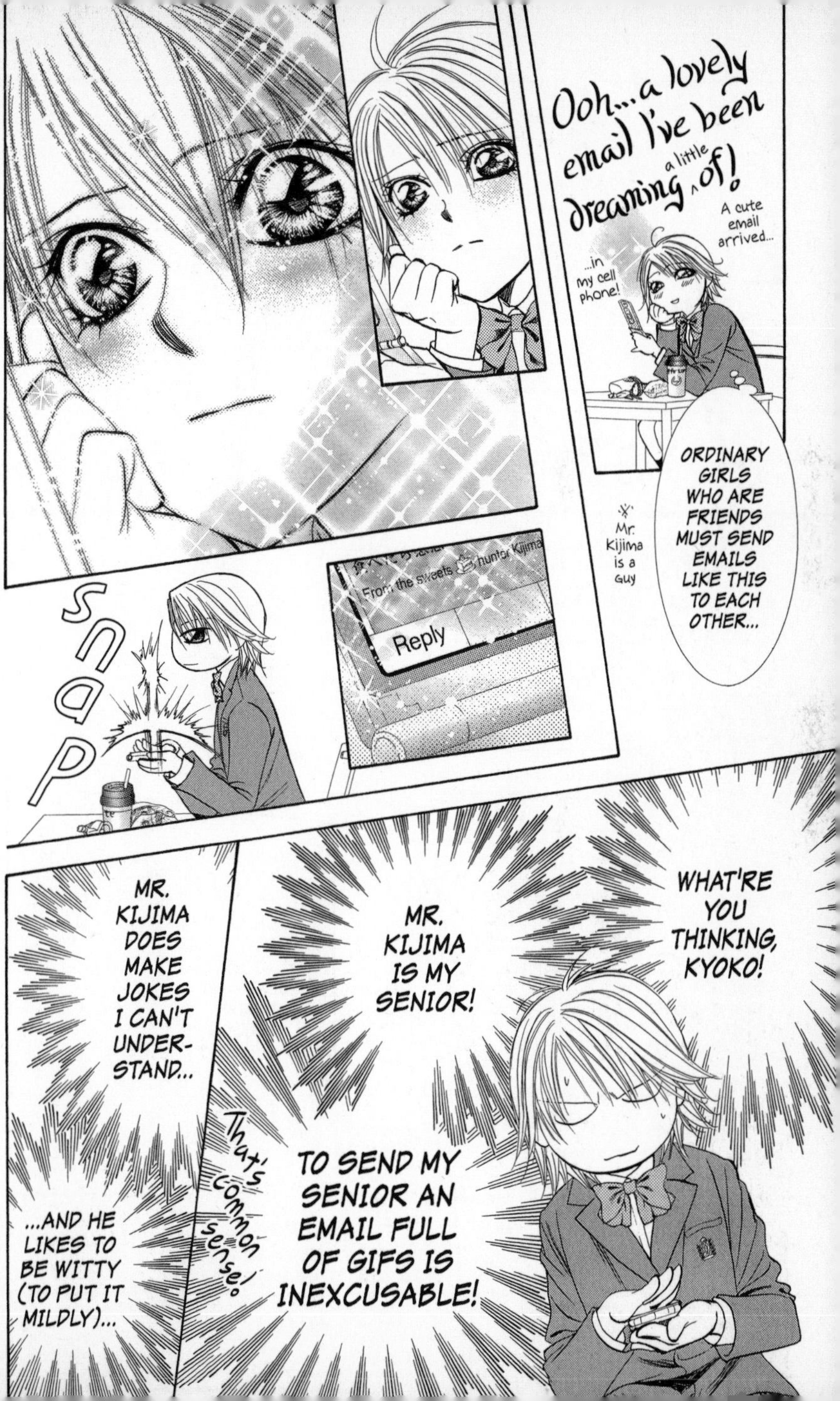

Ooh...a lovely email I've been dreaming a little of!
A cute email arrived...
...in my cell phone!
ORDINARY GIRLS WHO ARE FRIENDS MUST SEND EMAILS LIKE THIS TO EACH OTHER...
※Mr. Kijima is a Guy
From the sweets hunter Kijima
Reply
snap
WHAT'RE YOU THINKING, KYOKO!
MR. KIJIMA IS MY SENIOR!
TO SEND MY SENIOR AN EMAIL FULL OF GIFS IS INEXCUSABLE!
That's common sense!
MR. KIJIMA DOES MAKE JOKES I CAN'T UNDER-STAND...
...AND HE LIKES TO BE WITTY (TO PUT IT MILDLY)...

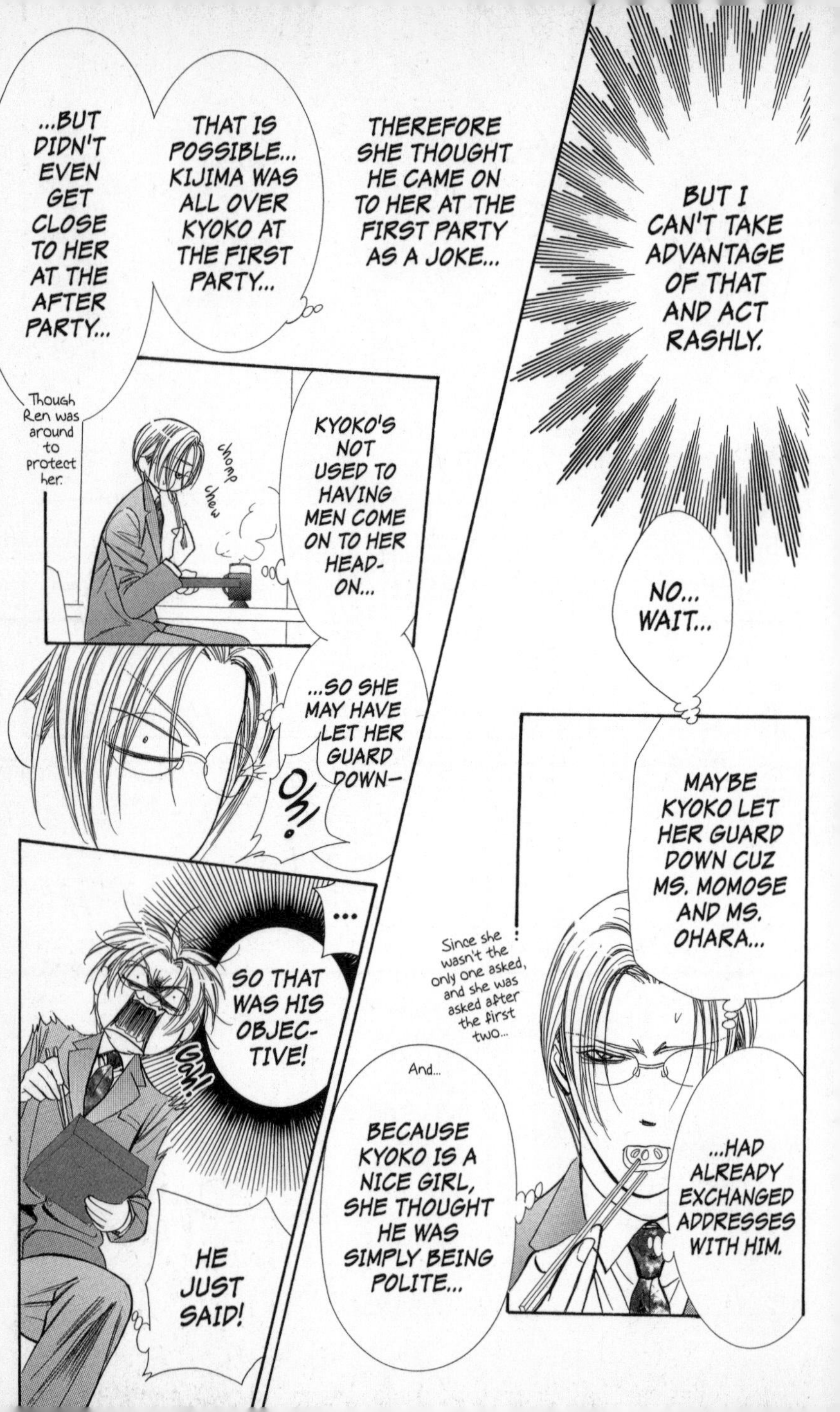
THAT IS POSSIBLE... KIJIMA WAS ALL OVER KYOKO AT THE FIRST PARTY...
...BUT DIDN'T EVEN GET CLOSE TO HER AT THE AFTER PARTY...
Though Ren was around to protect her.
THEREFORE SHE THOUGHT HE CAME ON TO HER AT THE FIRST PARTY AS A JOKE...
BUT I CAN'T TAKE ADVANTAGE OF THAT AND ACT RASHLY.
NO... WAIT...
MAYBE KYOKO LET HER GUARD DOWN CUZ MS. MOMOSE AND MS. OHARA...
...HAD ALREADY EXCHANGED ADDRESSES WITH HIM.
Since she wasn't the only one asked, and she was asked after the first two...
And...
BECAUSE KYOKO IS A NICE GIRL, SHE THOUGHT HE WAS SIMPLY BEING POLITE...
chomp
chew
KYOKO'S NOT USED TO HAVING MEN COME ON TO HER HEAD-ON...
...SO SHE MAY HAVE LET HER GUARD DOWN—
Oh!!
...
SO THAT WAS HIS OBJECTIVE!
Gah!
HE JUST SAID!

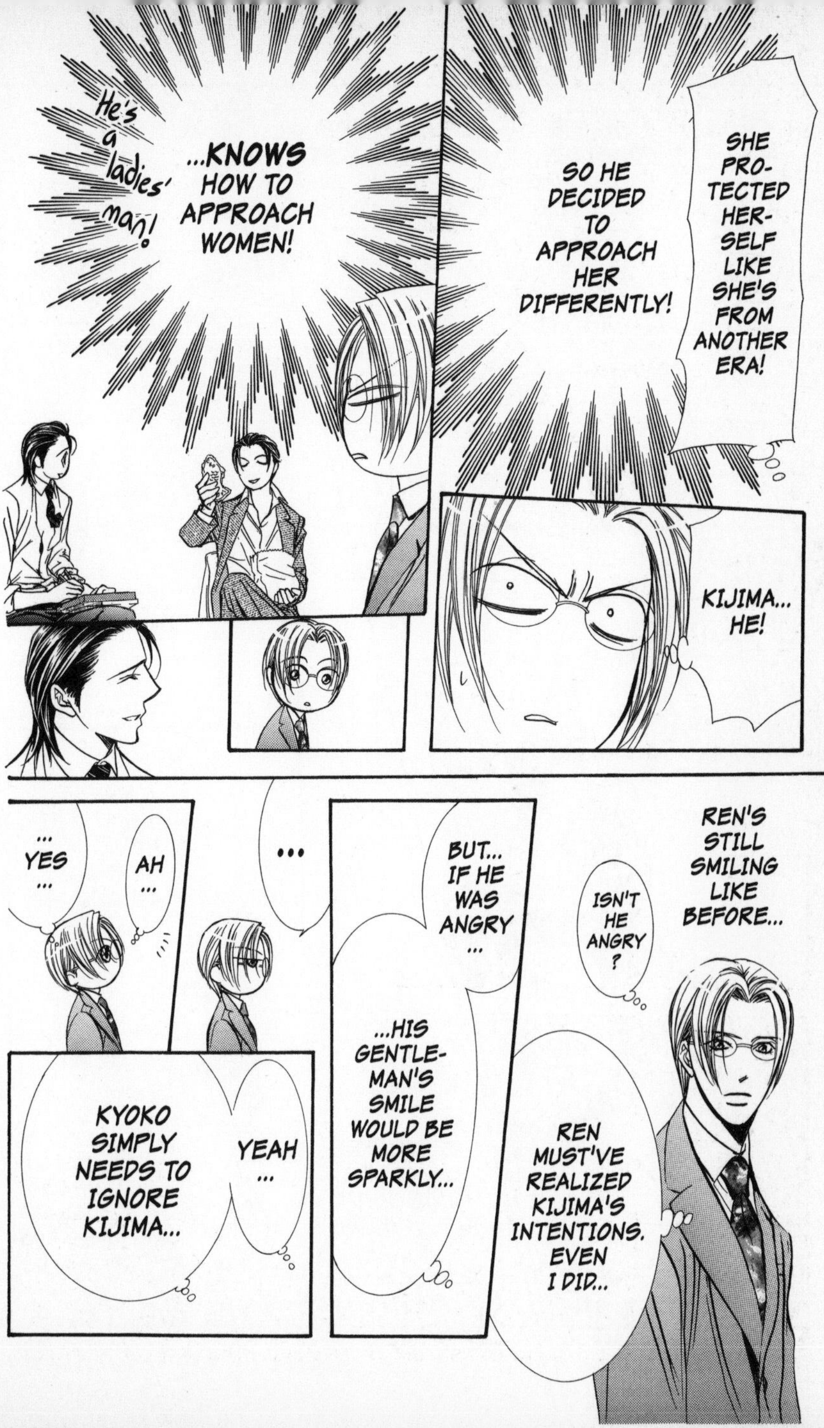
SHE PROTECTED HERSELF LIKE SHE'S FROM ANOTHER ERA!
SO HE DECIDED TO APPROACH HER DIFFERENTLY!
...KNOWS HOW TO APPROACH WOMEN!
He's a ladies' man!
KIJIMA... HE!
REN'S STILL SMILING LIKE BEFORE...
ISN'T HE ANGRY?
REN MUST'VE REALIZED KIJIMA'S INTENTIONS. EVEN I DID...
BUT... IF HE WAS ANGRY...
...HIS GENTLEMAN'S SMILE WOULD BE MORE SPARKLY...
...
AH...
...YES...
YEAH...
KYOKO SIMPLY NEEDS TO IGNORE KIJIMA...

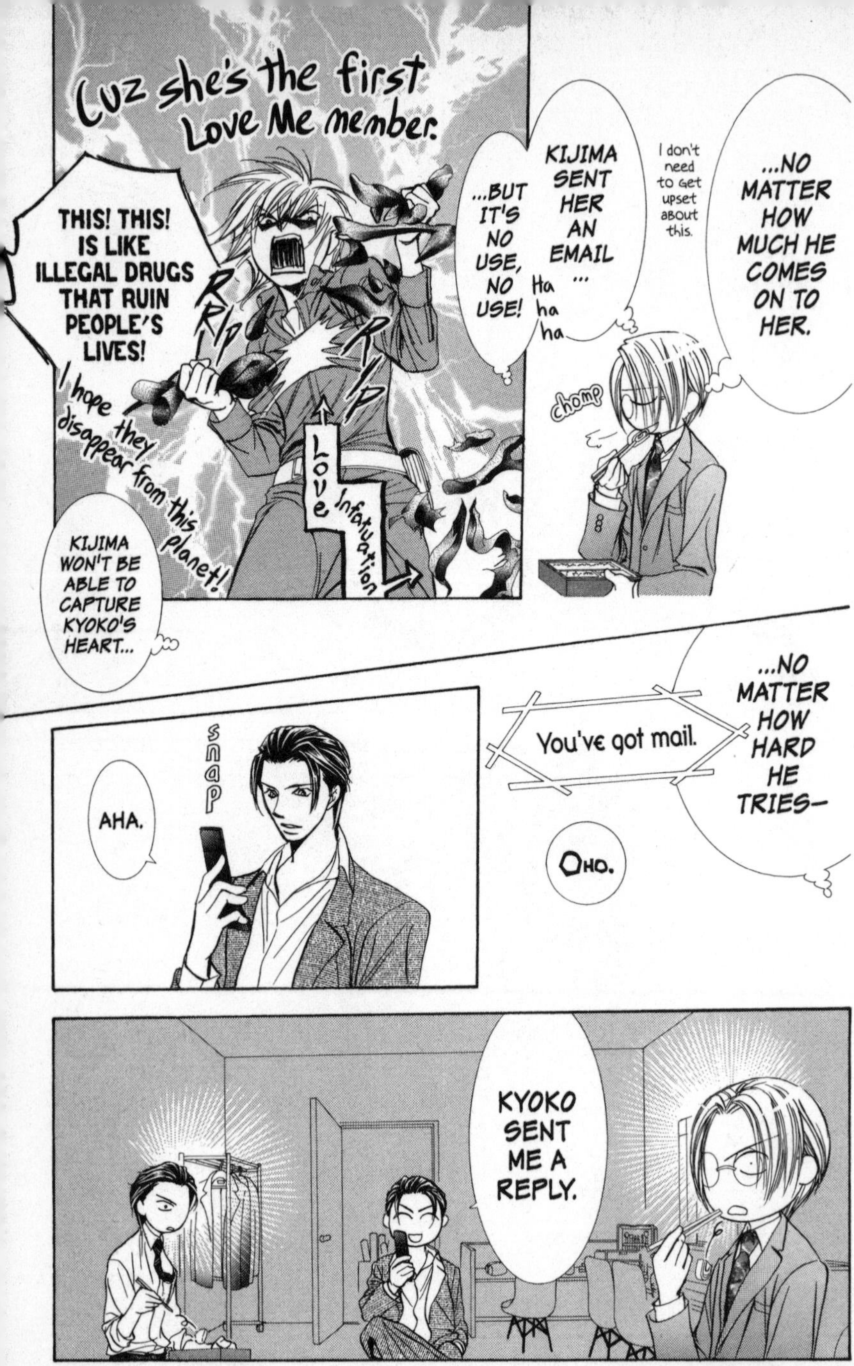
...NO MATTER HOW MUCH HE COMES ON TO HER.
I don't need to get upset about this.
KIJIMA SENT HER AN EMAIL...
...BUT IT'S NO USE, NO USE!
Ha ha ha
chomp
Cuz she's the first Love Me member.
THIS! THIS! IS LIKE ILLEGAL DRUGS THAT RUIN PEOPLE'S LIVES!
RRIP
RIP
Love
Infatuation
I hope they disappear from this planet!
KIJIMA WON'T BE ABLE TO CAPTURE KYOKO'S HEART...
...NO MATTER HOW HARD HE TRIES—
You've got mail.
OHO.
snap
AHA.
KYOKO SENT ME A REPLY.

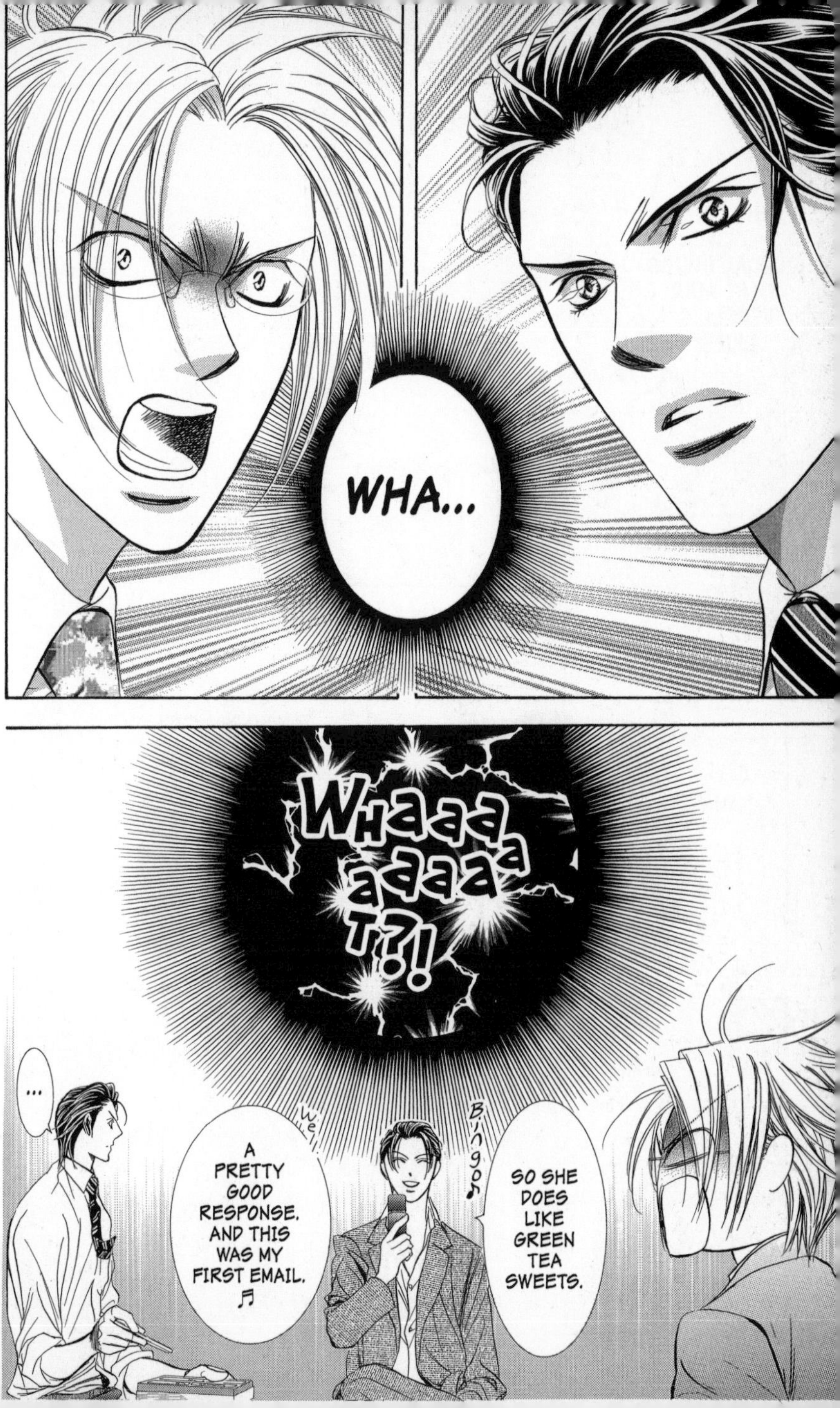
WHA...
WHAAAAAAAAT?!
Bingo♪
SO SHE DOES LIKE GREEN TEA SWEETS.
Well.
A PRETTY GOOD RESPONSE. AND THIS WAS MY FIRST EMAIL. ♬
...

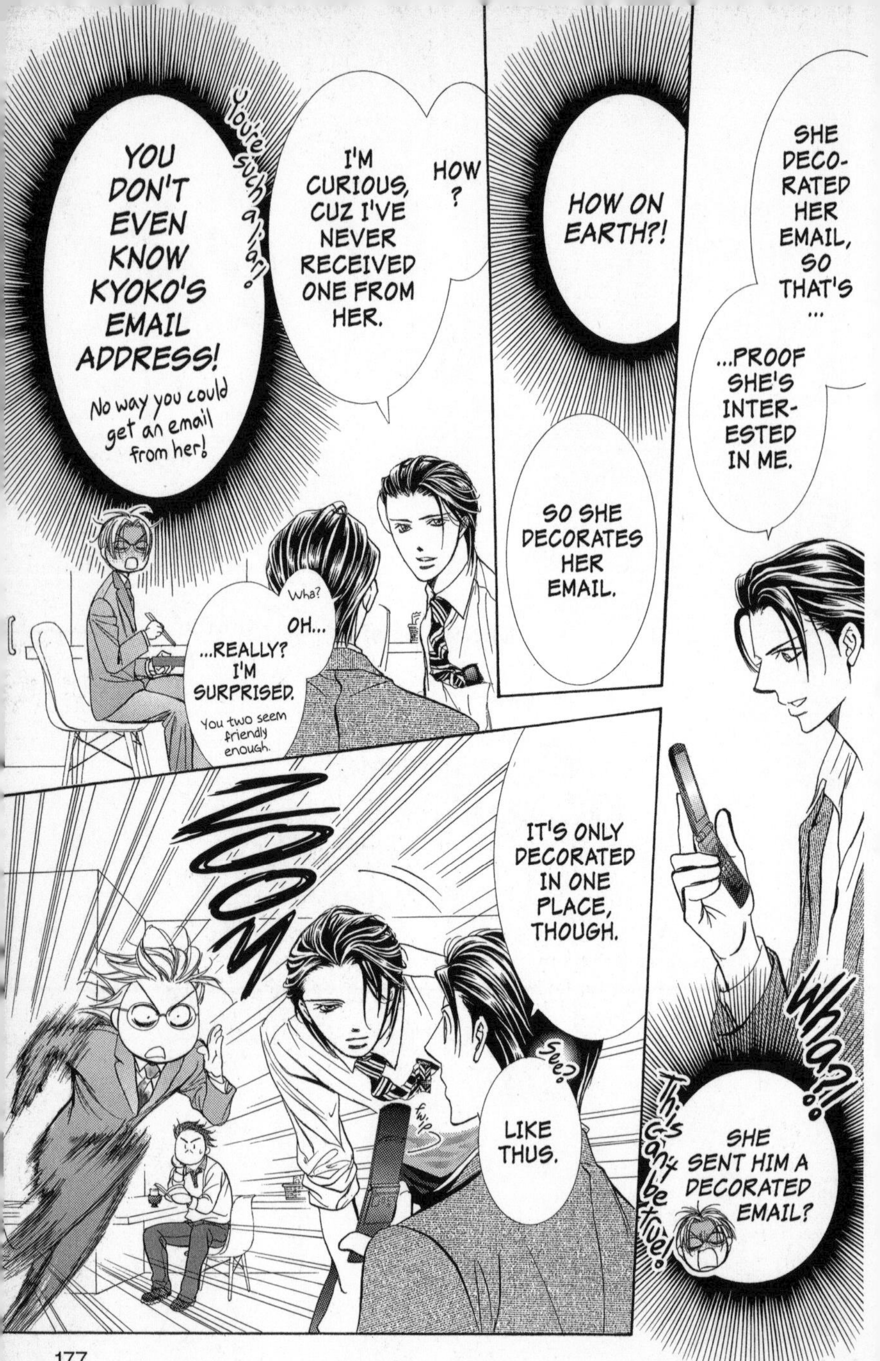
SHE DECORATED HER EMAIL, SO THAT'S ...
...PROOF SHE'S INTERESTED IN ME.
HOW ON EARTH?!
SO SHE DECORATES HER EMAIL.
HOW?
I'M CURIOUS, CUZ I'VE NEVER RECEIVED ONE FROM HER.
You're such a liar!
YOU DON'T EVEN KNOW KYOKO'S EMAIL ADDRESS!
No way you could get an email from her!
Wha?
OH...
...REALLY? I'M SURPRISED.
You two seem friendly enough.
Wha?!!
SHE SENT HIM A DECORATED EMAIL?
This can't be true!
IT'S ONLY DECORATED IN ONE PLACE, THOUGH.
See?
LIKE THUS.
fwip
ZOOM

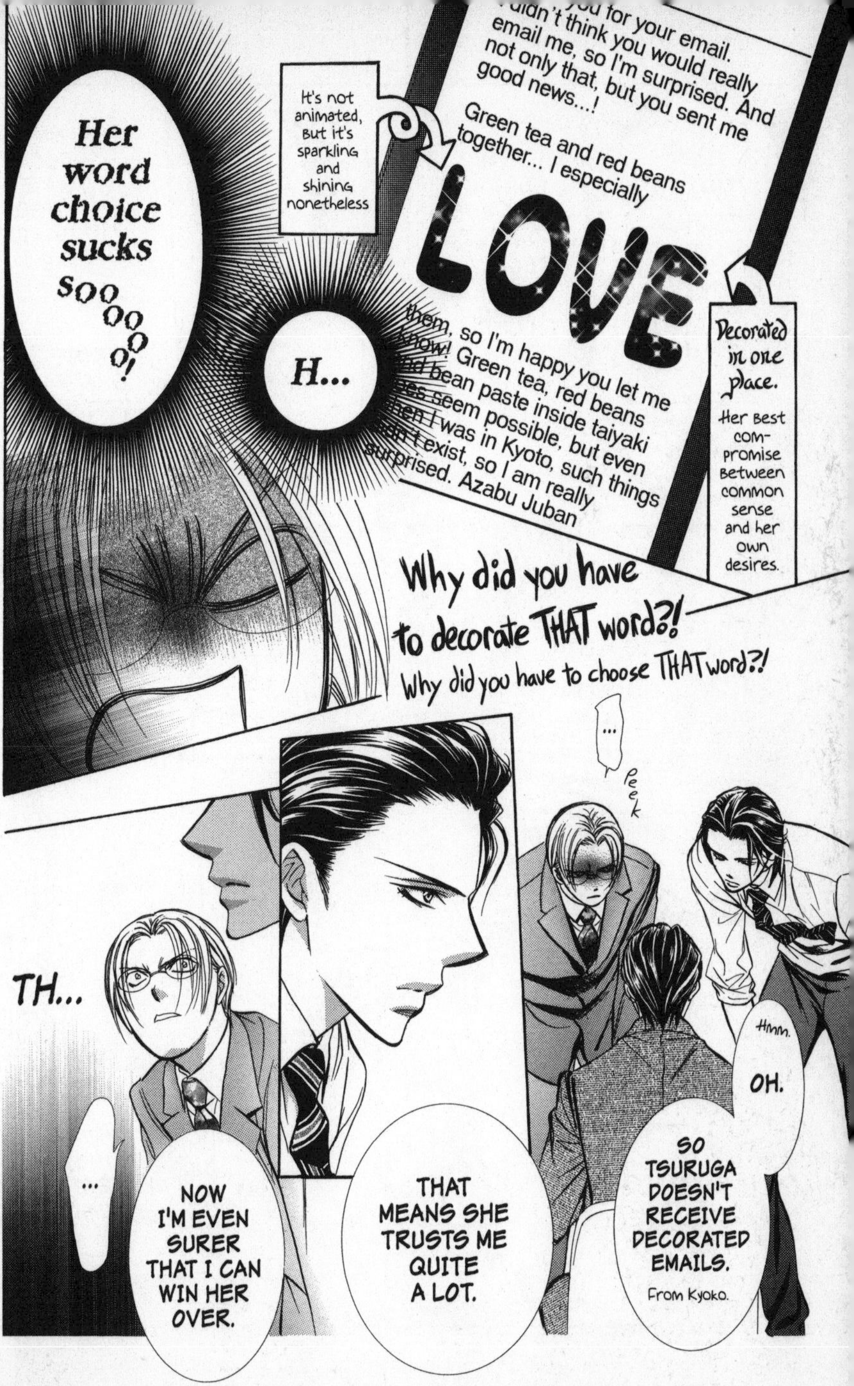
you for your email.
uldn't think you would really email me, so I'm surprised. And not only that, but you sent me good news...!
Green tea and red beans together... I especially
LOVE
them, so I'm happy you let me know! Green tea, red beans and bean paste inside taiyaki does seem possible, but even when I was in Kyoto, such things didn't exist, so I am really surprised. Azabu Juban
Decorated in one place.
Her best compromise between common sense and her own desires.
It's not animated, but it's sparkling and shining nonetheless
H...
Her word choice sucks soooooo!
Why did you have to decorate THAT word?!
Why did you have to choose THAT word?!
...
Peek
Hmm.
OH.
SO TSURUGA DOESN'T RECEIVE DECORATED EMAILS.
From Kyoko.
THAT MEANS SHE TRUSTS ME QUITE A LOT.
TH...
...
NOW I'M EVEN SURER THAT I CAN WIN HER OVER.

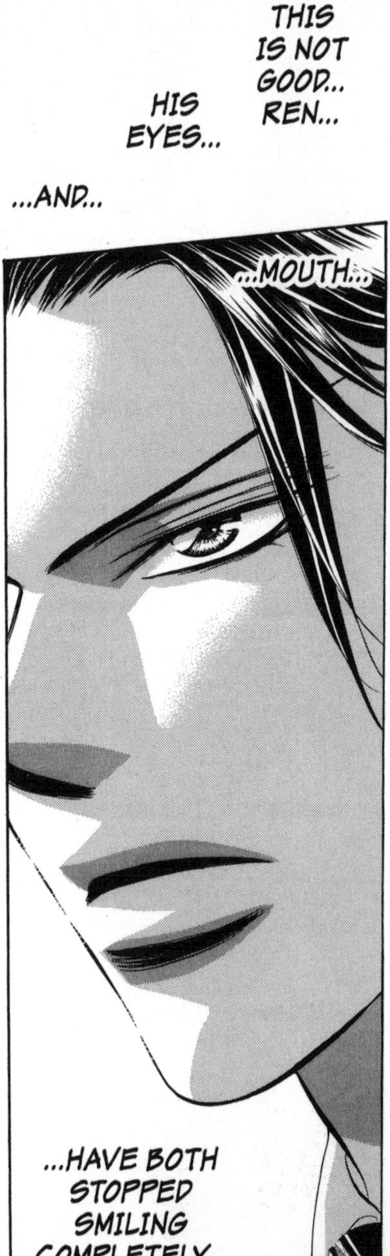
THIS IS NOT GOOD... REN...
HIS EYES...
...AND...
...MOUTH...
...HAVE BOTH STOPPED SMILING COMPLETELY...

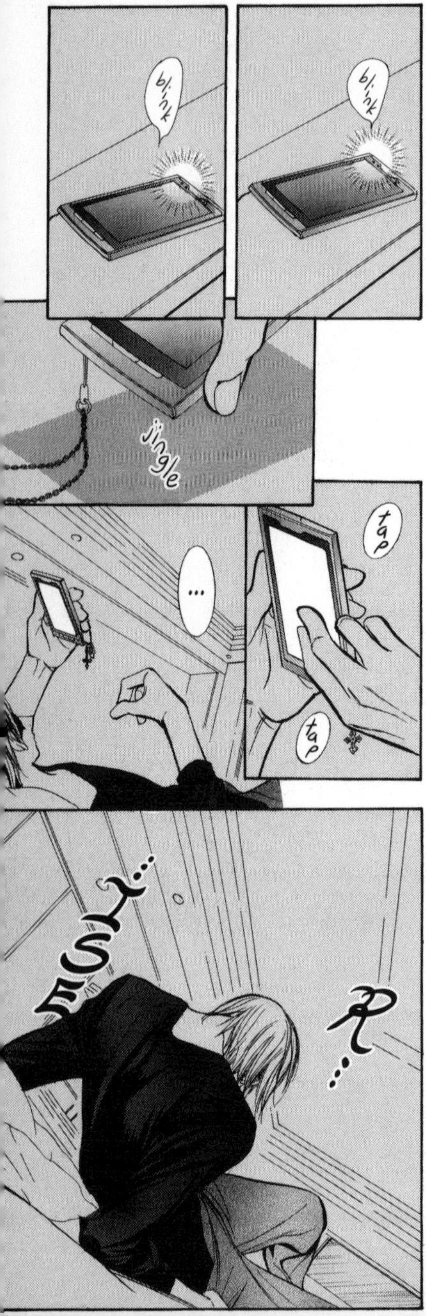
blink
blink
jingle
tap
tap
...
R...

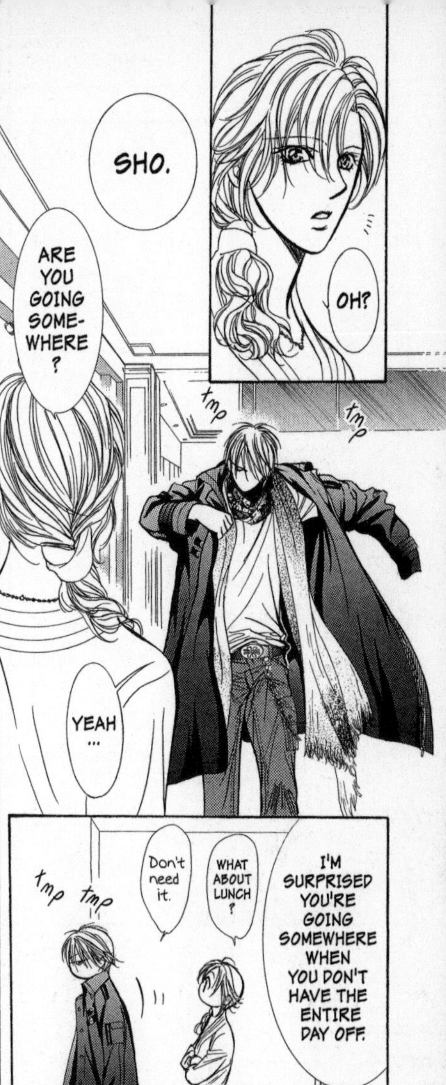
OH?
SHO.
ARE YOU GOING SOME-WHERE?
xmp
xmp
YEAH...
I'M SURPRISED YOU'RE GOING SOMEWHERE WHEN YOU DON'T HAVE THE ENTIRE DAY OFF.
WHAT ABOUT LUNCH?
Don't need it.
xmp tmp
YOU CAN GET TO MUSIC HEAVEN AT 7 PM BY YOURSELF, RIGHT?
Mmm.

End of Act 188

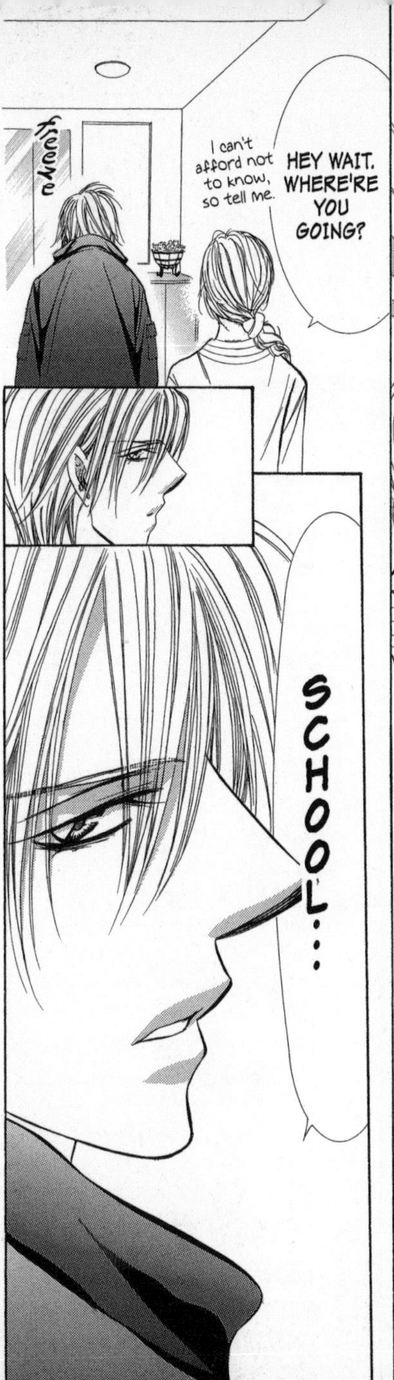
HEY WAIT. WHERE'RE YOU GOING?
I can't afford not to know, so tell me.
freeze
SCHOOL...

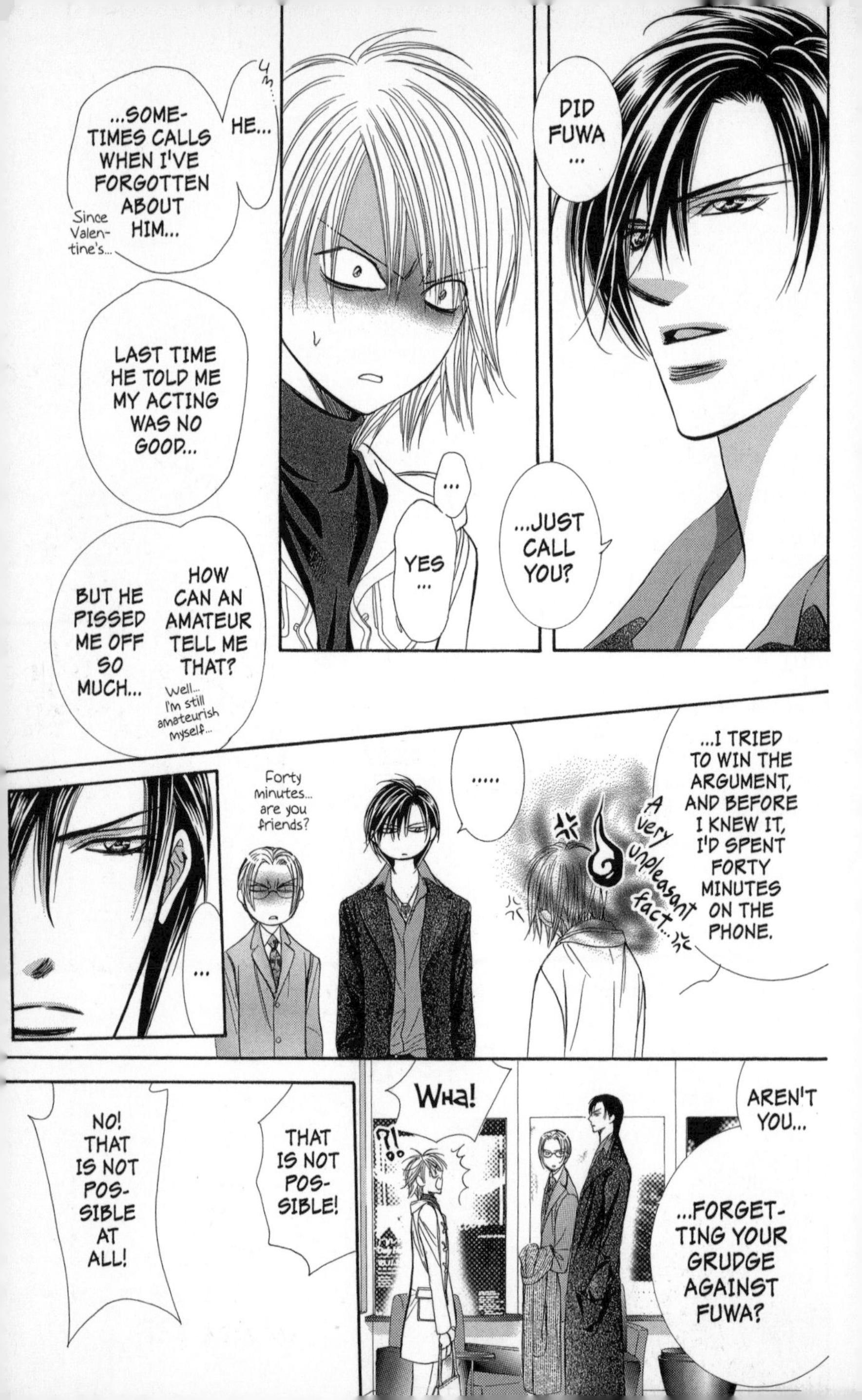
DID FUWA ...
...JUST CALL YOU?
Um...
...
YES ...
HE...
...SOME-TIMES CALLS WHEN I'VE FORGOTTEN ABOUT HIM...
Since Valen-tine's...
LAST TIME HE TOLD ME MY ACTING WAS NO GOOD...
HOW CAN AN AMATEUR TELL ME THAT?
BUT HE PISSED ME OFF SO MUCH...
Well... I'm still amateurish myself...
...I TRIED TO WIN THE ARGUMENT, AND BEFORE I KNEW IT, I'D SPENT FORTY MINUTES ON THE PHONE.
A very unpleasant fact...
.....
Forty minutes... are you friends?
...
AREN'T YOU...
...FORGET-TING YOUR GRUDGE AGAINST FUWA?
WHA!
?!
THAT IS NOT POS-SIBLE!
NO! THAT IS NOT POS-SIBLE AT ALL!

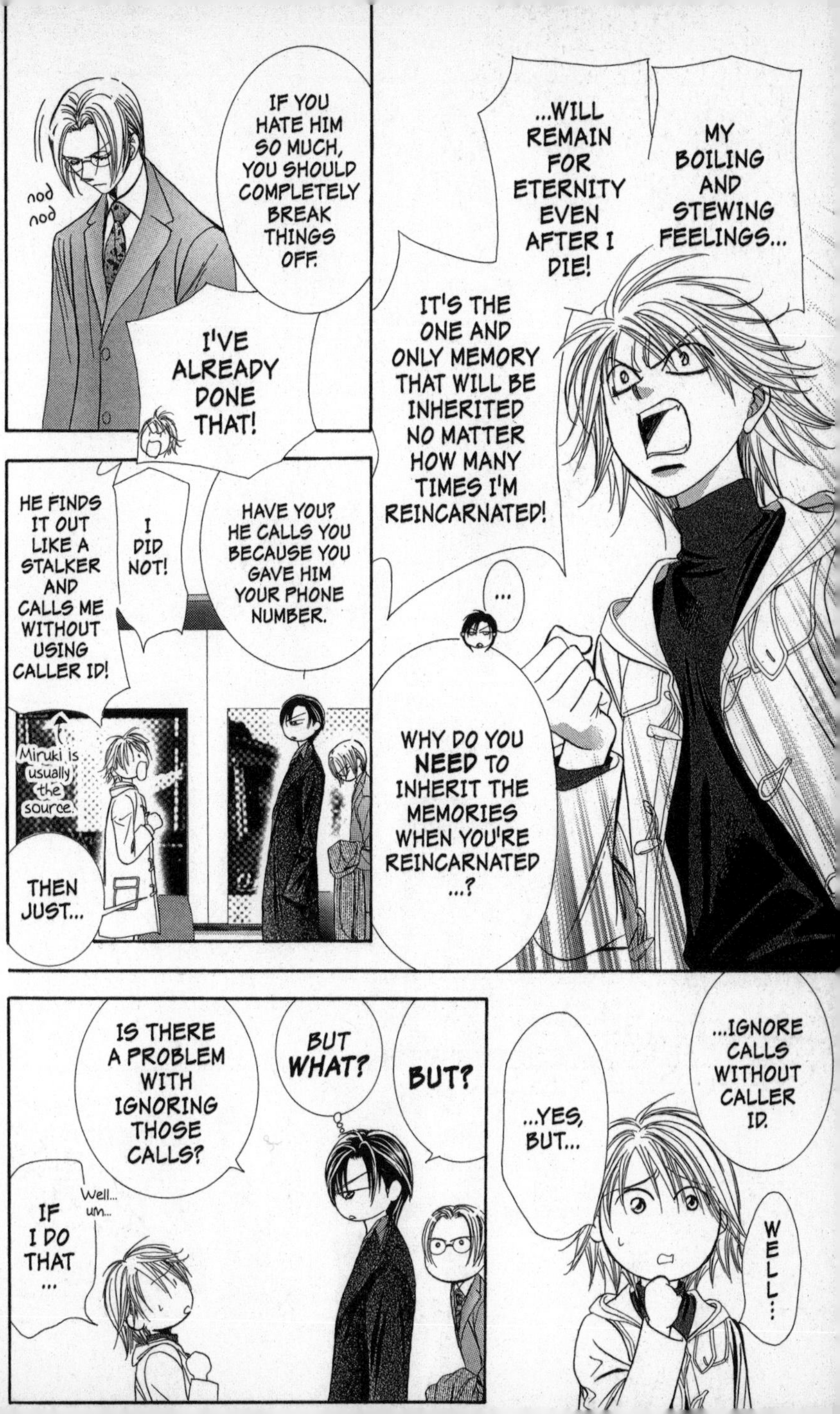
MY BOILING AND STEWING FEELINGS...
...WILL REMAIN FOR ETERNITY EVEN AFTER I DIE!
IT'S THE ONE AND ONLY MEMORY THAT WILL BE INHERITED NO MATTER HOW MANY TIMES I'M REINCARNATED!
...
WHY DO YOU NEED TO INHERIT THE MEMORIES WHEN YOU'RE REINCARNATED ...?
IF YOU HATE HIM SO MUCH, YOU SHOULD COMPLETELY BREAK THINGS OFF.
nod nod
I'VE ALREADY DONE THAT!
HAVE YOU? HE CALLS YOU BECAUSE YOU GAVE HIM YOUR PHONE NUMBER.
I DID NOT!
HE FINDS IT OUT LIKE A STALKER AND CALLS ME WITHOUT USING CALLER ID!
Miruki is usually the source.
THEN JUST...
...IGNORE CALLS WITHOUT CALLER ID.
...YES, BUT...
WELL...
BUT?
BUT WHAT?
IS THERE A PROBLEM WITH IGNORING THOSE CALLS?
Well... um...
IF I DO THAT ...

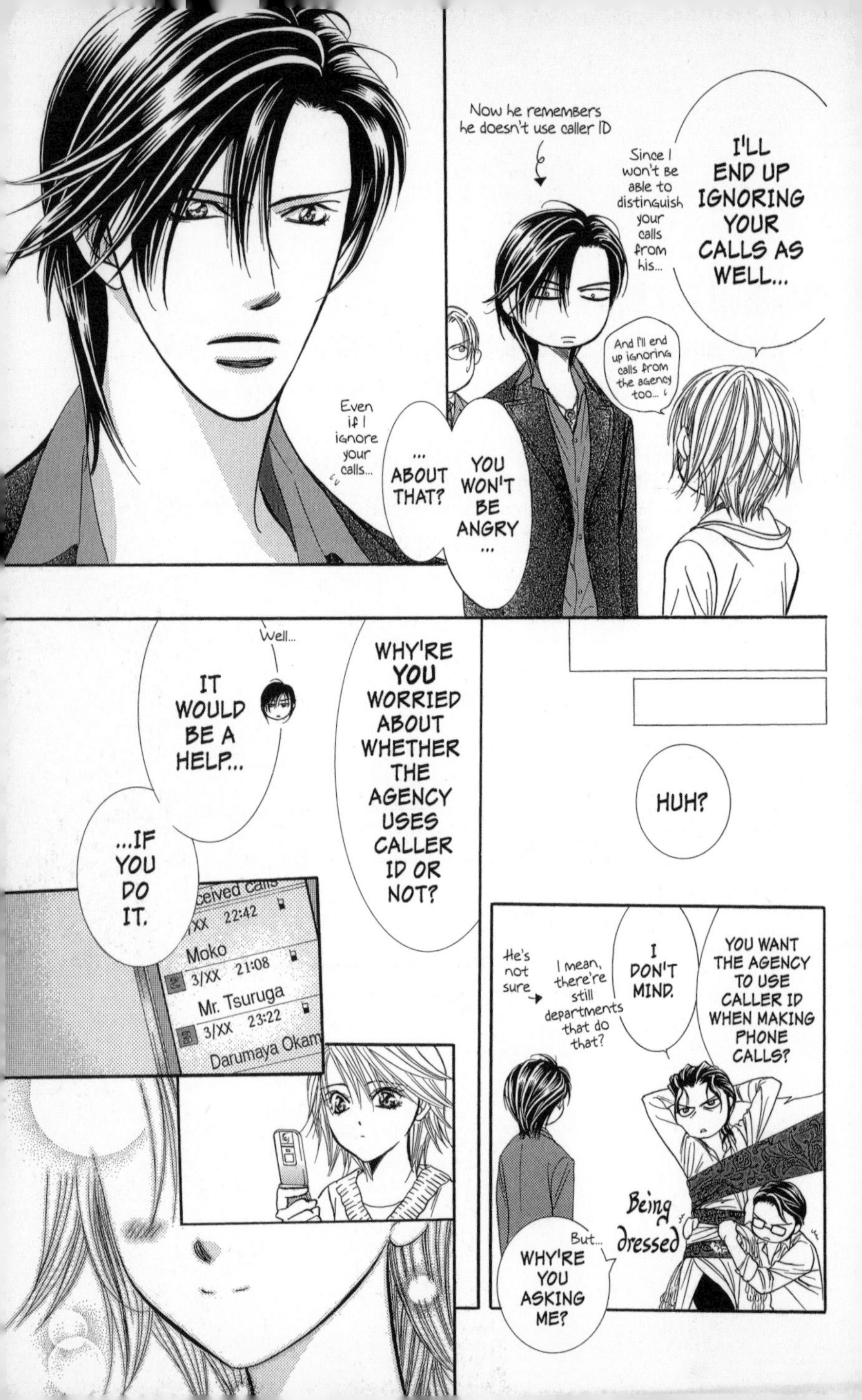
I'LL END UP IGNORING YOUR CALLS AS WELL...
Since I won't be able to distinguish your calls from his...
Now he remembers he doesn't use caller ID
And I'll end up ignoring calls from the agency too...
YOU WON'T BE ANGRY...
...ABOUT THAT?
Even if I ignore your calls...
HUH?
YOU WANT THE AGENCY TO USE CALLER ID WHEN MAKING PHONE CALLS?
I DON'T MIND.
I mean, there're still departments that do that?
He's not sure
Being dressed
But...
WHY'RE YOU ASKING ME?
WHY'RE YOU WORRIED ABOUT WHETHER THE AGENCY USES CALLER ID OR NOT?
Well...
IT WOULD BE A HELP...
...IF YOU DO IT.
Moko
3/XX 21:08
Mr. Tsuruga
3/XX 23:22

Skip-Beat! End Notes
Everyone knows how to be a fan, but sometimes cool things from other cultures need a little help crossing the language barrier.

Page 68, panel 1: Nio Statue, Un version
Statues of guardian gods that are placed at temple gates. The Un version has its mouth closed.

Page 68, panel 5: Ah version
Nio statue version with its mouth open.

Page 164, panel 3: Taiyaki
Fish-shaped cakes, usually filled with sweet black bean paste.

Page 171, panel 1: Azabu Juban
A trendy and lively residential area in central Tokyo.

Page 171, panel 1: "Dance ★Taiyaki-kun!"
"Dance! Taiyaki-kun" is a 1975 remake of the hit song "Oyoge! Taiyaki-kun (Swim! Taiyaki-kun)."

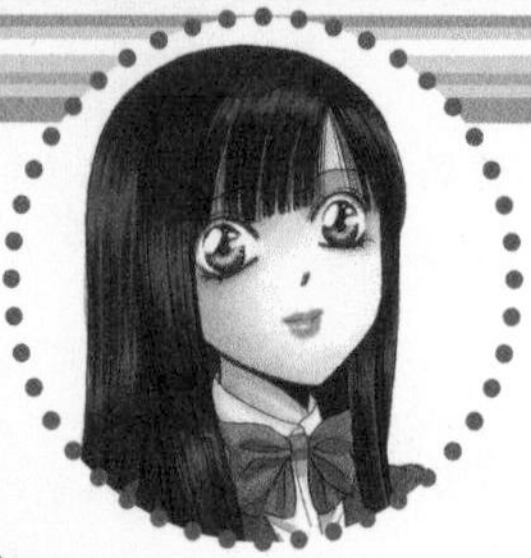

Yoshiki Nakamura is originally from Tokushima Prefecture. She started drawing manga in elementary school, which eventually led to her 1993 debut of *Yume de Au yori Suteki* (Better than Seeing in a Dream) in *Hana to Yume* magazine. Her other works include the basketball series *Saint Love, MVP wa Yuzurenai* (Can't Give Up MVP), *Blue Wars* and *Tokyo Crazy Paradise*, a series about a female bodyguard in 2020 Tokyo.

Shojo Beat

SKIP·BEAT!

Vol. 31

Shojo Beat Edition

STORY AND ART BY YOSHIKI NAKAMURA

English Translation & Adaptation/Tomo Kimura
Touch-up Art & Lettering/Sabrina Heep
Design/Ronnie Casson
Editor/Pancha Diaz

Printed in the U.S.A.

Published by VIZ Media, LLC
P.O. Box 77010
San Francisco, CA 94107

www.viz.com

www.shojobeat.com

10 9 8 7 6 5 4 3 2 1
First printing, June 2013

RATED T FOR TEEN

PARENTAL ADVISORY
SKIP·BEAT! is rated T for Teen and is recommended for ages 13 and up. This volume contains a grudge.

ratings.viz.com

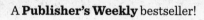
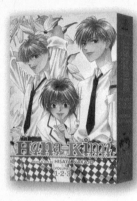
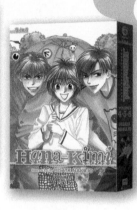
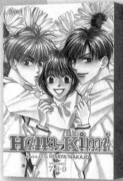
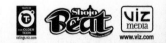

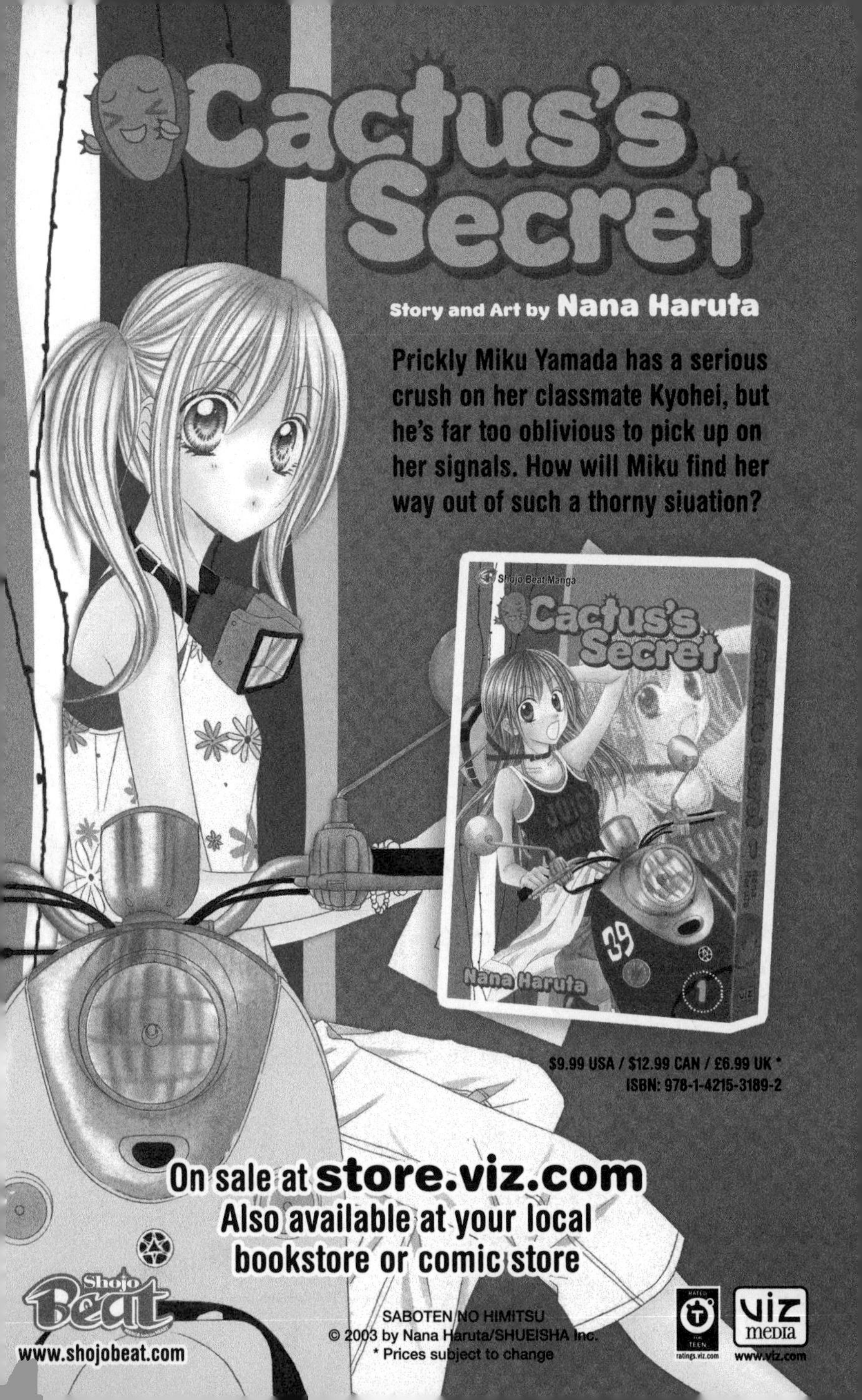
Cactus's Secret
Story and Art by Nana Haruta
Prickly Miku Yamada has a serious crush on her classmate Kyohei, but he's far too oblivious to pick up on her signals. How will Miku find her way out of such a thorny siuation?
Shojo Beat Manga
Cactus's Secret
Nana Haruta
1
$9.99 USA / $12.99 CAN / £6.99 UK *
ISBN: 978-1-4215-3189-2
On sale at store.viz.com
Also available at your local bookstore or comic store
Shojo Beat
www.shojobeat.com
SABOTEN NO HIMITSU
© 2003 by Nana Haruta/SHUEISHA Inc.
* Prices subject to change
RATED T FOR TEEN
ratings.viz.com
VIZ media
www.viz.com

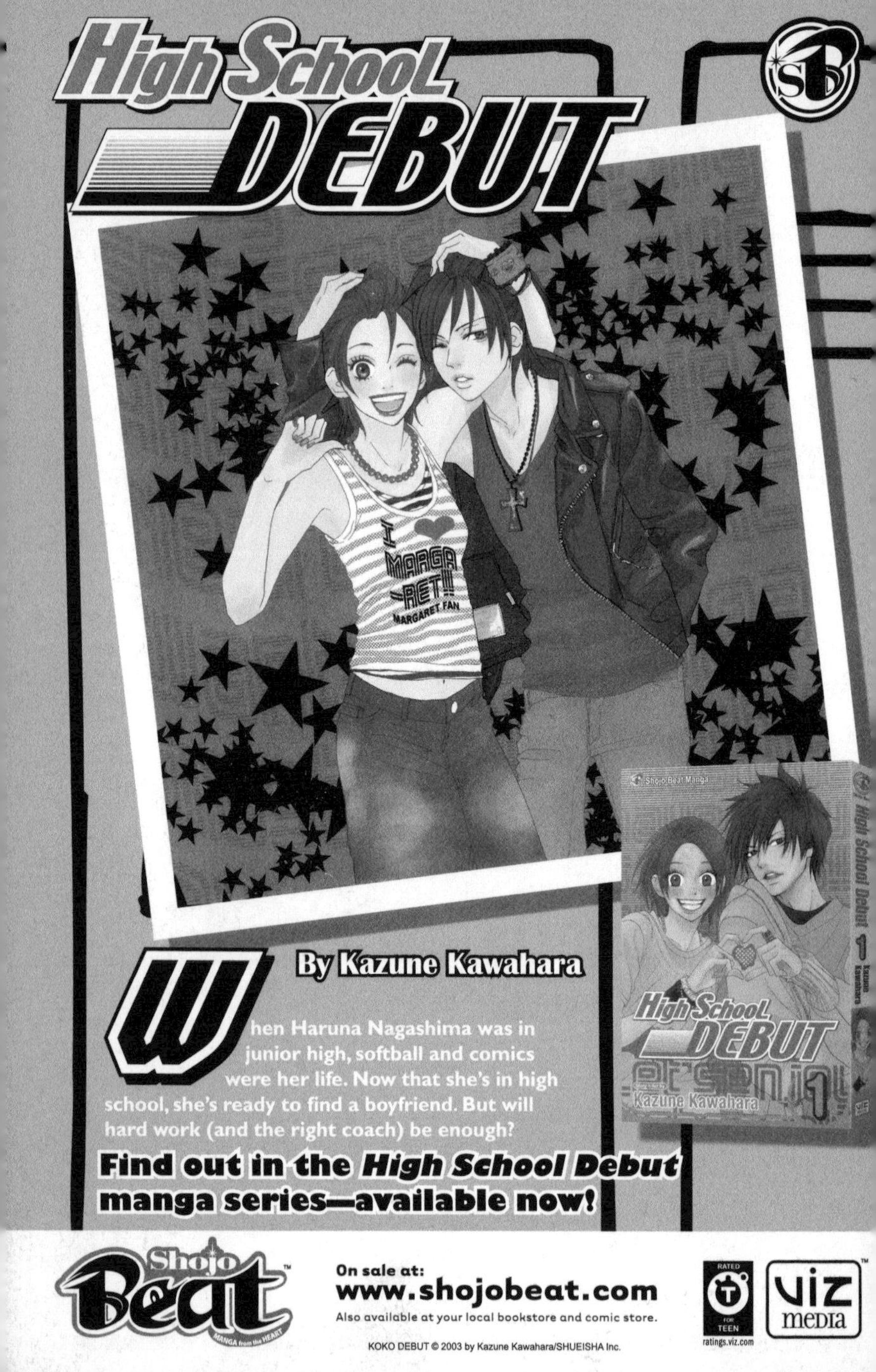
High School DEBUT
I ♥ MARGA-RET!! MARGARET FAN
Shojo Beat Manga
High School Debut 1
Kazune Kawahara
By Kazune Kawahara
When Haruna Nagashima was in junior high, softball and comics were her life. Now that she's in high school, she's ready to find a boyfriend. But will hard work (and the right coach) be enough?
Find out in the High School Debut manga series—available now!
Shojo Beat
MANGA from the HEART
On sale at:
www.shojobeat.com
Also available at your local bookstore and comic store.
RATED T FOR TEEN
ratings.viz.com
VIZ media
KOKO DEBUT © 2003 by Kazune Kawahara/SHUEISHA Inc.

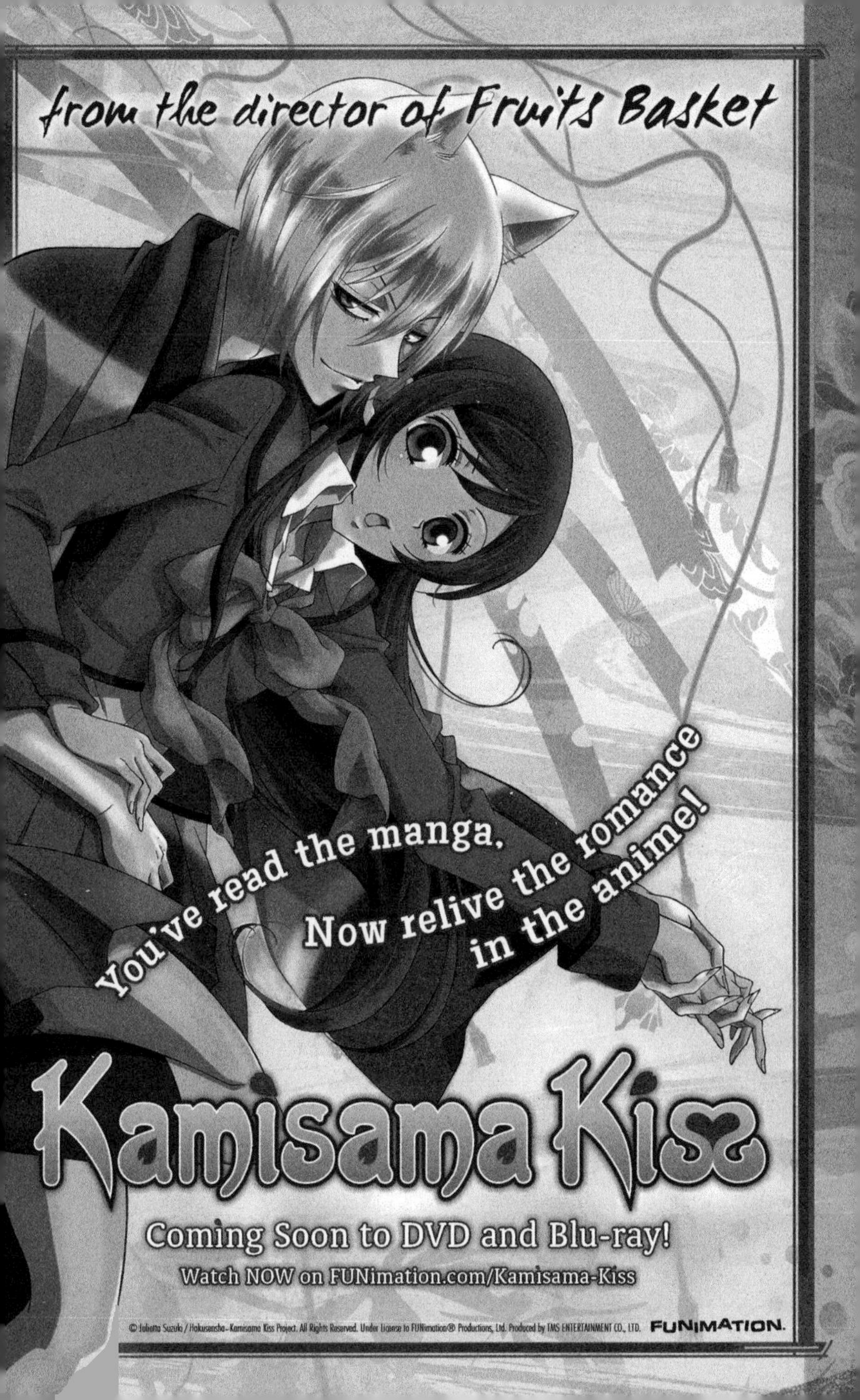

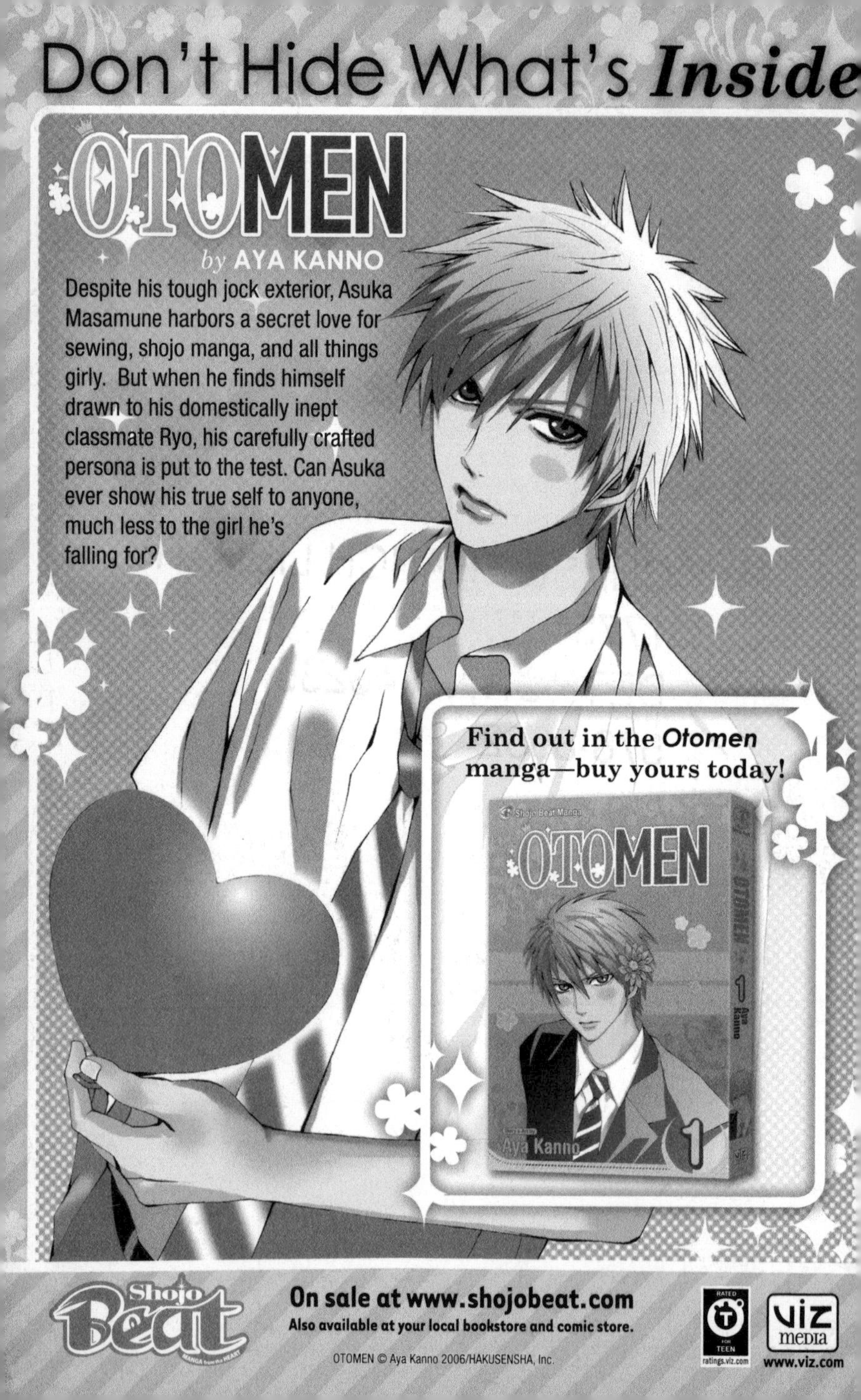
Don't Hide What's Inside
OTOMEN
by AYA KANNO
Despite his tough jock exterior, Asuka Masamune harbors a secret love for sewing, shojo manga, and all things girly. But when he finds himself drawn to his domestically inept classmate Ryo, his carefully crafted persona is put to the test. Can Asuka ever show his true self to anyone, much less to the girl he's falling for?
Find out in the Otomen manga—buy yours today!
Shojo Beat Manga
OTOMEN
Aya Kanno
1
Shojo Beat
On sale at www.shojobeat.com
Also available at your local bookstore and comic store.
OTOMEN © Aya Kanno 2006/HAKUSENSHA, Inc.
RATED T FOR TEEN
ratings.viz.com
VIZ media
www.viz.com

SURPRISE!

You may be reading the wrong way!

It's true: In keeping with the original Japanese comic format, this book reads from right to left—so action, sound effects, and word balloons are completely reversed. This preserves the orientation of the original artwork—plus, it's fun! Check out the diagram shown here to get the hang of things, and then turn to the other side of the book to get started!

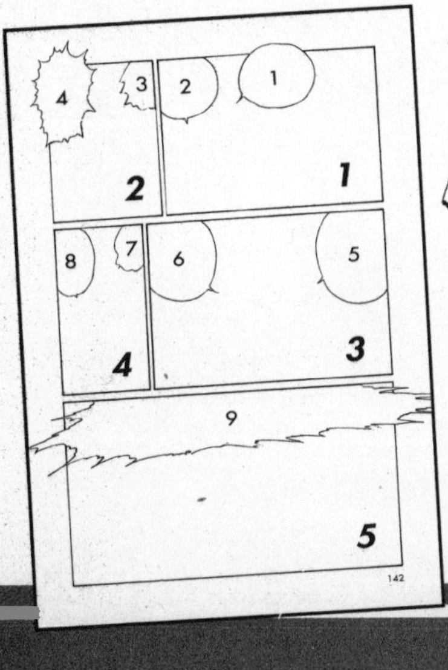
1
2
3
4
1
2
5
6
7
8
3
4
9
5
142

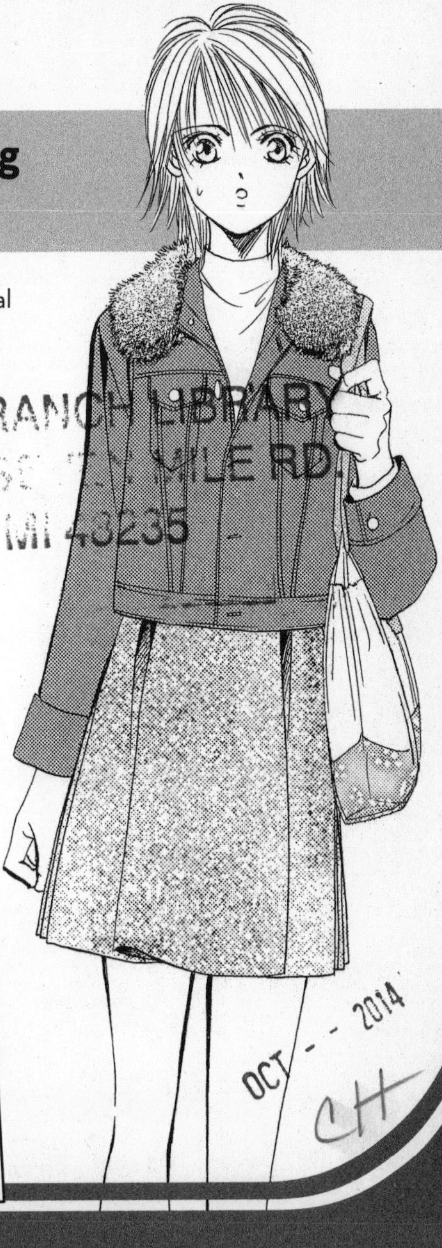